Money and the Governance of Punishment

Money is the most frequently used means in the legal system to punish and regulate. Monetary penalties outnumber all other sanctions delivered by criminal justice in many jurisdictions, imprisonment included. More people pay fines than go to prison and in some jurisdictions many of those in prison are there because of failure to pay their fines. Therefore, it is surprising how little has been written in the Anglophone academic world about the nature of money sanctions and their specific characteristics as legal sanctions.

In many ways, legal innovations related to money sanctions have been poorly understood. This book argues that they are a direct consequence of the changing meaning of money. Considering the 'meaninglessness' of modern money, the book aims to examine the history of changing conceptions in how fines have been conceived and used. Using a set of interpretative techniques sensitive to how money and freedom are perceived, the genealogy of the penal fine is presented as a story of constant reformulation in response to shifting political pressures and changes in intellectual developments that influenced ideological commitments of legislators and practitioners.

This book is multidisciplinary and will appeal to those engaged with criminology, sociology and philosophy of punishment, socio-legal studies, and criminal law.

Patricia Faraldo-Cabana is Professor of Criminal Law at the University of A Coruña, in Spain, and Adjunct Professor at the Queensland University of Technology in Brisbane, Australia.

Routledge Studies in Crime and Society

For a full list of titles in this series, please visit www.routledge.com

23 Regulation and Social Control of Incivilities
Edited by Nina Peršak

24 Skinhead History, Identity, and Culture
Kevin Borgeson and Robin Valeri

25 Homicide, Gender and Responsibility
Edited by Sandra Walklate and Kate Fitz-Gibbon

26 Cybercrime through an Interdisciplinary Lens
Edited by Thomas J. Holt

27 Domestic Violence in International Context
Edited by Diana Scharff Peterson and Julie A. Schroeder

28 Child Trafficking in the EU
Policing and protecting Europe's most vulnerable
Pete Fussey and Paddy Rawlinson

29 Resettlement of Sex Offenders after Custody
Circles of support and accountability
David Thompson and Terry Thomas with Susanne Karstedt

30 Cybercrime and Its Victims
Edited by Elena Martellozzo and Emma A. Jane

31 Gender, Technology and Violence
Edited by Marie Segrave and Laura Vitis

32 Money and the Governance of Punishment
A Genealogy of the Penal Fine
Patricia Faraldo-Cabana

Money and the Governance of Punishment

A Genealogy of the Penal Fine

Patricia Faraldo-Cabana

Routledge
Taylor & Francis Group
LONDON AND NEW YORK

First published 2017 by Routledge

2 Park Square, Milton Park, Abingdon, Oxfordshire OX14 4RN
52 Vanderbilt Avenue, New York, NY 10017

Routledge is an imprint of the Taylor & Francis Group, an informa business

First issued in paperback 2019

British Library Cataloguing-in-Publication Data
A catalogue record for this book is available from the British Library

Library of Congress Cataloging-in-Publication Data
Names: Faraldo Cabana, Patricia, author.
Title: Money and the governance of punishment : a genealogy of the penal fine / Patricia Faraldo Cabana.
Description: 1 Edition. | New York : Routledge, 2017. | Series: Routledge studies in crime and society ; 32 | Includes bibliographical references and index.
Identifiers: LCCN 2016057647 | ISBN 9781138686236 (hardback) | ISBN 9781315542720 (ebook)
Subjects: LCSH: Fines (Penalties)—History.
Classification: LCC HV9277 .F37 2017 | DDC 364.6/8—dc23
LC record available at https://lccn.loc.gov/2016057647

ISBN: 978-1-138-68623-6 (hbk)
ISBN: 978-0-367-22708-1 (pbk)

Typeset in Times New Roman
by Apex CoVantage, LLC

Contents

Figures

Tables

Acknowledgements

During the four years of my concerted interest in money and punishment I have benefited enormously from exchanges with many colleagues. I want to single out the regular conversations with José Ángel Brandariz García, professor of criminal law at the University of A Coruña, who has generously allowed me to make use of his wide knowledge on the sociology of punishment and kindly commented on the draft of this book. My thanks to him for his corrections and suggestions. Needless to say, the remaining errors are my own. Among the individuals who responded to my (mainly statistical) queries, I would like to use this opportunity to thank Beatriz Cruz Márquez, professor at the University of Cádiz (Spain), Britta Küst, scientific coordinator at the Freiburg Institute for Advanced Studies (Germany), and Carmen Lamela Viera, professor at the University of A Coruña (Spain). Many thanks also to Gregg Dubow for his proof-reading.

This book was written while I was in receipt of a Marie Curie Intra-European Fellowship from the European Research Council (ERC) under award number PIEF-GA-2012-326780, which allowed me to make a 13-month research stay (August 2013 to September 2014) at the Max Planck Institute for Foreign and International Criminal Law in Freiburg, Germany; and a EURIAS (European Institutes for Advanced Studies) senior fellowship, which granted me a second research stay of 10 months (October 2015 to July 2016) at the Freiburg Institute for Advanced Studies, also in Germany, under award number 10.13039/501100003190 REA, grant agreement no. 609400. I was able to take on these fellowships thanks to my colleagues in the Department of Public Law in A Coruña. This work was also supported by research projects GRC2015/021, financed by the regional government of Galicia, and DER2014/52674-R, financed by the Spanish Ministry of Economy and Competitiveness. Without this support it would have been impossible to finish this book.

Lastly, this book is dedicated to the man who guided me from childhood into maturity, my father, Antonio Faraldo Tenreiro, who died during the writing. And to my son, Max Heim-Faraldo, whom I hope to help through this difficult phase as my own father did with me.

Preface

It has been said that 'money is probably the most frequently used means of punishing, deterring, compensating and regulating throughout the legal system' (O'Malley 2009: 1). In particular, the penal fine outnumbers other penal sanctions, including custodial sentences, in many European jurisdictions, with just a few notable exceptions in countries like Italy or Spain. In light of its extensive use, the small amount of attention sociologists of punishment and social control, legal scholars, and criminologists give to the role of money in the criminal system is extremely surprising, with conceptual and empirical priority having been given to other sanctions that statistically speaking are less common (Beristain Ipiña 1976: 15; Bottoms 1983: 168; Young 1989: 47 and 1999: 182–183; O'Malley 2009; McCallum 2011: 541; Lappi-Seppälä 2014: 1637). As Grover (2008: 178) puts it, 'there appears to be an inverse relationship between the amount of literature regarding particular punishments and their incidence. In other words, a great deal has been written about imprisonment, but far less has been written about fines'. One could think this assertion is not entirely correct, on the one hand, because there is a vast amount of literature on the specific characteristics of fines as a legal sanction. However, much of this literature fails to address the historical development of fines and their changing place in the criminal justice system, once again with some notable exceptions (i.e., Rusche and Kirchheimer 1939 [2003]; Padovani 1981; Roldán Barbero 1983; Young 1989; O'Malley 2009).

On the other hand, although it could be possible to agree with this assertion regarding two Anglophone countries (United Kingdom and the United States of America), in continental Europe there is at least one outstanding exception: Germany. The quantity and quality of works relating to the penal fine in this country are vast. They cover the entire codification period to the present while often taking a historical perspective. This intense attention devoted to the fine was well known in countries profoundly influenced by Germany, such as neighbouring German-speaking countries, Austria and Switzerland, as well as in other European countries that experienced waves of German legal influence in their academic history, such as Spain and Italy, and to a lesser extent, Portugal and the Scandinavian countries. In both Southern and Northern Europe, there has been a lively academic debate and numerous works devoted to the fine. While it can be argued that some works are too much centred on the legal characteristics of the fine within a concrete national criminal justice system, others extend their attention to the historical development of the penal fine from very interesting points of view. As a Spanish legal scholar who speaks or reads English, German, Italian, Portuguese, and some French, my purpose is to make this vast amount of 'non-English-speaking' literature about the penal fine known to the Anglophone academic world, in the context of a work aimed at studying the role of fines in criminal law.

In order to do so, I will pose larger questions about institutions and practices in five of the most populated countries in Western Europe: namely, Germany, France, United Kingdom – mostly England and Wales – Italy, and Spain, adding now and then interesting developments in Austria, Portugal, Switzerland, and the Scandinavian countries. But I will make no attempt to systematically compare all these countries – neither by comparing the present circumstances in a longer historical perspective nor by analysing contemporary differences of place and legal culture. To proceed otherwise would be simply impossible in a single book. These countries had both striking similarities and great differences. I will refer to national experiences and developments when sources allow and as appropriate for the advance of my argument. I will also stress the interaction and sometimes simultaneous development of ideas, movements, and socio-legal trends inside Europe. I will try to identify patterns of punishment that are robust across time and space, but at the same time the exceptions to these patterns. The reason why is that although generally speaking nineteenth- and twentieth-century national penal policies regarding fines appear to be similar in their design, certain developments took place earlier in some places than in others, and did not occur in certain countries at all. There were processes that drove different countries towards the same solutions, but there were also limits to transfers of criminal sanctions and methods of corrections that can be explained by reference to history, culture, political or penal ideologies, or inertia. International communication and legal transplants do not necessarily insure that mistakes made by one country would not be repeated in another, or that a national success would not end in a sad failure in another place.

Of course, any understanding of change or innovation in penal law should involve a historically informed appreciation of the situation, and of the often conflicting pressures which confront scholars, courts, and policymakers. I do not pretend to conduct a comprehensive analysis of the ideological and cultural differences between the legal systems involved, but to explain the present by offering an explanation of the past. In fact, as a legal scholar, I *am* interested in asking 'how it really was' in a particular historical moment (from the late eighteenth century onwards) and country (mainly the five aforementioned countries, but also Western Europe in general). I intend to pursue this question not from the perspective Garland (1997: 207) called 'sociological realism', but from the viewpoint of the legal discussion and regulation in the countries that will be addressed in this study, not forgetting the ways in which the practices always diverge from the pattern implicit in the law and in the rationalities behind it. As Rusche and Kirchmeier (1939 [2003]: 5) put it, 'Punishment as such does not exist; only concrete systems of punishment and specific criminal practices exist'. As we will see, there were reasonable and foolish statutes, and there were also more or less fortunate interpreters of the legal norms and proposers of reforms. This research aims to analyse the opinion of the thinkers of the time, since in any case it is their opinions which spiritually characterize the epoch they lived in. Moreover, I want to discover if the more philosophical discourse exerted any influence on legislation and if it did, to what extent it permeated to both legal regulations and their practices. Legal change cannot be fully understood by only reading the preparatory reports preceding the passing of a new enactment, however interesting. The pro and con arguments must often be seen as nothing more than legitimation for the procurement of other goals and interests that are not clearly or explicitly expressed. From the perspective that the processes leading to our present practices and institutions in the criminal justice system were neither inevitable nor linear and continuous, this research intends to reveal not only how things came to be – that is, the conditions of possibility of a penal fine that is considered to be 'fair' – but also how they could have been otherwise by looking at failed drafts, useless statutes, rejected approaches, and academic debates. This means that this book does not intend to detail the history of changes in the use of money as punishment – although many historical aspects will be addressed, it makes no pretence to be such – but rather it aims to examine the history of changing conceptions in how fines have been conceived and used. Furthermore, this book describes the importance that certain penal and extra-penal aspects had in the theoretical and practical configuration of the law, setting aside the systematic study of a particular criminal justice system.

A further caveat is necessary. Properly speaking, I am not interested in dealing with the history of juridical theories and even less so with the overall history of jurisprudence as they pertain to the penal fine. What I will try to do is document a history of punitive rationalities and their transformations with regard to the penal fine and only marginally to other penalties, such as imprisonment or community service: a mapping of chronologically distinct rationalities and practices that immediately renders clear their modes of functioning, and their limits. With few exceptions, dramatic changes in punishment are better seen when looking not at short periods of time but at centuries. I will strive to analyse the discourses that unfolded from around the end of early modern times until now, from the viewpoint that the legal discussions during the nineteenth century set the stage for the profound reforms initiated by the emergence of the consumer society. As we will see, the genealogy of the penal fine is a story of constant reformulation in response to shifting political pressures, changes in institutional and administrative arrangements, and intellectual developments that changed ideological commitments of legislators and practitioners. Within this chronicle of reformulation, broad transformations since the late 1800s are discernible. Some of them were fuelled by the international nature of the science of punishment, which had its roots in the Enlightenment cosmopolitanism of the preceding century. These legal transformations, mostly widely discussed and debated, help us to delimitate old and new forms of punishment and, to some degree, different modes of constructing punishment inside the criminal law. But it would be inappropriate to stop here. Other more subtle, hidden changes had to do with the changing meaning of money. As will be shown, a series of associations based on the idea of money, its essence, and its capabilities had a profound impact on modern legal culture. Against the background of Simmel's work (1907 [1990]) on the characteristics of money, I will explore two interwoven hypotheses: first, that the meanings of money influenced the perceived appropriateness of fines as a punishment; and second, that different perceptions of what money sanctions are and how they work decisively influenced the development of criminal law during the nineteenth and twentieth centuries. To this end I will take an interdisciplinary approach in the fields of criminal justice and legal history, assigning a relevant role to criminology and the sociology of punishment.[1]

As statistical knowledge feeds bio-political technologies – and is produced by them (Hacking 1990, 1991)–, statistical information is an important part of this work. Criminal statistics were born in some eighteenth-century countries, and were in use in most nineteenth-century countries. The scarcity of data about the use of penal fines prior to the twentieth century is a problem in Italy and Spain, but there are relatively good data with regard to England and Wales, France, Germany, and the Scandinavian countries. Nevertheless, there are some important limitations due not only to the absence of available data and historical records but also to the comparability of the existing ones. The selection of the particular comparative study cases has been made taking into account these problems, although it is clear that they raise questions about the generalization of the conclusions.

Last but not least, this book is centred on the penal fine, understood as a sum of money required to be paid to the state as a penalty for a criminal offence. I will take into account only other 'monetized sanctions' (confiscation, civil forfeiture, punitive damages, liquidated damages, regulatory fines, court fees, probation supervision fees, costs, bonds), as O'Malley (2009: 1ff.) calls them, as a means to analyse the penal fine. Although all of them include an order to pay an amount of money, meaning no difference for the offender's pocket, their specific rationale varies (Klein 1997: 213ff.). On the contrary, deprivation of liberty is widely mentioned. The fact that this work mainly focuses on the penal fine justifies, in itself, paying careful attention to custodial penalties, most noticeably imprisonment. Penal policy is neither formulated in a vacuum nor necessarily the product of a coherent and consistent consensus. There is very little evidence for concerted, carefully planned policymaking in criminal law (Garland 1985: 208). On the contrary, when we search for the 'origins' of a concrete form of punishment, what is often found is not a clearly identified problem and the proposal of an universally accepted solution but the dissension of other things. In the case of fines, this 'other thing' is the penalty of imprisonment. As will be shown, the theoretical justification and practical application of the fine depend largely on whether the penalty of imprisonment, and especially short-term imprisonment, is seen as an eligible, positive option capable of fulfilling the purpose of punishment. In the European experience, prison and fines are essentially alternatives. From this perspective, this research on the genealogy of the penal fine is based on the conviction that the use of money as a sanction has contributed and can still greatly contribute to the reduction of imprisonment in Western European criminal justice systems.

Note

1 I will not use a Foucauldian approach, although I certainly aim to anatomize the past and contemporary practice on the penal fine, revealing the ways in which its modes of exercising power depend upon specific ways of thinking (rationalities) and specific ways of acting (technologies), as well as upon specific ways of 'subjectifying' individuals, not only criminals, and governing populations. By being inspired by a recent Foucauldian application to the field of monetary punishments – O'Malley's work on *The Currency of Justice* – I still intend to analyse discourses, norms, and practices, and the consequences in terms of governing crime and punishment. I will also problematize these practices of governing, located in a variety of different sites, by subjecting them to a 'genealogical' analysis, tracing their historical lineage in order to understand not only why and how we arrived at the present situation but also how the future might take shape. But I am too interested in legal developments to use the Foucauldian model. And I am even more interested in making the non-English-speaking literature about fines better known to the Anglophone/international academic world, improving the visibility of other European legal cultures and traditions, which explains the vast number of references in other languages than English.

References

Beristain Ipiña, A. (1976) 'La multa penal y la administrativa en relación con las sanciones privativas de libertad'. In AA.VV (ed.) *III Jornadas de Profesores de Derecho Penal*. Madrid: Universidad de Santiago de Compostela, 11–56.

Bottoms, A. E. (1983) 'Some Neglected Features of Contemporary Penal Systems'. In Garland, D. and P. Young (eds.) *The Power to Punish*. London: Heinemann, 166–202.

Garland, D. (1985) *Punishment and Welfare*. Aldershot: Gower.

Garland, D. (1997) '"Governmentality" and the Problem of Crime: Foucault, Criminology, Sociology'. *Theoretical Criminology* 1(2): 173–214.

Grover, C. (2008) *Crime and inequality*. Cullompton: Willan.

Hacking, I. (1990) *The Taming of Chance*. Cambridge: Cambridge University Press.

Hacking, I. (1991) 'How Should We Do the History of Statistics'. In Burchell, G., Gordon, C. and P. Miller (eds.) *The Foucault Effect*. Hemel Hempstead: Harvester Wheatsheaf, 181–196.

Klein, A. R. (1997) *Alternative Sentencing, Intermediate Sanctions and Probation*. 2nd ed. Cincinnati: Anderson.

Lappi-Seppälä, T. (2014) 'Fines in Europe'. In Bruinsma, G. and D. Weisburd (eds.) *Encyclopedia of Criminology and Criminal Justice*. New York: Springer, 1637–1648.

McCallum, D. (2011) 'Money, Discipline, and Liberal Political Reason'. *Social & Legal Studies* 20(4): 540–545.

O'Malley, P. (2009) *The Currency of Justice: Fines and Damages in Consumer Societies*. New York: Routledge-Cavendish.

Padovani, T. (1981) *L'utopia punitiva*. Milan: Giuffrè.

Roldán Barbero, H. (1983) *El dinero, objeto fundamental de la sanción penal*. Madrid: Akal.

Rusche, G. and O. Kirchheimer (1939 [2003]) *Punishment and Social Structure*. New Brunswick: Transaction.

Simmel, G. (1907 [1990]) *The Philosophy of Money*. New York: Routledge.

Young, P. (1989) 'Punishment, Money and a Sense of Justice'. In Carlen, P. and D. Cook (eds.) *Paying for Crime*. Milton Keynes: Open University Press, 46–65.

Young, P. (1999) 'The Fine as an Auto-Punishment: Power, Money and Discipline'. In Duff, P. and N. Hutton (eds.) *Criminal Justice in Scotland*. Aldershot: Dartmouth, 182–197.

Glossary

Day-fine system (also called unit-fine system): In the day-fine system, the amount of the fine imposed is based on the seriousness of the offence as well as the offender's ability to pay. The fine amount is arrived at through the application of a two-stage process. The number of days or units depends on the seriousness of the offence, usually between a minimum and a maximum. The amount of money to be paid every day depends on the offender's ability to pay, also usually between a minimum and a maximum. The final amount is the result of the multiplication of the number of days of the first step by the amount of money to be paid every day of the second step. As a result, wealthy individuals are given a larger fine compared to poor individuals who committed the exact same crime. This increases fines' punitive potential and makes them more appropriate for more serious offences.

Fixed-fine or tariff-fine system: In the fixed-fine system, the amount of the fine to be paid is fixed for any particular offence based on the seriousness of the offence. Some statutes establish a minimum and a maximum between which courts may discretionally decide the appropriate amount. If the tariff is set high, poor offenders are disproportionately impacted and suffer more frequently the consequences of default for non-payment. If the fine is set low, wealthier offenders are not deterred. Because most offenders tend to be poor and unemployed, tariffs are typically set at the lower end of the range. This decreases fines' punitive potential and makes them less appropriate for more serious offences.

Imprisonment for default: It is a consecutive prison term which the offender may be required to serve if he or she fails to satisfy the imposed fine. It substitutes the payment of the fine.

1 Making offenders pay

Introduction

Time and money are the great scarcities of modern life. Therefore, it should come as no surprise that loss of time, in the form of imprisonment, and loss of money, in the form of a fine, have become the two basic foundations of most Western European criminal justice systems. Fines outnumber any other penal sanction, including imprisonment, in many countries. However, legal scholars, criminologists and sociologists write about prisons and imprisonment as if fines did not exist. This trend makes it almost impossible to fully understand the historical evolution of the penalty of imprisonment, since it is intimately related to the reasons why fines were first abandoned and then re-established. At the same time, a more comprehensive analysis of the uses of money as a sanction is also needed, because views on money influence the perceived appropriateness of fines as a punishment for every type of offence, or only certain offences. More than a century ago, Simmel's seminal study on the philosophy of money suggested the need for a closer and more detailed interpretative analysis of the meaning of money, since the effects of money transcend the market (Simmel 1907 [1990]). This remains more urgent than ever in the fields of criminal law, criminology, and the sociology of punishment, in which the nature of the very special monetary relation between the offender and the state that constitutes the essence of the fine has been generally neglected by literature.

In fact, an accurate analysis of the fine must contain a set of interpretative techniques sensitive to how money, time, and freedom are perceived and to the range of dispositions and expectations which inform how they are used. As we will see, a series of associations based on the idea of money, its essence, and its capabilities had a profound impact on modern legal culture.[1] These associations generated a pattern of practices and dispositions that have strongly influenced the way we see the compulsory payment of a sum of money to the state as a 'suitable' punishment only for some offences or offenders. Quite surprisingly, although we could say that money is essentially the measure of all things in market societies, and as a pure medium it could be thought that loss of money would be an appropriate equivalent even for long periods of deprivation of freedom, in practice the changing meaning of money in the last two centuries has undermined the use of fines as a punishment for serious crimes, while promoting them as the perfect sanction for regulatory offences and misdemeanours. The purpose of this chapter is to contribute to this line of research and present some of the key aspects that will be addressed in the next chapters.

Money as the measure of all things

It is a generally accepted fact that the fine is a less severe punishment than imprisonment, and that it is even less severe than other intermediate punishments (Von Hirsh et al. 1992), which makes it unsuitable for punishing serious crimes. The reason for this is, apparently, quite straightforward. The commodity affected by the fine, money, does not have the same value as what is usually attributed to freedom. In Western societies, freedom and its deprivation have a phenomenal importance that money and fines do not. Only exceptionally can we find some authors striving to point out that wealth, which the offender would be deprived of by applying the fine,

> is, in its infinite gradations, an extremely important asset for man, and the punishment affecting the offender regarding this asset he has, is identical in nature to other punishments and may take on gradual and overwhelming importance, the same as the relevant asset may be gradual and large.
>
> (Bertola 1893: 549)

Such opinions were absolutely in the minority and harshly criticized (e.g., Ciccarelli 1897: 653–654). Generally, it was agreed that money and freedom are unequal assets, with freedom being held in higher esteem than money (Merkel 1895: 389–390; Conti 1910: 457; Stooß 1916: 5).

And yet, to explain the rise of the fine since the early twentieth century, many authors argue that 'money had become the measure of all things', and therefore 'it was only right that the state, which extends positive privileges in the form of monetary grants, should also introduce the negative privilege of taking wealth away in punishment for delinquency' (Rusche and Kirchheimer 1939 [2003]: 168). In market societies one could say that money is indeed the measure of all things. It turns all aspects of social life into marketable commodities. It 'makes up for lost wages, profits or other lost opportunities for financial gain', but also 'for pain and suffering, mental anguish, ridicule and contempt' (O'Malley 2009: 6). In contrast to earlier forms of society, market economies use money for every possible purpose known to economics (Ilmonen 2011). It serves as a medium of exchange, but also as a standard of value used in reckoning prices, costs, and values – what is usually called 'money of account' – as a store of value, and as a standard of deferred payment. As a general symbol of value, money serves more purposes than ever before. If this is true, why is it not the same in criminal law?

Simmel's general view of money as an unconditionally interchangeable, qualitatively neutral, infinitely divisible, and entirely homogeneous medium of exchange, expressing no value of its own other than as a representation of other objects

(Simmel 1907 [1990]), explains the nineteenth-century conceptualization of money as exclusively determined by quantity and free from any quality. Certainly, Simmel's approach to money helps to explain the discrediting of the fine as a punishment for serious crimes since the end of the eighteenth century. As we will see, at that time, money no longer had personal connotations. It gradually came to be considered a universal equivalent, 'a medium that could express the significance of any feature of human experience' (Reddy 1987: 77). Money became a widespread medium of exchange, despite the fact that it was possessed in large amounts by very few people. Nevertheless, Simmel's general approach to money does not explain other points, such as the indivisibility of the monetary unit when the fine is to be replaced with a subsidiary prison sentence. If money is allegedly divisible, does it really matter if a few unpaid cents are substituted by a day or an hour in prison?[2] What about the concern that grew in the nineteenth century about how to prevent the fine from being paid by an innocent third party? If money is impersonal, does it really matter who pays the fine? How can we explain the effort made to prevent the payment of the fine from affecting the most basic needs of the individual and his or her family? Or the late eighteenth- and nineteenth-century emergence of a school of thought that professed that the amount of the fine must be calculated so that it leaves the offender the means necessary to support himself, 'excluding the amount that serves to satisfy pleasures, whatever these may be, such as wine, spirits and tobacco' (Garofalo 1887: 108)? Again, if money is unlimited and easily substitutable, does it really matter what the offender and his or her family have to deprive themselves of to pay it?

The answer is yes. It does matter. Zelizer (1997: 18ff.) points out that Simmel's general viewpoint fails to capture the complex range of characteristics of money as a social medium. For her, in certain domains another coding is necessary, for the money used there can be indivisible, non-fungible, deeply subjective, and therefore qualitatively heterogeneous. This perspective is not embodied in Simmel's general approach to money, but in his much more nuanced study of money *as a punishment*, contained in the fifth chapter of *The Philosophy of Money*. He recognized there that 'fines can, in fact, produce an individual trait that is alien to money as such', overcoming the classical underestimation of the importance of individuals' perceptions of how they actually use money. Following this approach, my argument is that one of the domains Zelizer refers to is the criminal law, where money's significance thus lies in the synthesis it promotes between impersonal abstraction and the principle of personality of penalties, qualitative neutrality and the very different cultural resonances and connotations of imprisonment and fines, absolute interchangeability and the impossibility of substitution of long custodial sentences by fines.

Equating money and freedom through criminal law

In criminal law, loss of money is the bearer of qualitatively different meanings compared with loss of freedom. One should rationally conclude that money cannot be equated with freedom. However, the criminal justice system establishes rates of exchange between the time served and the payment of a sum of money using two approaches: first, through the mechanism of imprisonment by default; second, through substituting the originally imposed prison sentence with a penal fine. One could think that Marx was right when he warned that money, 'confounding and compounding [. . .] all natural and human qualities [. . .] serves to exchange every property for every other, even contradictory, property and object: it is the fraternization of impossibilities' (1844 [1975]: 325–326). In fact, money seems to reduce the priceless itself to price. As Marx said, from an extremely negative perspective on money (Campbell 2011), 'not even the bones of saints [. . .] are *extra commercium hominum* able to withstand the alchemy' (1867 [1996]: 142).

Yet, when we analyse the rationale of these equivalences, we can see that it is not actually a matter of equating an amount of money with an amount of time. Money and freedom are not interchangeable because they are thought to have equal value – quite the opposite. Regarding imprisonment for fine defaulters, the offender must be threatened with a prison sentence that is *more severe* than the fine. Imprisonment by default ensures that the offender will pay whatever fine is levied. The purpose of imprisonment here is not to punish the offender but to coerce collection of the fine – the idea being that if there is no difference in severity, the offender will be indifferent between the two forms of punishment. The very premise of the established equation between time and money is thus to reinforce the use of fines as a method of punishment.

The substitution of (usually short-term) prison sentences by fines is also based on the superiority of fines to imprisonment – namely, on the belief that the benefits gained from short-term prison sentences in preventive terms are not as great as the damage caused to both the offender and society through imprisonment. It is impossible to speak here of an essential equality of all trading goods and therefore of the neutrality of money and monetary exchange.

In sum, the establishment of rates of exchange between time and money through imprisonment for fine defaulters or the substitution of short-term prison sentences by fines fails to consider any equivalence between the fine and the period of the deprivation of freedom, although in both cases the fine remains articulated to imprisonment through the metrics of quantity.

As in the cases mentioned before, it could also be deemed necessary to establish some equivalence between time and money when it comes to defining criminal law, when the legislator decides which punishment is the most appropriate for each offence. Sadly enough, just then penalties are not themselves the product of an accurate theoretical analysis and calculation, but are only the roughest of guesses, too often influenced by extra-legal considerations, such as political concerns, social fears, moral panics, and changes in the willingness to bring prosecutions. We must not forget the issue of how 'serious crime' is defined. The vast majority of crimes punished with medium and long terms of imprisonment are those crimes which are characteristically associated with the poor, while, for example, white-collar crime is neglected. 'The wrongdoings of the affluent are paid for mainly by money' (Hudson 2000: 199), as we will see later on with more detail. In sum, we cannot extract any equation from penal codes.

Only the law and economy movement has strongly defended the notion that fines and imprisonment are perfectly equivalent in terms of punitivism. When facing the problem of measuring the cost of punishments as different as fines and imprisonment, Becker (1974: 13) maintained '[t]he cost of different punishments to an offender can be made comparable by converting them into their monetary equivalent or worth, which, of course, is directly measured only for fines'. As Posner (1980: 415–416) said, 'For every prison sentence there is some fine equivalent; if the fine is so large that it cannot be collected, then the offender should be imprisoned'. He added that 'even if, improbably, imprisonment produced a stigma effect which no magnitude of fine could duplicate, only the rate of exchange between fine and imprisonment, and not the principle of equivalence, would be affected'. The only difference between imprisonment and fines is in the units of measurement: fines are prices measured in monetary units, and imprisonments are prices measured in time units. Becker and Posner used words like 'price', 'cost', or 'profit' in ways that imply acceptance of money as a valid instrument of numerical measurement of the seriousness of a crime and the cost of a punishment. For them, the problem arises only when some crimes, such as murder, are so serious that even the affluent cannot pay adequate fines, solvency limitations precluding the imposition of very large fines for such crimes, although they are the optimal sentence. In this case, fines have to be supplemented with imprisonment or other punishments in order to discourage offences optimally. They extract the obvious conclusion: 'This analysis implies that if some offenders could pay the fine for a given offense and others could not, the former should be punished solely by fine and the latter partly by other methods' (Becker 1974: 31). 'Since water cannot be squeezed out of a stone, it may seem that incarceration must continue to be used for indigent offenders, who predominate in theft and in crimes of violence' (Posner 1972: 363). The first consequence of this proposal is the selection of punishments not by the seriousness of the crime but by the impossibility of the offender to pay the fine. The second one is that a rich offender should not go to prison as long as he pays the fine. Becker justified these striking conclusions by determining a 'fair' length of the prison term compared to the fine, and suggesting 'a policy of leniency toward persons who are imprisoned because they cannot pay fines' (Becker 1974: 32).

Despite having become the neo-liberal rationality of government par excellence, the perspective adopted by the economic analysis of law by treating criminal law as a pricing mechanism and sanctions as prices for doing what is forbidden did not change the relative position of fines in the panoply of punishments. Dependence on economic terms that obscure the fundamental difference between deprivation of money and deprivation of freedom makes it extremely difficult to fully appreciate the widespread rejection of a wholly monetized punishment. At this level, there exists a profound dissociation: although the penal fine is the most common punitive sanction, deprivation of money fails to fulfil general cultural expectations of what punishment ought to be like in many important ways. Why?

Both time and money are quantifiable and divisible. This circumstance gives the modern penalty, the one emerging from the Enlightenment, the character of an abstract and equal sanction that can be legally predetermined in both nature and content as the deprivation of a *quantum*: a specific time period of freedom in the case of custodial sentences, and a specific sum of money in the case of a fine (Ferrajoli 1990: 388–389). This abstract and measurable character of both penalties, imprisonment and fine, allows them to be applied as a calculation, aimed specifically at quantitatively determining them in accordance with the circumstances of the case, within the legal limits, which ensures proportionality. However, the Enlightened concept of the principle of equality, based on a formal understanding that did not allow the offender's personal circumstances to be taken into account when determining the appropriate punishment, particularly those arising from belonging to a specific social class, had and indeed still has a considerable impact on the way we understand the fine as an appropriate sanction. Let us see why.

Why is the fine inappropriate to punish serious crimes?

Several thinkers have raised this question in different times and places (see Marcos Gutiérrez 1826: 147; Young 1989; Doob and Marinos 1995; Marinos 2005). Its persistence shows that relationships between money and punishment are complex. They have 'very different connotations and are underpinned by very different cultural values' (Easton and Piper 2005: 222). As we will see here, a 'cultural separation' or estrangement exists between punishment and money, so that 'an ambivalent, even contradictory, set of cultural values form the context in which money is used as a judicial punishment' (Young 1994: 187). Although money is the measure of all things, there exist a certain number of crimes in which the use of money as the only means of punishment is rejected, purporting that fines are not equitable with all prison sentences, but just short-term sentences. This happens not because 'there are some things which are still placed beyond the reach of monetary exchange' (Young 1989: 65), nor because 'the whole development of the value of life out of predominantly Christian doctrine is based on the idea that man has an *absolute* value' that 'cannot possibly be measured by any quantitative standard and cannot be compensated for merely by more or less of another value' (Simmel 1907 [1990]: 360). In most areas of law, human life, health, freedom, and dignity – the highest and most sacred human values – are routinely rendered into monetary amounts. 'Thus the priceless itself surrenders to price' (Zelizer 1997: 8). Only in the field of criminal law is imprisonment generally seen as the only proper punishment when crimes affect central aspects of our notion of 'personhood', with fines failing symbolically to serve the functions of punishment for such crimes.

This was not always the case. It is true that the widespread rejection of punishing serious crimes with just a fine has been supported by specialized literature since the nineteenth century (e.g., Wahlberg 1877: 264; Friedmann 1892: 100ff.; Brenn 1945: 12; Driendl 1983: 669), normally without explanation for this rejection, as it was considered to be so obvious that there was no need for clarification. For example, while holding that there were 'a few instances where fixed fines were appropriate to more serious crime', the Seventh Report of Her Majesty's

Commissioners on the Criminal Law sustained the belief that 'fines should be restricted to cases of minor delinquency punishable by summary jurisdiction' (Commission on Criminal Law 1843: 174–175), without giving a reason for this restriction. Another example: for Bumke (1928: 16–17), 'when dealing with serious infringements of the law the fine is not a sufficient punishment according to current opinion. Therefore, in accordance with the law in force it is not possible to punish any crime with just a fine'. Very few proposed that murder and other serious crimes should be sanctioned with a fine, accompanied by imprisonment only in the most serious cases (e.g., Ferri 1900: 454, following Rossi 1853), without success.

The use of fines only for minor offences is also evident right from the very first criminal statistics. For example, the fine was imposed as a single punishment in 14.1 per cent of cases, mostly for minor offences between 1891 and 1895 in Italy (Direzione Generale della Statistica 1899: xxvi–xxvii). In turn, in England, aggregate figures for the lower court's use of sanctions for non-indictable offences are not easily available for this period, but it seems that the fine was the predominant sanction used only in these cases (Garland 1985: 8).

This situation clearly differs from the one under ancient Celtic, Slav, and Germanic laws. These laws, under the *lex talionis*, considered the deprivation of money through a fine or confiscation, together with redressing the damage, as punishment enough even for the more serious crimes.[3] *Talio* is Latin for 'equivalent to' or 'equal', so that the *lex talionis* requires punishment equal to the offence. This concern for equality between the offence and the punishment of the offender was expressed during the Middle Ages in lists that assigned a monetary value not only to every part of the human anatomy but also to human life, in accord with the severity of the injury and with the status of the person injured or slain – that is, whether the victim was freeborn, a slave, an aristocrat, male or female, adult or child. That is to say that the level of payment for such debts was specified by a hierarchy of value by which an individual's position and status in society were established. Simmel explained: 'This tendency not only makes money the measure of man, but it also makes man the measure of the value of money' (1907 [1990]: 356). Money provided a quantitative concept of the value of human life. As soon as the amount of money to be paid for one particular person was permanently fixed according to his or her position in the social order, and the same payment was expected even for vastly different persons and cases within this social order, the notion was formed that man in himself was worth such and such an amount. These types of tariffs transcended subjective assessments of a person's value based on how his or her kin valued the personal loss associated with the injury to, or death of, their kinsperson (Peacock 2013: 107).

> This indifference to personal differences no longer allows a person's value as a whole to consist of what other individuals enjoy and lose by them; their value is, as it were, embodied in themselves as an objective quality expressible in money. The fixing of *wergild* carried out in the interests of social peace and in order to avoid endless feuds therefore seems to be the psychological

> origin of the transformation of the originally subjective utilitarian valuation of human life into the objective notion that man has this specific value.
> (Simmel 1907 [1990]: 359)

However, these payments were never imagined to be material equivalents of the loss of life or limb, since such injuries were seen as incalculable. Rather they emerged from 'the need to assuage the anger of the injured party and make good his loss in public reputation' (Grierson 1977: 20–21). As Graeber (2009: 124) pointed out, 'The conversion of an unpayable debt into the "price" of a man or woman, then, appears to have been brought about principally through an alchemy of violence'. Moreover, we should remember that the feudal economy was extensively non-monetary: despite the wide use of money by merchants and others frequenting markets and fairs, money was not strategic in economic life, nor was it broadly distributed in large amounts between individuals (Spufford 1988). In such a society, 'money could be the bearer of meaning, because it was unusual and thereby, in degree, distanced from everyday life' (O'Malley 2009: 10). *Wergeld* codified elements of social structure into a hierarchy of value, in which the use of fines was saturated with sacral, moral meaning. Outside the boundaries of market exchange but on the terrain of law, it offered for the first time standardized scales of value, so that money could serve to denominate payments in units of value (Grierson 1977). These scales disappeared during the Enlightenment, being based as they were on characteristics that were considered no longer suitable to inform the quantity and quality of punishments. The penal fine lost its meaning as a collective representation of order analogous to the structure of society, since modern, liberal societies based their ideas on the principle of equality of all men in the eyes of the law. In this way, the Enlightened conceptualization of the equality principle, based on a formal understanding that did not allow the offender's personal circumstances to be taken into account when determining the appropriate punishment, particularly those arising from belonging to a specific social class, strongly impacted how fines were understood. We should remember that under the *ancien régime* punishment was measured based on the offender's economic circumstances or personality (Sbriccoli 1990 [2009]: 408). The dominant opinion around the middle of the eighteenth century still saw the social status of the delinquent as a central aspect to be considered when selecting the type of punishment, and partly also the severity of punishment. Differentiation of punishments according to status was rejected 50 years later. New codifications from the beginning of the nineteenth century onwards avoided references to social class or economic status due to the influence of the equality principle, which was in part constitutionally guaranteed. Under the banner of the equality principle, legislative parity was centred on the value of 'freedom', which is presumed to be possessed in the same *quantum* by all subjects, excepting deeper probing into the inner feelings of each prisoner – which was considered at the time to be a forbidden intrusion. The position regarding the fine is very different. In fact, it is exactly the reverse of that which can be presumed in the use of imprisonment (Young 1989: 63). Nobody presumes that individuals are in an equal position with regard to the commodity, money, they are about to be deprived of. It was not the relatively equal amount of what was paid for a certain offence that set up the fairness of the sentence. It was the fact that the amount paid was insignificant for one offender but substantial for the other. Formal equality combined with brutal inequities in practice. As we will see, this put fines outside the cultural boundaries of nineteenth-century liberalism.

Imprisonment, on the contrary, was considered a more equal punishment than the fine, and soon after, also a more rehabilitative one. As we will see, since the beginning of the nineteenth century a direct link has been established between the fine and the prison, so that the expectations placed on the latter, in terms of the possibility that offenders could be reformed by hygienic, strictly regulated prison regimes, undermined the use of the fine. As King (1996: 64) explained, 'the acceptance of the penalty of imprisonment first relegated the fine to a comparatively minor role as a punishment for light misdemeanours and police offences'. But also the changing importance of money should be considered. During the nineteenth century, there were a number of changes in the meaning of money that influenced not only the establishment of the consumer society but also the use of fines. In contrast to freedom, money is now thought to be not personal. The monetary penalty was regarded and experienced differently because of the changing meaning and value that liberal societies attributed to money and, correspondingly, to its deprivation in the form of a fine: 'the progressive differentiation of people and the equally progressive indifference of money combine to make expiation for murder and other serious crimes by money completely impossible' (Simmel 1907 [1990]: 365–366). Simmel correctly contended that our sense of human worth and developments in the meaning of money moved in opposite directions.

> The increasing valuation of the human soul with its uniqueness and individuality meets with the opposite trend in the development of money [so that i]t is precisely because money represents the value of incommensurable things and has become colourless and indifferent that it cannot be used as an equivalent in very special and uncommon conditions where the inner most and most basic aspects of the person are concerned.
>
> (Simmel 1907 [1990]: 365)

As Seagle (1948: 250) puts it, in contrast to ancient and medieval times when pecuniary penalties often had to be discharged in highly valuable domestic animals or agricultural goods, 'a money economy now made it particularly easy to measure and secure the fair price of an offense, but for that very reason it must have been felt that the deterrent value of such a punishment as the fine was bound to be small'. The lack of meaning is in itself the most important meaning of modern money, shaped by the cultural matrix in which it is embedded and characterized by a market system in which private and not only public debts like fines and taxes are monetized. As money is a commodity held in less esteem than liberty, it is believed that fines run the risk of commercializing criminal law. Their use gives the impression that everything can be fixed with money and that money can be used to avoid the weight of the repressive power of the state, or at least to reach a deal. Furthermore, the undifferentiated quality of money makes it impossible to establish whose money is paying a fine imposed on the condemned criminal. As we will see in Chapter 3, for a large part of the nineteenth century, in some cases well into the twentieth century, several European countries permitted payment to be made by third parties, including the offender's heirs. Although transferability of fines to the offender's heirs could be legislatively avoided, the impossibility to control whose money really pays the fine has since then been considered a qualitative defect of the fine as a punishment: 'the fine affects an impersonal [*unpersönliches*] asset and therefore there is no guarantee that it is the perpetrator himself who pays the fine [. . .] This fault of the penal fine is impossible to avoid, whatever the regulations in force may be' (Zipf 1965: 633). In sum, the fact that it is impossible to prevent a third party from paying the fine, based as it is on the impersonality of money, combined with money's lack of meaning, affected the idea of the pecuniary penalty as a proper punishment for serious and medium-range crimes. The different perception of the significance – or lack of significance – of money in contrast to freedom explains the rise of imprisonment in the nineteenth century and the correlative relegation of the fine to a comparatively minor role in the law. The corresponding disappearance of the fine also in the law in practice – in those countries where it was included in the penal codes, but could not be effectively applied because of the offenders' insolvency, which led automatically to imprisonment for fine default – is to be bound up with the unequal distribution of money in liberal societies.

Should petty offences be punished or regulated?

The opposite problem also arises. Today many criminal offences are punishable only with a fine. The perceived 'leniency' of this penalty has led many past authors to propose the decriminalization of these offences (see already Wahlberg 1877: 240, and Birkmeyer 1901: 1067, but also recent ones, such as Driendl 1978: 31ff.; Ferrajoli 1990: 415–416; Padovani 1994: 449ff.). The main reason is that they should be not punished but regulated. There is no shortage of arguments for this: from the inflation they cause, giving rise to the criminal law being discredited, to the development of administrative forms of justice that relativize penal and procedural guarantees, and also their default 'disproportion' regarding the severity determined by the criminal infringement.

Some of these aspects will be addressed in other chapters. Here I am interested in two different but related questions: first, how the perceived leniency of money sanctions influenced the rise of regulatory law; and second, whether there are differences attributable to the option of a penal or administrative nature of the sanction.[4] There are many differences, but I will highlight only those which are the most significant for the purposes of this section.

Since the separation of regulatory law and criminal law, there has been a unanimous proposal to punish infringements of the first – *mala quia prohibita* – via a fine, with imprisonment being reserved as a punishment for criminal offences of greater ethical importance – *prohibita quia mala* (Merkel 1893: 340; Saltelli

1939: 703; Nowakowski 1973: 2; Driendl 1983: 669; Ogus 2010: 29). When an action is viewed as wrong only because it is contrary to a statute, although not inherently evil – not a *malum in se* – we tend to think that there is nothing unfair about allowing a third party to pay the fine, such as a parking ticket. We do not, however, allow third parties to be sent to prison in the place of those who have committed a crime. Whenever guilt, responsibility, and culpability are at play punishment becomes personal by its very nature. And since culpability as a penal – not moral – notion is personal, not something that can freely be transferred from one person to another, it informs our understanding of the principle of personality of punishments.

This different perception leads to other differences in the regulation of penal and regulatory fines. I have already noted that it is difficult to give the fine a strictly penal nature due to the interchangeability of money. The fine's monetary nature makes it a sanction that is especially useful for implementing in other branches of the legal system.[5] The fine is transversal; it permeates through all aspects of law. Its proportionality to the seriousness of the unlawful act and the possibility that it can be paid by a third party, thereby satisfying the financial interests of the state, are two characteristics which stand out.

If we disregard strictly formal classification criteria, such as the criteria for determining the penal or regulatory nature of a fine according to the range of the relevant regulation, the competent authority to impose it, and the appropriate corresponding procedure, the only substantial aspect that nowadays characterizes the penal fine compared to the regulatory fine is the possibility to replace it with a term of imprisonment in the case of non-payment (see already Saltelli 1939: 704). Such a conversion is not possible in the case of the regulatory fine.[6] Disarticulation of the regulatory fine from the possibility of imprisonment in the case of default is its most vital characteristic (O'Malley 2009: 73). It is true that this characteristic is in practice very relativized by the provision of alternatives to short-term imprisonment, which has led to imprisonment for fine default being replaced with other intermediate sanctions, such as community service, as we will explore in Chapter 4. But it is also true that, ultimately, a penal fine can end up as a custodial sentence if the alternative sanctions fail, while a regulatory fine cannot: there are no other substantial differences.

Decoupling from the possibility of imprisonment for fine defaulters leads to other consequences, the most important of which is the lack of concern for adapting the fine to the offender's financial circumstances, unlike what happened with the penal fine, as will be addressed in Chapter 4.[7] Usually regulatory fines are imposed using tariff and fixed-fine systems, which do not vary the amount to be paid according to the offender's means.[8] This difference between penal and regulatory fines is not only attributable to the different recipients of one and the other. It is true that the main recipients of the harshest punishments in criminal law are members of the poorer classes. A simple sociological analysis of prison inmates is clear proof of this (Hudson 2000: 197). It is also true that, originally, regulatory fines appeared to resolve class, technical, and ideological problems associated with prosecuting respectable businessmen and managers, who do not usually pose the problem of inability to pay. The regulatory fine was not and 'is not directed at the traditional categories of offenders at whom the penal fine was and is directed' (O'Malley 2009: 100). Fines emerged as the appropriate sanction for the 'respectable' offender in the late nineteenth century, when they were used to punish the new economic offences of white-collar criminals. In these cases, only the fine was considered acceptable as it did not involve prison for the businessmen affected. As O'Malley (2009: 65) pointed out, 'The fine, in other words, with the implication of its reduced stigma, and the fact that it did not lay hands on the bodies of the middle classes, made this regulation politically palatable'. Although sometimes imprisonment was provided in law, it was not generally applied in practice. Extra-legal factors operated to mitigate the severity of formal penalties (Levi 1989; Croall 1991; Wilson 2006; Taylor 2013). This lack of application of custodial sentences, and the reactions of outraged astonishment that ensued in the rare cases in which businessmen were sentenced to imprisonment,[9] led to the widespread use of fines in the new regulatory laws applicable to industry and in economic criminal law. As O'Malley (2009: 97) put it,

> In this way, 'decent citizens' would avoid stigmatization as the money penalty was given a certain 'acceptable' meaning by linking it to what Rusche and Kirchheimer might regard as a 'technical' question: distanced from bad motives and moral condemnation; distanced from the taint of prison that demolished good character.

But the use of the regulatory fine increased significantly when it began to be applied to mass traffic violations. In half a century the invention of the internal combustion engine completely changed road-based transport,[10] remaking the European landscape and economic structure. It also posed new questions to European criminal justice systems. In all of them ever-expanding vehicle ownership generated major social and regulatory problems, from the control and regulation of road traffic to the problem of road accidents, the expensive adaptation of roads and bridges to the new conditions, the spreading of the population over the countryside, the need of regulating speed limits, and the increasing parking difficulties in the cities. The definition and sanction of a new type of offence dependent on the use of motor vehicles were a high-profile political issue that revolutionized the business of criminal courts as soon as car ownership became widespread (Walker 1968: 32; Emsley 1993: 357; Simon 1998). Criminal courts were called upon to deal with a sheer volume of cases which threatened to collapse them.[11]

The need to alleviate the pressure on the courts led to the introduction of a procedural wedge between 'routine' infractions and 'criminal' offences. With the exception of drunken and dangerous driving, most of road traffic offences, such as the enforcement of speeding and parking time limits, were considered a nuisance, a mere 'technicality'. They were regarded as neither morally problematic nor affecting public safety. Adopting summary proceedings and fixed penalty procedures became a common phenomenon across Europe, with fines directly imposed either by the police or by the prosecutors. By then, these fines were imposed on members of the middle *and* lower classes, who certainly can experience problems when it comes to payment (Warner 2012: 237; Ashworth 2015: 266). Traffic fines have an inequitable impact on low-income offenders. In fact, this is the area where inequity is most pronounced. Despite this, the regulatory fine was not adjusted to suit the offender's financial ability to pay.[12] One might think that this lack of adjustment is attributable to a reasonable order of values whereby penal fines are higher than regulatory ones. However, this cannot be the reason: regulatory fines often involve much higher sums than penal fines, despite being the sanction for acts that in theory are less serious than those involving criminal law (Grebing 1982: 166–167). Penalties for regulatory offences are not invariably less serious than those for criminal offences. Indeed, in many jurisdictions even traffic fines have overtaken the quantum of fines handed out for many criminal offences. Thus the penalty provisions set out in the respective legislation do not necessarily reflect the differences between 'true' crimes and regulatory offences. And fixed fines are set at standard rates, which means they cannot possibly have an equal impact upon offenders with different economic circumstances: they impact disproportionately hard upon poorer people.

There is another reason for not taking into account the offender's financial circumstances. It is not that the money sanction applied as a regulatory fine is in anyway meaningless. Quite the contrary – it has a significantly different meaning.

The difference between meanings of the regulatory fine and the penal fine seems to lie in the establishment of regulatory law as a form of regulation of sheer volumes of minor infractions through the monetization of the sanction. The use of fines enables a reduction of safeguards and protections for the defendant because fines do not affect liberty, not even in the case of non-payment.[13] As O'Malley (2009: 82–83) explains, 'it is difficult to pass by the point that because the regulatory fine short-circuits the likelihood of imprisonment in default, it is liberated from the traditional onerous procedural rules that are intended to protect the accused in the otherwise uneven contest with the state'. Mostly, regulatory sanctions can be imposed without an oral hearing or other formalities, and to a lower standard of proof compared with what is used in criminal procedures. They deliver what is seen as swift, simple, effective justice. In contrast, a criminal penalty can be imposed only by a criminal court and only following prescribed procedures, usually with a burden of proof on the prosecution to a standard higher than the one used in non-criminal cases, with rules of evidence protecting the defendant. As Ogus (2010: 35) pointed out,

> The principal purpose of the criminal procedural requirements is to reduce the number of errors that can result from the adjudication process, including notably the wrongful imposition of a penalty on those who are innocent, and the costs that arise from such errors.

These costs are much higher if the wrongful sentence imposed is imprisonment instead of a fine (Ogus 2004: 51). The latter is obviously easier to compensate, for two reasons: first, because as it affects an 'impersonal' commodity it is easier to return the offender to the situation he or she was in before experiencing the punishment; second, because the loss of freedom imposed upon a prisoner deprives him or her of a finite resource – namely, time – while the loss of money 'need not to be viewed in this way: an individual may be able to create opportunities to obtain more money' (Ashworth and Player 1998: 259–260). Therefore, it is easy to conclude that time-consuming procedures are associated with protection of the accused from a wrongful *prison* sentence (O'Malley 2013: 380).

Furthermore, calculating the offender's financial ability to pay would excessively complicate an administrative procedure that is required to be expeditious. Administrative procedures are established the way they are, precisely, because the fine is the regulatory sanction par excellence. Standardization to achieve rapid processing of large numbers of cases is regarded as a necessary sacrifice in the cause of administrative efficiency (Lappi-Seppälä 2014: 1638–1639; Vormbaum 2014: 135). Assessing the financial circumstances of the offender would be an obstacle to streamlined procedures (Albrecht 2001: 309).

But the line that distinguishes regulatory from penal offences is wavering and blurry, in particular if we use a substantive, non-formal approach.[14] In German-speaking countries (Germany, Austria) and other countries influenced by German legal thinking, like Italy, Portugal, and Spain, the principle of guilt prevents strict liability offences from having a penal nature. They lack moral content and, thus, can only be administrative. But regulatory law also includes reckless and wilful violations that could easily be classified as penal, and in fact they are or have been in some countries during certain periods. Just think of road traffic offences. Regulatory and criminal offences simply overlap in many criminal justice systems.

Therefore, the difference between criminal offences, *mala in se*, and regulatory ones, *mala quia prohibita*, is not always easy to apply. What is then the difference between punishing and regulating? The example of road traffic offences is very telling. Whenever there is a safety problem for others, the possibilities of an incident becoming a criminal matter and ending with a prison sentence increase (Samuels 1970: 202–203). For example, in cases of driving under the influence, the offence may be regarded by law as sufficiently serious to incur imprisonment – even if few motoring offences measure up to the layman's conception of a criminal offence, since illegal behaviour on the road is not heavily stigmatized. In contrast, when a problem is regarded as one of public inconvenience rather than safety, it becomes an administrative matter instead of a criminal one. For cases of parking infringements fines can be imposed without an oral hearing or other formalities, and to a lower standard of proof compared with what is used in criminal procedures. They are accompanied by measures such as discouragement of attendance at court by extra fees and risks of extra penalties if disputing the infraction, discounts in case of payment of the penalty within a short period of time, no criminal records at all, and, in general, the possibility of handling everything out of court. Fines take up the character of a regulatory governmental technique, aimed at regulating flows and distributions (O'Malley 2009: 105–106). In sum, deprivation of liberty, even of a relatively low duration, makes the proceedings and related offences 'criminal', because only imprisonment is deemed to be the proper punishment for serious crimes, and only serious crimes are properly punished with a prison sentence, following a classic dog-chasing-its-own-tail argument.

Notwithstanding the foregoing, 'it is best to treat the matter as on a spectrum between the two concepts' (Ogus 2010: 29, citing Sutherland 1945). I will do so by taking into account that fines and the way they are used show the fluidity and ambiguity of this distinction. We will come back to this topic when analysing the expansion of fines in the twentieth century (in Chapter 5). To properly understand this phenomenon we first have to look at the liberal approach to imprisonment and fines (Chapter 2) and the way in which the impersonality and unequal distribution of money affected how fines were perceived and used during the nineteenth century (Chapters 3 and 4).

Notes

1 I will not address here the difficult topic of the concept of money. Economists have grappled with its definition for centuries. It is interesting to know, however, that 'money' is usually described through the functions it fulfils, following Hicks's core idea, according to which money is what money does (Hicks 1967: 1). If a commodity functions as a medium of exchange, a unit of account, a store of value, and a unit of deferred payment, then it can be considered money. This approach must be completed by taking into account that money expresses a social relation (Foley 1987; Ingham 1996). To see money as a social relationship stresses the significance of money as a unit of account in which obligations are both created and extinguished: 'Money then represents a relation between those who claim these obligations and those who must service those claims' (Henry 2004: 70–71). This perspective is particularly interesting when analysing the penal fine, here understood as the *obligation* to pay a certain quantity of money to the state as a punishment for an offence. Notice that Innes (1913: 392) notes that the verb 'to pay' has the root meaning 'to appease', 'pacify', or 'satisfy'.

2 When implementing imprisonment for fine defaulters, a conversion rate equates, for any given individual, a quantity of money with a number of days in prison. Usually the time unit (never less than a day) as well as the monetary unit (never in fractions, such as cents) is considered indivisible in this regard. See, for example, Article 135 of the 1930 Italian Penal Code – known as Rocco Code after Alfredo Rocco, the Fascist minister of justice under whose direction it was drafted – or Article 49 of the 1937 Swiss Penal Code.

3 A situation which Carrara (1871: 458) explained by stating that it was not a penalty that was imposed but rather the need to redress the damage. But it was not always or just a case of redress, not by a long way. Germanic law believed that the crime offended an individual and breached social order. Therefore, it established a pecuniary penalty (*Busse*) with two recipients: the *Wergeld*, or 'worth payment' (Grierson 1977: 28), was paid to the offended person or family for the concept of *capitis aestimacio* or price of the injured man; the *Friedgeld*, or 'price of peace', was paid to the tax authority for the concept of the remedy owed to society (His 1928: 54, 96–97; Von Hentig 1955: 401). The same happened in ancient Anglo-Saxon codes, where the monetary sanction was divided into *Wer*, the value of the injured party, and *Wite*, a fine payable to the king or to some other public authority (Pollock and Maitland 1898: 53–54; Westen 1969: 780ff.). In turn, in the Spanish law of the High and Late Middle Ages, of Germanic origin, many jurisdictions also set a pecuniary penalty – the *caloña* – which was usually split into three parts: *prima querimonioso, secunda palatio, tertia vero concilio*. In other words, one part went to the injured party or the family, another went to the king,

and the third went to the municipality. This was a unique pecuniary penalty in which the *Wergeld* of the relatives changed its nature, as it did not put an end to the enmity, but rather it was a public, official penalty (Orlandis 1947: 88ff.; López-Amo 1956: 560–561). By the sixteenth century the fine was divided only into two parts: one went to the king and the other one to cover expenses of the justice system (Alonso Romero 1985: 28–34). On the use of specific payments (fines) to victims of torts or crimes (or to their kin) in accord with the severity of an injury and with the status of the person injured or slain in the ancient Slav law code known as *Pravda Russkaja* (in three versions), see Baranowski (2005: 167ff.), where he explains that it is still not clear who was the recipient of the money.

4 It is not the aim here to explain recent historical development, well known to legal scholars, which has led to pecuniary sanctions, up until not long ago exclusively confined to the criminal field, being introduced, multiplied, and rediscovered in various sectors of the legal system, in both public law and private law. The privatization of sanctions in terms of decriminalization has been discussed extensively in Italian literature, which refers to 'private penalties'. See Paliero (1985: 487ff.), Bernardi (1993: 514ff.), and papers contained in Busnelli and Scalfi (1985). In part, the Anglo-Saxon equivalent is punitive damages, which have also been widely analysed (O'Malley 2009).

5 We should not forget that the observation that sanctions that exclusively affect the offender's wealth are not inherently criminal in nature is supported by mainstream literature (O'Malley 2009: 20).

6 O'Malley opposed this (2009: 80), explaining that in many jurisdictions regulatory fines may be enforced in default with a term of imprisonment. This is not the case in Western Europe, the main object of this study, although there are exceptions, like the Austrian regulation (§ 16 of the Administrative Penal Act 1991, *Verwaltungsstrafgesetz*, which in case the fine cannot be collected allows a substitute prison sentence that 'must not exceed the maximum possible prison term applicable for the administrative offence and, if prison sentence or anything else is not provided for, it must not exceed two weeks'). In any case, O'Malley (2009: 81) also recognizes that, for the most part, in marked contrast to penal fines, regulatory fine defaults are dealt with by other means than imprisonment.

7 That is what happened at least until fines began to be used against legal entities, and then a determinate percentage of either the sales volume or the equity of the entity was established as a system for calculating the sum of the fine.

8 Only in Finland, Norway, Sweden, and Switzerland the amount of the regulatory fine can be in some cases a function of the net income of the offender. In Austria there was a lively discussion about the possible extension of the day-fine system to the field of administrative penal law during the 1970s and 1980s (Driendl 1983: 692–693), but the possibility was finally rejected.

9 As noted by Emsley (2005: 57), while contemporaries came to recognize 'that men of wealth and social standing committed offences [. . .] such offenders, however common in fiction, newspaper accounts, and journal literature, were not perceived as members of a criminal class and were categorised as "criminal" with some difficulty'.

About the challenge of respectable crime to the understandings and interpretations of 'the criminal' in the late nineteenth century, see Locker (2008: 115ff.) and Wilson (2014).

10 Whereas in the early 1900s there were only a few thousand cars in Great Britain (16,000 in 1905), in 1918 there were already 189,000 motor vehicles in use. The number increased to 551,000 in 1920, to 1,141,000 in 1923, to just over 2,000,000 in 1928, and to 2,416,000 in 1934 (British Association for the Advancement of Science 1935: 213). This growth was boosted by the fact that the automobile, besides being a practical and efficient means of transport, became a symbol of wealth and power, even after the steady fall in the cost of motoring transformed cars in a middle-class luxury.

The situation was very different in other countries. Let me give just an example. In Spain, during the first half of the 1930s, domestic travel for passengers and goods was still primarily carried out using the railroad system and cabotage. Road transport had not undergone any significant progress given the predominance of traditional vehicles, the poor condition of the roads, and high cost of fuel, to the point that in 1936 there were only 334,801 motor vehicles in use, a number that would considerably decrease after the civil war. This fact did not, however, place Spain at the back of the queue for the number of vehicles per capita in developed countries: it had 8.62 vehicles for every 1,000 inhabitants, obviously a long way behind France and Great Britain (37.03 each), but still well ahead of Austria (6.02), Italy (5.53), and Portugal (5.23) (Cayón García and Muñoz Rubio 2005: 4). In these three countries only the second post-war period brought an exponential increase in the number of motor vehicles. The change that other countries had seen decades before came to Spain in the mid-1960s – from 93,000 cars in 1950 to 290,000 in 1960, 2,400,000 in 1970, and 7,600,000 in 1980. Until then, the Spanish vehicle fleet was that of a developing country.

11 Let me provide just one example. In the British statistics, the percentage of persons tried for offences against Highway Acts of all persons tried for indictable and non-indictable offences increased constantly since the early twentieth century. In the 1930s it was already almost 50 per cent.

Table 1.1 Offences against Highway Acts (annual averages and percentages), United Kingdom: 1900–1933

Year	*All persons tried*	*All persons tried for offences against Highway Acts*	*Percentage of persons tried for traffic offences to all persons tried*
1900–1909	767,458	48,512	6.3
1910–1919	630,096	70,167	11.1
1920–1924	617,112	161,410	26.1
1925–1929	666,852	246,561	36.9
1930–1933	643,572	278,610	43.2

Source: Criminal Statistics 1934.

12 Renowned authors defended the necessity of establishing this clear difference between penal and regulatory fines (e.g., Mittelstädt 1891: 63, Rosenfeld 1892: 189, Schmölder 1902: 17, Goldschmidt 1908: 401–402, or Mittelbach 1957: 1139).

13 This idea was already advanced by Rusche and Kirchheimer in *Punishment and Social Structure* (1939 [2003]). They had the extraordinary merit of foreseeing the steady growth in punishing minor offences with regulatory fines and the corresponding increase in bureaucratic regulations during the twentieth century (1939 [2003]: 206). They also linked it with the new meanings of money in such societies. On the one hand, they recognized that, '[u]nlike imprisonment, the fine needs not to have the negative effect of penetrating one's whole life' (1939 [2003]: 175). This perspective would be retaken first by Bottoms's account of the limited competence of bureaucracies (1983: 189–190) originally proposed by Berger et al. (1973), and more recently by O'Malley's thesis about fines governing distributions of action rather than correcting offenders and the 'dividual' as the subject of such regulation (2009: 78–85; 2013: 379–381). On the other hand, from the perspective Rusche and Kirchheimer called the moral defence of the fine system, they recognized the rise of the consumer society as a factor that was giving force to the use of fines. They also linked it with the changing meaning of money as an explanatory factor of the expansion of fines during the

second half of the nineteenth century. In particular, they viewed the steady growth of regulatory fines as quite positive: 'The great mass of minor offences against the existing social order is growing steadily with the growing economic difficulties and the increase in bureaucratic regulations, *but it's not followed by a corresponding intensification of the repressive program*' (1939 [2003]: 206, italics added).

The reason why regulatory fines do not intensify repression is left unexplained, but it can be easily linked with the aforementioned decoupling of fines from the possibility of imprisonment in case of default and with the deprivation of offenders of the more ample procedural guarantees that apply in serious criminal cases, as O'Malley does.

14 The problem addressed here reflects to some extent two important historical traditions. Continental legal theory makes a clear distinction between criminal and administrative offences, with far-reaching consequences for the imposition and enforcement of sanctions. In Germany, a general concept of administrative offences (*Ordnungswidrigkeiten*), procedurally different from criminal offences, was introduced in 1949 (Ohana 2014). Administrative authorities have the power to impose a monetary penalty and other non-custodial sanctions for a violation of an administrative offence, with the substantive and procedural aspects of the process being contained in the Administrative Offences Act (*Ordnungswidrigkeitengesetz*). It is very clear what a criminal offence is and what an administrative offence is. Something similar happens in Italy, Portugal, Spain, or Sweden, where administrative offences are contained in administrative laws which also regulate an administrative procedure, while criminal offences are either in the penal code or in special criminal law statutes. Here the problem of differentiation exists only during the legislative process, when the legislator has to decide whether a new offence should be included in the penal legislation. The situation is very different in France, but also in Anglo-Saxon countries.

References

Albrecht, H.-J. (2001) 'Post-Adjudication Dispositions in Comparative Perspective'. In Tonry, M. and R. S. Frase (eds.) *Sentencing and Sanctions in Western Countries*. New York: Oxford University Press, 293–330.

Alonso Romero, M. P. (1985) 'Aproximación al estudio de las penas pecuniarias en Castilla (siglos XIII–XVIII)'. *Anuario de Historia del Derecho Español* 55: 9–94.

Ashworth, A. (2015) *Sentencing and Criminal Justice*. 6th ed. Cambridge: Cambridge University Press.

Ashworth, A. and E. Player (1998) 'Sentencing, Equal Treatment and the Impact of Sanctions'. In Ashworth, A. and M. Wasik (eds.) *Fundamentals of Sentencing Theory*. Oxford: Clarendon Press, 252–272.

Baranowski, G. (2005) *Die Russkaja Pravda – ein mittelalterliches Rechtsdenkmal*. Frankfurt: Lang.

Becker, G. (1974) 'Crime and Punishment: An Economic Approach'. In Becker, G. and W. Landes (eds.) *Essays in the Economics of Crime and Punishment*. New York: Columbia University Press, 1–54.

Berger, P. L., Berger, B. and H. Kellner (1973) *The Homeless Mind: Modernization and Consciousness*. New York: Random House.

Bernardi, A. (1993) 'Natura penale e retaggi civilistici della pena pecuniaria'. *Rivista Italiana di Diritto e Procedura Penale* 36: 514–568.

Bertola, E. (1893) 'Della pena pecuniaria'. *Rivista Penale* 1: 548–553.

Birkmeyer, K. (1901) 'Das Strafrecht'. In Birkmeyer, K. (ed.) *Enzyklopädie der Rechtswissenschaft in systematischer und alphabetischer Bearbeitung*. Berlin: D. Häring, 1025–1092.

Bottoms, A. E. (1983) 'Some Neglected Features of Contemporary Penal Systems'. In Garland, D. and P. Young (eds.) *The Power to Punish*. London: Heinemann, 166–202.

Brenn, A. (1945) *Die Busse und ihr Vollzug nach dem Schweizerischen Strafgesetzbuch*. Affoltern am Albis: Dr. J. Weiss.

British Association for the Advancement of Sciences. Economic Science and Statistics Section, The (1935) *Britain in Depression: A Record of British Industries since 1929*. London: Pitman & Sons.

Bumke, E. (1928) 'Die Freiheitsstrafe als Problem der Gesetzgebung'. In Bumke, E. (ed.) *Deutsches Gefängniswesen: Ein Handbuch*. Berlin: Verlag von Franz Vahlen, 16–32.

Busnelli, F. D. and G. Scalfi (eds.) (1985) *Le pene private*. Milan: Giuffrè.

Carrara, F. (1871) *Programa del Corso di Diritto Criminale dettato nella R. Università di Pisa. Parte Generale*. 4th ed. Lucca: Tipografia Giusti.

Cayón García, F. and M. Muñoz Rubio (2005) 'Los transportes y las comunicaciones durante la guerra civil'. Paper available at www.usc.es/estaticos/congresos/histec05/a2_cayon_munoz.pdf

Ciccarelli, A. (1897) 'Per l'abolizione della pena pecuniaria'. *La Scuola Positiva* 7: 577–598.

The Commission on Criminal Law (1843) *Seventh Report of Her Majesty's Commissioners on Criminal Law: Dated the 11th Day of March 1843. Presented to Both Houses of Parliament by Command of Her Majesty*. London: W. Clowes and Sons.

Conti, U. (1910) 'La pena e il sistema penale del codice italiano'. In Pessina, E. (ed.) *Enciclopedia del diritto penale italiano. Volume IV*. Milan: Società Editrice Libraria, 1–970.

Croall, H. (1991) 'Sentencing the Business Offender'. *The Howard Journal of Criminal Justice* 30(4): 280–292.

Direzione Generale della Statistica (1899) *Notizie complementari alle Statistiche Giudiziarie Penali degli anni 1890–1895*. Rome: Tipografia Nazionale di G. Bertero.

Doob, A. N. and V. Marinos (1995) 'Reconceptualizing Punishment: Understanding the Limitation on the Use of Intermediate Sanctions'. *University of Chicago Law School Roundtable* 2(2): 413–433.

Driendl, J. (1978) *Die Reform der Geldstrafe in Österreich*. Baden-Baden: Nomos.

Driendl, J. (1983) 'Entwicklung und Neuregelung der Geldstrafe nach dem Tagessatzsystem in Österreich'. In Jescheck, H.-H. and G. Grebing (eds.) *Die Geldstrafe im deutschen und ausländischen Recht*. Baden-Baden: Nomos, 659–737.

Easton, S. and C. Piper (2005) *Sentencing and Punishment: The Quest for Justice*. Oxford: Oxford University Press.

Emsley, C. (1993) 'Mother, What Did the Police Do before There Were Motors? The Law, the Police and the Regulation of Motor Transport in England 1891–1939'. *Historical Journal* 36: 357–381.

Emsley, C. (2005) *Crime and Society in England, 1750–1900*. 3rd ed. Harlow: Longman.

Ferrajoli, L. (1990). *Diritto e raggione: Teoria del garantismo penale*. Rome: Laterza.

Ferri, E. (1900) *Sociologia Criminale*. 4th ed. Turin: Fratelli Bocca Editori.

Foley, D. (1987) 'Money in Economic Activity'. In Eatwell, J., Milgate, M. and P. Newman (eds.) *The New Palgrave: Money*. New York: W. W. Norton, 519–525.

Friedmann, O. (1892) 'Sind Änderungen des geltendes Recht erwünscht in Betreff des Verhältnisses zwischen Geld- und Freiheitsstrafen?' In Deutscher Juristentag (ed.) *Verhandlungen des Zweiundzwanzigsten Deutschen Juristentages: Zweiter Band*. Berlin: Guttentag, 95–183.

Garland, D. (1985) *Punishment and Welfare*. Aldershot: Gower.

Garofalo, R. (1887 [2002]) *Indemnización a las víctimas del delito: Traducción y estudio crítico*. Pamplona: Analecta (*Riparazione alle vittime del delitto*. Turin: Bocca, 1887).

Goldschmidt, J. (1908) 'Die Geldstrafe'. In Heimberger, J. (ed.) *Vergleichende Darstellung des deutschen und ausländischen Strafrechts: Vorarbeiten zur deutschen Strafrechtsreform. Allgemeiner Teil. 4*. Berlin: Liebmann, 398–411.

Graeber, D. (2009) 'Debt, Violence, and Impersonal Markets: Polanyian Meditations'. In Hann, C. and K. Hart (eds.) *Market and Society: The Great Transformation Today*. Cambridge: Cambridge University Press, 106–132.

Grebing, G. (1982) *The Fine in Comparative Law: A Survey of 21 Countries*. Cambridge: Institute of Criminology Occasional Papers no. 9.

Grierson, P. (1977) *The Origins of Money*. London: Athlone Press.

Henry, J. F. (2004) 'The Social Origins of Money: The Case of Egypt'. In Wray, L. R. (ed.) *Credit and State Theories of Money: The Contributions of A. Mitchell Innes*. Cheltenham: Edward Elgar, 79–98.

Hicks, J. R. (1967) *A Contribution to the Theory of the Trade Cycle*. London: Oxford University Press.

His, R. (1928) *Geschichte des deutschen Strafrechts bis zur Karolina*. Munich: Oldenbourg.

Hudson, B. (2000) 'Punishing the Poor: Dilemmas of Justice and Difference'. In Heffernan, W. C. and J. Kleinig (eds.) *From Social Justice to Criminal Justice: Poverty and the Administration of Criminal Law*. New York: Oxford University Press, 189–216.

Ilmonen, K. (2011) *A Social and Economic Theory of Consumption*. Basingstoke: Palgrave Macmillan.

Ingham, G. (1996) 'Money is a Social Relation'. *Review of Social Economy* 54(4): 507–529.

Innes, A. M. (1913) 'What Is Money?' *The Banking Law Journal* 30: 377–408.

King, P. (1996) 'Punishing Assault: The Transformation of Attitudes in the English Courts'. *Journal of Interdisciplinary History* 27(1): 43–74.

Lappi-Seppälä, T. (2014) 'Fines in Europe'. In Bruinsma, G. and D. Weisburd (eds.) *Encyclopedia of Criminology and Criminal Justice*. Heidelberg: Springer, 1637–1648.

Levi, M. (1989) 'Suite Justice: Sentencing for Fraud'. *The Criminal Law Review*, June: 420–434.

Locker, J. P. (2008) 'The Paradox of the "Respectable Offender": Responding to the Problem of White-Collar Crime in Victorian and Edwardian England'. In Johnston, H. (ed.) *Punishment and Control in Historical Perspective*. New York: Palgrave MacMillan, 115–134.

López-Amo Marín, A. (1956) 'El Derecho penal español de la Baja Edad Media'. *Anuario de Historia del Derecho Español* 26: 337–368.

Marcos Gutiérrez, J. (1826) *Práctica criminal de España: Tomo III*. 4th ed. Madrid: Imprenta de Don Fermín Villalpando.

Marinos, V. (2005) 'Thinking about Penal Equivalents'. *Punishment and Society* 7(4): 441–455.

Marx, K. (1844/1975) 'Economic and Philosophical Manuscripts of 1844'. In Marx, K. and F. Engels (eds.) *Collected Works. Volume* 3. London: Lawrence and Wishart, 229–346.

Marx, K. (1867 [1996]) 'Capital, vol. 1'. In Marx, K and F. Engels (eds.) *Collected Works. Volume 35*. London: Lawrence and Wishart.

Merkel, A. (1893) 'Sind Aenderungen des geltenden Rechts erwünscht in Betreff des Verhältnisses zwischen Geld- und Freiheitsstrafen?' In Deutscher Juristentag (ed.) *22. Verhandlungen des Deutschen Juristentages: Vierter Band*. Berlin: Guttentag, 336–360.

Merkel, A. (1895) 'Empfiehlt sich die Einführung von Verschärfungen der Freiheitsstrafen im Sinne des österreichischen Entwurfs?' In Deutscher Juristentag (ed.) *23. Verhandlungen des Deutschen Juristentages. Zweiter Band*. Berlin: Guttentag, 350–425.

Mittelbach, H. H. (1957) 'Ersatzfreiheitsstrafe (§ 29 StGB)'. *Neue Juristische Wochenschrift* 10: 1138–1139.

Mittelstädt, O. (1891) 'Sind Änderungen des geltenden Rechts erwünscht in Betreff des Verhältnisses zwischen Geld- und Freiheitsstrafe?' In Deutscher Juristentag (ed.) *Verhandlungen des Einundzwanzigsten Deutschen Juristentages. Zweiter Band.* Berlin: Guttentag, 49–69.

Nowakowski, F. (1973) 'Die Zurückdrängung der kurzen Freiheitsstrafe in der RV 1971'. *Österreichische Juristen-Zeitung* 28: 1–4.

Ogus, A. (2004) 'Enforcing Regulation: Do We Need the Criminal Law?' In Skögren, H. and G. Skogh (eds.) *New Perspectives on Economic Crime*. Cheltenham: Edward Elgar, 42–56.

Ogus, A. (2010) 'Regulation and Its Relationship with the Criminal Justice Process'. In Quirk, H., Seddon, T. and G. Smith (eds.) *Regulation and Criminal Justice: Innovations in Policy and Research.* Cambridge: Cambridge University Press, 27–41.

Ohana, D. (2014) 'Administrative Penalties in the Rechtsstaat: On the Emergence of the Ordnungswidrigkeit Sanctioning in Post-War Germany'. *University of Toronto Law Journal* 64(2): 243–290.

O'Malley, P. (2009) *The Currency of Justice: Fines and Damages in Consumer Societies.* New York: Routledge-Cavendish.

O'Malley, P. (2013) 'Monetized Justice: Money and Punishment in Consumer Societies'. In Simon, J. and R. Sparks (eds.) *The SAGE Handbook of Punishment and Society.* London: SAGE, 375–392.

Orlandis Rovira, J. (1947) 'Las consecuencias del delito en el Derecho de la Alta Edad Media'. *Anuario de Historia del Derecho Español* 18: 61–166.

Padovani, T. (1994) *Diritto penale del lavoro: Profili generali.* 4th ed. Milan: FrancoAngeli.

Paliero, C. E. (1985) *'Minima non curat praetor': Ipertrofia del diritto penale e decriminalizzazione dei reati bagatellari.* Padova: Cedam.

Peacock, M. (2013) *Introducing Money.* London: Routledge.

Pollock, F. and F. W. Maitland (1898) *The History of English Law Before the Time of Edward I. Volumes I and II.* London: Cambridge University Press.

Posner, R. A. (1972) *Economic Analysis of Law.* Boston: Little, Brown.

Posner, R. A. (1980) 'Optimal Sentences for White-Collar Criminals'. *American Criminal Law Review* 17: 409–418.

Reddy, W. M. (1987) *Money and Liberty in Modern Europe.* New York: Cambridge University Press.

Rosenfeld, E. (1892) 'Die Regelung der Geldstrafe'. In International Union of Penal Law/ Deutsche Landesgruppe (ed.) *Mitteilungen der Internationalen Kriminalistischen Vereinigung: Bulletin de l'Union internationale de droit pénal.* Berlin: Guttentag, 135–221.

Rossi, P.L.O. (1853) *Trattato di diritto penale.* Turin: Società Editrice.

Rusche, G. and O. Kirchheimer (1939 [2003]) *Punishment and Social Structure.* New Brunswick: Transaction.

Saltelli, C. (1939) 'Pene pecuniarie'. In D'Amelio, M. (ed.) *Nuovo digesto italiano. Volume IX.* 2nd ed. Turin: Unione Tipografico-Editrice Torinese, 703–705.

Samuels, A. (1970) 'The Fine: The Principles'. *The Criminal Law Review*, May: 201–210, 268–272.

Sbriccoli, M. (1990 [2009]) 'La penalistica civile: Teorie e ideologie del diritto penale nell'Italia unita'. In Sbriccoli, M. (ed.). *Storia del diritto penale e della giustizia: Scritti editi e inediti (1972–2007). Tomo I.* Milan: Giuffrè, 493–590.

Schmölder, R. (1902) *Die Geldstrafe: Vortrag, gehalten auf der 74. Jahresversammlung der Rheinisch-westfälischen Gefängnissgesellschaft in Düsseldorf am 15. Oktober 1902*. Hamm: Griebsch.

Seagle, W. (1948) 'Fines'. In Seligman, E. and A. Johnson (eds.) *Encyclopaedia of the Social Sciences. Volume 6*. New York: Macmillan, 249–252.

Simmel, G. (1907 [1990]) *The Philosophy of Money*. New York: Routledge.

Simon, J. (1998) 'Driving Governmentality: Automobile Accidents, Insurance and the Challenge to Social Order in the Inter-War Years 1919–1941'. *Connecticut Insurance Law Journal* 4: 522–588.

Spufford, P. (1988) *Money and Its Use in Medieval Europe*. Cambridge: Cambridge University Press.

Stooß, C. (1916) 'Geldstrafe und Bußenabdiener'. *Zeitschrift für Schweizer Strafrecht* 29: 1–36.

Taylor, J. (2013) *Boardroom Scandal: The Criminalization of Company Fraud in Nineteenth-Century Britain*. Oxford: Oxford University Press.

Von Hentig, H. (1955) *Die Strafe. Band 2*. Berlin: Springer.

Von Hirsh, A., Wasik, M. and J. Greene (1992) 'Scaling Community Punishments'. In Von Hirsch, A. and A. Ashworth (eds.) *Principled Sentencing: Readings on Theory and Policy*. Boston: Northeastern University Press, 368–387.

Vormbaum, T. (2014) *A Modern History of German Criminal Law*, ed. by M. Bohlander. New York: Springer.

Wahlberg, W. E. (1877) 'Nationalökonomische Gesichtspunkte im Strafrecht mit besonderer Rücksicht auf die Geldstrafe'. In Wahlberg, W. E. (ed.). *Gesammelte kleinere Schriften und Bruchstücke über Strafrecht, Strafprozess, Gefängnisskunde, Literatur und Dogmengeschichte der Rechtslehre in Oesterreich*. Vienna: Alfred Hölder, 231–264.

Walker, N. (1968) *Crime and Punishment in Britain: The Penal System in Theory, Law, and Practice*. 2nd ed. New Brunswick: Aldine Transaction.

Warner, K. (2012) 'Equality Before the Law and Equal Impact of Sanctions: Doing Justice to Differences in Wealth and Employment Status'. In Zedner, L. (ed.) *Principles and Values in Criminal Law and Criminal Justice: Essays in Honour of Andrew Ashworth*. Oxford: Oxford University Press, 225–244.

Westen, D. A. (1969) 'Fines, Imprisonment, and the Poor: Thirty Dollars or Thirty Days'. *California Law Review* 57(3): 778–820.

Wilson, S. (2006) 'Law, Morality and Regulation: Victorian Experiences of Financial Crime'. *British Journal of Criminology* 46(6): 1073–1090.

Wilson, S. (2014) *The Origins of Modern Financial Crime*. London: Routledge.

Young, P. (1989) 'Punishment, Money and a Sense of Justice'. In Carlen, P. and D. Cook (eds.) *Paying for Crime*. Milton Keynes: Open University Press, 46–65.

Young, P. (1994) 'Putting a Price on Harm: The Fine as a Punishment'. In Duff, A., S. Marshall, R. Emerson Dobash, and R. P. Dobash (eds.) *Penal Theory and Practice: Tradition and Innovation in Criminal Justice*. Manchester: Manchester University Press, 185–198.

Zelizer, V. (1997) *The Social Meaning of Money*. Princeton, NJ: Princeton University Press.

Zipf, H. (1965) 'Abwälzung der Geldstrafe auf einen Dritten und Erreichbarkeit des Strafzweckes'. *Monatsschrift für Deutsches Recht* 8: 632–633.

2 The fine as the ideal penal sanction in the age of the Enlightenment

Liberal governmentality on fines

In the eighteenth century, after the abusive use the *ancien régime* made of pecuniary sanctions, including fines and confiscation, they were subjected to severe criticism by some intellectuals and philosophers we could include in a general category called 'Enlightenment'. I do not want to assume a characterization of the Enlightenment as a single cultural formation in which liberalism, rationalism, capitalism, and humanitarianism came together to form a common liberal and capitalist 'modernity'. The late refinements in historical accounts of 'the Enlightenment' show us that we have not just one Enlightenment but many, produced by many national cultures (Wood 2012: 289ff.). The argument that follows here is intended to present some of these disparate threads through the works of two authors most commonly associated with the 'Enlightenment(s)' and the distinctive culture of capitalism, Cesare Bonesana Marquis of Beccaria and Jeremy Bentham. They formed the basis of two philosophies that competed with each other, almost in terms of sectarianism, throughout the whole nineteenth century. Beccaria was a firm defender of individual rights and guarantees and, consequently, he defended proportionality in the imposition of punishments. Influenced by the contractarian theories, he believed, following Rousseau (1762 [1913]: Book 2, Chapter 5), that applying punishments that went beyond what was necessary to maintain the social contract was always a sign of weakness or remissness on the part of the government, and therefore counterproductive. In his work, he makes almost no mention of the existence of confinement, asylums, or imprisonment. The intended preventive message of punishment is provided simply by representations and signs, since there is no specific penal administrative apparatus designed to mould offenders into obedient subjects (Bottoms 1983: 176). He did not care what went on in daily life inside prisons. He agreed with other Enlightenment thinkers, who believed that punishing an offence with specific fine amounts was appropriate only for those offences caused by greed – punishment should correspond with the offence in nature and scope, but he saw a number of practical difficulties in the fines' administration, given the poverty among large sections of the population. Instead, Bentham, the founder of classical criminology, focused on the execution of punishments, and imprisonment in particular. In his most famous work in the criminal field, *The Panopticon*, he immersed himself in meticulous regulation of the space and time spent in prison. But he abandoned the idea of the 'terror' of imprisonment, as exposed in his *Panopticon*, in his middle years and shifted towards other forms of punishment. In particular, as we will see, he advocated for the widespread use of monetary or 'pecuniary' sanctions.

This is striking, since we tend to think that the Enlightenment humanism promoted prison as a more humane penalty than the corporal punishments used so commonly under the *ancien régime*. This assumption is not in line with historical reality. It is true that the Enlightenment thinkers proposed a humanization of punishments, but as a by-product of their quest for proportionate, appropriate, and useful punishments, rather than as something desirable for its own sake. And only a minority sought this objective through punitive imprisonment, through the loss of freedom as a penal sanction. The terrible state of the prisons at that time prevented any illusions on this matter. And although the prison now appears to be the epitome of liberal thinking on punishment – largely due to the works of Foucault and Melossi and Pavarini – the truth is that for Beccaria, one of its maximal exponents, imprisonment was not even a punishment, while for Bentham, one of the most influential thinkers of this period, the fine was the ideal penal sanction.

Cesare Bonesana Marquis of Beccaria

Beccaria is one of the main exponents of juridical Enlightenment, as defined by Foucault (1977). His most celebrated work – and also his sole but undeniable claim to lasting fame – *Dei delitti e delle pene*, was first published anonymously in Italian in 1764, because of the author's fear of reprisals, and quickly translated into German in 1766 (*Abhandlung von den Verbrechen und den Strafen*, Hamburg: Bock),[1] English in 1767 (*An Essay on Crimes and Punishments*, London: J. Almon, here cited through the English translation from 1872),[2] and Spanish in 1774 (*Tratado de los delitos y de las penas*, Madrid: Joachin Ibarra).[3] This brief treatise was the first full-scale work to tackle criminal reform and to suggest that criminal justice should conform to rational principles. The principles to which Beccaria appealed were reason, an understanding of civil society as a form of contract and, above all, the principle of utility, or of the greatest happiness for the greatest number. Beccaria had elaborated this principle in conjunction with Pietro Verri, and greatly influenced Jeremy Bentham to develop it into the full-scale doctrine of utilitarianism.[4] His thinking cannot really be considered very original; he was not actually the first person to express many of the ideas he formulated in his treatise – as he himself admitted, for example, with regards to the work of Montesquieu *De l'Esprit des lois* (Beccaria 1764 [1872]: Introduction, Chapter 2). When compared with the works of other great reformers of the eighteenth century, such as Voltaire or Bentham, Beccaria's works are less profound, and in many ways full of irresoluble contradictions. However, it must be acknowledged that he knew how to express his thesis succinctly and passionately, presenting, along with the complaints about the excesses of the *ancien régime*, a convincing programme of principles upon which a new penal system should be built.

Beccaria summarized them in his conclusion: 'That a punishment may not be an act of violence, of one or of many, against a private member of society, it should be public, immediate and necessary; the least possible in the case given; proportioned to the crime, and determined by the laws' (1764 [1872]: Chapter 47). In order to concretize his idea of proportionality he proposed only a whole scale of punitive sanctions: corporal – including death – and pecuniary punishments, infamy, banishment, slavery, but not prison. He did not consider the deprivation of liberty to be a punishment, but rather a precautionary measure: 'Imprisonment is a punishment, which differs from all other in this particular, that it necessarily precedes conviction' (1764 [1872]: Chapter 29). Regarding fines, their application in the context of the *ancien régime* received all kinds of criticisms:

> There was a time when all punishments were pecuniary. The crimes of the subjects were the inheritance of the prince. An injury done to society was a favour to the crown; and the sovereign and magistrates, those guardians of the public security, were interested in the violation of the laws. Crimes were tried, at that time, in a court of Exchequer, and the cause became a civil suit between the person accused and the crown. The magistrate then had other powers than were necessary for the public welfare, and the criminal suffered other punishments than the necessity of example required. The judge was rather a collector for the crown, an agent for the treasury, than a protector and minister of the laws. But, according to this system, for a man to confess himself guilty, was to acknowledge himself a debtor to the crown; which was, and is at present (the effects continuing after the causes have ceased) the intent of all criminal causes.
>
> (1764 [1872]: Chapter 17)

Further on, he implies that while crimes related to persons ought to be punished corporally, so that 'the great and rich should by no means have it in their power to set a price on the security of the weak and indigent', punishment for crimes related to property should be pecuniary. His views coincided with the widespread opinion of the time stating that punishments should bear some relation to the crimes (in Denmark Ørsted 1818: 371ff.; in Italy Filangieri 1788: Book 3, second part, Chapter 32; in Germany Von Soden 1792: 103, or Von Feuerbach 1804: 228; in Spain Lardizábal 1782: Chapter 5 § V.3, or Marcos Gutiérrez 1826: 145–147), since it was thought that all arbitrary treatment would cease once punishment was determined by the nature of the particular crime (Montesquieu 1748: Book 12, Chapter 4). Such a viewpoint was accepted in many of the early penal codes and compilations: the 1791 French Penal Code, the 1787 Austrian Code (*Allgemeines Gesetzbuch über Verbrechen und derselben Bestrafung*, known as Josephine Code, because it was enacted by Joseph II) and the 1803 Austrian Code (*Gesetzbuch über Verbrechen und schwere Polizeyübertretungen*), the 1794 Prussian *Allgemeines Landrecht*, the 1799 Swiss Penal Code (*Peinliches Gesetzbuch*), or the 1813 Penal Law Code for the Kingdom of Bavaria. The poverty of those who committed these types of crimes against property, or to which they were subjected after the execution of the punishment, as well as the effect on innocent third parties, did not lead him to propose bringing the fine in line with the offender's financial situation. He simply preferred slavery in these cases, as it was understood that the obligation to work allowed society to take advantage of the criminal's labour and the victim to recover the damages suffered:

> The punishment of robbery, not accompanied with violence, should be pecuniary. He who endeavours to enrich himself with the property of another, should be deprived of part of his own. But this crime, alas! is commonly the effect of misery and despair; the crime of that unhappy part of mankind, to whom the right of exclusive property, a terrible, and perhaps unnecessary right, has left but a bare existence. Besides, as pecuniary punishment may increase the number of poor, and may deprive an innocent family of subsistence, the most proper punishment will be that kind of slavery, which alone can be called just; that is, which makes the society, for a time, absolute master of the person and labour of the criminal, in order to oblige him to repair, by this dependence, the unjust despotism he usurped over the property of another, and his violation of the social compact.
>
> (1764 [1872]: Chapter 22)

As we can see, although Beccaria adopted the liberal dogma of the formal nature of equality, recognition of its flaws compelled him to introduce some sort of alternative punishment. Rusche and Kirchheimer (1939 [2003]: 76) said on this matter,

> this passage is significant in the first place because it calls for fines in the interest of property. But since the payment of a fine is not possible for the lower classes, imprisonment is recommended in its place. The deprivation of liberty is considered a natural result of the invasion of property, that is to say, property and personal liberty are assigned equal value.

However, Beccaria did not recommend prison but slavery, understood as appropriation of the offender's work: deprivation of liberty is used only to compel offenders to recompense society for their transgressions with a period of hard labour visible to the public. Therefore, the equation proposed by the Italian author and followed by many others during the period (see, e.g., Eden 1771: 44ff., 60ff.) does not strictly equate property and personal liberty – money and freedom – but property and labour, an equivalence that even now, more than two centuries later, still seems perfectly acceptable.

Beccaria's influence was huge already during his life. He had an enormous impact on the reforms adopted by Enlightened absolutist monarchs – for example, Frederick the Great of Prussia or Joseph II of Austria – as in the American and French Revolutions and the first penal codes of the nineteenth century, although his influence's extent, its nature, and its effectiveness differed in such different political settings. While he was very influential in Spain, Sweden, Austria, and Tuscany, where his proposals were quickly embodied in the legislation, England constituted a relevant exception. The 'Bloody Code' was to maintain extremely hard penalties until Bentham added his great influence to reform.

Jeremy Bentham

The influence exerted by the English philosopher Jeremy Bentham on the subsequent literature, as well as on the codification processes carried out from the start of the nineteenth century in Europe and America, is undeniable. His extraordinary reach was largely due to the early translations of his works into French, Spanish, Italian, and German.[5] The *Panopticon*, despite being the work for which this author is most remembered in the fields of criminology and criminal and penitentiary law – mostly because of the central role that it plays in Foucault's *Discipline and Punish*, 1977 – is not the definitive expression of his thought on this matter, which is partly due to the fact that it was one of his early works. In fact, it was written in the year 1787, in a series of letters from Crechoff in White Russia to a friend in England (one volume, Dublin: Thomas Byrne, 1791; two volumes with a postscript in two parts, London: T. Payne, 1791). His affiliation with the disciplinary techniques characteristic of the police state, especially his insistence upon the 'terror' of imprisonment, with its delivery of corporal pain, resulted in a far more utilitarian vision of punishment in his later works, so that 'it would be quite possible to argue that, rather than the Panopticon, the twinned punishment of the fine and monetary compensation was the ideal liberal criminal justice sanction' (O'Malley 2009a: 29). His arguments reappeared in innumerable variations during the nineteenth century and beyond. This makes it especially interesting to analyse in detail the Benthamite way of thinking regarding fines as a punishment.

Bentham dedicated Chapter 4, 'Of Pecuniary Forfeiture', of Book 3, 'Of Privative Punishments, or Forfeitures', of his work *The Rationale of Punishment* to analyse the advantages and disadvantages of what he called 'pecuniary forfeiture'. His assessment could not be more positive. He enumerated six advantages:

1 First, being convertible to profit,
2 Second, equality, since:

> no punishment can be made to sit more equally than this can be made to sit on different individuals; so as the quantum of it be proportioned to the means which the delinquent has of bearing it. For money (that is, the ratio of a given sum of money to the total sum of a man's capital) we have already shown to be the most accurate measure of the quantity of pain or pleasure a man can be made to receive,

3 Third, variability, intended as the non-production of other infamy than what is necessarily attached to the offence, in contrast to corporal punishment,
4 Fourth, economy or frugality, intended as the perfect balance of the original pain produced to innocent parties comprised within the circle of the criminal's dependents by the consciousness of the loss in which themselves are likely to incur, with the pleasure that goes to those persons, whosoever they

be, to whose profit the money is applied, in a clear application of his greatest-happiness principle,

5 Fifth, remissibility, because, in contrast to punishment, '[u]nder no other mode of punishment can reparation be made for an unjust sentence with equal facility',

6 And sixth, popularity, because '[i]t is the only one of any consequence against which some objection or other of the popular cast has not been made'.

The only important disadvantage he observed has to do with exemplarity:

> At the execution of it, no spectacle is exhibited: the transfer of a sum of money on this account has nothing to distinguish it from the case of an ordinary payment. It is not furnished with any of those symbolical helps to exemplarity which belong to most punishments of the corporal kind.
>
> (Bentham 1830: Book 3, Chapter 4)

In short, money sanctions are preferred because they deliver punishment with 'the greatest economy of force and the most exactitude of suffering'. But Bentham recognized the principal problem of fines imposed by fixed amounts:

> When a man of large fortune, and a man of moderate fortune, are condemned to the same fine, is the punishment the same? do they suffer the same evil? The manifest inequality of such treatment, is it not rendered more hateful by the derisory equality? Is not the design of the law missed, since the one may lose the means of his existence, whilst the other escapes with triumph?
>
> (Bentham 1789: Chapter 6)

Bentham pointed to the possibility that the amount of the fine be related to 'the fortune of the offender' – an idea already advanced by Montesquieu, Filangieri, and many others, although not by Beccaria – as well as to the profit of the offence, the value of the thing which is the subject matter of the offence, and the amount of the injury. The first two terms of comparison, the profit of the offence and the value of the thing, are typical of the current proportional fines, and the third one, the amount of the injury, is typical of damages. In fact, Bentham stated that it is best to set a percentage of the offender's fortune:

> The pleasures which two men will be deprived of, by being made to lose each a given part (suppose a tenth) of their respective fortunes, will in specie perhaps be very different; but this does not hinder but that, on taking into the account quantity on the one hand and actual expectations and probable burthens on the other, they may be the same; they will be the same as nearly as any two quantities can be made to be so by any rule of measuring. It is from his money that a man derives the main part of his pleasures; the only part that lies open to estimation. The supposition we are forced to follow is, that the quantities of pleasure men are capable of purchasing with their respective

> capitals are respectively equal. This supposition is, it must be supposed, very loose indeed, and inaccurate, because the quantity of a man's capital is subject to infinite fluctuations, and because there is great reason to suppose that a richer man is apt to be happier upon an average than a poorer man. It is, however, after all nearer to the truth than any other general suppositions that for the purpose in question can be made.
>
> (Bentham 1830: Book 3, Chapter 4, Section 2.3)

In a more concise way, he explained, 'The same *nominal* punishment is not, for different individuals, the same *real* punishment. Let the punishment in question be a fine: the sum that would not be felt by a rich man would be ruin to a poor one' (1830: Book 1, Chapter 6). Bentham also addressed the subsidiary punishment for non-payment of fines. He asked,

> [B]y what standard are we to estimate a sum of money by a sum of imprisonment? for what debt, or part of a debt, is each day's imprisonment to be reckoned as an equivalent?
>
> Let us say that the amount of the debt struck off by each day's imprisonment shall be equal to what each day the patient might have earned, had he remained in a state of liberty.
>
> . . . The points that then require to be determined, are the three following:
>
> 1 The income being given, what portion of the debt shall be considered as being abolished by imprisonment of a certain duration?
> 2 From what period, anterior to the contracting of the debt, ought the value of the income to be estimated?
> 3 What proofs ought to be required, by which to fix the amount of the income in question? It would be the interest of the debtor to make it appear as great as possible. During the examination, the creditor ought to be present, and to be at liberty, either by himself or his counsel, to examine the defaulter.
>
> (Bentham 1830: Book 6, Chapter 2)

This passage clearly demonstrates the Benthamite concern about the delimitation of the exact terms of the equation that equates money to time in prison. The calculation is made based on the amount the subject could have earned had he not been imprisoned. In other words, as with Beccaria, the specific terms of the comparison are labour power and money. To calculate a fine in terms of labour value by units of time is possible only when imprisonment is filled with this significance, when offenders work in prison or are trained to work, in the sense of wage labour, as we will see later on.

It should be highlighted that Bentham transferred his felicity calculus of the rational choice actor to the penal system, considering money as a means to provide pleasure and inflict pain. Within his own liberal and utilitarian governmental framework, he prefigured the future acceptability of fines as the perfect sanction in the work of the law and economics movement. It has been said that the poverty of the lower classes, given the tariff and fixed-fine systems, remained a successful obstacle to its introduction on a broad basis before the middle of the nineteenth century. However, the problem, as we will see, did not concern the poverty of the lower classes so much as the scant doctrinal acceptance of a punishment that was all too reminiscent of the ability of the upper classes in the pre-Enlightenment era to buy their freedom and, once this prejudice had been overcome, there was the difficulty of establishing a coercive means of enforcing the fine without reinstating this privilege. As Rusche and Kirchheimer (1939 [2003]: 167) put it, 'It was necessary to establish an equation between the money of the upper classes and the time of the lower classes; what loss of time by the latter is equivalent to a given sum of money?' The final answer to this question was more related to the liberal approach to short-term punishment and less so to the rising living standard towards the second half of the nineteenth century.

The liberal approach to short-term imprisonment

The Enlightenment and the need to punish 'better'

In general, it can be said that it was after the first French Penal Code, in 1791,[6] when the punishment of imprisonment began to be widely implemented throughout the Western world. The justification of imprisonment as a punishment, beyond its traditional function as a precautionary measure, is usually associated with the criticism of the paraphernalia that went with enforcing the death penalty and corporal punishments. As Radzinowicz (1966: 11) highlighted, comprehensively expressing this idea, '[t]he savage penalties of the past were to give place to the punishments most suited to an age that valued liberty above everything, the punishment of imprisonment'. But the origin and application of imprisonment as we know it today were not a contribution of the Enlightenment. Enlightenment is not attached to a specific penology, not even to codification techniques,[7] but to the analysis of social and political processes in the context of rationality. It is important to remember that Beccaria never justified imprisonment as a punishment, although he tried to reduce its use and improve its conditions when it was implemented as a precautionary measure, as did other Enlightenment thinkers of the time (e.g., Eden 1771: 50–55). At that time imprisonment was recognized as having an essentially preventive function in Spain, although it was also used as a punishment for some not very serious offences (Lardizábal 1782: Chapter 5 § 3.27, who, because of the hard conditions of enforcement, considered it one of the most severe afflictive corporal punishments; Marcos Gutiérrez 1826: 207ff.). In Italy, where imprisonment was not used as a punishment, Filangieri (1788: Book 3, second part, Chapter 33) proposed that when it was applied for this purpose it should have a maximum duration of three months. In England neither the debtors' prison, nor the county gaol, nor the house of correction was an actual prison in the modern sense of the word (Finzsch 1996: 220). Incarceration was not thought to be a useful punishment in the century after the Restoration (Beattie 1986: 460). Well into the eighteenth century, imprisonment was a penalty for minor offences, and only from the 1770s was it used more frequently for more serious crimes. In Germany it was not until the eighteenth century that we saw imprisonment finally becoming an accepted criminal sanction (Spierenburg 1996: 24). In the Austrian Empire, the 1768 *Constitutio Criminalis Theresiana* noted that imprisonment, though not a primary punishment, could be handed down by the ruler by way of commutation, but how or where it would then be served was not specified (Sellin 1976: 56). Imprisonment was considered a corporal punishment, defined as 'the [punishment] which, apart from direct physical pain, subsequently causes suffering and torments the body by subjecting it to public labour'. I do not wish to spend too much time on this point, which has been analysed in detail many times before. I am, however, interested in analysing the liberal thinking concerning the appropriateness of imposing punishments of short-term imprisonment, because the extent to which fines are implemented depends on the acceptance of this, as we will see later.

It is striking that only the first purely theoretical approaches to short-term prison sentences were based on a positive perspective (e.g., Filangieri 1788: Book 3, second part, Chapter 33). In contrast, those who came down from their ivory towers to discover the reality of imprisonment were not at all optimistic. Optimism was hindered by the terrible state of the establishments of the time (denounced by Howard 1777 and Wedderburn 1793 in England, but also by Jovellanos 1779 [1945]: 463–468, Lardizábal 1782, and Marcos Gutiérrez 1826 in Spain, Petitti di Roreto 1840 in Italy, and Von Arnim 1803 in Prussia). It is not true, in general, that the Enlightenment thinkers proposed imprisonment as a more humane punishment than the corporal punishments and death penalty used during the *ancien régime*. But by what measure should we conclude today that prison was milder than the several corporal punishments applied in the eighteenth century and before? The reasoning behind promoting imprisonment as a more appropriate punishment was not based on it being a milder, more humane punishment, but on a utilitarian concern about the need for maximum economy in the use of pain. Montesquieu, Beccaria, Voltaire, and Filangieri agreed that legislative cruelty might defeat itself by preventing law enforcement. They thought that most corporal punishments, including the death penalty, were inappropriate because they made it impossible to establish an exact proportion between crime and punishment. They understood that, despite the existing variety of torments a criminal can 'suffer only to a certain degree, beyond which it is impossible to proceed, be the enormity of the crime ever so great' (Beccaria 1764 [1872]: Chapter 27), and that the death of a criminal 'is a terrible but momentary spectacle, and therefore a less efficacious method of deterring others, than the continued example of a man deprived of his liberty, condemned as a beast of burden, to repair, by his labour, the injury he has done to society' (Beccaria 1764 [1872]: Chapter 28).

Clearly, the criticism of the death penalty and of the majority of corporal punishments is based not on their cruelty but on their *useless* cruelty (Tomás y Valiente 1969: 365; Sellin 1976: 65–66; Sbriccoli 1990 [2009]: 412–413).

The reformers wanted 'not to punish less, but to punish better' (Foucault 1977: 82). From this viewpoint, imprisonment is not seen as a less cruel punishment,[8] and even less as a punishment consisting of being locked up, without further ado. Imprisonment means the obligation to work. Work legitimizes prison as a penal sanction, as it confirms that this is the way in which it achieves its aim of correcting and disciplining prisoners (Carrara 1871: 446–447; Wahlberg 1877: 233; Florian 1934: 819). It is the means necessary to make the offender, through his labour, redress the damage caused to society, cover the enormous maintenance costs of the prison system, and reform along the way.[9] And to do this, different types of custodial sentences were established, which varied in length and intensity – that is, in their enforcement regime, of greater or lesser harshness – depending on the severity of the crime committed. In other words, the punishment was not simply to work;[10] the work that was provided for the inmates was deliberately 'irksome', and it was accompanied by penalties, such as isolation, public humiliations, the fitting of chains on hands and/or feet, and extremely frugal amounts of food. It responded to an interpretation of the idea of rehabilitation which permitted its fusion with the more direct concerns of rational deterrence:

> This consisted of an adaptation of the Protestant ethic albeit in a grossly distorted form; work was to be equated with virtue, and idleness (which included economic survival through crime) with vice. Thus if prisoners could be put to work it would be positively good for them in permitting them to act virtuously while if the work were irksome it would provide that element of deterrence that would dissuade them from continuing in crime.
>
> (Morris 1978: 83)

Why, then, do we tend to associate the Enlightenment with a more widespread use of imprisonment? The effort made by many Enlightenment thinkers to establish a proportionalist ideology – as a means to fight against arbitrariness – explains the preference for punishments whose numbers are widely divisible and multipliable, such as prison, arrest, and bail. Imprisonment lent itself extremely well to an exact gradation of the degree of punishment to the offence, much better than the death penalty or most of the corporal punishments, an observation that was still upheld at the end of the nineteenth century (Carrara 1871: 451).

But the same advantages could be attributed to the fine (Tarello 1976; Driendl 1983: 668). The fine was a very important sanction in most European countries until the late eighteenth century.[11] As O'Malley (2009b: 70) explains, 'It was not simply corporal punishment that prisons displaced, but also and even more so, fines'. Why then was the use of fines as a punishment abandoned? The generalized acceptance of the programme of reformation through hard labour by the end of the eighteenth century helps to explain the further rapid development of the idea of imprisonment over the next century. The fine was considered in this regard to have no reformative value at all. Deprivation of money could not be conceived as a morally improving factor in the same way imprisonment was, at least during the first half of the nineteenth century, when the use of the prison system responded to a philosophy of individual transformation and correction.

This may have been an important factor. However, in my opinion the shift is to be seen in the acceptance of the penalty of imprisonment as a more equal punishment than the fine, because of the way liberty was regarded from the end of the eighteenth century. Liberty is something that every person should be deemed to possess in the same amount, except for deeper probing into the inner feelings of each prisoner – which was considered at the time to be a forbidden intrusion. In contrast, the use of fines as a punishment did not sit well with the formal understanding of the equality principle. Admittedly, it could be said, and some (Carrara 1871; Merkel 1889: 227; Samuels 1970: 201) in fact did say, that the law is equal for all when the same amount of money is set to be paid, regardless of the class or socio-economic status of the offender. But even from a formal perspective this argument was not upheld: imprisonment could be applied with more equal force than fines to those with means and those without. And it could be done without directly affecting the prisoner's family, unlike fines. This led to fines being relegated to the periphery of the catalogue of punishments until the critics of short-term imprisonment, while pointing out the pernicious practical effects of this, reawakened interest in finding a more egalitarian pecuniary punishment. Such a reformulated fine would allow for individualization in line with personal inequalities, and be understood as a punishment that would adapt to the financial situation of the offender so that it would no longer be necessary to impose prison sentences for non-payment. This took place within the framework of a new concept of equality, which was no longer formal but material instead (Friedmann 1892: 96; Brenn 1945: 21ff.).

Expansion of the prison system and first criticisms

In brief, after the Enlightened criticisms of the penal panoply of the *ancien régime*, the sanction par excellence became imprisonment. It could be said that by inventing liberty, the French Revolution also gave birth to its opposite (Perrot 1978: 214). When imprisonment started to become more widespread as a punishment it was immediately accompanied by a reformist trend of a humanist nature: a philanthropic penitentiary movement arose that focused on the living conditions of the existing prisoners and demanded that they be improved. This trend aimed to give imprisonment a new justification, as well as to develop a new type of confinement that was still punitive but also productive (see references in Padovani 1981: 24). A more rationalized and uniform system of punishment began to be advocated. And for it to be implemented two changes were needed, which took place at different times in different countries during the nineteenth century: on the one hand, the rise of a centrally administered state control apparatus that included the prison system; on the other hand, the implementation of a rigorous prison discipline, oriented to the offender's rehabilitation.

Centralization

At the beginning of the nineteenth century, most prisons in England (Webb and Webb 1922: 14–15; Kilcommins 2002: 62ff.), France (Perrot 1978), Germany (Krohne 1889: 138ff.; Kriegsmann 1912: 8ff.), Italy (Beltrani-Scalia 1867: 401–402; Bernabò-Silorata 1926: 309ff.), and Spain (Burillo Albacete 1999: 61–64, 89ff.) had few or no trained officers – most of whom received no salaries, but were paid through the appropriation of gaol fees and the payment of fees or gratuities by the prisoners – and poor auditing and account-keeping, and operated as private ventures. The first prison regulations influenced by the Enlightenment aimed to improve the state of the buildings, the behaviour and conduct of the prison officers, and the treatment and condition of the prisoners, including the amount of their earnings and the expenses involving such prisons, but they usually created no mechanism by which the legislation could be enforced and lacked effective sanctions. The result was that there was little or no attempt to comply with the regulations and they were widely ignored. For example, that was the case with the first legislation to prescribe rules for all prisons in England and Wales, the Gaols Act 1791 (Playfair 1971: 73), but the same happened with the Gaol Fees Abolition Act 1815 (Harding 1985: 163–164), Peel's Gaol Act 1823 (Webb and Webb 1922: 73–75; Harding 1985: 144; Emsley 1987: 222), and the Prison Act 1835 – although this one went a step further by allowing the appointment of government inspectors to visit prisons and make reports to the secretary of state. In 1863 a Report for the Select Committee on Prison Discipline stated,

> many and wide differences, as regards construction, labour, diet and general discipline, exist in the various gaols and houses of correction in England and Wales, leading to an inequality, uncertainty and inefficiency of punishment, productive of the most prejudicial results.
>
> (Select Committee 1863: iii)

In fact, the question of centralization of local gaols and government prisons was still an issue at the first international penal and penitentiary congress held in London in 1872, where Hastings stated that there was considerable doubt in Great Britain that this would be an advantage (Pears 1872: 432). A further Prison Act had to be enacted in 1877 because the rationalizing and centralizing process was by no means completed by the Prison Act 1865 (Garland 1985: 9–10). It intended to promote uniformity in the management of prisons and to relieve the burden of local rates, and it succeeded by nationalizing the entire prison system (McConville 1981: 482; Harding 1985: 205). Critics of the prison system, who first targeted prison conditions, disciplinary techniques, and prison design, began to question the use of imprisonment as a punitive technique after 1877.

A similar evolution could be seen in Spain (Burillo Albacete 1999; Ramos Vázquez 2013), Germany (Kriegsmann 1912: 78ff.; Smaus 1996: 186–188), and Italy (Bernabò-Silorata 1926). It was even more complicated in the latter two countries with the additional problem of the long process of unification of the

German Empire, on the one hand, and the Kingdom of Italy, on the other. The German prison service, which was run by the federated states until 1935, exemplifies this complication. In 1879 an attempt was made to enact a Prison Code for the whole empire, but it failed since some of the states feared that such an act might entail a costly obligation to build new and expensive cellular prisons (Grünhut 1944: 7). In 1897 an Inter-State Agreement was made to bring about certain general administrative principles, in order to achieve some degree of uniformity in the execution of prison sentences, but prison administration remained decentralized for decades. In 1923 the agreement of 1897 was replaced by a new system of Principles of Prison Discipline (*Grundsätze für den Vollzug von Freiheitsstrafen*), but the administration of German prisons rested with the member states. As for France, 'neither architecture nor penal practice in the nineteenth century reflected an immediate or sharp rupture with old-regime practices, the transformation extended over a longer period of time than has been commonly supposed' (O'Brien 1982: 17). Hospitals, beggars' prisons, and workhouses were the first institutional remedies for social problems, such as the growing hordes of beggars and vagrants produced in the transition from traditional to modern society. The first major wave of penitentiary reform took place from 1790 through the 1820s. The main legal instrument was an imperial decree of September 22, 1810, which set aside millions of francs for the organization of a centralized prison system in France. The essential characteristics of the penitentiary system were legally defined through work, rehabilitation, and differentiation. In the next decade, eight central prisons of detention (*maisons centrales*) were built throughout France. Construction and renovation continued during the Restoration and July Monarchy, so that at mid-century the number of central prisons expanded to 19 (O'Brien 1982: 22). The second wave of reforms took place in the 1830s and 1840s, with central prisons converted into laboratories for testing the new principles of organization and treatment to be applied to the whole prison system (Perrot 1978: 232–233). Nevertheless, we should take into account that in 1842 there were only 19 *maisons centrales*, but many departmental and cantonal prisons – 86 *maisons de justice*, 362 *maisons d'arret*, 2,800 cantonal prisons, and 2,238 cells in police headquarters (O'Brien 1982: 23). On the whole, however, it is possible to speak of a single, centralized, and highly homogeneous prison regime before mid-century. The third major period of reform, which followed the revolution of 1848, was bolstered by the fear of an urban, dangerous criminal class with high rates of recidivism. 'Tighter standards of operation were imposed on existing institutions and the building of new prisons was halted' (O'Brien 1982: 24). There was greater attention now paid to prison personnel, with reforms promoting the bureaucratization of punishment. Prison administrators became a professionalized and specialized civil-service group. These tendencies were preserved by the fourth wave of penal reforms in the nineteenth century. Following the repression of the Commune of 1871, the two main structural reforms were the 1875 law for the solitary confinement of departmental inmates and the 1885 law on the relegation of recidivists for life to penal colonies. As Perrot (1978: 214) put it, 'The failure of the prison spelled the triumph of exclusion'. By then, an even higher degree of state centralization was achieved, although very few departmental prisons conformed to the state requirements, mainly because of a lack of means to do so. In Sweden, town and district jails were still administered by the respective communities in the 1930s – although they were compelled by law to observe uniform rules and regulations issued by the state government concerning the cells and their equipment, food, medical care, and so forth – while central prisons, prisons, and crown prisons, as well as the workhouses and institutions for care and internment, belonged to the state (Almquist 1931: 198). Danish and Norwegian prison administration was organized approximately in the same manner as in Sweden.

Correction

It was not only a mere matter of centralization but also a perceived need to improve techniques. Since little attempt had been made to regulate the day-to-day life of prisoners, it was proposed that the prisoner should serve his or her sentence in isolation, subjected to rigorous discipline, with or without the obligation to work depending on the different systems.[12] Correction was to be achieved through hard work, discipline, moral instruction, and constant surveillance. This philosophy of punishment – the origins of which dated back to the seventeenth century (see Paley 1787 2: 291), although not put into practice at the time due to a lack of resources – did bring about the need to adapt the architecture of prisons, because the buildings were not suitably designed to enable proper control or reformation. This required money, which was always scarce, and even more so when it was to be spent on improving the situation of criminals. As clearly explained by Vingtrinier (1840: 21), 'Anyone today would laugh at a man speaking [of the need to] improve the physical lot of prisoners'. The debate concerning penitentiary systems, at least in France, Germany, Italy, or Spain, was limited to intellectual circles, scarcely touching pragmatic policy. Prisons continued to be places where people were left to rot alive. With their roots in the early modern workhouses, prisons originally functioned as a congregation point for the poor and the jobless. Influencing this was the fact that the dominant penal ideology in the first half of the nineteenth century was retributionism, at least in the German-speaking countries and other countries under the intellectual influence of Germany, where the theories of Kant and Hegel provided a good philosophical foundation. All the enthusiasm shown by certain scholars for ideas such as protection, custody, and prisoner reform was rendered in legislation in purely retributionist terms, to the point where the penal codes of the era, such as the 1810 French Penal Code – known as 'Code Napoleon', extended in 1812 to all Italian regions under French rule –, the 1813 Penal Law Code for the Kingdom of Bavaria and the 1848 Spanish Penal Code, followed in this regard by the 1870 Spanish Penal Code, did not allow for the slightest reduction in sentences for reformed or well-behaved prisoners. Under the rule of retributionism, the punishment must be imposed within the limits, however strict these may be, that the law allows the judge, with there being no cause or reason, aside from the right to grant pardons, justifying the suspension, reduction, or substitution of the punishment. As a reminder of this we have the words of Von Buri (1894: 321), who expressed the following regarding suspended sentences:

> Current criminal law has the following two alternatives: either the perpetrator deserves a punishment, or he does not. In the first case the punishment should be enforced without fail, because a punishment that is not enforced is no punishment at all. In the second case, however, the defendant must be acquitted. There are no grounds for a suspended sentence in either case.

Meanwhile, the idea of isolation, developed to serve the sense of creating discipline, is a unique technique of a prison system that responds to a philosophy of individual transformation and correction. It is true that the idea of correction or reformation was already present in the execution of punishment centuries before. The English houses of correction are a good example of this, as their name leads one to believe. But what then was an idea barely sketched and more than often impeded by a lack of endeavour, intention, and homogeneity of practice (Kilcommins 2002: 149–150) now became the main objective, a new philosophy that should inspire the execution of punishments. Optimism about the moral improvement of offenders through the control of environment was high.

Unfulfilled promises

In practice, the gap between promise and achievement was great. Although cellular confinement, the great panacea for the ills of the prison and a key idea of prison reform, was not widespread in most of the countries under study because of the enormous cost of the renovation or new construction of appropriate establishments,[13] criticism was soon forthcoming for the pernicious effect that isolation had on prisoners serving long-term sentences. Even its partisans relate the disastrous effects of the Philadelphian system: penitentiary insanity and an increasing rate of suicides (Petitti di Roreto 1840: 462; Notaristefani 1924: 84). There was scientific evidence of an increased incidence of the physical and mental deterioration of prisoners subjected to such a regime. In the middle of the nineteenth century this situation led to the first doubts about the possibility of effectively re-educating prisoners within a prison environment being voiced (e.g., Posada de Herrera 1843: 89–90; Cattaneo 1906: 99–100, despite being a declared partisan of the Philadelphian system). The failure of the revolutionary movements of 1848 saw the end of the enthusiasm for reform, and laid the groundwork that would culminate in the movement criticizing short-term imprisonment and cellular isolation. Specialists played a very important role in the controversies surrounding the prison system, as well as in the rising awareness that prisons neither prevented crime nor corrected offenders. For example, criticism from Mittelstädt (1879) and Ferri (1900) was devastating. What is left is, on the one hand, a handful of Panopticon-style prisons,[14] and on the other hand, a ferocious prison discipline, with military influence in some countries like Spain, where the militarized administration of the prison system did not end until 1903 (Roldán Barbero 1988: 95–104; Ramos Vázquez 2012).

It has been said that a peculiar relationship was gradually established between prisons and factories that would affect the development of imprisonment within a context of increasingly bureaucratized and rationalized punitive power. The legal system was centralized as it started to produce people, activities, proceedings, and criminality while simultaneously experimenting with ways to reduce or eliminate it – let us not forget that the bourgeois ideology believed it possible to radically eliminate crime. For Foucault, prisons became the emblem of the new organization model of disciplinary power exerted within the social context of those who held the power in their hands. The prison was an instrument to control, measure, and train individuals, to make them docile and at the same time useful. The prison became a factory, in which the very special working conditions gave rise to a system of brutal exploitation. It was a model which, for Foucault, took on a universal and quasi-metaphysical aspect, and which lost, specifically because of its abstraction and generalization, a precise historical dimension. It is true that Foucault examined the birth of the prison institution and of the other internment institutions in France during the period covering the end of the seventeenth century and the first decades of the eighteenth, but the significance he attributes to the discovery of the disciplinary model of prison organization makes it a truly universal model.

This interpretative model does not fit with the prison ideologies or the real living conditions of the prisoners throughout most of Western Europe. The differences between the countries considered here were enormous. In France, many prisons were pestholes with the worst living conditions. For example, the prison of Pau: 'Misfortune, misfortune for the prisoner whom justice calls to this horrible place! [. . .] He will recover his liberty someday, but he has probably lost his health forever' (Michau, quoted by Villermé 1820: vi). Almost 25 years later, it still could be said,

> [i]t is only common sense that a system of imprisonment which increases the odds of mortality among prisoners should weaken the constitutions of those it does not kill and should make those individuals more susceptible to a greater number of sicknesses.
>
> (Faucher 1844: 388)

In fact, changes were slow. As highlighted by O'Brien (1982: 47–48), a parliamentary inquest conducted between 1873 and 1875 on the quality of life in prison (*Enquête parlementaire sur le régime des établissements pénitentiaires*) reached conclusions similar to the Decazes report (*Rapport au Roi sur les prisons et pièces à l'appui du rapport*) in 1819:

> Unfortunately it is a fact that in the majority of departmental prisons the privations imposed on the prisoners by their position get worse and worse. There remains much to do for the sake of cleanliness, order, morals, and the fundamental reform of convicts.

Nevertheless, the central prisons, under the Auburn system, relied heavily on prison contracting. The industrial prison model functioned quite well until the general decline in the 1880s, due to political attack from businessmen and workers alike.

The rest of the continent was not so successful. In England and Wales, the house of correction ideal did contain a reformatory element based on the correction of the inmates' habits of idleness by replacing them with habits of industry directed to achieve an honest livelihood. They soon lost their reformative role. By the mid- to late seventeenth century they were simply appropriated 'to the cheap custodial punishment of minor offenders and financed and administered accordingly' (McConville 1981: 48). In the eighteenth century workhouses[15] never produced an output 'which even repaid the purchase of raw materials, nor did they meet the vaunted secondary objective of training the poor in habits of industry' (Rule 1992: 128). It proved impossible to provide the inmates with sufficient labour. At the same time, neither Germany nor other countries of Western Europe managed to develop a training function for industrial work and for the control-regulation of the labour market through prison. In the German-speaking countries, the first wave of enthusiasm for the system of the house of correction led to the founding of several establishments in the Hanseatic cities – Bremen in 1609, Lübeck in 1613, Hamburg in 1622, Danzig in 1629 – and other parts of the territory – Breslau and Vienna in 1670, Frankfurt in 1679, Munich in 1682 – modelled after Amsterdam and therefore with a strong impact on the correction of the poor and the idle. With the start of the eighteenth century came a distinction between the punishment of imprisonment (*Gefängnisstrafe*) for criminals and internment in workhouses for the poor and idle, both of which prescribed work. The boundaries between them were poorly defined. The punishment of confinement in a fortress without the obligation of working (*Festungsstrafe*) was reserved for offenders whose motives were recognized as honourable (Wächter 1786). In general, the state of the establishments used for the execution of these penalties was such that inmates were often physically unable to work *ex squalore carceris* (Von Arnim 1803: 135; Kriegsmann 1912: 19) or were given nothing to do (Von Hippel 1925: 138–139).

In Spain, the houses of correction, or to be more accurate, the departments of correction of the hospices – which was the closest thing that existed to the English workhouses or the Dutch *Rusphuis*, albeit with a clear manufacturing bias that made them similar to a 'type of prison and factory', as astutely defined by Howard during his visit to Spain – were practically non-existent. The scant labour provided in the hospices and their correctional annexes served only a purely internal function, to help cover the costs of the institution itself. This objective was, of course, never achieved. Nor was there any pressure from the employment market calling for an increase in the number of workers, which meant that the emphasis was always placed more on learning moral values rather than manual skills. In turn, there was never a real drive to turn gaols and military prisons into factories, with scholars offering up proposals to engage prisoners in beneficial public works 'diverting them away from idleness, which was the main reason for their lawlessness' (Elizondo 1784: 175), as well as expressing regret over the 'continuous and disastrous idleness' that prevailed in prison establishments (Marcos Gutiérrez 1826: 230–231; Posada de Herrera 1843: 89–90). In fact, until the middle of the century the only noticeable intervention involving the prison system concerned the field of public works, such as building roads or draining marshes.[16] The 1848 Spanish Penal Code established imprisonment (*prisión*) and ordinary imprisonment (*reclusión*), punishments in which the confinement itself was the essential aspect, meaning that if the prisoner could afford to pay his own way he was not obliged to work (Burillo Albacete 1999: 275–277). This was explicit recognition of the fact that labour, without the up until then inconceivable deprivation of freedom, was no longer the underlying element. This loss of importance was confirmed by the Spanish Law establishing the basis for the reform and improvement of prisons and imprisonment, and the approach for a good penitentiary system of October 11, 1869 (*Ley fijando las bases para la reforma y mejora de las cárceles y presidios, y para el planteamiento de un buen sistema penitenciario*), which suppressed compulsory work inside the prison.

In turn, the Italian prison system never saw an extensive use of industrial labour (Melossi and Pavarini 1981: 69; Neppi Modona 1985: 58). Attempts were made in legislation, but in reality it was never really implemented (Florian 1934: 826–827, with more references). There were some early attempts to use people locked in charitable institutions (*ospedali*) and houses of correction for the youth. At the end of the eighteenth century Howard (1792: 122–123) could write that the inmates did not generally work but were sent to the galleys, and by the middle of the nineteenth century the situation had not improved in the slightest, which sustained a system of living together with no productive occupation (Petitti di Roreto 1840) – despite the emphatic proclamation of the obligation to work in the various prison regulations of the Italian states (Bernabò-Silorata 1926). The same situation could be seen at the end of the century (Beltrani-Scalia 1879: 307–308), despite the introduction of the isolation system by the 1853 Penal Code of Tuscany, and of the mixed one in 1860. Not until the General Regulations on Prison Institutions and Reformatories no. 260 of February 1, 1891 (*Regolamento generale degli stabilimenti carcerari e dei riformatori*), was the cornerstone laid for the prison system of liberal Italy. Until then, all the reform projects stalled in Parliament, weighed down by useless debates and discussions between the partisans of the different prison systems, preventing any real reform (Beltrani-Scalia 1879: 12–50; Neppi Modona 1985: 59). Despite all these efforts Italian prisons were still considered 'cemeteries for the living' in 1904, according to Turati (cited by Bosch 1984: 333).

Along with the generalized delay and lack of real implementation of the new prison systems that advocated labour as an instrument of reform for the offender, there was also the socialist concern for the unwanted competition of industrial prison labour, ironically condemned by Mittelstädt (1879: 42–43) and naively dismissed by Garofalo (1887 [2002]: 109), based on the fact that the prisoners would continue to do the same trade that they had done before being sentenced – against the evidence drawn from statistical data (Assirelli and Santangelo 1928: 190–192). The proposals to limit this competition ranged from limiting prison production to state-owned industries (Aschaffenburg 1903: 218–219; Bernabò-Silorata 1926: 322) to using it exclusively for the internal needs of the prison (Beltrani-Scalia

1867: 445). Both enjoyed support from the international congresses and had some level of legal implementation (e.g., Law April 14, 1898, of the State of Massachusetts), as well as the control of the type of work and the price of products (French Ordinance of April 19, 1819) and the prohibition of importation of goods made or produced wholly or in part in any foreign prison, gaol, house of correction, or penitentiary (English Foreign Prison-Made Goods Act 1897).

Without even considering the minimum impact prison labour had on the national product (pointed out by many; see Assirelli and Santangelo 1928: 196ff., and confirmed by statistics), it was attacked by the working class *and* employers alike. The protests were particularly virulent in Spain, where the representatives of a rickety and technologically backward industry expressed their fear that prison manufacturing, once developed, could compete with local industry, if due only to the scarcity of wages (Burillo Albacete 1999: 277). But also in Germany, one of the most industrialized countries, the Trade Council decided in 1878 that prisons were not to be allowed to contract out their inmates as cheap labour force to private companies, or to engage them in factory work (Streng 1886: 144; O'Brien 1995: 204). The progressive decommissioning of prison labour[17] led to the bankruptcy of the system as it was impossible for the state to justify to citizens the enormous costs involved in supporting the prisoners.[18]

The creation of crime statistics in the middle of the nineteenth century helped to increase the criticism aimed at prisons. The statistics gave people a more accurate idea of the number of offenders sentenced to imprisonment, the degree of overcrowding in prison institutions, the level of (non-)compliance with the legal obligation to separate prisoners according to the severity of their crimes and the type of custodial sentence imposed, the cost involved in maintaining the prison system, and other interesting aspects used to assess the effectiveness of prison sentences, like the percentage of repeat or habitual offenders. As this statistical information became widespread, a bleak image was propagated of the different types of custodial sentences governed by law and their effects. Awareness grew in leading circles that the prisons were in abominable condition and that the situation of the inmates was unacceptable.

The search for a change

In sum, from the middle of the nineteenth century there was widespread criticism of the living conditions in prisons and the forced labour of the era, which in the majority of countries had not changed much in comparison to those put forward by Howard. The succession of criticism against the retributionist-based penal codes, resulting from the *avant-garde* of correctionalist intellectuals, eventually created the right environment for prison reform to finally become something more than a grandiloquent gesture. For the first time, however, the criticism led to a review of the punishment of imprisonment and its fundamental and almost exclusive role (Padovani 1981: 44). The literature from all the European countries studied herein no longer limited itself to discussing the reality of prisons, demanding their transformation in line with the establishment of a specified prison system under which punishment could effectively achieve its purpose and deploy its efficiency. Doubts started to emerge about the appropriateness of actually employing this type of sanction. Leading academics in the campaign against short-term imprisonment from European countries – Austria, England, France, Germany, Italy, Portugal, Scandinavia, Spain, Switzerland – expressed their uneasiness about the drawbacks they perceived in custodial sentences, which they did not believe were outweighed by the prospective benefits that could be derived from imprisonment.[19] This led to a series of international penitentiary congresses, the first one in London in 1872, the second one in Stockholm in 1878, and the third one in Rome in 1885, as well as the inaugural meeting of the International Union of Penal Law in Brussels in 1889, and the third one in Christiania (later Oslo) in 1891, in which short imprisonments were deplored and fines, especially when levied against the poor, were decried, because of non-payment of fines leading to short sentences of imprisonment. The substitutive sanctions suggested for both short-term imprisonment *and* fines were forced labour with deprivation of liberty or voluntary labour outside prison. Fines were considered to be a replacement punishment for short-term imprisonment only when insolvency did not end in imprisonment for fine defaulters (Von Ihering 1877 [1904]: 39, 48, 53, 90, 292–293). Usually, fine supporters limited its use to less severe crimes, petty offences and misdemeanours (Krohne 1889: 235; Von Liszt 1889: 45; Zürcher 1891: 268; Bertola 1893: 553; Schmölder 1902: 11; Silvela 1903: 318; Conti 1910: 462; Vila Miquel 1917: 163; but not Merkel 1889: 225–226, who said that the legal maximum pointed to the possibility of also using them for serious crimes). As the Seventh Report of Her Majesty's Commissioners on the Criminal Law pointed out, there were 'a few instances where fixed fines were appropriate to more serious crimes', but the general belief was that 'fixed and absolute fines should be restricted to cases of minor delinquency punishable by summary jurisdiction' (Commission on Criminal Law 1843: 109–111). The fine was not considered to be an appropriate punishment when the crime was committed out of necessity, because then it would have criminogenic effects (Carrara 1871: 463; Ferri 1900: 454; Rauh 1912), an observation that had already been put forth by Enlightenment thinkers, like Beccaria (1764 [1872]: Chapter 22) or Kleinschrod (1794). This greatly limited the scope of fines, given the poverty of those who committed the most applied crimes, particularly theft.

Padovani pointed out (1981: 134) that only radical and socialist-inspired doctrine promoted the use of fines as a punishment aimed at overcoming social resistance to the infamy of imprisonment on *honnêtes gens*. For crimes typical of their social class, this literature further argued for replacing imprisonment with a punishment in line with their status, insofar as it affected the asset that held the greatest importance for them, money (Gómez Rodríguez 1864: 45; Ciccarelli 1897: 577–578 and 631–632; Conti 1907: 199). This viewpoint should explain how pecuniary punishments appeared, as effectively expressed by Heilborn (1908: 57), as 'the heart-breaking punishment for the rich bourgeois'. It should be taken into account, nonetheless, that the fine was *generally* considered to be an appropriate – 'mirroring' – punishment for crimes committed out of greed (Puccioni 1855

1: 204; Maffei 1875: 406; Wahlberg 1877: 236–237; Mittelstädt 1879: 86; Krohne 1889: 235; Merkel 1889: 227; Zürcher 1891: 268; Friedmann 1892: 136; Conti 1910: 462; Saldaña 1931: 206; 7th International Penal and Penitentiary Congress held in Budapest in 1905, see Barrows 1907). It was not a matter of extending the use of fines to all types of criminality, but rather putting forth a counterbalance to the logic of unlawful gain. This meant that fines came to the fore with respect to business regulation through criminal and regulatory law (Mittelstädt 1879: 86; Rauh 1912: 58). The fine was considered to be most appropriate when offences linked to productive processes of industry involved omissions or reckless actions, caused by selfish improvidence, or criminal neglect from certain industrialists and capitalists, when

> in order to save money, due to simple greed, they disregarded precautions, the measures they were obliged to observe: when they commit this neglect, and by doing so become criminals, let's hit them hard, by taking from them the very capital they aim to increase even with the blood of their fellow men.
> (Angiolini 1897: 668–669)

In fact, fining came to take on new significance with the growth of regulatory offences and economic, white-collar crime (Briggs et al. 1996: 172). The fine was to be an important tool in resolving the paradox of 'the respectable offender'.[20] It helped to rebuild the symbolic divide between criminal and non-criminal by asserting the 'special nature' of economic crime.[21]

With the aforementioned exception of economic crimes, the proposals formulated in the international congresses and conferences of reformers that flourished in the second half of the nineteenth century in Western Europe mainly focused on introducing or increasing the use of suspended sentences. Very few could predict the increase in the use of fines that would occur throughout the twentieth century. For the fine to get to that point it had to undergo a clean-up process of two of the most criticized characteristics derived from its monetary nature: the impersonality which allowed the fine to be paid by an innocent third party (Chapter 3) and the unequal impact on offenders caused by the unequal distribution of money between individuals in society (Chapter 4).

Notes

1 Despite the speed with which it was translated and published in Germany, and after influencing the first compilation of common law in Prussia – the Prussian *Allgemeines Landrecht* – and being acknowledged by Von Feuerbach, the subsequent rejection by Kant (1797: 331–332) and Hegel (1820: § 100) led to its omission from the current German criminal law books, which do not mention Beccaria at all, not even when analysing the principle of legality or the functions of punishment.

2 The book was very favourably received in England, where its popularity is clearly shown by the four editions it achieved by the turn of the century.

3 It was published with a note at the beginning of the work indicating that publication was permitted only 'for public education, without affecting the Laws of the Kingdom, and their strict adherence', and a prologue in which the translator, J.A. de las Casas,

explains that the work corresponds to Christian values and royal decrees. This did not prevent the Inquisition from banning it in 1777. This ban was upheld in Spain until the abolition of this court system in 1813 (Defourneaux 1973: 90ff.). In fact, not the legislator but the Catholic Church turned out to be Beccaria's opponent. In the territories of the Habsburg monarchy – it should be remembered that Beccaria was an Austrian state official, for at that time Milan belonged to the Austrian Empire – after putting his book on the *Index Librorum Prohibitorum Typis Polyglottis Vaticanis* already in 1766, it remained there for 200 years up to its abolition in 1966.

4 It has been suggested that Bentham was a disciple of Beccaria. Hart (1982: 49) has shown, however, that although Bentham admired Beccaria's work because it was based on reason, he also was highly critical of Beccaria's failure to develop his general points in detail.

5 The most important ones in this regard were *Principles of Civil Law* and *Principles of Penal Law*, both published originally in 1802 in French, translated by his Swiss disciple Etienne Dumont (*Traités de legislation civile et pénale*, Paris: Boussange, Masson & Besson). They appeared in Italian in 1818 (*Trattati di legislazione civile e penale: Preceduti da'principi generali di legislazione, e da un proggetto di un corpo completo di diritto*, Naples: A. Trani, in three volumes). In Spain they emerged in 1821 under the title *Tratados de la Legislación Civil y Penal*, translated by Ramón de Salas (Madrid: Imprenta de Fermín Villalpando, in five volumes), in time to influence the preparatory work for the first 1822 Spanish Penal Code (*Diario de las Discusiones y Actas de las Cortes extraordinarias de 1821: Discusión del Proyecto de Código Penal*, Volume 1, Madrid: Imprenta Nacional, 1822, assembly of November 23, 1821, 210–211; Sánchez Oses 1967: 540; Puyol Montero 1997: 113), and from there the Hispano-American codification process (Schwartz 1978; Cajas Sarria 2010). Already before the translation of his works into Spanish Toribio Núñez Sessé, a jurist from Salamanca, had published his *Espíritu de Bentham: Sistema de la Ciencia social* in 1820 (Salamanca: Imprenta Nueva de D. Bernardo Martín), as well as *Principios de la Ciencia Social o de las Ciencias Morales y Políticas* in 1821 (Salamanca: Imprenta Nueva de D. Bernardo Martín), raising awareness of the thinking of the English author with whom he corresponded and of whom he considered himself a disciple. They were published in Germany in 1830 in two volumes under the title *Grundsätze der Civil- und Criminal-Gesetzgebung*, translated by the anti-Hegelian thinker Friedrich Eduard Beneke (Berlin: Amelang).

In turn, *The Rationale of Punishment* was first published in French as *Théorie des peines et des récompenses*, in two volumes, translated once again by Dumont (London: B. Dulau, 1811); first published in English as *The Rationale of Reward*, translated and edited by Richard Smith (London: J. & H. Hunt, 1825), and *The Rationale of Punishment*, translated and edited also by Smith (R. Heward, 1830). The *Teoría de las penas legales* was first published in Spanish in 1825 (Paris: Masson e hijo), and one year later it was published in full as *Teoría de las penas y de las recompensas*, in two volumes. And *Jeremias Bentham's Grundsätze der Criminalpolitik in einem Auszuge und systematischen Zusammenhange* was first published in German in 1839 (Tübingen: Osiander), edited by Ferdinand Hepp.

The relatively late dates of the German translations of Bentham's works are proof of the fact that he was accepted in the German legal world considerably later than in Spain or England, only from the middle of the nineteenth century. This was due to the initial rejection of his utilitarian thinking in German literature, imbued with idealism and conservatism, which criticized him as an example of non-philosophy, dismissing his empirical approach and the model of Man he proposed (see references in Luik 2003: 94ff.).

6 Drawn up by Le Pelletier de Saint Fargeau, its Article 1 established the following: 'The punishments meted out by the jury against those defendants found guilty, are the death

penalty, branding, confinement in workhouses, imprisonment, detention, banishment, civic degradation, the pillory'. Fines were not included. The same happened in other penal codes that were mere translations of the French one, like the 1799 Swiss *Peinliches Gesetzbuch* (Lang 1983: 8). Nevertheless, in France a very advanced regulation of fines was established by the Law of July 19–22, 1791, regarding the organization of a municipal police (*Loi du 19–22 juillet 1791, relative à l'organisation d'une police municipal*), which based the fine on the value of a day's work in each town, and then this amount was doubled, trebled, quadrupled . . . in accordance with the nature of the offence, but regardless of the fortune of the offender.

7 In fact, some of the early Enlightenment criminal or penal codes were made within the framework of non-liberal, despotic political systems, like the 1794 Prussian *Allgemeines Landrecht*. Subsequent literature tended to magnify the political significance of codification, associating this technique with the idea of an absolute, revolutionary change compared to the previous state of affairs. 'The system of codification, the system of absolute change, was the only legitimate and indeed, the only possible system', in opposition to tradition and compilation, affirmed the Spanish commentator Pacheco (1856: lii).

8 Despite the ideas upheld by numerous authors who believed that the disappearance of corporal punishments and the extension of imprisonment would lead to a general development of criminal law towards milder, more humane penalties. See, for instance, Von Hippel (1928: 3).

9 See, for example, Filangieri (1788: Book 3, second part, Chapter 33). However, it must be remembered that on numerous occasions the statements proclaiming the multiple advantages attributed to prison sentences were based on abstract reasoning, far removed from the real institutions, with some authors going so far as to admit that the benefits attributed to custodial sentences in reality did not result from the sentences that were executed in the existing prisons (Rossi 1853: 475ff.), where it was common practice for there to be no prison regime whatsoever, despite the solemn legal proclamations.

10 Although work was undoubtedly a large part of the prison regime, next to the loss of freedom (Spierenburg 1991: 173–175), to the point where the prison regulations of some countries considered it necessary to explain that 'the inability to work will not exempt prisoners from serving the custodial sentences' (Articles 119 and 298 of the 1834 Spanish Prison Ordinance, *Ordenanza General de los Presidios del Reino*). As late as in 1895 the fifth international penal and penitentiary congress held in Paris still discussed if cases of imprisonment could be admitted without compulsory labour, and the answer was that manual labour ought, as a general rule, to be made compulsory for all sentences involving deprivation of liberty.

11 See in England Sharpe (1990: 20–25) and Briggs et al. (1996); in Germany Neumaier (1947); in Spain Roldán Barbero (1988: 176); in Italy del Giudice (1905: 507) and Cecchini (1991: 282ff.).

12 The initial experience of Auburn consisted of solitary confinement with no occupation that would distract the prisoner from his meditation. It was soon discovered that exclusive dedication to thinking all day did not produce positive effects on the prisoners. Experiments introducing labour were carried out, but as an activity to be performed individually, inside the cell. The Pennsylvanian system was defined by complete isolation day and night with work carried out in the cell. This then gave way to isolation in the cell at night but during the day the prisoners worked together in workshops, in complete silence. The disciplinary function of work in the Auburn system is evident, as is the intention to make the prisoners' labour profitable, which was a new approach. Various systems were proposed to exploit the labour performed in prisons, with the most relevant being the piece-price system and the contract system. They are both variations of the same idea, but they were executed with subtle differences that in practice

produced very different consequences. They were both based on a system of leasing the work out to a private manufacturer, but under the piece-price system the contractor provided the material and bought the finished product at a fixed price per unit, but the work was managed and supervised by the prison staff. Under the contract system, the contractor supplied the material and supervised the prisoners' work, so the prison staff had to deal only with the internal order of the prison. The difference between the pedagogical concept of labour and the idea of labour being a productive activity is what distinguishes these two systems of organizing prison labour.

13 Referring to Italy, Melossi and Pavarini (1981: 87) said that 'in 1849, the adoption of the Philadelphian system of solitary confinement became widespread'. It is true that this system was sanctioned by a general regulation of 1850 and then by the 1853 Penal Code of Tuscany, which remained in effect after Italian unification, but despite responding to the proposals in literature (Petitti di Roreto 1840) it was not actually applied. The same can be said about Spain (Roldán Barbero 1988: 94), where cellular confinement was almost unknown in practice. Only in 1867 cellular prisons were built in Navalcarnero (Madrid), with 24 cells, and Cieza (Murcia), with 38 (Cadalso 1896: 172). For Germany, see Glauning (1905: 278), while for Austria Dearing (1983: 605–606). On the contrary, some northern countries were able to hold most or all prisoners in solitary confinement. That was the case of Denmark, Norway, and Sweden (Nilsson 2003; Scharff Smith 2012: 51–53), where isolation practices were established in the 1800s and persisted well into the twentieth century. As for France, although the Philadelphian system enjoyed a very strong support between 1840 and 1847, when it seemed that total isolation of prisoners would achieve parliamentary support, the system finally adopted was the Auburn one, with modifications: total separation of prisoners only at night and a communal rule of silence during the day (O'Brien 1982: 23). However, a half-century was to elapse before these measures were put into practice. Around 1875 only three French prisons enforced around-the-clock cellular isolation, while 52 institutions chose not to do so, despite being equipped to follow such a regime. See in this regard the report presented by Bérenguer and the subsequent parliamentary debate preceding passage of the law of June 4, 1875, in the *Journal Officiel* of May 21, 1875, which reinstated solitary confinement.

14 In Italy, a panopticon prison was already established in 1795. In Switzerland, a prison modelled on the Panopticon was built in Geneva in 1825. In Germany the prison cell in Moabit Berlin was built in the 1840s. In Norway, although the panoptic principles were discarded before they were implemented, the new Oslo prison opened in 1851, Botsfengselet, was built as a panopticon institution. The first Spanish panopticon prison was built in Vitoria in 1861 and the second one in Madrid in 1883. The model was never built in England, despite Bentham's efforts.

15 The workhouse, an institution evolving from the Houses of Correction created by English law in 1576 and the Dutch *Tuchthuisen*, created in Amsterdam in 1596, spread throughout Western Europe during the seventeenth and eighteenth centuries (Von Hippel 1898: 419 ff.; Rusche and Kirchheimer 1939 [2003]: 41–52; Foucault 1977; Melossi and Pavarini 1981; Roldán Barbero 1988: 70ff.). It should be noted, however, that workhouses may be distinguished from houses of correction in relation to forced labour, since it is possible to argue that they did not involve forced labour as there was an element of implied consent: paupers had to work in order to assist in financing their upkeep, but they could leave the institution whenever they desired (Kilcommins 2002: 228). Anyway, in terms of capitalistic exploitation, both workhouses and houses of correction proved to be dismal failures.

16 Despite the fact that the eighteenth-century theoreticians did not generally recommend this practice, they believed that workers assigned to the programmes of public works should be labourers untarnished by the stigma of crime: the idle (Feijóo 1739: discourse 13; Cabarrús 1808: 95–96).

17 Prison labour was abolished in France on March 24, 1848, although it was reintroduced after the defeat of the revolution. In Spain the concentration of prison manpower on a few large-scale public works, particularly on the Canal of Castile and the roads of Andalusia, continued up until the first governments of the reign of Isabel II (approx. mid-nineteenth century).

18 Although Western European countries remained committed to the goal of the prison as a financially self-sustaining institution, many of them had ruinous balance sheets of prisoner income and expenditure. For example, Salillas (1904: 115) calculated that in 1890 the maintenance expenses cost Spain 2,102,763 pesetas, while the profits amounted to 95,370 pesetas. Meanwhile, Notaristefani (1924: 85) offered some data for the Italian prison system in 1899–1900: the maintenance costs of the prisoners amounted to 5,273,816.63 lire, while the profits from the prisoners' work for the state and for private businessmen amounted to 1,075,514.86 lire, of which 332,781.16 lire were industrial profit. Equally telling are the figures provided by Assirelli and Santangelo (1928: 204–205) for the 1894–1900 period in Italy. On the contrary, among German states,

> Brunswick claimed that its system of inmate labor contracted out to local businessmen nearly covered the cost of operating the prison, whereas Baden, under a work system administered by the state, was said to have supplied two-thirds of the institution costs and taught useful trades to inmates.
>
> (O'Brien 1995: 204)

19 Interestingly, this critical viewpoint led a doctrinal sector to request a greater use of the punishments 'of old'. For example, Mittelstädt (1879) supported a greater use of the death penalty and flogging, forced labour without imprisonment, banishment, symbolic sanctions, and, of course, fines. See also Rosenfeld (1890) or Merkel (1889: 220–221), although only for young criminals. Another direction driven by scepticism of the usefulness of short-term prison sentences was the advocacy of a more rigorous prison regime: hard beds, restricted diet, confinement in darkness, and so on (Lucchini 1882: 467; Fuld 1890: 449–453; Heilborn 1908: 31–45). Following this trend, the revision of the 1844 Swedish draft criminal code took the 'advanced' step, according to Von Bar (1916: 369), of recognizing only one kind of punishment – namely, simple imprisonment in seven grades. It was not accepted by Parliament.

20 As noted by Emsley (2005: 57), while contemporaries came to recognize

> that men of wealth and social standing committed offences [. . .] such offenders, however common in fiction, newspaper accounts, and journal literature, were not perceived as members of a criminal class and were categorised as 'criminal' with some difficulty.

About the challenge of respectable crime to the understandings and interpretations of 'the criminal' in the late nineteenth century, see Locker (2008: 115ff.) and Wilson (2014).

21 For example, in England 97 per cent of all those convicted in 1928 for violating labour laws were fined. No one was imprisoned for more than three months (Home Office 1928: 66). In Germany 99.97 per cent of all those convicted in 1933 for violating the regulations about hours of labour were fined, while the rest, 0.03 per cent, were sentenced to prison for less than three months (Deutsches Reich 1933: 182). With strong criticism, see Rusche and Kirchheimer (1939 [2003]: 173–174).

References

Almquist, V. (1931) 'Scandinavian Prisons'. *The Annals of the American Academy of Political and Social Science* 157: 197–207.

Angiolini, A. (1897) 'Nota a Ciccarelli, Per l'abolizione della pena pecuniaria'. *La Scuola Positiva* 7: 641–670.

Aschaffenburg, G. (1903) *Das Verbrechen und seine Bekämpfung: Kriminalpsychologie für Mediziner, Juristen und Soziologen, ein Beitrag zur Reform der Strafgesetzgebung.* Heidelberg: Carl Winter's Universitätsbuchhandlung.

Assirelli, P. G. and I. Santangelo Spoto (1928) 'Lavoro carcerario'. In Lucchini, L. (ed.) *Il Digesto Italiano: Enciclopedia metodica e alfabetica di legislazione, dottrina e giurisprudenza. Volume XIV.* Turin: Unione Tipografico-Editrice Torinese, 176–210.

Barrows, S. J. (1907) *Report of Proceedings of the Seventh International Prison Congress, Budapest, Hungary, September, 1905, by Samuel J. Barrows, commissioner for the United States on the International Prison Commission.* Washington: Govt. Print. Off.

Beattie, J. M. (1986) *Crime and the Courts in England. 1660–1800.* Princeton, NJ: Princeton University Press.

Beccaria, C. Bonesana di (1764 [1872]) *An Essay on Crimes and Punishments: By the Marquis Beccaria of Milan. With a Commentary by M. de Voltaire. A New Edition Corrected.* Albany: W. C. Little.

Beltrani-Scalia, M. (1867) *Sul governo e sulla riforma delle carceri in Italia: saggio storico e teorico.* Turin: Favale.

Beltrani-Scalia, M. (1879) *La riforma penitenziaria in Italia: Studi e proposte.* Rome: Tipografia Artero e comp.

Bentham, J. (1789) *An Introduction to the Principles of Morals and Legislation.* London: Payne.

Bentham, J. (1830) *The Rationale of Punishment.* London: Robert Heward.

Bernabò-Silorata, A. (1926) 'Case penali'. In Lucchini, L. (ed.) *Il Digesto Italiano: Enciclopedia metodica e alfabetica di legislazione, dottrina e giurisprudenza. Volume VI, parte seconda.* Turin: Unione Tipografico-Editrice Torinese, 307–323.

Bertola, E. (1893) 'Della pena pecuniaria'. *Rivista Penale* 1: 548–553.

Bosch, J. (1984) 'Die Freiheitsstrafe und ihre Surrogate in Italien'. In Jescheck, H.-H. (ed.) *Die Freiheitsstrafe und ihre Surrogate im deutschen und ausländischen Recht.* Baden-Baden: Nomos, 327–372.

Bottoms, A. E. (1983) 'Some Neglected Features of Contemporary Penal Systems'. In Garland, D. and P. Young (eds.) *The Power to Punish.* London: Heinemann, 166–202.

Brenn, A. (1945) *Die Busse und ihr Vollzug nach dem Schweizerischen Strafgesetzbuch.* Affoltern am Albis: Dr. J. Weiss.

Briggs, J., Harrison, C., McInnes, A. and D. Vincent (1996) *Crime and Punishment in England: An Introductory History.* New York: St. Martin's Press.

Burillo Albacete, F. J. (1999) *El nacimiento de la pena privativa de libertad.* Madrid: Edersa.

Cabarrús, F. Conde de (1808) *Cartas sobre los obstáculos que la naturaleza, la opinión y las leyes oponen a la felicidad pública.* Vitoria: Imprenta de Don Pedro Real.

Cadalso y Manzano, F. (1896) *Diccionario de legislación penal, procesal y de prisiones. Volumen I.* Madrid: J. Góngora y Álvarez.

Cajas Sarria, M. A. (2010) 'Usos locales de Tratados de Legislación Civil y Penal de Jeremy Bentham en los inicios de la República'. *Revista de Derecho: Universidad del Norte* 34: 21–41.

Carrara, F. (1871) *Programma del Corso di Diritto Criminale dettato nella R. Università di Pisa. Parte Generale.* 4th ed. Lucca: Tipografia Giusti.

Cattaneo, C. (1906) *Della riforma penale.* Milan: Società Editrice Sonzogno.

Cecchini, B. M. (1991) 'Il reato e la condanna nel sistema della Leopoldina: Mutamenti e variazioni nella struttura della pena (1781–1790)'. In Berlinguer, L. and F. Colao (eds.) *Criminalità e società in età moderna.* Milan: Giuffrè, 259–306.

Ciccarelli, A. (1897) 'Per l'abolizione della pena pecuniaria'. *La Scuola Positiva* 7: 577–598.

The Commission on Criminal Law (1843) *Seventh Report of Her Majesty's Commissioners on Criminal Law: Dated the 11th Day of March 1843. Presented to Both Houses of Parliament by Command of Her Majesty*. London: W. Clowes and Sons.

Conti, U. (1907) 'Delle riforme alla legislazione penale'. *Rivista di diritto penale e sociología criminale* 8: 196–212, 287–307.

Conti, U. (1910) 'La pena e il sistema penale del codice italiano'. In Pessina, E. (ed.) *Enciclopedia del diritto penale italiano. Volume IV*. Milan: Società Editrice Libraria, 1–970.

Dearing, A. (1983) 'Die Freiheitsstrafe und ihre Surrogate in Österreich'. In Jescheck, H.-H. and G. Grebing (eds.) *Die Freiheitsstrafe und ihre Surrogate im deutschen und ausländischen Recht. Band 1*. Baden-Baden: Nomos, 599–720.

Defourneaux, M. (1973) *Inquisición y censura de los libros en la España del siglo XVIII*. Madrid: Taurus.

Deutsches Reich (1933) *Kriminalstatistik*. Berlin: P. Schmidt.

Driendl, J. (1983) 'Entwicklung und Neuregelung der Geldstrafe nach dem Tagessatzsystem in Österreich'. In Jescheck, H.-H. and G. Grebing (eds.) *Die Geldstrafe im deutschen und ausländischen Recht*. Baden-Baden: Nomos, 659–737.

Eden, W., Baron Auckland (1771) *Principles of Penal Law*. 2nd ed. London: B. White and T. Cadell.

Elizondo, F. A. de (1784) *Práctica universal forense de los tribunales de España e Indias. Volume IV*. Madrid: Imprenta de Joaquín Ibarra.

Emsley, C. (1987) *Crime and Society in England 1750–1900*. London: Longman.

Emsley, C. (2005) *Crime and Society in England, 1750–1900*. 3rd ed. Harlow: Longman.

Faucher, L. (1844) 'Du Projet de loi sur la réforme des prisons'. *Revue des Deux Mondes* 5: 373–408.

Feijóo y Montenegro, B. J. (1739) *Theatro crítico universal, o Discursos varios en todo género de materias para desengaño de errores comunes. Tomo 8*. Madrid: del Hierro.

Ferri, E. (1900) *Sociologia Criminale*. 4th ed. Turin: Fratelli Bocca Editori.

Filangieri, G. (1788) *La scienza della legislazione*. Catania: Pastore.

Finzsch, N. (1996) '"Comparing Apples and Oranges?" The History of Early Prisons in Germany and the United States, 1800–1860'. In Finzsch, N. and R. Jütte (eds.) *Institutions of Confinement: Hospitals, Asylums, and Prisons in Western Europe and North America, 1500–1950*. Cambridge: Cambridge University Press, 213–234.

Florian, E. (1934) *Parte generale del Diritto penale. II*. 4th ed. Milan: Casa Editrice Dottor Francesco Vallardi.

Foucault, M. (1977) *Discipline and Punish*. New York: Pantheon Books.

Friedmann, O. (1892) 'Sind Änderungen des geltendes Recht erwünscht in Betreff des Verhältnisses zwischen Geld- und Freiheitsstrafen?' In Deutscher Juristentag (ed.) *Verhandlungen des Zweiundzwanzigsten Deutschen Juristentages. Zweiter Band*. Berlin: Guttentag, 95–183.

Fuld, L. (1890) 'Die kurzzeitigen Freiheitsstrafen und ihr Ersatz'. *Der Gerichtssaal* 43: 444–480.

Garland, D. (1985) *Punishment and Welfare*. Aldershot: Gower.

Garofalo, R. (1887 [2002]) *Indemnización a las víctimas del delito: Traducción y estudio crítico*. Pamplona: Analecta.

Giudice, P. del (1905) 'Diritto penale germanico rispetto all'Italia'. In Pessina, E. (ed.) *Enciclopedia del diritto penale italiano. Volume I*. Milan: Società Editrice Libraria, 431–611.

Glauning, D. (1905) 'Zur "Reform der Geldstrafe"'. *Blätter für Gefängnisskunde* 39: 277–289.

Gómez Rodríguez, T. (1864) 'Detención y prisión preventiva'. *Revista General de Legislación y Jurisprudencia* 24: 38–47.

Grünhut, M. (1944) *The Development of the German Penal System 1920–1932*. Toronto: The Canadian Bar Association.

Harding, C., Hines, B., Ireland, R. and P. Rawlings (eds.) (1985) *Imprisonment in England and Wales: A Concise History*. London: Croom Helm.

Hart, H.L.A. (1982) *Essays on Bentham*. New York: Oxford University Press.

Hegel, G.W.F. (1820) *Grundlinien der Philosophie des Rechts oder Naturrecht und Staatswissenschaft im Grundrisse*. Berlin: Nicolai.

Heilborn, P. (1908) *Die kurze Freiheitstrafe*. Leipzig: Engelmann.

Home Office (1928) *Criminal Statistics, England and Wales*. London: HMSO.

Howard, J. (1777) *The State of Prisons in England and Wales with Preliminary Observations, and an Account of Some Foreign Prisons*. London: Warrington.

Howard, J. (1792) *The Works of John Howard, Esq.: Containing the History of Prisons. Volume 2: An Account of the Principal lazarettos in Europe*. 2nd ed. London: Johnson, Dilly, and Cadell.

Jovellanos, G. Marqués de (1779 [1945]) *Informe de la Real Sala al Consejo de Castilla, sobre indultos generales*. Madrid: Biblioteca de Autores Españoles.

Kant, I. (1797) *Die Metaphysik der Sitten*. Königsberg: Nicolovius.

Kilcommins, S. (2002) *The Introduction of Community Service Orders: An Historical Interpretation*. Chichester: Barry Rose Law.

Kleinschrod, G.A.K. (1794) *Systematische Entwicklung der Grundbegriffe und Grundwahrheiten des peinlichen Rechts nach der Natur der Sache und der positiven Gesetzgebung. Volume II*. Erlangen: Palm.

Kriegsmann, N. H. (1912) *Einführung in die Gefängniskunde*. Heidelberg: Winter.

Krohne, K. (1889) *Lehrbuch der Gefängniskunde unter Berücksichtigung der Kriminalstatistik und Kriminalpolitik*. Stuttgart: Verlag von Ferdinand Enke.

Lardizábal y Uribe, M. de (1782) *Discurso sobre las penas, contraído a las leyes criminales de España, para facilitar su reforma*. Madrid: Joachin Ibarra.

Locker, J. P. (2008) 'The Paradox of the "Respectable Offender": Responding to the Problem of White-Collar Crime in Victorian and Edwardian England'. In Johnston, H. (ed.) *Punishment and Control in Historical Perspective*. New York: Palgrave MacMillan, 115–134.

Lucchini, L. (1882) 'Sull'antico progetto del nuovo Codice penale italiano: Considerazioni generali'. *Rivista Penale* 15: 457–474.

Luik, S. (2003) *Die Rezeption Jeremy Benthams in der deutschen Rechtswissenschaft*. Köln: Böhlau Verlag.

Maffei, N. (1875) 'Intorno al progetto 24 febbraio 1874 di un nuovo codice penale italiano'. *Rivista Penale* 1: 399–416.

Marcos Gutiérrez, J. (1826) *Práctica criminal de España: Tomos I a III*. 4th ed. Madrid: Imprenta de Don Fermín Villalpando.

McConville, S. (1981) *A History of English Prison Administration, 1750–1877. Volume I*. London: Routledge and Kegan Paul.

Melossi, D. and M. Pavarini (1981) *The Prison and the Factory: Origins of the Penitentiary System*. London: Macmillan.

Merkel, A. (1889) *Lehrbuch des Deutschen Strafrechts*. Stuttgart: Verlag von Ferdinand Ente.

Mittelstädt, O. (1879) *Gegen die Freiheitsstrafe: Ein Beitrag zur Kritik des heutigen Strafensystems*. Leipzig: Hirzel.

Montesquieu, Charles de Secondat, Baron de (1748) *De l'esprit des lois*. Geneva: chez Barrilot & fils.

Morris, T. (1978) 'The Parlous State of Prisons'. In Freeman, J. (ed.) *Prisons Past and Future*. London: Heinemann, 81–92.

Neppi Modona, G. (1985) 'Il sistema penitenziario italiano nel XIX secolo: Ideologia dell'istituzione e condizioni di vita dei detenuti'. In Levra, U. (ed.) *La scienza e la colpa: Crimini criminali criminologi: un volto dell'Ottocento*. Milan: Electa, 57–69.

Neumaier, R. (1947) *Die geschichtliche Entwicklung der Geldstrafe vom 15*. Jahrhundert bis zum StGB. Tübingen: Univ. Diss.

Nilsson, R. (2003) 'The Swedish Prison System in Historical Perspective: A Story of Successful Failure?' *Journal of Scandinavian Studies in Criminology and Crime Prevention* 4(1): 1–20.

Notaristefani, R. de (1924) 'Penitenziari (sistemi)'. In Lucchini, L. (ed.) *Il Digesto Italiano: Enciclopedia metodica e alfabetica di legislazione, dottrina e giurisprudenza. Volume XVIII, parte seconda*. Turin: Unione Tipografico-Editrice Torinese, 1–94.

Núñez Sessé, T. (1820) *Espíritu de Bentham: Sistema de la Ciencia Social*. Salamanca: Imprenta Nueva de D. Bernardo Martín.

Núñez Sessé, T. (1821) *Principios de la Ciencia Social o de las Ciencias Morales y Políticas*. Salamanca: Imprenta Nueva de D. Bernardo Martín.

O'Brien, P. (1982) *The Promise of Punishment: Prisons in Nineteenth-Century France*. Princeton, NJ: Princeton University Press.

O'Brien, P. (1995) 'The Prison on the Continent: Europe, 1865–1965'. In Morris, N. and D. J. Rothman (eds.) *The Oxford History of the Prison: The Practice of Punishment in Western Society*. New York: Oxford University Press, 199–225.

O'Malley, P. (2009a) *The Currency of Justice. Fines and Damages in Consumer Societies*. New York: Routledge-Cavendish.

O'Malley, P. (2009b) 'Theorizing Fines'. *Punishment and Society* 11(1): 65–83.

Ørsted, A. S. (1818) *Ueber die Grundregeln der Strafgesetzgebung. Band 1*. Copenhagen: Gyldendal.

Pacheco, J. F. (1856) *El Código penal: Concordado y comentado. Tomo I*. 2nd ed. Madrid: Imprenta de la Viuda de Perinat y Compañía.

Padovani, T. (1981) *L'utopia punitiva*. Milan: Giuffrè.

Paley, W. (1787) *The Principles of Moral and Political Philosophy*. London: Collins.

Pears, E. (1872) *Prisons and Reformatories at Home and Abroad, being the Transactions of the International Penitentiary Congress held in London, July 3–13, 1872, Including Official Documents, Discussions, and Papers Presented to the Congress*. London: Longmans, Green.

Perrot, M. (1978) 'Delinquency and the Penitentiary System in Nineteenth-Century France'. In Forster, R. and O. Ranum (eds.) *Deviants and the Abandoned in French Society*. Baltimore: Hopkins, 213–245.

Petitti di Roreto, C. I. (1840) *Della condizione attuale delle carceri e dei mezzi di migliorarla. Trattato*. Turin: G. Pomba e Comp.

Playfair, G. (1971) *The Punitive Obsession: An Unvarnished History of the English Prison System*. London: Tavistock.

Posada de Herrera, J. (1843) *Lecciones de Administración. Tomo II*. Madrid: Establecimiento Tipográfico.

Puccioni, G. (1855) *Il Codice penale toscano illustrato sulla scorta delle fonti, del diritto e della giurisprudenza. Tomo I*. Pistoia: Tipografia Cino.

Puyol Montero, J. M. (1997) 'La abolición de la pena de horca en España'. *Cuadernos de Historia del Derecho* 4: 91–140.

Radzinowicz, L. (1966) *Ideology and Crime: A Study of Crime in Its Social and Historical Context*. London: Heinemann.

Ramos Vázquez, I. (2012) 'La Administración Civil Penitenciaria: militarismo y administrativismo en los orígenes del Estado de Derecho'. *Anuario de Historia del Derecho Español* 82: 471–520.

Ramos Vázquez, I. (2013) *La reforma penitenciaria en la historia contemporánea española*. Madrid: Dykinson.

Rauh, M. F. (1912) *Die Vermögensstrafen des Reichsstrafrechts und ihre Reform*. Breslau: Schlatter.

Roldán Barbero, H. (1988) *Historia de la Prisión en España*. Barcelona: PPU.

Rosenfeld, E. (1890) 'Welche Strafmittel können an die Stelle der kurzzeitigen Freiheitstrafe gesetzt werden?' In Von Liszt, F. (ed.) *Abhandlungen des kriminalistisches Seminars zu Halle. Zweiter Band, 2. Heft*. Berlin: Guttentag, 110–355.

Rossi, P.L.O. (1853) *Trattato di diritto penale*. Turin: Società Editrice.

Rousseau, J. J. (1762 [1913]) *The Social Contract: Or Principles of Political Right*. New York: E. P. Dutton.

Rule, J. (1992) *Albion's People: English Society, 1714–1815*. London: Longman.

Rusche, G. and O. Kirchheimer (1939 [2003]) *Punishment and Social Structure*. New Brunswick: Transaction.

Saldaña, Q. (1931) *Nueva penología (penas y medidas de seguridad)*. Madrid: Librería y Casa Editorial Hernando.

Salillas y Panzano, R. (1904) 'Informe del negociado de sanidad penitenciaria'. In Dirección General de Prisiones (ed.) *Expediente general para preparar la reforma penitenciaria*. Madrid: Hijos de J. A. García, 102–232.

Samuels, A. (1970) 'The Fine: The Principles'. *The Criminal Law Review*, May: 201–210, 268–272.

Sánchez Oses, J. (1967) 'Jeremías Bentham y el Derecho Penal'. *Anuario de Derecho Penal y Ciencias Penales* 20: 539–562.

Sbriccoli, M. (1990 [2009]) 'La penalistica civile: Teorie e ideologie del diritto penale nell'Italia unita'. In Sbriccoli, M. (ed.) *Storia del diritto penale e della giustizia: Scritti editi e inediti (1972–2007). Tomo I*. Milan: Giuffrè, 493–590.

Scharff Smith, P. (2012) 'A Critical Look at Scandinavian Exceptionalism: Welfare State Theories, Penal Populism and Prison Conditions in Denmark and Scandinavia'. In Ugelvik, T. and J. Dullum (eds.) *Penal Exceptionalism? Nordic Prison Policy and Practice*. Abingdon: Routledge, 38–57.

Schmölder, R. (1902) *Die Geldstrafe: Vortrag, gehalten auf der 74. Jahresversammlung der Rheinisch-westfälischen Gefängnissgesellschaft in Düsseldorf am 15. Oktober 1902*. Hamm: Griebsch.

Schwartz, P. (1978) 'Bentham's Influence in Spain, Portugal and Latin America'. *The Bentham Newsletter* 1: 34.

Select Committee of the House of Lords (1863) *Report on the Present State of Discipline in Gaols and Houses of Correction*. London: HMSO, iii–xvii.

Sellin, J. T. (1976) *Slavery and the Penal System*. New York: Elsevier.

Sharpe, J. (1990) *Judicial Punishment in England*. London: Faber and Faber.

Silvela, L. (1903) *El derecho penal estudiado en principios y en la legislación vigente en España. Segunda parte*. Madrid: Establecimiento Tipográfico de Ricardo Fé.

Smaus, G. (1996) 'The History of Ideas and Its Significance for the Prison System'. In Finzsch, N. and R. Jütte (eds.) *Institutions of Confinement: Hospitals, Asylums, and Prisons in Western*

Europe and North America, 1500–1950. Washington, DC: Cambridge University Press, 175–190.

Spierenburg, P. (1991) *The Prison Experience: Disciplinary Institutions and Their Inmates in Early Modern Europe*. New Brunswick: Rutgers University Press.

Spierenburg, P. (1996) 'Four Centuries of Prison History: Punishment, Suffering, the Body, and Power'. In Finzsch, N. and R. Jütte (eds.) *Institutions of Confinement: Hospitals, Asylums, and Prisons in Western Europe and North America, 1500–1950*. Cambridge: Cambridge University Press, 17–35.

Streng, A. (1886) *Studien über Entwicklung, Ergebnisse und Gestaltung des Vollzugs der Freiheitsstrafe in Deutschland*. Stuttgart: Enke.

Tarello, G. (1976) *Storia della cultura giuridica moderna: Assolutismo e codificazione del diritto*. Bologna: Il Mulino.

Tomás y Valiente, F. (1969) *El Derecho penal de la monarquía absoluta (siglos XVI, XVII y XVIII)*. Madrid: Tecnos.

Vila Miquel, E. (1917) *De la necesidad y medios de sustituir las penas cortas de privación de libertad*. Madrid: Imprenta de Juan Pueyo.

Villermé, L.-R. (1820) *Des Prisons telles qu'elles sont, et telles qu'elles devraient être, ouvrage dans lequel on les considère par rapport à l'hygiène, à la morale et à l'économie politique*. Paris: Chey Méquignon-Marvis.

Vingtrinier, A.-B. (1840) *Des prisons et des prisonniers*. Versailles: Klefer.

Von Arnim, A. H. (1803) *Bruchstücke über Verbrechen und Strafen, oder Gedanken über die in den preussischen Staaten bemerkte Vermehrung der Verbrecher gegen die Sicherheit des Eigenthums: nebst Vorschlägen der Gefangenanstalten, wie derselben durch zweckmässige Einrichtung der Gefangenanstalten zu steuern seyn dürfte; zum Gebrauch der höheren Behörden*. Frankfurt: Frommann & Wessenlhöft.

Von Bar, C. L. (1916) *A History of Continental Criminal Law*. Boston: Little, Brown.

Von Buri, M. (1894) *Beiträge zur Theorie des Strafrechts und zum Strafgesetzbuch. Gesammelte Abhandlungen*. Leipzig: Veit.

Von Feuerbach, A. (1804) *Kritik des Kleinschrodischen Entwurfs zu einem peinlichen Gesetzbuche für die Chur-Pfalz-Bayrischen Staaten*. Giesen: Tasché § Müller.

Von Hippel, R. (1898) 'Beiträge zur Geschichte der Freiheitsstrafe'. *Zeitschrift für die gesamte Strafrechtswissenschaft* 18: 419–494.

Von Hippel, R. (1925) *Deutsches Strafrecht. Band 1*. Allgemeiner Grundlagen. Berlin: Springer.

Von Hippel, R. (1928) 'Die geschichtliche Entwicklung der Freiheitsstrafe'. In Bumke, E. (ed.) *Deutsches Gefängniswesen. Ein Handbuch*. Berlin: Franz Vahlen, 1–15.

Von Ihering, R. (1877 [1904]) *Der Zweck im Recht*. Leipzig: Breitkopf & Haertel.

Von Liszt, F. (1889) 'Welche Maßregeln können dem Gesetzgeber zur Einschränkung der kurzzeitigen Freiheitsstrafe empfohlen werden?'. In International Union of Penal Law/ Deutsche Landesgruppe (ed.) *Mitteilungen der Internationalen Kriminalistischen Vereinigung: Bulletin de l'Union internationale de droit pénal*. Berlin: Guttentag, 44–51.

Von Soden, J. (1792) *Geist der peinlichen Gesetzgebung Teutschlands*. Band I. Frankfurt: s.n.

Wächter, C. E. (1786) *Über Zuchthäuser und Zuchthausstrafen: wie jene zweckmäßig einzurichten, und diese solcher Einrichtung gemäß zu bestimmen und anzuwenden seyen*. Stuttgart: Buchdr. d. Hohen Carls-Schule.

Wahlberg, W. E. (1877) 'Nationalökonomische Gesichtspunkte im Strafrecht mit besonderer Rücksicht auf die Geldstrafe'. In Wahlberg, W. E. (ed.) *Gesammelte kleinere Schriften und Bruchstücke über Strafrecht, Strafprozess, Gefängnisskunde, Literatur und Dogmengeschichte der Rechtslehre in Oesterreich*. Vienna: Alfred Hölder, 231–264.

Webb, S. and B. Webb (1922) *English Prisons under Local Government*. London: Longman.

Wedderburn, A., Earl of Rosslyn (1793) *Observations on the State of the English Prisons, and the Means of Improving Them*. London: Printed for John Stockdale.
Wilson, S. (2014) *The Origins of Modern Financial Crime*. London: Routledge.
Wood, E. M. (2012) *Liberty and Property: A Social History of Western Political Thought from Renaissance to Enlightenment*. London: Verso.
Zürcher, E. (1891) 'Thesen zu den Fragen betreffend die Geldstrafe'. *Zeitschrift für Schweizer Strafrecht* 4: 268–270.

3 The impersonality of money

Why and how fines paid by an innocent third party were prohibited

The impersonality of money and fines

Economic exchange, Simmel argued, can best be understood as a form of social interaction. When monetary transactions replaced earlier forms of barter, significant changes occurred in the forms of interactions between social actors. Money was subject to precise division and manipulation and permitted exact measurement of equivalents. It became impersonal in a manner in which objects of barter could never be and thus helped promote rational calculation in human affairs and further the rationalization that is characteristic of modern society. Beyond its economic functions, money began to symbolize and embody the modern spirit of rationality, of calculability, of impersonality. How did the characteristic impersonality of money influence monetary sanctions?

For a large part of the early and mid-nineteenth century literature it seemed quite obvious that the fine was *not* a personal punishment (Stooß 1878: 7). The impersonality of the fine stems from the impersonal nature of money, the object with which the fine is paid, which then makes the payment of the fine akin to the payment of any other debt of a civil type. Already Bentham (1830: Book 3, Chapter 4, Section 2) had stressed that in the execution of the fine, 'no spectacle is exhibited: the transfer of a sum of money on this account has nothing to distinguish it from the case of an ordinary payment'. Consequently, few people at the time objected to an innocent third party paying the fine, either voluntarily or through the imposition of a joint or vicarious obligation. There was also minimal objection to the fine being transferred to an innocent third party, as occurs when an offender dies before making payment.

On the other hand, the impersonality of money also makes it impossible to know whose money is paying the fine. For a large part of the nineteenth century, and in some cases well into the twentieth century, faced with the knowledge that it is impossible to control the source of the money used to pay the fine, several countries permitted payment by third parties. This was justified on the basis that either the fine is a punishment imposed against the offender's wealth and not his or her person – thereby the fine is imposed as an 'impersonal' sanction – or the fine becomes a civil or public debt as soon as the offender is sentenced or as soon as he or she dies, thereby justifying that in the first case it may be paid by a third party and in the second case it may be transferred to the offender's heirs. The underlying reason upholding these theories is again the impersonal nature of money. As Simmel (1907 [1990]: 297) explained, '[money] is conducive to the removal of the personal element from human relationships through its indifferent and objective nature'. In contrast, nowadays, based on the personality principle of penalties, it is generally considered unfair to punish an innocent person in place of some other guilty individual, even if the innocent person unequivocally accepts punishment. Even if it may be useful to accept payment by a third party so as to avoid imprisonment for fine default and even collect money for the state, even if this shift of punishment may have some deterrent effect because the affected relatives or friends may pressure the offender to avoid further crime, 'it offends our sense of fairness to punish the innocent as a means of deterring the guilty' (Westen 1969: 792).

I will start by analysing the question of the *legal* admissibility of payment made by a third party, since a substantial change has taken place regarding this issue. I will analyse how the problem of the impersonality and transferability of money, and therefore fines, has been addressed – that is, what effects this aspect has had on legal regulations and the use of the fine as a punishment. After that, the legal possibility of transferring the obligation of payment of the penal fine to the deceased offender's heirs will be explained, as well as the legal reasoning behind such legislative provisions. The reasons for the abolition of the transferability of penalties will also be addressed, taking into account that at the beginning they did not refer to the fine, but only to another pecuniary punishment – namely, confiscation. Both the question of payment by a third party and by the offender's heirs are clear examples of how some characteristics of money 'tainted' the penal fine and cast doubts on its nature, because of their absolute incompatibility with the principle of personality of punishments.

Why and how the principle of personality of penalties extended to the fine

Allowing a third party to pay the fine

All punishments may indirectly affect third parties, which has never prevented punishments from being considered personal in the sense that they should befall the perpetrator of the offence, and lead to his or her punishment, whether it be imprisonment, deprivation of rights, or sentencing to community work. It is not considered acceptable for an innocent third party to bear punishment while the offender is spared punishment. This principle of guilt, expressed in the Latin aphorism *poena non alios quam suos teneat auctores* (misconduct should bind only its own authors), has been considered a cornerstone of the theories of crime and punishment since the Enlightenment (Beccaria 1764 [1872]: Chapters 17 and 35; Von Feuerbach 1805: § 138).

Compared to other punishments, the fine is characterized by the fact that its *direct* effects – the distress of the punishment – that is, the payment of a sum of money to the state – can be borne entirely by an innocent third party, which is what happens when a third party pays the fine with liberating effects for the offender (Von Lilienthal 1892: 87; Westen 1969: 792; Beristain Ipiña 1976: 19; Pradel 1977: 566; Driendl 1978: 31; Molinari 1983: 25–27; Musco 1984: 39; Hillenkamp 1987: 459). As we will see, the principle of personality of penalties understood in its material sense – in other words, from the perspective that the distress of the punishment should befall the perpetrator – is difficult to apply to the fine. Although this is fulfilled in theory – by imposing the punishment on the perpetrator, who may well be the only person able to pay it with liberating effects – it seems impossible to prevent these effects when payment is made by a third party directly to the offender. Anyone can give the offender the money to pay the fine, and subsequently free him or her of suffering punishment – that is, the reduction of his or her wealth. When money changes hands it forms part of the wealth of the receiver, which makes it impossible to prevent a third party from materially bearing the payment. While there is a minority view that either regards it as an advantage to the state (Von Lilienthal 1897: 489) or simply completely ignores the issue (Binding 1905: 651), most scholars view it as a qualitative defect of the fine as a punishment (Friedmann 1892: 107–108; Hassan 1959: 70ff.; Westen 1969: 791–792; Grebing 1982: 19–20; Musco 1984: 39; Hillenkamp 1987: 458; Warner 2012: 233).

When it comes to imprisonment, this division between the formal imposition of the punishment and the person who materially suffers the deprivation of liberty is impossible. It has never been permitted, nor is it possible, for another person to materially serve a prison sentence in place of the offender. This characteristic introduces a fundamental difference between the fine and imprisonment (Zipf 1974: 529; Von Spiegel 1979: 25–28; Young 1999), which affects the element of personality attributed to both penalties. In essence, money is not personal, but life, liberty, and bodily indemnity certainly are (very clearly Wahlberg 1890: 54; Groß 1894: 328; Baumann 1969: 115; Young 1999: 185), as I have analysed in Chapter 1.

From the start of the nineteenth century in Germany a theory negating the personality of the fine was upheld: the theory of non-personality, or *Unpersönlichkeitstheorie*, according to which the fine consists of a 'wrong' against the offender's wealth, not his actual person, thereby being established as an 'impersonal' punishment (Waldthausen 1881: 395). While this theory completely separated the punishment from the offender's person, the obligation theories, or *Obligationstheorien*, understood that the fine befell the offender personally, but as soon as it was sentenced it became a civil obligation, which then permitted payment to be made by a third party or, in the event of the offender's death, the transfer of the fine to his or her heirs (Heffter 1833: 211–212; Berner 1857 and 1869: 15–16; Bozi 1896: 258; Rauh 1912: 34).

For much of the nineteenth century, these theories resulted in legislative acceptance for allowing payment of the fine by a third party not responsible for the offence. Some of these regulations are still in force today, despite the generalized acceptance of the principle of personality of penalties. Leaving aside the admission of the transferability of fines to heirs, which we will look at in more detail in the following section, there were three mechanisms used to accept payment by a third party: the imposition of a civil liability for a third party to pay the penal fine in the case of the offender's insolvency, either as a vicarious liability or a joint one; the use of the legal concept of the guarantor for the payment of a penal fine; and the direct admission of the payment of the fine by a third party. As we will see, it is only in this last case that the fine is officially imposed on the offender and officially paid by another person.

Vicarious and joint liability for the payment of fines

In France, Article 55 of the 1810 Penal Code established that '[a]ll the individuals condemned for the same crime, or the same delict, shall be jointly and severally bound with each other for the payment of the fines, restitutions, damages and costs'. It followed the precedent set by Article 42 of the Law of July 19–22, 1791, regarding the organization of a municipal police (*Loi du 19–22 juillet 1791, relative à l'organisation d'une police municipal*), which established that fines imposed by correctional and municipal police were to be jointly and severally distributed between accomplices of the crime. Until the 1975 Act, which reformed the system of fines and suspended sentences and instituted a number of alternatives to imprisonment, this joint and several liability for fines was recognized in statute. In addition, the literature tended to support the impossibility of avoiding the shift of the financial burden to a third party (as indicated by Teufel and Pradel 1983: 407, 431–432), with justification based on the higher severity of a crime organized and committed by more than one offender (Perret 1941: 77ff.; see, however, with strong criticism, Ortolan 1874: 246, affirming the personal nature of the monetary penalty; Schütz 1967: 352–353; Merle and Vitu 1967). Something similar can be seen in Article 101.1 of the 1852 Portuguese Penal Code, with literature recognizing the French influence (Jordão 1853: 226).

One century later in Italy, Articles 196 and 197 of the 1930 Rocco Penal Code included the legal concept of the civil liability of the payment of the *ammenda* – which is the name given traditionally in Italy to the pecuniary penalty when it is imposed for an infringement, while it is called a fine, *multa*, when imposed for a crime. Article 196 considered the case of an infringement committed by a person subject to the authority, orders, or supervision of another person to be a breach of a rule that the authoritative person must enforce, without being criminally liable for offence of the subordinate. Article 197 included the case of an infringement committed by a person acting as a representative or administrator of a corporate body – that is, not the state, a province, or a town council – or who works for a corporate body, stating that this implied the breach of an obligation inherent to the status assumed by the offender. In both cases, in the event of the offender being found insolvent, the person providing the authority, orders, or supervision, or the corporate body was obliged to pay a sum equivalent to the amount of the *ammenda*. If they paid, the offender was exempted from the obligation to pay the fine. If they did not pay due to insolvency, the fine would be converted into a prison sentence for the offender, not for the vicariously obliged party. The Italian legislature has upheld the civil nature of this vicarious and possible financial obligation. The most widespread doctrine accepted this characterization (Florian 1934: 831, 1098–1100; Manzini 1910: 99; Spasari 1966: 78), with many dissenting voices (Rossi 1954: 180–181; Bricola 1964: 206–207; Dolcini 1972: 422ff.). The thesis of the civil nature was confirmed by the Italian Constitutional Court (decree of the Constitutional Court of May 14, 1966, no. 40, published in *Giurisprudenza Costituzionale* 1966: 229–231). The truth is that, despite it being considered a civil obligation, some authors introduced certain striking peculiarities in their approach. For example, Florian (1934: 1102) stated that, as there is an unquestionably penal motive and substratum, it is not lawful to forego the public and penal nature; hence it is a personal obligation that cannot be passed on to heirs of the vicariously obliged party.

In Germany there were also examples of vicarious and joint liability for the payment of fines. Cases of vicarious liability, in which a person who was a relative or in a position of authority over the offender was vicariously liable for payment of the fine, were included in the Prussian Fisheries Act (*Fischereigesetz*) of May 30, 1874, § 52, the Prussian Forest Theft Act (*Forstdiebstahlgesetz*) of April 15, 1878, § 11, the Tobacco Duty Act (*Tabaksteuergesetz*) of September 12, 1919, § 72, or in the Spirits Monopoly Law (*Reichgesetz über das Branntweinmonopol*) of April 8, 1922, in the 1939 drafting, § 110. As a matter of fact, some of these regulations were still in force until the 1960s, despite sharp criticism aimed at both the offender not paying the fine and the offender being exempted since the obligation to pay is transferred to an innocent party (Kronecker 1879: 16; Binding 1885: 490). In turn, the Tax Law for Itinerant Companies (*Gesetz betreffend die Besteuerung des Gewerbebetriebes im Umherziehen*) of July 3, 1876, established that the fine should be paid jointly by the perpetrator and the person on whose behalf and in whose interest the offence was committed. Similar provisions can be found primarily in tax law: the Spirit Duty Act (*Gesetz betreffend die Besteuerung des Branntweins*) of July 8, 1868, § 67 III, the Tobacco Duty Act (*Gesetz betreffend die Besteuerung des Tabaks*) of July 16, 1879, § 42 II, the Beer Brewing Duty Act (*Brausteuergesetz*) of June 3, 1906, § 48 II, and so forth. Furthermore, in the absence of regulations, case law has also led to very similar results despite doctrinal opposition (see Von Spiegel 1979: 76ff. and 107ff.; Hillenkamp 1987: 463ff.). For example, it was admitted for a businessman to transfer the effects of the fine imposed on the worker who did not prevent the offence from being committed, as was his duty (RAG 27, 43ff.); or a client could civilly demand a refund of the sum paid towards a penal fine from the financial adviser who incorrectly advised against using voluntary disclosure to exempt the client from the penalty (*Reichsgericht in Zivilsachen* 169, 267); or a board member of a public limited company could demand the company to refund any fine he may have had to pay for a financial offence committed on behalf of the corporation (*Entscheidungssammlung des Bundesgerichtshof in Zivilsachen* 41, 223). Similar regulations were seen in France (Article 184 of Book 2 of the *Code du travail et de la prévoyance sociale* of December 28, 1910; Article L. 21 of the *Code de la route* of December 15, 1958, etc.), where the concept of civil liability for fines imposed on a third party was used (Teufel and Pradel 1983: 407).

It seems clear that in the debate between whether the fine serves as a civil duty to the state or as an effective reduction of the offender's wealth, the aforementioned cases are based on the idea that in the enforcement phase the fine is nothing more than the offender's debt to the state as the person given the fine is allowed to service the debt without suffering a real reduction of his wealth. This is clearly an approach which makes it easier to establish the fine as simply an obligation of the offender and, jointly or vicariously, other third parties under the relevant criteria.

Guarantees for the payment of fines

Second, again in Italy, Article 237 of the royal decree no. 2701 of December 23, 1865, which regulates the law *di tariffa penale*, established the legal concept of *fidejussore* or guarantor for the person fined who requested an extended payment period or was allowed to pay the fine in instalments. The guarantor was obliged to pay the fine and the costs if the extension was not granted or if the principal debtor breached the agreed terms, without the need to confirm his insolvency. Some European penal procedure codes also included the existence of a bondsman for the payment of the fine while the process was pending. Hence, the 1882 Spanish Criminal Procedure Act, still in force today, established in Article 589 that '[w]hen the summary proceedings reveal evidence of criminality against a person, the Judge will order a bond to be paid to cover the pecuniary liabilities that may ultimately be deemed appropriate'. Note that no mention is made of civil liabilities, just 'pecuniary' liabilities, which included fines, as accepted in literature (Aguilera de Paz 1913: 365). In accordance with this provision, the fine could end up being paid by a third party not responsible for the offence, although this was considered incompatible with the principle of personality of penalties (Manzanares Samaniego 1983: 127). However, strictly speaking, we find ourselves once again faced with a situation in which this principle has not been formally breached, given that the punishment as such is imposed on the offender.

Payment of fines by a third party

If the two mechanisms already mentioned can be considered as particular forms of civil obligation, which do not involve an inculpatory reproach regarding the third party liable to make the payment, the third mechanism certainly cannot. The same Italian law of *tariffa penale* mentioned earlier established that the court clerks, to whom the fine had to be paid, could not refuse to accept 'the sum of the amount due from an insolvent debtor under the terms of the fine or *ammenda* [. . .] even if the payment was offered by a third party'. This was an explicit refusal to control the payer's identity (Manzini 1934: 120; Saltelli 1939: 705). Precisely in one of the few cases in which the source of the money does not seem problematic, legislation prohibited measures being adopted to prevent payment by a third party (Dolcini 1972: 427). The law abandoned all concern for the principle of personality of the pecuniary penalty, which literature recognized as not having been rigorously applied (Manzini 1910: 99; Frosali 1958: 276–277).

This Italian regulation is striking, in particular for its apparent contradiction with Article 27 I of the 1947 Italian Constitution, which states that penal liability is personal. In literature it was generally understood that the personality of penalties is linked to their essentially depriving or restricting nature concerning the personal freedom of the perpetrator of the crime (Bricola 1964 [1973]: 283). The pecuniary punishment is potentially a deprivation of freedom as it can be replaced with a prison sentence if the obligation to pay is breached, and they are all strictly personal in the sense that they can be imposed only on the offender 'with it opposing the rationale of penal liability to apportion blame to the heirs of the offender as well as those who were not involved in the commission of the illicit offence' (Spasari 1966: 63). A fourth mechanism is found in criminal justice systems which allow parents or guardians of a minor offender to pay the fine. The reasoning that justifies this regulation is concerned not so much with the financial benefit of recovering the fine but rather with encouraging parents and guardians to adopt a more vigilant attitude to prevent their minors from committing repeat offences. This was obvious in the 1933 English Children and Young Persons Act, which was the first act to empower the court to order parents or guardian to pay fines, damages, or costs imposed on a child or young person, including recovering the fine from the parent or guardian by distress or imprisonment, unless the court is satisfied that the parent or guardian cannot be found or that he has not aided the commission of the offence by neglecting to exercise due care of the child or young person (Section 55[1]). This provision was intended to encourage the courts to assert the duty of parents and guardians to act responsibly towards their children, taking all steps within their power to prevent them committing criminal offences and in case of failure to take some responsibility for their misdoings (Bathurst 1996: 201–202).[1] Despite the statutory duty to order parents or guardians to pay, this power was not widely used. The literature criticized the questionable nature of the governmental assumption that the order requiring parental payment alerts them to real consequences of their children's behaviour and the implications for their own actions (Ball et al. 1995: 168). And in all cases, rather than payment of the fine by a third party, it seems clear that the aim is to punish parents' negligence when it comes to raising their children.

Towards a strict understanding of the principle of personality of penalties

At the end of the nineteenth century and early twentieth century voices were still being heard in academic and judicial circles in favour of allowing third-party payment. Hence, in its report of 1906 the Prosecutor's Office of the Supreme Court of Spain declared itself in favour of admitting it on the following basis:

> the fine as a punishment is of a mixed nature: criminal insofar as it is a penalty and represents a fair punishment imposed on the perpetrator of an offence,

> and civil, insofar as it involves an obligation to serve or to give that affects the assets of the convicted offender.
>
> (Ruiz Valarino 1906: 90)

The idea behind this admission was that if payment by a third party were not admitted 'the State will no longer receive a sum with no benefit or use for anybody, except perhaps the fact that the offender pays in prison, not just to pay for his crime but also to pay for his poverty, unlike what happens with rich people'. Even in the middle of the twentieth century there were still people who claimed that the fine 'because it involves non-personal assets, it is not essentially personal in its enforcement, it can be paid by another and become a civil debt' (Miguel Garcilópez 1940: 320); therefore 'it can be vicariously extended to other people: to parents, for offences committed by their children; to corporate entities, for crimes committed by their employees, etcetera' (Antón Oneca 1949: 540; also Montes 1929: 389). This observation partially coincided with the German courts, which in 1967 still allowed the offender's mother to pay the fine with liberating effects, on the basis, once again, that the fine as a punishment 'is not strictly personal in nature [*keine höchspersönliche Leistung*]' (*Oberlandesgericht* Düsseldorf, published in Monatschrift für Deutsches Recht 1969, 70). These ideas were supported by the civil concept of the fine. However, the majority held the view that it was incompatible for a third party to pay a penal fine (Lehmann 1871: 788; Wahlberg 1877: 248–250; Von Buri 1878: 241ff.; Merkel 1889: 224; Von der Decken 1892: 109; Stooβ 1898; Kohler 1902: 180; Berolzheimer 1907: 256; Höh 1909: 5ff.; Rauh 1912: 28; and the conclusions of the 7th International Penal and Penitentiary Congress held in Budapest in 1905, in Barrows 1907), given the general acceptance of the principle of personality of penalties. As Carrara (1871: 465–466) stated, 'The idea of *penalty* that goes with the fine gives it the concept of *personality* [. . .] At this point [. . .] as a scientific principle, no distinction can be allowed between corporal and pecuniary punishments' (italics in the original). Payment by a third party

> opposes the nature and purposes of all punishments: it opposes the nature because the punishment is intensely personal and does not admit substitutions; and it opposes the purposes because these include the correction of the offender by means of the punishment personally imposed on him.
>
> (Ruiz Valarino 1906: 89)

Two reasons justify the gradual shift in legislation. First, imprisonment for fine defaulters created a considerable obstacle to the legal admission of payment of the fine by a third party (Gutmann 1909: 94–95; Spasari 1966: 76), because if a third party took on the obligation to pay, could he end up in prison if he did not pay the fine? The pecuniary punishment, which in essence has an impact on a non-personal asset like money, takes on a quality similar to a custodial sentence from the moment it can become a prison sentence in the case of insolvency. Second, by having to take the offender's financial situation into account during sentencing in order to adjust the amount of the fine to his or her real capacity to pay, it is clear that payment by a third party is conceptually incompatible with the new system (Kruse 1934: 11–12).

However, the undifferentiated quality of money, which is the object of the fine, makes it impossible to establish whose money is paying a fine imposed on the condemned offender. And although it has been said that 'courts do not often concern themselves with who pays a fine, or who pays damages – as long as they are paid' (O'Malley 2009: 20), the truth is that criminal and constitutional courts and penal literature have indeed concerned themselves with this topic. They did it sometimes from an optimistic perspective, confident that payment by a third party can be prevented (Figueiredo Dias 1989: 298). For example, López-Rey and Álvarez-Valdés (1933: 91) stated,

> the difficulties for preventing this are considerable, but not insurmountable, if the summary proceedings include all the data pertaining not only to the offence, but also to the situation, environment, etc., in which the offender lives, and from which it can be concluded that it will not be him, but a third party or parties who pay, or that, even if he does pay, other people will feel the effects more.

At other times, they took on a much more negative perspective, pointing out that this fault of the penal fine is impossible to avoid, whatever the regulations in force may be (Manzini 1910: 99; Saltelli 1939: 705; Zipf 1965: 633; Samuels 1970: 202; Göppinger 1975: 319; Beristain Ipiña 1979: 708; Manzanares Samaniego 1983: 110–116; Ferrajoli 1990: 415; Bernardi 1993: 536).

The impossibility of preventing a third party from paying the fine has, in turn, led to multiple legal adjustments. Initially there were proposals that the fine should always be sentenced along with a 'little corporal punishment' (Von Sonnenfels 1820: 190). Later on it was suggested that the possibility of third-party payment should be taken into account when choosing the sanction to impose (Von Lilienthal 1892: 87; Von Spiegel 1979: 183; Albrecht 1980: 164). In this regard, community service was proposed as an alternative punishment (Hillenkamp 1987: 465), even without the need for consent from the offender (Baumann 1968: 49). When, due to the scant means of the offender, the fine was expected to be paid by a third party, like the offender's parents, it also led to doubts being raised about the aims of the penal sanctions. Zipf (1965: 632–633) actually commented on such a case in which a fine was imposed on a child with no means to pay it. Contrary to the view originally held by the German Imperial Supreme Court (*Reichsgerichts-Entscheidungen in Strafsachen* 65, 308), which stated that when it was clear that the fine would be paid by a third party, the court should refrain from using that mode of punishment, the Supreme Court of Bavaria held that such sentencing would cause injustice by discrimination. For the Bavarian court, 'the choice between a custodial sentence and a fine should not depend on the financial situation of the offender' (Zipf 1965: 633). It also remarked that the penal aim is often achieved *by* the mere fact of conviction rather than *by* the actual execution thereof. This approach is quite different from that of Bentham, which is based on the assumption that the effectiveness of punishment lies in a simple pleasure-pain principle. In the Bavarian ruling conviction and sentence are considered to be a symbolic process of stigmatization, placing less stress on who is effectively paying the fine (Packer 1968: 40). 'But it is submitted that when, after due consideration of all the circumstances, the court chooses to impose a real punishment, execution of sentence should not be frustrated' (Bein 1974: 340).

In other countries, the possibility of the fine being paid by another serves as grounds to reduce the amount of fine or eliminate it, such as when the offender is a minor or a young adult with no income and the burden of the fine would fall upon his or her parents. In over 200 years of Spanish legislation for juveniles the fine has never been used as a penalty, precisely because of this problem.

The possibility of categorizing third-party payment of fines as an offence has also been considered. In Spanish, French, Italian, German, and English criminal law there was no special offence dealing directly and comprehensively with the payment of a fine by a person other than the defendant.[2] The question, therefore, was whether such conduct was covered by any general offences, especially by any one of the offences whose aim is to ensure proper administration of justice. Proposals were made for the law to include a clause under which the court could accept only the money handed to it by the offender himself. Proposals also included the possibility of sanctioning any third party who tried to pay the imposed fine in place of the offender; the third party could be characterized either as the perpetrator of a new offence, as an instigator or accomplice to the crime committed by the offender, or as an accessory after the fact (Stooβ 1878: 9–11; 1898: 364ff.). And in fact, in Germany and Switzerland the payment of fines by a third party, either directly or indirectly via giving the money to the offender, was considered punishable as 'assistance after the fact' or *Begünstigung* until recently (for all, Lehmann 1871: 794; Friedmann 1898: 821ff.; Brenn 1945: 68ff.; and Zipf 1965: 633; against it Waldthausen 1881: 395). Other legal scholars (Grebing 1978: 45) believed labelling such third-party conduct as a crime of assistance in avoiding prosecution or punishment, *Strafvereitelung*, would be more explicit. The ruling of the German Supreme Federal Court of November 7, 1990 (*Entscheidungssammlung des Bundesgerichtshof in Strafsachen* 37, 226), could have put an end to this controversy. It denied the possibility of subsuming the payment of the fine by a third party in the crime of assistance in avoiding prosecution or punishment. The Supreme Court believed that this overrode the literal meaning of the precept. Such meaning was linked, seemingly, to the external frustration of the administrative process – following a view that was systematically expounded by Engels (1981: 581ff.), with abundant references, and also upheld in other countries of German influence (in Spain, see Manzanares Samaniego 1977: 250–252). However, the majority of scholars still maintains the material reasons that make it intolerable for a third party to pay the offender's fine. Therefore, the literal argument of the German Supreme Federal Court itself has been subject to intense criticism (Hillenkamp 1992: 75). In any case, German literature, while applauding the existence of these offences and confirming the need to regulate them (Stree 1964: 588; Brüggemann 1968: 161; Engels 1981: 581; Schönke and Schröder 2010: § 258 Rn. 28), acknowledges the difficulties in implementing them as well as the ease with which the prohibition of payment by an innocent third party can be circumvented – for example, by granting a personal loan with interest that can be waived at a later date. In the other studied countries there is no reported case of a person being brought to trial for such conduct,[3] although some authors believe that the payment of a fine by a third party can imply the offence of 'assistance after the fact' (in Switzerland Schwander 1969: 192) or complicity (in Italy Manzini 1910: 99–100).

The gradual acceptance of the principle of personality of penalties, including those of a pecuniary nature, also prevented the solidarity of the fine. As we have seen, some penal codes, such as the French one (Article 55), still established that all the individuals sentenced for one and the same offence would be jointly liable for paying the fines, as well as redressing the damages and losses and paying the costs. However, following the conclusions of the 7th International Penal and Penitentiary Congress held in Budapest in 1905 (Barrows 1907), the majority of European delegates – with the relevant exception of the French – stood against joint responsibility with reference to fines, based precisely on the principle of personality of penalties.

As far as I have been able to ascertain, the problem of the impersonality of the penal fine has never been comprehensively dealt with. And despite all the efforts undertaken so far, this issue has still not been satisfactorily resolved to date. In fact, it has been called the 'constitutive failure of the fine' (Zipf 1965: 633).

Payment of the fine by the offender's heirs

As already shown, faced with the theory of impersonality, which denied the penal nature of the fine, defenders of the obligation theory or *Obligationstheorie* emerged. There were different versions of this theory. The most radical version maintained that the conviction turned the fine into a monetary debt of a civil nature that encumbered the offender's wealth (Jordão 1853: 226–227; Berner 1857: 220–221). The more moderate version, in turn, was based on the penal nature of the fine. The existence of a link between the sanction and the sanctioned person was acknowledged, insofar as the fine was supposed to cause the perpetrator of the offence some damage. However, in both versions, if the offender died after being sentenced and before paying the fine, the fine became a civil obligation that was passed on to the heirs (Jordão 1853: 227; Von Stenglein 1861: 600; Merkel 1889: 224–225; Höh 1909: 8; Rauh 1912: 34). Thus an older doctrinal tradition was upheld which proposed that in the event of the offender's death, the pecuniary penalty did not follow the rules of other penalties – that is, it was not annulled (Kleinschrod 1794: 80–81; Von Quistorps 1796: 127; Álvarez Posadilla 1797: 38–48; Von Feuerbach 1805: § 139). Despite identifying the joint responsibility that extended criminal liability to the offender's relatives or to his associates in a way typical of 'people mired in barbarism or that were taking their first steps on the road to civilisation', Groizard (1872: 587) emphasized,

> if death occurs after a definitive ruling has been passed and the commission of the crime and the participation therein of the offender is declared a legal truth, the civil liability must fall on his fortune and assets, and they must be put to this purpose. The same occurs with regards pecuniary penalties. *Everything that is not personal does not disappear with death.* Fines are payable after the death of the offender, whenever he leaves assets that may be used for this purpose.
>
> (italics added)

As we can see, the fundamental idea is that payment of a sum of money is not personal. What this means is that money does not threaten life, personal safety, honour, or liberty. It was obviously not taken into account that in cases of default the fine was turned into a deprivation of liberty and, therefore, into a much more personal punishment. An obvious yet undesired consequence of this approach was that if the fine was passed on to the heir and left unpaid there was no other solution than to impose the subsidiary punishment of imprisonment. Although considered 'absurd', handing down a prison sentence to heirs was recognized as responding to 'the strict logic of inadmissible principles' (Ramiro Rueda 1898: 494; in a similar vein, Dorado Montero 1915: 144–146). As Silvela (1903: 340–341) pointed out – contrary to the transferability of the fine to heirs with the understanding that '[i]f the penalty has to be personal in nature, it must be annulled by the death of he who, having breached the law, cannot now redress this fact' – the transformation of the pecuniary penalty into a *personal* penalty, understood to be a term of imprisonment, is nothing more than adjusting the pecuniary penalty to the conditions of the person who must pay it:

> the offender who dies without having paid the fine in one way or another and who passes the obligation to pay it on to his heirs should pass it on as it was imposed on himself, in other words, to pay it with money or by serving a term of imprisonment.

This is, however, a logical consequence which the courts should never adopt, since although 'the duty to pay the fine may be transferred and may live on after the offender's death [. . .] paying it with a personal subsidiary penalty must never be passed on' (Silvela 1903: 340–341).

Some legal scholars opposed the strictly penal nature of the fine and advocated converting the fine into a public or civil obligation. Within this particular interpretation there were two lines of thought. The first one, more radical, advocated turning the penalty into a monetary debt of a public nature owed to the state, which was different from other penalties of the same nature in its form of execution, but not in its formal nature (Fuchs 1881: 432). The second line, more moderate, understood that the death of an offender after a definitive ruling converted the fine into a public debt, not a private one, which encumbered the inheritance. From this perspective, death led to the transformation of the fine, a component of criminal law, into a debt of public nature, which is not part of criminal law: the *ius puniendi* disappeared and a public debt appeared in its place (Binding 1885: 497, and 1907: 299; Bozi 1896: 257–258). The justification for this transformation lies in the financial interest of the state. Also the idea that the offender's death transformed the unpaid fine into a civil debt that passively encumbered his estate was defended (Von Buri 1894; Combaldieu 1929: 117; Donnedieu de Vabres 1937: no. 668).

The idea that death transformed the fine into a different type of obligation, either civil or public, to be enforced under the terms of non-criminal proceedings led to two logical conclusions: not only was it inappropriate to replace the fine with a term of imprisonment in the case of non-payment (an idea rejected by all the German literature; see Kruse 1934: 15), but also it would be perfectly admissible for an non-obliged third party to pay the fine.

Similarly, doubts about whether the penal fine became part of the inherited duties and obligations and, therefore, whether the benefits of deliberation and inventory were applicable (Silvela 1903: 340–341; Cuello Calón 1929: 254) could be suitably resolved with the idea that the penal nature was transformed into something different, which consequently led to these benefits having to be admitted. However, the possibility of pardoning fines passed on to heirs was also admitted (Spanish Pardon Law of June 18, 1870), which favoured the penal nature of the heirs' obligation to pay over the civil nature. Pardons are never extended to civil liabilities resulting from offences.

But, also based on the essentially penal nature of the fine, it could be argued that the death of the offender did not cancel out the obligation of payment. Hence, it was stated that the death of the offender made it factually, but not conceptually, impossible to enforce the penalty. If the fine does not need the offender to be alive and his 'estate' lives on, it is possible to enforce the penalty using his legacy. This implied accepting the argument that the personality of the deceased lived on through his estate, which formed the 'intermediate instrument of his will' (Köstlin 1845: 900). It also meant that the fine could be justifiably collected from an inheritance without contradicting the principle of personality of penalties. Contrarily, if 'the essence of the penalty lies in the reaction against the will of the offender' and, consequently, 'the death of the offender precludes the enforcement of the penalty', it would be useless to collect the pecuniary penalty from the unsettled inheritance or demand it from heirs, given that it was not possible to accept the fictitious idea that the personality of the offender lives on in his heirs (Stooß 1878: 4–5).

These opinions resulted in the legal provision of the transferability of the obligation to pay a fine passed on to the heirs of the offender, a provision found in various European penal and civil codes of the nineteenth and early twentieth centuries.[4] The same position was defended even in default of legal regulation by case law and majority opinion in France (Grebing 1982: 262; Teufel and Pradel

1983: 431). Transferability of the obligation to pay a fine on to the heirs received support from different experts. In Spain, as we have seen, the prosecutor of the Supreme Court, Trinitario Ruiz Valarino, believed it was 'indisputable' that

> the fine is of a mixed nature: criminal, insofar as it is a penalty and represents the fair punishment imposed on the perpetrator of the offence; and civil, in that it involves an obligation to serve or to give that affects the assets of the convicted offender and which, as such a civil obligation resulting from a criminal act, is passed on to the heirs.
>
> (Ruiz Valarino 1906: 90)

Two of the most famous Spanish commentators of that time, Groizard (1872: 585ff.) and Viada (1890: 565ff.), defended the legal solution from a different perspective: they understood that everything that is not personal does not disappear with death, provided that assets are left that may be used for this purpose.

The transferability of the fine to the deceased offender's family is much more striking since the personal character of the punishments, which by virtue of the sentence could be applied only to the offender, was an important principle of criminal law already established in the legislation of the *ancien régime* and in the first constitutional texts. Let me provide just one example. The express abolition of the transferability of penalties, already included in the *Partidas*,[5] was so definitively established in the 1812 Cadiz Constitution[6] that none of the subsequent Spanish constitutions referenced it. And yet the penal codes stated that a fine that remained unpaid upon the death of the offender should be paid by the heirs. The explanation for this was that the aforementioned principle did not refer to the fine – or to the penalty of infamy, which was upheld until the 1848 Spanish Penal Code[7] – but to the penalty of confiscation. Consequently, confiscation was also abolished in the Cadiz Constitution. As Masferrer Domingo (2009: 108) says, the main reason for abolition was crystal clear to those who drafted the first Spanish Constitution: 'it is not fair that the punishments reach the innocent offspring, the honest relative' (Official Journal of the General and Extraordinary Courts, Legislature of 1810 to 1813, IV, no. 437, p. 2419, Madrid, 1870). From these words it is inferred that confiscation had to be abolished, not to soften the penalties the offenders deserved – in other words, not for humanitarian reasons – but rather to ensure the principle of personality of penalties, preventing any impact on third parties (Alonso Romero 1985: 14; Pino Abad 1999: 391–392). The same idea is found not only in the progressive literature of the time but also in the more moderate sector (Marcos Gutiérrez 1826: 149–150, or Pacheco 1854: 302–303; see, however, Lardizábal 1782), and even in the absolutist legislation of King Fernando VII.[8]

Similar expressions are found in other countries: the 1786 Penal Code for the Grand Duchy of Tuscany – known as Leopoldina after the Great Duke Pietro Leopoldo II – which also abolished confiscation; the French Decree of the Constituent Assembly of January 21, 1790; the 1818 Baden Constitution; the 1822, 1826, and 1838 Portuguese Constitutions; the 1831 Hessen Constitution; and the 1848 Prussian Constitution. This notion of the injustice of the complete confiscation of assets based on the impact on innocent third parties (reflected in the works of Beccaria 1764 [1872], Robespierre 1785, Von Soden 1792: 103, Von Feuerbach 1804: 163–164, Henke 1823: 485, 487, Von Abegg 1836: 206–207, Jordão 1853: 231, or Puccioni 1855 1: 203–204) was so generally accepted in European literature that when the German Imperial Penal Code was passed in 1871, it even stated in its reasoning that 'confiscation should only apply to certain objects. We do not consider it necessary to emphasise this'. As a matter of fact, prohibiting total confiscation was not even mentioned in the final text.

Towards the non-transferability of the penal fine

The disappearance of the transcendental nature of specific penalties should be considered one of the most important contributions of liberal reform regarding punitive matters. It supported the numerous criticisms dating back to the *ancien régime* and Enlightened authors, which had been launched against a reality that threatened the most basic principle of guilt. However, we must ask why the reason behind abolishing penalties of infamy and confiscation – the impact on innocent third parties – was not extended, initially at least, to the fine, given that it was possible for heirs to find themselves obliged to pay it. It was not until the second half of the nineteenth century and early twentieth century that a strong doctrinal opposition to the penalties of infamy and confiscation can be found (e.g., Puccioni 1855: 317–318; Birkmeyer 1901: 1064; Kohler 1902), and it took even longer until this view was reflected in legal reforms. It is all the more striking given that the effects on the personality of penalties, uncertain and indirect in cases of infamy and confiscation, are certain and direct in the payment of the fine by heirs (as noted by Carrara 1871: 462). It is true that some codes, such as the 1787 Josephine Code and the 1803 Penal Code, emphatically proclaimed the principle of personality of penalties, consequently abolished confiscation and the transferability of infamy, and reduced the use of the fine to a minimum. Nevertheless, these were in the minority. It was not until several decades later that widespread concern emerged for the impact on innocent third parties regarding the use of the fine.

Around the same time other legal texts were based on different criteria. In Italy and Portugal the death of the offender meant that any unpaid pecuniary liability was annulled (see the 1855 Portuguese Criminal Code, Article 102; or the 1889 Italian Penal Code – known as Zanardelli Code after the then Italian minister of justice, Giuseppe Zanardelli – Article 85;[9] much later the 1937 Swiss Criminal Code, Article 48). Therefore, it was possible to see only the penal nature of the fine, denying its enforcement when the offender no longer existed. The dominant line of thought was broken after 1870, when Puccioni (1855 2: 318) and Carrara (1871: 462) in Italy, Silvela (1886: 67–75) in Spain, Wahlberg (1877: 249–250) in Austria, Stooβ (1878: 20) in Switzerland, and Von Liszt (1908: 284) in Germany emphatically stated that passing the fine on to the offender's heirs was a 'national injustice and immoral'. This view was included in the pre-legislative texts of the 1893 Swiss Penal Code, written by Stooβ (1893: 81), of the 1882 Spanish Penal Code, submitted to the Senate by Alonso Martínez, and of 1884, by Silvela, and of an amendment to the German Imperial Penal Code submitted to the *Reichstag* in 1909. The 7th International Penal and Penitentiary Congress held in Budapest in 1905 concluded that 'the fine is not to be exacted from the heirs of a deceased delinquent' (Barrows 1907: 32). The definitive argument to this effect was the principle of personality of the penalty: '[F]rom the aim of the penalty the highly personal nature of the penal proceedings is deduced and, consequently, the need for the penalty to befall the perpetrator of the offence' (Von Liszt 1908: 284). If the penalty is paid by the heirs, the penalty is not suffered by the offender, but by the heirs, who are deprived of what is theirs under the right of succession and are impoverished for a crime they did not commit (Puccioni 1855 2: 318; Carrara 1871: 462). This observation connected with another and most subtly exposed argument, that the fine is directed against the condemned person (Von Liszt 1908: 262). That is to recognize that the fine is also personal. Therefore it was considered that passing the fine on to the heirs

> is to deny and contradict, with no practical purpose that adequately explains it, the personality of the penalty itself, which is a fundamental and undeniable principle of modern law, bringing upon the heirs the inexplicable burden of having to pay for the crimes of another, and thereby confusing the offender's debt with the inherited right and the disrupted legal order, with liabilities of a civil nature that should legitimately befall the inherited asset.
>
> (Preamble of the draft by Silvela 1884; also Ramiro Rueda 1898: 493; Dorado Montero 1915: 144ff.)

Despite the growing doctrinal opposition, the transferability of the fine to heirs was upheld in Spain until the 1932 Penal Code came into effect. Although the preamble explained that 'death means the end of any liability for the pecuniary penalty', its articles do not mention the matter 'as it is notoriously tautological to state that the penalty is annulled by the death of the offender (cancelling the exception of the surviving heirs in the case of the fine) and by fulfilment'. Until the 1950s there were still those who believed that the heirs should pay the fine if a definitive ruling had been passed before the offender died, to the point of reaching the inheritance accepted under benefit of inventory (Sánchez Tejerina 1948: 168), but this was now only a minority opinion. Despite harsh criticism (Von Buri 1878; Prenner 1897; Gutmann 1909: 131), transferability of the fine was upheld in Germany until December 31, 1974, the date on which it was suppressed as a result of the Second Criminal Law Reform Act (*Zweites Gesetz zur Reform des Strafrechts*) of July 4, 1969, coming into effect. In France, the practice of recovering the unpaid fine imposed before death from the offender's estate was supported by case law and majority opinion until the 1970s (e.g., Bouzat and Pinatel 1970: 591) to the point that the preliminary draft of 1976 expressly proposed that it should be adopted as law (Grebing 1982: 262; Teufel and Pradel 1983: 431). The joint and several liabilities of principal offenders and other participants for the payment of a fine – not for damages or victim compensation – were abolished for all but exceptional cases in 1975 (see Decocq 1976: 22–23).

Nevertheless, the idea that the fine is an impersonal penalty is still quite widespread in contemporary literature. And until recently there were still some criminal justice systems that allowed the transferability of the imposed fine to the offender's heirs, prohibiting it only if the sentence was not imposed before the offender's death. See, for instance, § 548 of the Austrian General Civil Code in the pre-2015 version, very criticized because it was considered irreconcilable with the individual nature of the penalty (Driendl 1978: 124).

Notes

1 The same happened with others of similar content, like the one in the 1969 Children and Young Persons Act, in regard to a fine imposed for failure to comply with a supervision order, or under the 1991 Criminal Justice Act, for breaching a requirement of a community service order, because it has been retained since then.

2 There were some drafts. For instance, the 1909 Austrian draft penal code, § 195, established that 'He who instigates or undertakes a public collection to be used to pay or reimburse a pecuniary penalty imposed by the judge will be punished with a detention of three months or a fine of up to 1,000 kronen'. The Polish Penal Code had a similar regulation in the 1980s, considering a public collection for the payment of a fine punishable as a petty misdemeanour (Grebing: 1982: 185).

3 I have found an important exception in the Israeli Penal Law 5737/1977, where there is a crime called 'payment of fine imposed on another':

252A (a) 'A body corporate shall not pay – directly or indirectly – a fine imposed on another person, and an employer shall not pay a fine imposed on his employee; if a person violated any provision in this subsection, then he is liable to one year imprisonment.

(b) If an offense under subsection (a) was committed by a body corporate, then every person who – when it was paid – was an active director, a partner other than a limited partner, or a ranking administrative employee responsible for payment of the fine shall also be accused thereof, unless he proved the following two points:

(1) that the offense was committed without his knowledge;
(2) that he took all reasonable steps to prevent commission of the offense.

(c) For purposes of this section, "body corporate" includes a non-incorporated body of persons, but excludes a body corporate whose members are obligated to place all their working capacity at its disposal and to transfer all their property to it'.

This provision is not directed against a person who assists a member of his or her family to pay a fine. It has been said

> [f]or the purpose of the payment of fines, the family member should be regarded as one and the same as the defendant himself. In most cases, such an assumption corresponds to reality, as the loss or discomfort caused to the family member who pays the fine affects the defendant himself.

But the most important reason for not incriminating this practice is probably that 'a rule which would prohibit the payment of a fine whether directly or indirectly, by a family member instead of the defendant could not be enforced' (Bein 1974: 341).

4 For example, in Germany, the 1794 Prussian *Allgemeines Landrecht*, § 363, and the 1871 German Imperial Criminal Code, § 30; in Austria, the 1852 Penal Code, § 527, which due to its confusing wording needed clarification from the Ministry of Justice on April 3, 1859, confirming that 'all fines and financial penalties are passed on to the

heirs of the offender in the event of his death after a definitive ruling has been passed', and the 1811 Austrian General Civil Code, § 548; in Portugal, the 1852 Penal Code, Article 101.2; in Spain, the 1870 Penal Code, Article 132, and the 1928 Penal Code, Article 192.

5 Law 9 Section 31 entry 7 established

> for mistakes made by the father, no penalties or exemplary damages should befall the children, or other relatives, nor should the wife pay for the husband's errors. It is not fair that the wrongdoing of one man should cause suffering to another; because the punishment should only affect and impact the miscreant.

6 Article 305 of the 1812 Cadiz Constitution: 'No punishment to be given, whatever the crime, should be transcendental in any term to the suffering family, but instead it will have its effect upon he who deserved it'.

7 Unlike other countries, such as France, in Spain the penalty of infamy was not generally passed on to descendants. The legal status of 'infamous' was to be inherited only by descendants of the offender condemned for a crime of high or royal treason or against his divine majesty (Masferrer Domingo 2001: 397; 2009: 105–106). Most of the authors seemed to have no doubts about the desirability of abolishing the inheritance of this penalty (Lardizábal 1782: ap. 4, title 5, 9–10, or Marcos Gutiérrez 1826: 141; see, however, Pérez López 1781: 172ff., who defended the transferability to descendants, but only with regard to the crime against the person of the Monarch). According to Elizondo (1784: 174),

> hence is derived the horror with which the penalty of infamy shall be observed, that it should not be personal, and only with respect to very serious crimes, when there is no possibility of reforming the offender and improving his behavior.

The widespread criticism of passing the effects of infamy on to the descendants of the offender for offences of high treason and against his divine majesty did not extend to the penalty itself. In fact, highly influential enlightened scholars, like Lardizábal himself (1782), strongly favoured upholding it, once its transferability to descendants had been eradicated, which explains the peaceful coexistence of this penalty with the 1812 Cadiz Constitution and its introduction in the first 1822 Spanish Penal Code. In fact, it has been noted that no other period in Spanish penal history had recorded so many offences punished with infamy, some of them new and others coming from historical law (Masferrer Domingo 2001: 381–382). It was not until the 1848 Spanish Penal Code that it was established that 'the law does not recognise any infamous penalty' (Article 23), although the 1843 project of the criminal code of the Third Assembly had already established that 'legal infamy for offences will never be passed on to the parents or children, nor to any other relative of the offender' (Article 74), thereby following the precedent set in France on January 21, 1790, the day on which the French Assembly passed three new articles to be added to the law requiring equality in punishment, which was effectively to abolish the attachment of infamy to the offender's family. Article 2 established that

> [o]ffences and crimes are personal. The punishment imposed on the offender, and whatever infaming judgments are visited upon the offender, do not impose any stigma on his family. The honor of those who are near to him is not stained in any way, and they shall continue to be admissible to any profession, employment, or dignity.

8 The royal decree of December 2, 1819, by virtue of which His Majesty Fernando VII ordered the Council to produce a new criminal code that clearly and simply classified the offences, and the just punishment to be applied to them, stated,

> some penalties contained in the *Partidas*, established in accordance with the opinions and critical circumstances of those times of constant troubles and turbulence,

lack severity that is completely incompatible with the civilisation and customs of the day, which is always the silent voice that always indicated the most appropriate legislation. The confiscation of assets, the transferal of infamy to the children for the offences of the father, with no other result than leaving the family perpetually disgraced [. . .].

9 The 1921 Ferri project proposed an Article 47, which, with the aim of benefitting the victims, established that

> if the offender dies before paying the fine, it will then encumber his estate. If the heirs are entitled to a legitimate share, this payment will be due to the extent that it does not deprive them of their
> livelihood [. . .] In the event of the heirs waiving the inheritance, the Fine Fund will fully replace the heir under the benefit of inventory.

However, the 1930 Rocco Penal Code, with regards to this point, simply stated that 'should the offender die after being convicted, the penalty will be cancelled', a precept which was considered, almost unanimously, applicable to the fine.

References

Aguilera de Paz, E. (1913) *Comentarios a la Ley de Enjuiciamiento Criminal. Tomo IV*. Madrid: Reus.

Albrecht, H.-J. (1980) *Strafzumessung und Vollstreckung bei Geldstrafen*. Berlin: Duncker & Humblot.

Alonso Romero, M. P. (1985) 'Aproximación al estudio de las penas pecuniarias en Castilla (siglos XIII–XVIII)'. *Anuario de Historia del Derecho Español* 55: 9–94.

Álvarez Posadilla, J. (1797) *Práctica criminal por principios; o modo y forma de instruir los procesos criminales de las causas de oficio de justicia contra los abusos introducidos*. n.p.: S/l.

Antón Oneca, J. (1949) *Derecho Penal: Tomo I. Parte General*. Madrid: Gráfica Administrativa.

Ball, C., McCormac, K. and N. Stone (1995) *Young Offenders: Law, Policy and Practice*. London: Sweet & Maxwell.

Barrows, S. J. (1907) *Report of Proceedings of the Seventh International Prison Congress, Budapest, Hungary, September, 1905, by Samuel J. Barrows, Commissioner for the United States on the International Prison Commission*. Washington, DC: Govt. Print. Off.

Bathurst, D. (1996) *Financial Penalties: Collection and Enforcement in Magistrates' Courts*. Chichester: Barry Rose Law.

Baumann, J. (1968) *Beschränkung des Lebensstandards anstatt kurzfristiger Freiheitsstrafe*. Neuwied: Luchterhand.

Baumann, J. (1969) 'Besteht heute die Möglichkeit, die Freiheitsstrafe bis zu 6 Monaten zu beseitigen?' *Österreichische Richterzeitung* 62: 112–118.

Beccaria, C. Bonesana di (1764 [1872]) *An Essay on Crimes and Punishments: By the Marquis Beccaria of Milan. With a Commentary by M. de Voltaire. A New Edition Corrected*. Albany: W. C. Little.

Bein, D. (1974) 'Payment of a Fine by a Person Other Than the Defendant'. *Israel Law Review* 9(3): 325–345.

Bentham, J. (1830) *The Rationale of Punishment*. London: Robert Heward.

Beristain Ipiña, A. (1976) 'La multa penal y la administrativa en relación con las sanciones privativas de libertad'. In AA.VV (ed.) *III Jornadas de Profesores de Derecho Penal*. Madrid: Universidad de Santiago de Compostela, 11–56.

Beristain Ipiña, A. (1979) 'Voz Multa penal'. In Pellisé Prats, B. (ed.) *Nueva Enciclopedia Jurídica. Tomo XVI*. Barcelona: Seix, 699–716.

Bernardi, A. (1993) 'Natura penale e retaggi civilistici della pena pecuniaria'. *Rivista Italiana di Diritto e Procedura Penale* 36: 514–568.

Berner, A. F. (1857) *Lehrbuch des deutschen Strafrechtes*. Leipzig: Tauchnitz.

Berner, A. F. (1869) *Kritik des Entwurfes eines Strafgesetzbuches für den Norddeutschen Bund*. Leipzig: Tauchnitz.

Berolzheimer, F. (1907) *System der Rechts- und Wirtschaftsphilosophie. 5. Strafrechtsphilosophie und Strafrechtsreform*. Munich: C. H. Beck.

Binding, K. (1885) *Handbuch des Strafrechts. Band I*. Leipzig: Duncker & Humblot.

Binding, K. (1905) *Lehrbuch des Gemeinen Deutschen Strafrechts Besonderer Teil: Zweiter Band. Zweite Abteilung*. Leipzig: Verlag von Wilhelm Engelmann.

Binding, K. (1907) *Grundriss des deutschen Strafrechts: Allgemeiner Teil*. 7th ed. Leipzig: Engelmann.

Birkmeyer, K. (1901) 'Das Strafrecht'. In Birkmeyer, K. (ed.) *Enzyklopädie der Rechtswissenschaft in systematischer und alphabetischer Bearbeitung*. Berlin: D. Häring, 1025–1092.

Bouzat, P. and J. Pinatel (1970) *Traité de droit pénal et de criminologie: 3. Criminologie*. 2nd ed. Paris: Dalloz.

Bozi, A. (1896) 'Zahlung der Geldstrafe durch Dritte'. *Deutsche Juristen-Zeitung* 13: 257–258.

Brenn, A. (1945) *Die Busse und ihr Vollzug nach dem Schweizerischen Strafgesetzbuch*. Affoltern am Albis: Dr. J. Weiss.

Bricola, F. (1964) 'Pene pecuniarie, pene fisse e finalità rieducativa'. In AA.VV (ed.) *Sul problema della rieducazione del condannato*. Padova: Cedam, 193–216. Cited through Bricola, F. (1997) *Scritti di Diritto Penale. Volume I. Dottrine generali: Teoria del reato e sistema sanzionatorio. Tomo I. Dal 1960 al 1973*. Milan: Giuffrè, 275–298.

Brüggemann, D. (1968) 'Abwälzung und Rückwälzung von Geldstrafen und Geldbußen mit den Mitteln des bürgerlichen Rechts?' *Goltdammer's Archiv für Strafrecht* 16: 161–176.

Carrara, F. (1871) *Programa del Corso di Diritto Criminale dettato nella R. Università di Pisa. Parte Generale*. 4th ed. Lucca: Tipografia Giusti.

Combaldieu, R. (1929) *Du recouvrement de l'amende pénale*. Toulouse: Cléder.

Cuello Calón, E. (1929) *Las faltas en el nuevo Código Penal (su exposición y comentario)*. Madrid: Librería General de Victoriano Suárez.

Decocq, A. (1976) 'Les modifications apportées par la loi du 11 juillet 1975 à la théorie générale du droit pénal'. *Revue de science criminelle et de droit pénal comparé* 31: 5–28.

Dolcini, E. (1972) 'Pena pecuniaria e principio costituzionale di eguglianza'. *Rivista Italiana di Diritto e Procedura Penale* 15: 408–459.

Donnedieu de Vabres, H. (1937) *Traité élémentaire de droit criminel et de législation pénale comparée*. Paris: Sirey.

Dorado Montero, P. (1915) *El Derecho protector de los criminales. Tomo II*. Madrid: Librería General de Victoriano Suárez.

Driendl, J. (1978) *Die Reform der Geldstrafe in Österreich*. Baden-Baden: Nomos.

Elizondo, F. A. de (1781) *Práctica universal forense de los tribunales de España e Indias. Volume IV*. Madrid: Imprenta de Joaquín Ibarra.

Engels, D. (1981) 'Vollstreckungsvereitelung (§258 Abs. 2 StGB) durch Zahlung fremder Geldstrafe?' *Jura* 3: 581–585.

Ferrajoli, L. (1990). *Diritto e raggione: Teoria del garantismo penale*. Rome: Laterza.

Figueiredo Dias, J. de (1989) 'Problemas de igualdade na estruturaçâo e aplicaçâo da pena de multa'. In AA.VV (ed.) *Estudios Penales en Memoria del Profesor Agustín Fernández-Albor*. Santiago de Compostela: Servicio de Publicaciones de la Universidad de Santiago de Compostela, 289–305.

Florian. E. (1934) *Parte generale del Diritto penale. II*. 4th ed. Milan: Casa Editrice Dottor Francesco Vallardi.

Friedmann, O. (1892) 'Sind Änderungen des geltendes Recht erwünscht in Betreff des Verhältnisses zwischen Geld- und Freiheitsstrafen?' In Deutscher Juristentag (ed.) *Verhandlungen des Zweiundzwanzigsten Deutschen Juristentages. Zweiter Band*. Berlin: Guttentag, 95–183.

Friedmann, O. (1898) 'Begünstigung durch Bezahlung einer gegen einen anderen erkannten Geldstrafe'. *Zeitschrift für die gesamte Strafrechtswissenschaft* 18: 821–829.

Frosali, R. A. (1958) *Sistema penale italiano: Parte 1. Diritto penale sostanziale. Volume 3*. Turin: UTET.

Fuchs, C. (1881) 'Kritische Erörterungen von Entscheidungen des Reichsgerichts in Strafsachen'. *Goltdammer's Archiv für Strafrecht* 29: 422–434.

Göppinger, H. (1971) *Kriminologie: Eine Einführung*. Munich: Beck.

Göppinger, H. (1975) *Criminología*. Madrid: Reus.

Grebing, G. (1978) 'Die Geldstrafe im deutschen Recht nach Einführung des Tagessatzsystems'. In Jescheck, H.-H. and G. Grebing (eds.) *Die Geldstrafe im deutschen und ausländischen Recht*. Baden-Baden: Nomos, 1–184.

Grebing. G. (1982) *The Fine in Comparative Law: A Survey of 21 Countries*. Cambridge: Institute of Criminology Occasional Papers n° 9.

Groizard y Gómez de la Serna, A. (1872) *El Código penal de 1870 concordado y comentado. Tomo II*. Burgos: Imprenta de D. Timoteo Arnaiz.

Groß, H. (1894) 'Zum Stooβ'chen Vorentwurf für ein "Schweizerisches Strafgesetzbuch" '. *Allgemeine österreichische Gerichtszeitung* 45: 325–329.

Gutmann, H. (1909) *Die Natur der Geldstrafe und ihre Verwendung im heutigen Reichsstrafrecht*. Leipzig: Druck von J. B. Hirschfeld.

Hassan, M. A. (1959) *L'amende pénale dans les droits modernes et spécialement dans le Code Pénal Suisse*. Paris: Librairie Générale de Droit et de Jurisprudence.

Heffter, A. W. (1833) *Lehrbuch des gemeinen Deutschen Criminalrechts mit Rücksicht auf die nicht exclusiven Landesrechte*. Halle: Schwetschte.

Henke, E. (1823) *Handbuch des Criminalrechts und der Criminalpolitik. Erster Theil*. Berlin-Stettin: Nicolai.

Hillenkamp, T. (1987) 'Zur Höchstpersönlichkeit der Geldstrafe'. In Küper, W., Puppe, I. and J. Tenckhoff (eds.) *Festschrift für K. Lackner zum 70. Geburtstag*. Berlin: Walter de Gruyter, 455–469.

Hillenkamp, T. (1992) 'Anmerkung'. *Juristische Rundschau* 46: 74–76.

Höh, F. (1909) *Zur juristischen Natur der Geldstrafe*. Borna-Leipzig: Univ. Diss.

Jordão, L. M. (1853) *Commentario ao Codigo Penal Portuguez. Tomo I*. Lisbon: Typographia de José Baptista Morando.

Kleinschrod, G.A.K. (1794) *Systematische Entwicklung der Grundbegriffe und Grundwahrheiten des peinlichen Rechts nach der Natur der Sache und der positiven Gesetzgebung. Volume II*. Erlangen: Palm.

Kohler, J. (1902) 'Geldstrafe'. *Goltdammer's Archiv für Strafrecht* 49: 177–184.

Köstlin, C. R. (1845) *Neue Revision der Grundbegriffe des Kriminalrechts*. Tübingen: Laup.

Kronecker (1879) 'Beiträge zur Lehre von der Geldstrafe'. *Goltdammer's Archiv für Strafrecht* 27: 1–18.

Kruse, W. (1934) *Die Mitwirkung Dritter bei Entrichtung von Geldstrafen*. Eisfeld i. Thür.: Carl Beck.

Lardizábal y Uribe, M. (1782) *Discurso sobre las penas, contraído a las leyes criminales de España, para facilitar su reforma*. Madrid: Joachin Ibarra.

Lehmann (1871) 'Bezahlung der Geldstrafe für den Verutheilten als Begünstigung der Strafthat'. *Goltdammer's Archiv für Strafrecht* 19: 784–788.

López Rey y Arrojo, M. and F. Álvarez-Valdés (1933) *El nuevo Código penal*. Madrid: Editorial Revista de Derecho Privado.

Manzanares Samaniego, J. L. (1977) *La pena de multa*. Madrid: Excma. Mancomunidad de Cabildos.

Manzanares Samaniego, J. L. (1983) *Las penas patrimoniales en el Código penal español tras la LO 8/1983*. Barcelona: Bosch.

Manzini, V. (1910) *Tratatto di diritto penale italiano. Volume III*. Milan: Fratelli Bocca Editori.

Manzini, V. (1934) *Tratatto di diritto penale italiano secondo il Codice del 1930. Volume III*. Turin: UTET.

Marcos Gutiérrez, J. (1826) *Práctica criminal de España. Tomo III*. 4th ed. Madrid: Imprenta de Don Fermín Villalpando.

Masferrer Domingo, A. (2001) *La pena de infamia en el Derecho histórico español: Contribución al estudio de la tradición penal europea en el marco del ius commune*. Madrid: Dykinson.

Masferrer Domingo, A. (2009) 'Codification of Spanish Criminal Law in the Nineteenth Century. A Comparative Legal History Approach'. *Journal of Comparative Law* 4(1): 96–139.

Merkel, A. (1889) *Lehrbuch des deutschen Strafrechts*. Stuttgart: Enke-Verlag.

Merle, R. and M. Vitu (1967) *Traité de droit criminel*. Paris: Cujas.

Miguel Garcilópez, A. de (1940) *Derecho Penal. Parte General*. Madrid: Reus.

Molinari, F. (1983) *La pena pecuniaria*. Verona: Team.

Montes, P. (1929) *Derecho Penal Español*. 2nd ed. San Lorenzo del Escorial: Imprenta del Real Monasterio.

Musco, E. (1984) *La pena pecuniaria*. Catania: C.U.L.C.

O'Malley, P. (2009) *The Currency of Justice: Fines and Damages in Consumer Societies*. New York: Routledge-Cavendish.

Ortolan, J.L.E. (1874) *Éléments de droit pénal*. 4th ed. Paris: Plon.

Pacheco, J. F. (1854) *Obras jurídicas de Don Joaquín Francisco Pacheco: Lecciones pronunciadas en el Ateneo de Madrid en 1839 y 1840. Tomo II. Estudios de Derecho penal*. 2nd ed. Madrid: Imprenta a cargo de D. S. Compagni.

Packer, H. L. (1968) *The Limits of the Criminal Sanction*. Stanford: Stanford University Press.

Pérez López, A. X. (1781) *Discurso sobre la honra y deshonra legal, en que se manifiesta el verdadero mérito de la Nobleza de sangre, y se prueba que todos los oficios necesarios, y útiles al Estado son honrados por las Leyes del Reyno, segun las quales solamente el delito propio disfama*. Madrid: Blas Román.

Perret, H. (1941) 'Le rôle pénal de la Solidarité entre les condamnés à une peine d'amende'. *Revue de science criminelle et de droit pénal comparé* 6: 77–119.

Pino Abad, M. (1999) *La pena de confiscación de bienes en el derecho histórico español*. Córdoba: Diputación Provincial de Córdoba.

Pradel, J. (1977) *Droit pénal. 1. Introduction générale, droit pénal général*. Paris: Cujas.

Prenner, J. B. (1897) *Die Vollstreckung der Geldstrafe in den Nachlaß der Schuldigen*. Munich: Ackermann.

Puccioni, G. (1855) *Il Codice penale toscano illustrato sulla scorta delle fonti, del diritto e della giurisprudenza. Tomo I e Tomo II*. Pistoia: Tipografia Cino.

Ramiro Rueda, R. (1898) *Elementos de Derecho penal. Tomo I*. 4th ed. Santiago de Compostela: Imprenta de José M. Paredes.

Rauh, M. F. (1912) *Die Vermögensstrafen des Reichsstrafrechts und ihre Reform*. Breslau: Schlatter.

Robespierre, M. (1785) *Discours couronné par la Société royale des arts et des sciences de Metz, sur les questions suivantes, proposées pour sujet du prix de l'année 1784. 1. Quelle est l'origine de l'opinion, qui étend sur tous les individus d'une même famille, une partie de la honte attachée aux peines infamantes que subit un coupable? 2. Cette opinion est-elle plus nuisible qu'utile? 3. Dans le cas ou` l'on se décideroit pour l'affirmative, quels seraient les moyens de parer aux inconvénients qui en résultent?* Amsterdam: Chez J. G. Merigot.

Rossi, P. (1954) *Lineamenti di diritto penale costituzionale*. Palermo: Priulla.

Ruiz Valarino, T. (1906) *Memoria elevada al Gobierno de Su Majestad el 15 de septiembre de 1906 por el Fiscal del Tribunal Supremo*. Madrid: Imprenta de la Revista de Legislación.

Saltelli, C. (1939) 'Pene pecuniarie'. In D'Amelio, M. (ed.) *Nuovo digesto italiano. Volume IX*. 2nd ed. Turin: Unione Tipografico-Editrice Torinese, 703–705.

Samuels, A. (1970) 'The Fine: The Principles'. *The Criminal Law Review*, May: 201–210, 268–272.

Sánchez-Tejerina, I. (1948) *Código penal anotado de 23 de diciembre de 1944, con las modificaciones introducidas hasta el momento actual, con un breve comentario y la más reciente jurisprudencia del Tribunal Supremo*. Madrid: Instituto Editorial Reus.

Schönke, A. and H. Schröder (2010) *Strafgesetzbuch Kommentar*. 28th ed. Munich: C. H. Beck.

Schütz, B. (1967) *Le principe de la personnalité des peines en droit pénal français*. Nancy: Univ. Diss.

Schwander, V. (1969) *Das Schweizerische Strafgesetzbuch*. 2nd ed. Zürich: Polygraphischer Verlag.

Silvela, L. (1886) *El Código penal y el sentido común*. Madrid: Tipografía Hernández.

Silvela, L. (1903) *El derecho penal estudiado en principios y en la legislación vigente en España. Segunda parte*. Madrid: Establecimiento Tipográfico de Ricardo Fé.

Simmel, G. (1907 [1990]) *The Philosophy of Money*. New York: Routledge.

Spasari, M. (1966) *Diritto Penale e Costituzione*. Milan: Giuffrè.

Stooβ, C. (1878) *Zur Natur der Vermögensstrafen*. Bern: M. Fiala.

Stooβ, C. (1893) *Motive zu dem Vorentwurf eines schweizerischen Strafgesetzbuches*. Basel-Geneva: Georg.

Stooβ, C. (1898) 'Geldstrafe und Begünstigung'. *Zeitschrift für Schweizer Strafrecht* 11: 364–370.

Stree, W. (1964) 'Anmerkung'. *Juristenzeitung* 64: 588–590.

Teufel, G. and J. Pradel (1983) 'Die Geldstrafe in Frankreich'. In Jescheck, H.-H. and G. Grebing (eds.) *Die Geldstrafe im deutschen und ausländischen Recht*. Baden-Baden: Nomos, 397–455.

Viada y Vilaseca, S. (1890) *Código Penal de 1870. Tomo I*. Madrid: Fernando Fe.

Von Abegg, J.F.H. (1836) *Lehrbuch der Strafrechtswissenschaft*. Neustadt a. d. Orla: Wagner.

Von Buri, M. (1878) 'Zur Natur der Vermögensstrafen'. *Der Gerichtssaal* 30: 1–8.

Von Buri, M. (1894) *Beiträge zur Theorie des Strafrechts und zum Strafgesetzbuch: Gesammelte Abhandlungen*. Leipzig: Veit.

Von der Decken (1892) 'Ist der Bezahlung einer Geldstrafe durch einen Dritten zulässig oder strafbar?'. *Zeitschrift für die gesamte Strafrechtswissenschaft* 12: 97–119.

Von Feuerbach, A. (1804) *Kritik des Kleinschrodischen Entwurfs zu einem peinlichen Gesetzbuche für die Chur-Pfalz-Bayrischen Staaten*. Giesen: Tasché & Müller.

Von Feuerbach, A. (1805) *Lehrbuch des gemeinen in Deutschland gültigen Peinlichen Rechts*. 3rd ed. Giesse: Georg Friedrich Heyer.

Von Lilienthal, K. (1892) 'Sind Aenderungen des geltenden Rechts erwünscht in Betreff des Verhältnisses zwischen Geld- und Freiheitsstrafe?'. In Deutscher Juristentag (ed.) *Verhandlungen des Zweiundzwanzigsten Deutschen Juristentages. Zweiter Band*. Berlin: Guttentag, 63–94.

Von Lilienthal, K. (1897) 'Begünstigung durch Bezahlung einer Geldstrafe für einen andern'. *Deutschen Juristen-Zeitung* 24: 489–491.

Von Liszt, F. (1908) *Lehrbuch des Deutschen Strafrechts*. 16th ed. Berlin: Guttentag.

Von Quistorps, J. C. (1796) *Grundsätze des deutschen Peinlichen Rechts. Band 1*. Würzburg: Rienner.

Von Soden, J. (1792) *Geist der peinlichen Gesetzgebung Teutschlands. Band I*. Frankfurt am Main: s.n.

Von Sonnenfels, J. (1787 [2003]) *Grundsätze der Polizey, Handlung und Finanz zum Gebrauche akademischer Vorlesungen*. 5th ed. Vienna: J. B. Strobel.

Von Sonnenfels, J. (1820) *Grundsätze der Polizey, Handlung und Finanz zum Gebrauche akademischer Vorlesungen*. 3rd ed. Tübingen: Osiander

Von Spiegel, H.-U. Frhr. (1979) *Drittwirkung der Geldstrafe*. Göttingen: Univ. Diss.

Von Stenglein, M. (1861) *Commentar über das Strafgesetzbuch für das Königreich Bayern und das Gesetz über die Einführung des Strafgesetzbuches und des Polizei-Strafgesetzbuches. 1. Das Einführungsgesetz und des Strafgesetzbuches allgemeine Bestimmungen*. Munich: Kaiser.

Wahlberg, W. E. (1877) 'Nationalökonomische Gesichtspunkte im Strafrecht mit besonderer Rücksicht auf die Geldstrafe'. In Wahlberg, W. E. (ed.) *Gesammelte kleinere Schriften und Bruchstücke über Strafrecht, Strafprozess, Gefängnisskunde, Literatur und Dogmengeschichte der Rechtslehre in Oesterreich*. Vienna: Alfred Hölder, 231–264.

Wahlberg, W. E. (1890) 'Betrachtungen über die Freiheitsstrafen in dem österreichischen Strafgesetzentwurf sowie über die Grundsätze der internationalen Criminalistischen Vereiningung'. *Juristische Blätter* 19: 1–3, 13–15, 25–27, 39–43.

Waldthausen (1881) 'Ueber Begünstigung'. *Archiv für Strafrecht* 29: 375–411.

Warner, K. (2012) 'Equality Before the Law and Equal Impact of Sanctions: Doing Justice to Differences in Wealth and Employment Status'. In Zedner, L. (ed.) *Principles and Values in Criminal Law and Criminal Justice: Essays in Honour of Andrew Ashworth*. Oxford: Oxford University Press, 225–244.

Westen, D. A. (1969) 'Fines, Imprisonment, and the Poor: Thirty Dollars or Thirty Days'. *California Law Review* 57(3): 778–820.

Young, P. (1999) 'The Fine as an Auto-Punishment: Power, Money and Discipline'. In Duff, P. and N. Hutton (eds.) *Criminal Justice in Scotland*. Aldershot: Darmouth, 182–197.

Zipf, H. (1965) 'Abwälzung der Geldstrafe auf einen Dritten und Erreichbarkeit des Strafzweckes'. *Monatsschrift für Deutsches Recht* 8: 632–633.

Zipf, H. (1974) 'Probleme der Neuregelung der Geldstrafe in Deutschland'. *Zeitschrift für die gesamte Strafrechtswissenschaft* 86: 513–544.

4 The unequal distribution of money and the (un)fairness of fines

Why and how fines were made affordable

Money distribution and the fairness of fines

As already said in Chapter 1, access to money is unequally distributed between individuals in society. In fact, the origins and evolution of money were closely intertwined with the rise and consolidation of class society and inequality. These factors mutually reinforced the development of one another, to the point where it has been said that 'the origins of money are to be found in the origins of inequality' (Semenova and Wray 2015: 1), with money playing a key role in establishing, maintaining, and exacerbating inequality and class division in societies (Henry 2004; Martin 2013: 60ff.). Money-based societies are more economically unequal as money is unevenly spread (Dodd 1994: 150), a state of things generated by the institutional system that produces money itself (Ingham 2000: 68). As clearly stated by Semenova and Wray (2015: 2),

> To put it simply, as soon as one witnesses the emergence of money, one observes the rise of class society and socioeconomic inequalities. Money, class society, and inequality came into being simultaneously, so it seems, mutually reinforcing the development of one another.

The unequal distribution of money puts a clear and definite limit on the fairness of tariff- and fixed-fine systems. Spanish author Pacheco wrote,

> The fine is a punishment of a singular kind, and has little in common with most other punishments established by law. While these cases encumber the person or freedom, which is almost the same person, those affect wealth only, which is something very different. The level of personality is the same for all men, and freedom is similar: wealth is so varied, men's fortunes are so disparate and diverse [. . .]. Therefore, if a personal punishment, death, custodial sentence, imprisonment, affects all men to an equal or similar extent, a pecuniary punishment is the most unequal that can be conceived, when it is applied in identical measures to two persons of different wealth.
>
> (Pacheco 1856: 414–415)

Fairness requires recognition that the same fine may have a disproportionately severe impact on certain offenders. If monetary penalties, like the fine, are set, they disproportionately affect those people whose income is limited. A high fine on a poor offender invites default. This means that it can result in imprisonment for an offence for which custody was not considered appropriate. Conversely, if the fine is set low, wealthier offenders can simply pay and go home, without having felt the 'bite' of punishment, which decreases fines' punitive potential. The problem of imposing fines which had to be appropriate both to the offence and to the offender was faced by all European criminal justice systems during the nineteenth century. A system had to be developed to subvert the inequality-inducing characteristic of the unequal distribution of money in society via the adaptation of the fine to the offender's financial circumstances, but without giving the impression that the court takes a lenient view of the offence. Equality of impact came to be widely accepted as a strong principle of fairness in the calculation of fines. As we will see in the next sections, this change was boosted by the wave of criticism against short-term prison sentences that reached its peak at the end of the nineteenth century.

The late nineteenth-century 'crusade' against short-term imprisonment

The year 1864 marks the start of the controversy over short-term imprisonment. In this year the French writer Bonneville de Marsangy focused his extensive criminal policy programme on a drastic downsizing of crimes punishable by imprisonment, recommending the fine in highly appreciative terms: 'Of all, the most liberal, the most divisible, the most economical, the most completely remissible, the most efficacious, really the punishment par excellence' (1864: 258–259). It was also the same year in which his enthusiastic German reviewer, Von Holtzendorff (1864: 652), proposed *tout court* the abolition of short-term imprisonment, warning that, if not done, there was a risk of 'devaluating the deterrent effectiveness of all the criminal justice system'. However, the most influential work at that time was Franz von Liszt's Marburg Programme (1882). It was a ferocious critique of short-term imprisonment. Specifically, when speaking of offenders in need of correction, he noted, 'the punishments herein involving a deprivation of freedom should always have a minimum duration, which must not be less than one year' (Von Liszt 1883: 11). And he added, 'There is nothing more immoral and more absurd than our short-term sentences of imprisonment for apprentices in crime' (Von Liszt 1889a: 743). The rationale behind this criticism is that a short-term prison sentence is 'worthless, indeed harmful. It does not deter, it does not improve, it contaminates' (Von Liszt 1905: 349).

The arguments are well known, and it is not my intention to discuss them extensively here. The widespread disillusion with imprisonment as a penal sanction can be traced to two main groups of reasoning, practical and theoretical. The need to reduce prison overcrowding was of a practical nature. It was believed that this would allow prisons to be reformed so that the buildings and prison personnel would be able to fulfil their true purpose, the offender's reform. The economy of means that could be achieved in managing prisoners – for example, supervision and medical care – was also based on practical considerations, given the economic stringencies during the period. In turn, arguments that short-term prison sentences vilified and corrupted inmates, thereby not leading to reform but to recidivism, were based on a theoretical rationale of a correctionalist and humanitarian nature (see in Austria Wahlberg 1869: 55ff., and Vargha 1896: 512; in Germany Von Ihering 1877 [1904], Mittelstädt 1879, Von Liszt 1889b: 292–293, or Berolzheimer 1907: 233ff.; in Italy Molinari-Tosatti 1888: 557ff., or Bertola 1893: 553; in Spain Arenal 1890: 313–314; in Sweden Thyrén 1910: 67). In fact, the triumph of correctionalism at the end of the nineteenth century exerted a considerable impact. Although this triumph was never complete (Garland 1985), correctionalist discourses strongly supported scepticism about the effectiveness of imprisonment as an instrument of treatment or a means of deterrence. Deprivation of freedom was viewed as both inappropriate for many offenders and harmful for all of them.

This wave of correctionalist criticism against the retributionist-based penal codes eventually created the right environment for prison reform to finally become something more than a grandiloquent gesture. For the first time, criticism led to a review of imprisonment and its fundamental and almost exclusive role in the liberal panoply of punishments (Padovani 1981: 44). Doubts started to emerge about the appropriateness of actually employing this type of sanction. The literature from all the European countries studied herein did not limit itself to discussing the reality of prisons. It went further and demanded transformation in line with the establishment of a specified prison system under which punishment could effectively achieve its purpose. Leading academics in Austria, England, Germany, Italy, Portugal, Scandinavia, Spain, and Switzerland expressed their uneasiness about the drawbacks they perceived in custodial sentences, since they thought that these disadvantages were not outweighed by the prospective benefits that could be derived from imprisonment. This became a widely held opinion, as evidenced by the conclusions stemming from a series of international penitentiary congresses held between 1872 and 1890, as well as meetings of the International Union of Penal Law, all of which focused on fines. In all of these meetings, short terms of imprisonment were deplored. But also fines, especially levied against the poor, were decried, because in case of non-payment they led to short sentences of imprisonment. As Grebing (1982: 8) pointed out,

> The common basis here, resulting from the intense national and international discussion that took place towards the end of the nineteenth century, was the widespread recognition of the harmfulness and futility of the almost universal practice of imposing short sentences of imprisonment [. . .]. Thus the abolition or, at the very least, the general restriction of short imprisonment was demanded. It was to be replaced by other types of sanction and, above all, by the fine and the conditional sentence. For this purpose, the fine would have to undergo a thorough improvement.

This provoked the re-emergence of the fine to substitute short terms of imprisonment, considered to have too damaging an effect on offenders. But not without difficulties, as will be shown ahead.

The problem of imprisonment for fine defaulters

Admittedly, in this context of harsh criticism against short terms of imprisonment penal fines could have been considered, in short, a 'progress . . . in culture' (Rauh 1912: 61) and their use 'rational' (Merkel 1889: 220). But criticism of short-term prison sentences did not initially correspond to a more positive view of the use of fines as a punishment.[1] Curiously, the first reason for this had nothing to do with the adverse effects of short-term imprisonment but rather with the idea that the punishment replacing the fine in case of default should maintain, to a certain degree, an element of pecuniary punishment. What was the rationale behind this opinion?

The first regulations of imprisonment for fine defaulters in European penal codes were applauded and considered an 'extremely fair and significant new development'.[2] They were based on the commonly accepted axiom *quod non habens in bonis luat in corpus* – 'let him who has nothing in purse pay in person'. But soon it was observed that

> [*m*]*oney* and *freedom* are *unequal* assets. Freedom should be held in higher esteem by the legislator and the citizen than money. Prison is a worst evil than a fine. If a fine turns into a custodial sentence, the offender suffers a greater evil than, according to his legal sentence, he deserves.
>
> (Stooß 1916: 5, italics in the original)

This criticism spread to nearly all the penal systems under German influence (see, e.g., in Austria Merkel 1895: 389–390; in Italy Conti 1910: 457). It was not without autochthonous precedent in countries like Spain, where Silvela (1874: 411) had already said,

> The injustice of completely changing the essence of the Punishment and turning it, as is commonly said, from that of a pecuniary nature into a personal one based on something entirely unrelated to the offence, should be something deemed worthier of consideration by our experts; and if a less irrational substitution than the one accepted to date is not possible in practice, the pecuniary punishment should be abolished with no excuse. But this substitution is fully appropriate in our opinion; in other words, the fine can change without losing its character. There is nobody whose spiritual or physical activity does not have any economic value and does not imply an income or wealth. Withholding part of the offender's wage, demanding – if he is not currently earning – that he works for the benefit of the State or the Municipality, does correspond to the idea of a pecuniary punishment, or rather it presents a new aspect under which the same punishment can be considered.

This passage underlines that the fairest substitute penalty would not be deprivation of freedom, but rather forced labour (Bonneville de Marsangy 1864: 293; Rosenfeld 1890: 316, 327). This notion, with precedents in Beccaria (1764 [1872]:

Chapter 22), was expressed as early as 1822 by Tittmann (1822: 134), for whom '[t]he substitute for a fine when it cannot be paid must be manual labour, not a corporal sentence which bears no relationship whatsoever with the fine'. As Von Liszt (1889b: 46) emphatically put it, 'compulsory work means a job carried out for the state which can be valued in money terms. It is by nature a pecuniary penalty. The restriction of personal freedom disappears almost entirely into the background therefore'. In this case the balance is no longer between time and money, or freedom and money, but between labour and money. Such an equation was also far more compatible with the emerging capitalist system of the time (Rusche and Kirchheimer 1939 [2003]). The same proposal can be found in Italy, where the arguments were based on the breach of the equality principle that occurred when the fine was replaced with imprisonment (Pessina, during the legislative meetings for a new penal code, quoted in *Rivista Penale* 1876: 527).

At the end of the nineteenth century the argument regarding the different nature of the subsidiary punishment was considered outdated. There was widespread consensus that subsidiary punishment had to be more severe than the one originally imposed, so the offender would not be given the option between one and the other. This viewpoint presumed, of course, the offender's ability to pay, since it was believed that many would rather go to prison than pay the fine (e.g., Castro y Orozco and Ortiz de Zúñiga 1848: 163; Maffei 1875: 405–406; Krohne 1889: 235–236; Rosenfeld 1890: 207). However, soon it was found that most offenders required to pay a fine did not do so simply because they lacked the financial means. Imprisonment for fine defaulters became widespread,[3] and therefore a central issue in criminal justice.

The fact that prisons were being filled with poor people who originally were fined precisely because their offences were *not* severe enough for imprisonment was commonly recognized in the second half of the nineteenth century. Soon, criticism of short-term prison sentences extended to the subsidiary punishment for fine defaulters, usually a form of short-term imprisonment (Bonneville de Marsangy 1864: 296–297; Felisch 1895: 300ff.; Galdo 1908: 55; Stooβ 1916: 5ff.). For example, Ferri (1900: 454) stated forcefully, 'substituting fines with imprisonment is an iniquitous leftover of barbaric laws, which allowed the debtor to first be ripped to shreds by his creditors and then personally arrested for debts, and which civilisation makes impossible today'. This statement reiterates the obvious inequality which ensued when fines were substituted by imprisonment in case of default. The problem with imprisonment for fine defaulters was no longer the nature of the penalty but the rate of exchange. A rate of exchange had to be found that equated, for any given individual, a quantity of money with a number of days in prison. Almost all criminal statutes established a rate of exchange highly favourable to people who had assets. For well-off individuals the loss of money to be paid as a fine was always a milder sanction than time to be spent in prison in case of default. The same could not be said for low-income people (Heilborn 1908: 58–59), because for them their 'money income is adequate only for the basic needs of life and allows almost no latitude in the choice of uses', a phenomenon due to the difference between the same amount of money as part of a large and of a small fortune (Simmel 1907 [1990]: 218–219). Therefore, the need to consider the offender's financial means when calculating the fine was justified with arguments based on the equalization of impact (see, e.g., Wahlberg 1869: 166; Von Liszt 1889b: 45; Getz 1893: 8ff.; Merkel 1893: 351; Groß 1894: 55; Felisch 1895: 300; Glauning 1905; Stooβ 1907; Goldschmidt 1908: 408–409; Navarro de Paiva 1915: 195). A new concept of equality, different from the one accepted during the Enlightenment, had to be taken into account. But the first attempts to enact this concept in the penal legislation were unsuccessful.

Experimentation with ways to manage the problem of default

There was some degree of legal experimentation to manage the problem of prisons being overcrowded with fine defaulters. Striking attempts were made to limit imprisonment to cases in which the offender did not pay the fine 'wilfully, through laziness, licentiousness, or negligence' (according to the 1918 Swiss project for a penal code, Article 46, based on the draft written by Stooß in 1893, in turn very influenced by the debates within the International Union for Penal Law). This kind of regulation, despite being welcome by literature (see Garofalo 1887: 105, Stooβ 1907: 245, Florian 1934: 807, or Baumann 1968: 74), was scarcely enacted in legislation or failed to reduce imprisonments.[4] Its inevitable consequence was the impossibility of imposing fines on those who were unable to pay.[5] And this was thought to lead to recidivism (Heüman 1938: 549ff.). To avoid then that the poor would be unpunishable, a compromise was reached: to limit the application of imprisonment for non-payment in cases of proven insolvency.

The compromise consisted of time limits that could not be exceeded in the case of an imposed fine being replaced with a prison sentence.[6] The justification given for this regulation was that if no time limit was set, 'the punishment would be very disproportionate to the offence', and it was advisable to establish imprisonment for fine default 'within certain limits based on fairness that had been neglected' (Vizmanos and Álvarez Martínez 1848: 270). But what was the extent of this disproportion if the module used to substitute a fine with a prison sentence was considered suitable? There was no clear explanation, but evidently it was linked to two aspects. First, those who were clearly unable to pay because of their lack of means should not be treated in the same way as those who fraudulently refused to pay. And second, a prison sentence becomes harder the longer it goes on, while the intensity of a fine penalty does not always increase with a larger amount, this depending on the financial situation of the offender. After all, depriving the offender of an amount he or she needs to live is not the same as depriving him or her of something that is superfluous to covering the most basic needs (see in this regard Rossi 1853: 495–496).

The length of the prison sentence was also limited in the case of small fines. For example, in England it was recommended that imprisonment should be prohibited for fines under five shillings, and detention for not more than 24 hours in police stations cells substituted (Thoday 1934: 32).

Additionally, in some countries it was considered inappropriate to impose imprisonment for fine default on prisoners who were already sentenced to long-term custodial sentences – for example, a whole year in the 1810 French Penal Code, Article 53, a period which could be reduced to six months in cases of less serious crimes, but with the precaution that the right to imprison the insolvent offender would revive if afterwards he became 'possessed of the means of payment' and still did not pay the fine. In Spain there was no imprisonment for default for offenders already condemned to at least four years or more, according to the 1848 Penal Code, Article 49. As Teruel Carralero (1956: 74–75) observed, it was

> the clear wish of the legislator not to lengthen the prison sentence excessively by applying this method of paying the fine, to limit it, as he does not dare to delete what, parodying Silvela, could be called the punishment of the poor, which is increasingly at odds with current legal ideas.

However, a way that was not explored at all was the reduction of fines to relatively affordable levels, as it had been the case in previous centuries. The explanation lies in the new use of fines as an alternative to imprisonment. As O'Malley (2009: 43; 2013: 377) explained,

> fines could not be reduced to trifling levels – unlike in the eighteenth century – because these fines were to appear as a plausible alternative to a significant deprivation of liberty. Basement-priced fines could only be legitimated where prison was not an alternative.

Only when committal to prison was an impossibility could very small fines be imposed – but for regulatory offences, not crimes.

The long route towards the day fine

The limited effect of the measures mentioned earlier led to the correctional criticism of short-term prison sentences being broadened to include fine penalties towards the end of the nineteenth century. For example, in Spain the literature, influenced by correctionalist approaches but also by the socio-economic reality, adopted viewpoints that were completely unfavourable towards pecuniary punishments (Vida 1885: 58, 68; Armengol y Cornet 1894: 57; Bernaldo de Quirós 1898: 306; Bernaldo de Quirós and Navarro de Palencia 1911: 598), or at the very most they expressed resigned acceptance considering them the lesser of two evils compared to short-term prison sentences (Arenal 1890: 321), with some notable exceptions (Silvela 1874: 318). In Italy it was also emphasized that given the fact that a large part of the population was trapped in abject poverty, the fine was a penalty that should be abolished since in reality it automatically turned into a prison sentence. Ciccarelli (1897: 655) described it as an 'iniquity', nothing more than a 'punishment of poverty'. The same view was held in Switzerland, where

Stooβ (1916: 5ff.) spoke of the fine as a 'privilege of the rich', and also in Austria and Germany, where Wahlberg (1877: 239), Felisch (1895: 300), and Merkel (1895: 387) pointed out that imprisonment for fine defaulters gave the administration of justice the nature of a justice of classes, since the rich man pays, while the poor man goes to prison. In the United Kingdom, the Commission on Criminal Law held in its Seventh Report on the Criminal Law of 1843 that 'the magnitude of a fine must in justice be proportioned to the offender's means'. By way of justification, it was stated, 'if a specific fine be set, the effect must still be oppressive and unequal in its operation. The same fine may be of little importance to the rich man, but ruinous to one in humbler circumstances' (Commission on Criminal Law 1843: 106). This negative viewpoint made it necessary to propose either abolishing the fine or making significant amendments to its regulations. Correctional rationale strongly supported innovations to deal with the problem of fine default (Seagle 1948: 250–252). A new juridical reasoning began to emerge. It was not related to a 'new' bourgeois philosophy on punishment, because most of the authors in the criminological and criminal field were still Benthamite in form and essence. The pivotal change was to be seen not only in their beliefs in the role of prisons as correctional institutions (Grebing 1982: 8) but also in the increased questioning of the idea of 'equal punishments for equal crimes'. In essence, many believed that the seriousness of the offence as well as the personality and unique circumstances of the offender had to be taken into account when determining the punishment (Saleilles 1911: 57–61 and 187–188), while simultaneously recognizing those who observed that the only merit of prisons in terms of the equality principle was that they were 'equally harmful for everybody' (Michaux 1872: 189). This shift promoted eliminating the aspects of fines that made payment difficult for low-income persons. In other words, the key idea was to adapt fines to the offender's financial situation in an effort to render prison sentences for non-payment unnecessary.

Three different techniques were adopted in order to avoid imprisonment for fine defaulters: taking the means of the offender into account, giving time to pay (payment by instalments), and paying off the fine by working. No solution was found for the cases of people with no income, since it was generally recognized that an endeavour to keep an offender out of prison by imposing a fine the offender cannot meet is entirely wrong. De facto, the fine simply worked as a deferred prison sentence. In this case only the alternative of working in public works was considered acceptable, with a minority asking for the remission of the penalty (Stooβ 1907: 246).

Taking into account the fortune of the offender

Some legislation of the *ancien régime* had already admitted clauses determining the amount of the fine based on the greater or lesser wealth of the offender,[7] and the same approach can be seen in some of the first European criminal codes.[8] In *The Rationale of Punishment* Bentham had also pointed to the possibility of the amount of the fine taking into account 'the fortune of the offender', as well as the profit of the offence, the value of the thing which is the subject matter of the offence, and the amount of the injury. Specifically, as we have seen, he stated that in order to guarantee equality of impact the most appropriate way of proceeding was to establish a percentage of the offender's wealth (1811: Chapter 4, Section 2.3). Montesquieu (1748: Book 6, Chapter 18), Blackstone (1769: Book 4, Chapter 29), Filangieri (1788: Book 3, second part, Chapter 32), Pastoret (1790: 149), Ørsted (1818: 373),[9] and others made similar assertions. At the time, theirs was a minority viewpoint in continental Europe, where two arguments supported the fact that the offender's financial situation was *not* to be taken into account when fixing the amount of the fine.

First, the establishment of fixed penalties that did not leave courts too much latitude was aimed at combatting the arbitrariness of the *ancien régime*. It was clearly desired that the fine did not become a type of general confiscation of the offender's assets, a measure that had been abused during the *ancien régime* and which, after the Enlightened criticisms (Beccaria 1764: Chapter 25; Voltaire's *Commentaries* of 1766: Chapter 21; Von Feuerbach 1804: 163–164), was forbidden in the first constitutions.[10] This is precisely why

> if the fine must not turn into confiscation, the judge must be given ample latitude to apply it, since the intensity of this penalty depends on the financial situation of the offender; consequently, [the Penal Code] gives the courts the authority to *make use of the full length of the law when imposing this penalty* [. . .] informs the judge which reason should be used to guide him when determining the amount of the fine; and without leading the courts to disregard the mitigating and aggravating circumstances of the offence, it advises them to consider *the wealth or affluence of the offender* [. . .] So, if the judicial equity takes into account the individual circumstances of the offender, this penalty can be applied to a fairer proportion, and only then can we avoid the situation of confiscation occurring and being concealed as a fine.
>
> (Vizmanos and Álvarez Martínez 1848: 306–307, italics in the original)

The need to break away from the *ancien régime* also bore some relation with the wish to prevent the courts from having to investigate thoroughly to determine what the offender possessed, as this procedure had inquisitorial overtones (Aurioles Montero 1849: 95–96; Rossi 1853: 496), and could be perceived by the offender as even harsher than the penalty itself (Ørsted 1818: 374–375).

Second, the equality principle, stated in the first constitutions, was understood to be a formal equality in terms of rights and obligations and in rewards and punishments, which prevented or advised against establishing differences based on the wealth of offenders.[11] This reaction was understandable given that the fine had been used as a privilege of the rich during the previous centuries. But what was considered at the time to be a manifestation of the equality principle – that punishments were imposed on everyone to the same extent – appeared as a manifestation of inequality at the end of the nineteenth century (Puccioni 1855: 204–205; Ortolan

1874: 245; Viada y Vilaseca 1890: 467; Bertola 1893: 549–550; Armengol y Cornet 1894: 56; Birkmeyer 1901: 1064, 1067; Vila Miquel 1917: 169–170). The reason why is that equality can pull in two directions: on the one hand, towards the achievement of formal equality related to the seriousness of the crime; and, on the other hand, towards material equality related to the offender's level of income. The latter followed the former during the transition into the twentieth century.

In practice, this first viewpoint led to the belief that it was unfair to determine the amount of the fine based on the financial capacity of the offender, because the amount set for the fine would not be proportionate to the seriousness of the offence, but rather would depend on external circumstances (Carrara 1871: 464–465). From the German perspective of the internal structure of the theory of crime and punishment, Von Stenglein (1892: 272–273), Merkel (1893: 351), and Berolzheimer (1907: 255) saw no sense in taking the offender's financial circumstances into account when determining the punishment as they bore no relation whatsoever to the level of culpability. They argued that the solvent offender was richer, not guiltier, and what should, in general, be considered positively must not be turned into a disadvantage in the penal domain. Arguments were lodged against this objection, stating that when determining the punishment, the level of culpability should be considered as well as the type of punishment that should be imposed. The key idea was that culpability, as an element of the crime related to retribution, cannot be considered in a purely objective manner and limited to the criminal act, but rather its subjective aspect must be taken into account, in the sense that the suffering inflicted must be truly felt by the offender. Therefore, the attention paid to the offender's financial capacity was not incompatible with the basis used for determining the punishment (Goldschmidt 1908: 402–403; Thyrén 1910: 74; Rauh 1912: 32). And there was no shortage of defenders of the idea that the rich man who committed a crime is, in fact, guiltier, because he has greater means and abilities to uphold the law than the person who does with fewer resources (Bonneville de Marsangy 1864: 289; Vila Miquel 1917: 143).[12]

Indeed, in the first half of the nineteenth century a formal conception of equality in the justification of the penal fine prevailed. As addressed before, the first penal codes adopted tariff and fixed-fine systems as a way of limiting the arbitrariness in the assessment of fines: the 1810 French Penal Code (followed by the 1822 Spanish Penal Code, and also by the Prussian Penal Code), abandoning the rejection of the fine in the first 1791 French Penal Code, established a fine penalty with an amount fixed between two precise limits from within which the judge, without having to consider the financial situation of the offender, must determine the exact amount. Tariff and fixed-fine systems were based upon understandings that the same or similar amounts of money should be imposed on all defendants coming before the court convicted of a particular offence. However, it was also clear that the same fine amount for all offenders sentenced for the same crime made the punitive impact of fine sentences comparatively less for more affluent offenders, since these systems tend to depress fine amounts in order to adapt them to the lowest common economic denominator of offenders in one determined country (a problem already identified by writers and thinkers across Europe, such as Filangieri 1788: Book 3, second part, Chapter 32; Carrara 1871: 464; and Gutmann 1909: 127–128).

In spite of the legal situation, the problem of imprisonment for fine defaulters made it necessary to propose either abolishing the fine or introducing significant innovations to deal with the problem of defaulters. If the courts were to impose fines fairly and if fines were to impact on the poor and the rich equally, then fines had to be set in light of the offender's financial situation. However, the primary difficulty was not in deciding that fines should be proportional, but in achieving this objective. Granting the progressive confluence of opinions regarding the need to take the offender's financial situation into account[13] did not spread to other relevant aspects of the fine, such as the concepts that had to be considered when determining the offender's financial capacity. For example, in most common-law countries there was a rather casual approach to performing the calculations, 'usually involving no more than a probation officer's or a social worker's report and thus not significantly slowing the administrative pace of the summary justice machine', according to O'Malley (2009: 53), whereas in continental Europe discussions arose about whether income or assets should be taken into account when determining the fine. The viewpoint of the growing industrial and commercial bourgeoisie, concerned about holding on to their wealth, was that the fine should be determined in accordance with income, as a guarantee against the confiscation of assets (Vizmanos and Álvarez Martínez 1848: 306–307; Aurioles Montero 1849: 96; Rossi 1853: 274–275; Wahlberg 1877: 262; Seidler 1890: 247–249; Goldschmidt 1908: 403). The spread of salaried work also tipped the balance in favour of income, which was relevant to a growing number of people, instead of assets, which concerned only a fairly small sector of the population (as highlighted by Von Lilienthal 1892: 80, who considered assets as a subsidiary criterion).

But it was one thing to say that the fine should be in line with the offender's income and another thing to determine what this income was. The concern for avoiding state intrusion into citizens' financial affairs led to the proposal that only known, manifest, or officially certified income should be taken into account (Wahlberg 1872: 136; Lammasch 1891: 232); the annually paid income tax (Krohne 1889: 236; Von Liszt 1889b: 45; Rosenfeld 1892: 187; Goldschmidt 1908: 402; Runkel-Langsdorff 1908: 43; Thyrén 1910: 79); or the census, which listed the people obliged to pay tax (Mittelstädt 1891: 63). Beyond these differences, these proposals were based on the need to rationalize the calculation system and to make it more predictable. This was opposed by those who believed that it was not the remit of criminal law to undertake financial investigations (e.g., Stooβ 1907: 243). In countries with a less developed tax system, such as Spain, it was proposed that disposable income would be certified by the mayor and four dignitaries (Vila Miquel 1917: 146), while in Italy a certificate from the local authorities was indeed required to prove the offender's insolvency (1865 Code of Criminal Procedure, Article 595). All this was aimed at avoiding enquiries into 'family secrets', thereby adding 'upheaval or indignity to the fine' (Vizmanos and Álvarez Martínez 1848: 307; also see Rossi 1853: 496), based on the fact that '[o]ur ideas do not allow for an inquisition into the possessions of each individual. The courts, on the other hand, would attempt this in vain. This cannot, and must not, happen' (Pacheco 1856: 415). Soon it was recommended to consider sufficient the information voluntarily provided by the offender (Getz 1893: 8ff.). However, proposals focusing on establishing the fine based on the income declared by the offender did not take hold. They tried to incorporate concepts which had been designed primarily for those who have money and would most likely be affected by tax law with other ideas which considered in particular people belonging to the poorer classes, who were more likely to be subjected to criminal law alone (Roldán Barbero 1983: 31). Taxes are not comparable to fines, although the sums of both are received by the state. As Von Buri (1878: 242) said,

> the exclusive essence of the fine is that the offender experiences, through its enforcement, a reduction of his wealth, that makes him poorer than he was previously. That a third party, especially the State, should accrete an asset upon payment of the fine is, in contrast, merely secondary. The money received from the offender could be appropriated, destroyed or thrown away, and the essence of the fine would still be intact.

The initial proposals regarding the proportion of the offender's income were quite demanding. For example, Garofalo (1887: 106–108) understood that, when dealing with solvent offenders, it was appropriate to take the proportion of their income that exceeded what was absolutely essential to cover their basic living needs, for board and lodging – what Albrecht (2001: 311) calls the principle of strict economy. These needs were calculated as what was strictly necessary to avoid starving, without the slightest consideration given to their social status and their accustomed lifestyle. However, opinions were soon expressed regarding the need to consider not only family duties but also the difference between what was superfluous and what was necessary, because 'a quarter of the daily income of a well-to-do gentleman is not the same proportion, although it may seem to be, as a quarter of the daily income of a manual worker' (Vizmanos and Álvarez Martínez 1848: 307, quoting Bentham to support this view). This concern, widespread in European literature,[14] foreshadowed the establishment of the fine as a penalty that deprives offenders of their income that is not strictly necessary for their personal maintenance and family duties – in other words, a penalty that deprives them of the *excess* that they could otherwise spend on consumption or leisure (as formulated by Baumann 1968: 71).

The difficulties inherent in determining the financial situation of the offender led to some penal codes and drafts initially adopting detailed formulas that were gradually simplified until they were mere programmatic declarations, without actually determining how they should be specified in judicial practice. That was the case in Norway, if we compare 1893 Getz's second draft for a penal code, § 22, and the final adopted formulation of the 1902 Norwegian General Civil Penal Code, Section 27.[15] Others, like the Spanish penal codes, experienced oscillating progress regarding this issue.[16] Some legislation, like the 1852 Portuguese Penal Code, Article 41, used from the beginning very general formulations which failed to offer a clue about how to calculate the offender's income, a fact that often resulted in courts imposing fines judging only 'by outward appearances' (Jordão 1853: 133–134). Another example is the 1871 German Imperial Penal Code, § 27c, which stated merely that the court had to 'consider the economic circumstances of the offender in calculating a fine'. Aside from these examples, we must not forget that there were countries that did not follow this path at all, like Italy.[17] The fact is that in the judicial practice of the European countries considered here the general tendency was not to make too many enquiries into the offender's level of income, essentially relying solely on information from the defendant and his or her counsel (Roldán Barbero 1983: 25). The high degree of confidence given to this self-reported information from average offenders was mostly supported by scarce verification efforts. It would have been possible, however, for the courts to have a great deal more information, and without major structural reforms, if they had asked for it. They did not, however, mostly because they lacked the time to do so. Nevertheless, courts were less confident about the accuracy of reports received from higher-income offenders, in which case they tended to use what they knew about the offender, including information about his or her residence, occupation, number of children, and so on. Anyway, in many cases it was not until the fined person defaulted that any real attempt was made to establish a means enquiry. This method of proceeding still goes on today, despite the enormous possibilities of cross-checking data offered by computer systems.

Giving time to pay: fine payment by instalments

If considering the financial means of the offender is linked to setting the amount of the fine, establishing instalments for split payments is related to the enforcement of the punishment once set, affecting the amount only indirectly.

The idea that a payment period had to be set in line with the offender's circumstances when immediate payment of the fine could lead to his or her ruin had already been discussed at the end of the eighteenth century. For example, Filangieri (1788: Book 3, second part, Chapter 32) suggested granting payment periods and reinforcing the obligation to pay by suspending civil rights until the offender had paid the fine imposed on him in full. In fact, the granting of payment periods had been introduced in some of the first nineteenth-century penal codes (e.g., the 1822 Spanish Penal Code, Article 91) and statutes (e.g., the Italian royal decree no. 2701 of December 23, 1865, of *tariffa penale*, Articles 237ff.). Therefore, it is not exactly true that the idea of payment of fines by instalments was a very innovative one, as O'Malley (2009: 52–53) maintains when he wrote, 'It was a high-profile commercial innovation that criminal justice would borrow and adapt – a manoeuvre that unintentionally brought paying a fine and purchasing a commodity one step closer to each other'. However, its expansion was indeed intimately related to the beginnings of a mass consumer culture. The invention of techniques of buying through instalments created a market where otherwise none could have existed. Modern instalment selling of durable goods was first introduced in the United States in 1807, the year in which a furniture store by the name of Cowperthwaite & Sons opened in New York City and immediately began offering instalment terms to its customers, but it was a very limited practice prior to the American Civil War (Seligman 1927: 14). After the war, manufacturers of pianos, organs, encyclopaedias, and stoves were quick to broaden their markets by providing for instalment payments. The automobile credit, which began in 1910, became the single largest component of consumer instalment credit, contributing decisively to the expansion of road traffic in the first half of the twentieth century. The instalment system also became rapidly common in criminal law, being enthusiastically supported by literature (Merkel 1889: 227). Granting payment periods expanded the penal market and enabled fines to be imposed on individuals who were unable to pay them previously. O'Malley (2009: 52) relates this innovation to the emergence of a speedier procedure that rendered it possible to enormously expand the volume of court-based governance: 'the fine and its correlative summary forms of justice were creating a condition of existence of a regulatory state'. This thesis is highly suggestive. However, it does not fully take into account the differences between the legal cultures of different countries. In late industrializing countries, such as Italy or Spain, this process, broadly related to the invention of the automobile and the need to regulate road traffic, as well as to the expansion of a consumer culture, took place much later, after the first third of the twentieth century, and only in regulatory law. Thus, in these countries the introduction of the instalment system in criminal law during the second half of the nineteenth century did not have the effect described by O'Malley (for Italy, see Puccioni 1855: 213; for Spain, Roldán Barbero 1983: 55).

But did the use of instalments reduce imprisonment for fine default? If at the beginning of the nineteenth century the concern was focused on whether paying the fine could deprive an offender of the means or instruments necessary for his trade or profession and thus disastrously ruin him and his family (Marcos Gutiérrez 1826: 148), the focus at the end of the nineteenth century and beginning of the twentieth had shifted to enabling the payment of the fine so that it was no longer necessary to impose prison sentences as a subsidiary punishment (Puccioni 1855: 213; Merkel 1889: 227; Glauning 1905: 288; Goldschmidt 1908: 407–408; Vila Miquel 1917: 150). Payment by instalments was introduced to avoid crowding the prisons with people who could not pay their fines, by helping to minimize the possibility of default. The experience of some countries shows, however, that legal reform is not enough. There also needs to be a change in mentality in those applying the law, and the appropriate national economic conditions to facilitate such reform. The case of England is a clear example of the need for a change of mind. Germany, on the other hand, is a good case of non-conducive economic conditions preventing the success of innovative legal changes.

It seems almost incredible today that in England in 1904 the total number of imprisonments for non-payment of fines was more than 108,000, 'equivalent to about 20 per cent of all those fined' (Radzinowicz and Hood 1986: 649; see also Bottoms 1983: 201). In 1913, 49.6 per cent of all males and 68.2 per cent of all females received in English prisons were there in default of fines (Fox 1936: 199; Rusche and Kirchheimer 1939 [2003]: 169). The fact is that although the 1879

Summary Jurisdiction Act first permitted English courts, when imposing fines, to allow time for payment, to authorize payment by instalment, to take security for payment, or to suspend collection of the fine subject to conditions, the courts did not take advantage of these provisions. Although the Home Office issued a lengthy circular in 1905 reminding courts of the serious hardships which would result from failure to use these provisions, the number of imprisonments for non-payment of fines remained approximately constant. It was reduced drastically during the next 30 years, even though the fine was the penalty with the greatest increase in the period. The tendency to reduce the number of defaulters in prison goes back to the 1914 Criminal Justice Administration Act, which was responsible for a sharp fall from an average of 83,187 prisoners in default of fines in the period 1909–1913 to 13,433 in the period 1925–1930 (Report of the Commissioners of Prisons and Directors of Convict Prisons for the year 1935: 8–9), while maintaining the number of people fined. As Sutherland (1934: 890) highlighted, 'The annual average number of persons fined in the period 1905–1909 was 498,958, of whom 19.6 percent were committed to prisons in default of payment, while in 1930 the number fined was 496,139, of whom only 2 percent were committed to prison in default'. In fact, imprisonment for default decreased abruptly after the enactment of the 1914 Act.

The 1914 Act provided that a court of summary jurisdiction, when imposing a fine, should grant the offender time to pay the fine unless the offender was able to pay the fine immediately or had no fixed abode within the jurisdiction of the court, or unless the court for other reasons decided that time should not be granted. This meant that the courts had to consider the means of the offender so far as they appeared or were known to them. On the other hand, the circumstances under which a warrant of commitment could be issued forthwith were restricted, these

Figure 4.1 Commitment to prison for non-payment of fines (total numbers), England: 1905–1930 (by five-year periods)

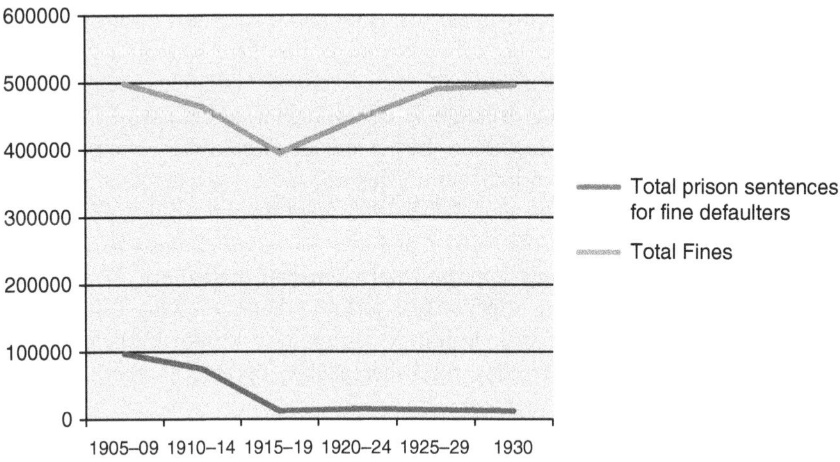

Source: Adapted from Sutherland (1934: 891).

Table 4.1 Commitment to prison for non-payment of fines (total numbers and percentages), England: 1905–1930 (by five-year periods)

Year (by five-year periods)	*Fines*	*Prison sentences for fine defaulters*	*% fines converted into imprisonment without giving time to pay*	*% fines converted into imprisonment after giving time to pay*
1905–09	498,958	97,858	19.6	0.0
1910–14	465,092	75,444	16.2	0.0
1915–19	394,913	12,253	2.7	0.4
1920–24	446,524	15,057	2.8	0.6
1925–29	490,790	13,842	1.9	0.9
1930	496,139	12,497	1.6	0.9

Source: Adapted from Sutherland (1934: 891).

circumstances being where the court was satisfied that the defendant was 'possessed of sufficient means to enable him to pay', where he expressed no desire for time to pay, where he failed to satisfy the court that he was of fixed abode, or where the court believed there was some other 'special reason' which warranted giving time to pay inappropriate. Based on the available statistical data, it is difficult to determine whether the decrease in imprisonment for defaulters is mainly due to the courts giving time to pay. The number of imprisoned fine defaulters who had not been granted time to pay their fines decreased from 97,859 – 19.6 per cent of fines imposed – in the period 1905–1909 to 8,063 – 1.6 per cent – in 1930. But the number committed in default *after* receiving time to pay the fine only slightly increased from 0 in 1905–1909 to 4,434 in 1930 – about 1 per cent of the total number of persons fined in that year (Sutherland 1934: 891–892).

We do not have the percentage of fines paid in full after receiving time to pay, but presumably that is the explanation. Sutherland (1934: 890) also considered the possibility of the decrease being due to better economic conditions, but in this regard he observed, 'Improvements in economic conditions during the War undoubtedly assisted in reducing this percentage, but there was no appreciable increase in the percentage after the War, when economic conditions became more difficult'. The fact is that the decrease in commitments in default of fines was approximately equal to the increase in the percentage of offenders who paid their fines in full, at least for non-indictable offences: '65.6 percent of all dispositions for non-indictable offenses in 1905–1909 were fines paid; this percentage increased slightly to 67.3 in 1910–1914, and then increased abruptly to 82.6 percent in 1915–1919, remaining approximately constant thereafter'. This means that the 1914 Act had a strong effect on less serious crimes, allowing a significant rise in the percentage of fines paid in full. As Briggs et al. (1996: 239) clearly put it, 'During the succeeding decades, fines increasingly became an alternative to, rather than a cause of, imprisonment'.

Additionally, the 1935 Money Payments (Justices' Procedure) Act gave the courts power to deal with applications for extensions to pay fines irrespective of whether the time originally allowed had expired. Courts were required, in dealing with such applications, to allow more time unless they believed that the failure to pay had been wilful or that the offender had no reasonable prospect of being able to pay if more time were allowed. Following the granting of time to pay, the Act also provided that a warrant of commitment could not be issued until a post-conviction means inquiry had been conducted in the offender's presence. Courts could still determine that 'special reason' made it expedient that the defaulter be imprisoned without such an inquiry. According to the aforementioned Report of the Commissioners of Prisons and Directors of Convict Prisons from 1935, imprisonments for non-payment of the fine numbered roughly 11,000 per annum during the first half of the 1930s. This figure was substantially reduced in the next years. The statistical data for 1936 show that the first year of the Money Payments (Justices' Procedure) Act brought about a fall of 3,401 in committals for default in payment of fines. In other words, imprisonments fell by approximately 30 per cent, and the number of people received in English prisons for non-payment of fines dropped to about 7,400 per annum (Report of the Commissioners of Prisons and Directors of Convict Prisons for the year 1935: 8; Thoday 1937: 389; Rusche and Kirchheimer 1939 [2003]: 170). The percentage of fined offenders imprisoned for default fell from 3.6 per cent in 1923 to 1.25 per cent in 1938, with a total of 7,936 imprisoned defaulters this year (Manchester 1980: 259). This happened in spite of the sharp increase in fine impositions at courts of summary jurisdiction, from 433,137 in 1923 to 633,929 in 1938. Grünhut (1948: 158) explained that this growth was due to the enforcement of regulations by fine. However, the change was due not only to legislative reforms but also to a new reluctance to impose imprisonment in cases deemed not merited, except as a last resort (Thoday 1937: 388). This reasoning had been observed since the early 1930s, soon after the Home Office Departmental Committee on Imprisonments by Courts of Summary Jurisdiction in default of payment of fines and other sums of money opined in their July 1934 report that not only was it inappropriately punitive to send offenders to prison only because of failure to pay the fine, but also not imprisoning fine defaulters was practical to considerably reduce the prison population.

It seems that once made mandatory *and* accepted, the instalment system may have the desired effect of keeping as many people as possible out of prison.[18] But this is true only while the offenders affected receive an income, no matter how small. If they do not, the correlation between total convictions and imprisonment in default of fines should increase. That was the case of Germany, where the instalment system introduced in the 1920s showed no positive impacts coinciding with a long period of economic crises.

In Germany the instalment system was introduced through legislation passed on October 20, 1923, and February 6, 1924, 20 years after the proposal of the 7th International Penal and Penitentiary Congress held in Budapest in 1905. From then on Paragraph 28 of the 1871 German Imperial Penal Code established that 'if it is not possible to force the offender to pay the fine quickly, given his economic conditions, the court must grant him a payment period or allow him to pay in specified instalments'. After an initial drop in fines levied, probably induced by the high level of inflation and subsequent hyperinflation of the immediate post-war years, up to 1923 and the currency reform of that year (Hellwig 1924: 23), the reforms produced a slow increase in the percentage of fines.

Table 4.2 Prison and fine sentences (total numbers and percentages), German Empire: 1922–1931

Year	*Total sentences*	*Prison*	*Fine*	*% prison*	*% fines*
1922	492,191	200,022	285,939	40.6	58.1
1923	649,495	249,987	391,238	38.4	60.2
1924	512,250	235,190	269,089	45.9	52.5
1925	393,787	174,133	212,347	44.2	53.9
1926	392,969	171,234	215,427	43.5	54.8
1927	389,912	159,811	224,761	40.9	57.6
1928	374,174	148,636	221,037	39.7	59.1
1929	397,472	156,455	236,938	39.3	59.6
1930	418,270	166,895	247,259	39.9	59.1
1931	422,085	178,748	239,218	42.3	56.6

Source: *Reichskriminalstatistik* (1925: 41–50; 1932: 35–56). Only offences against the Reich are included.

The proportionate approach in Figure 4.2 shows the balance between imprisonment and fines during the same period.

Figure 4.2 Prison and fine sentences (percentages), German Empire: 1922–1931

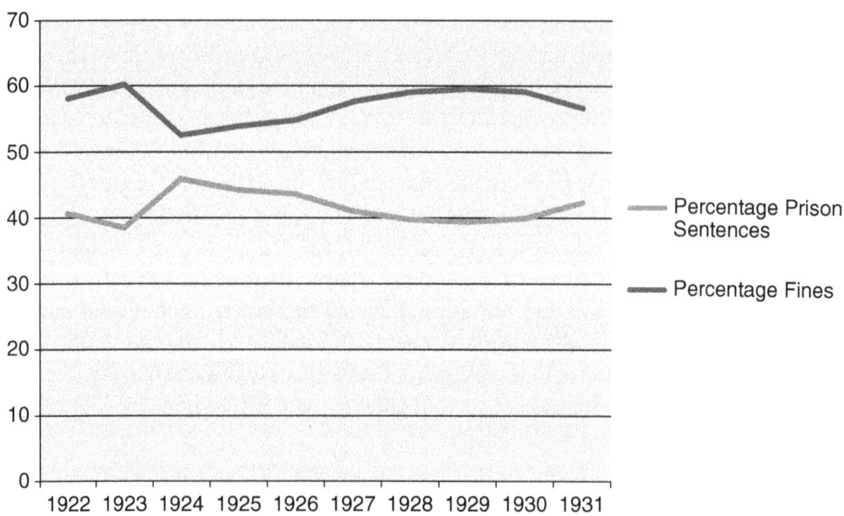

Source: *Reichskriminalstatistik* (1925: 41–50; 1932: 35–56). Only offences against the Reich are included.

But there was no corresponding drop in the percentage of imprisonment by fine default. This was partially due to the difficult economic situation of Germany during the interwar period. Periods of inflation at the beginning of the 1920s and severe unemployment induced by the Great Depression at the end of the decade limited the state's ability to collect fines. The number of defaults went up rapidly.

Table 4.3 Commitment to prison for non-payment of fines (total numbers and percentages), German Empire: 1925–1931

	Fines	*Prison sentences for fine defaulters*	*% fines converted into imprisonment*
1925	337,649	22,653	6.7
1926	437,325	40,186	9.1
1927	454,019	38,641	8.5
1928	461,718	37,360	8.1
1929	449,407	44,085	9.8
1930	440,140	53,027	12.0
1931	383,003	59,076	15.4

Source: *Statistik des deutschen Reichs* (1930: 44ff., 51). All offences against the Reich and the federated states are included.

In Figure 4.3 we can see graphically this development.

Figure 4.3 Imposed fines and commitment to prison for non-payment of fines (total numbers), German Empire: 1925–1931

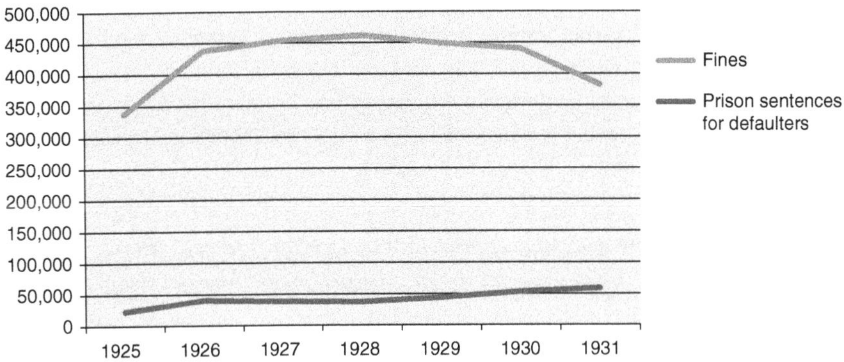

Source: *Statistik des deutschen Reichs* 1930, 44ff., 51. All offences against the Reich and the federated states are included.

However, it is surprising to see that the proportion of fines to total sentences did not decrease during this difficult period (O'Malley 2009: 39). As we will see in Chapter 5, only the ascension of the Nazis to power put a stop to the progress of the fine. This state of affairs continued until the 1970s, when the fine was relaunched with the introduction of the day-fine system.

In any case, the instalment system is applicable only if the offender can afford to meet the deferred payments – in other words, if he or she has sufficient assets or means. This became clear very early on. As with obtaining instalment credit for durable goods, granting time to pay the fine could be dependent on insurance through the repossession or mortgage of property or commercial establishments, if the offender owned such assets, or through the offender's employer garnishing part of his or her wages. Obviously, in these cases granting payment periods was a privilege for those who had the wealth to pay. That was the case in the 1928 Spanish Penal Code, Article 179: it was possible to grant payment periods for the fine to be paid in instalments only when the offender's solvency was clearly apparent (Cuello Calón 1929: 46).[19] This was also the case in Italy, where, pursuant to the royal decree no. 2701 of December 23, 1865, called *di tariffa penale*, payment by instalments was granted only to those who could offer real or personal guarantees (Goisis 2008: 63; Miedico 2008: 63). Only if there was no one who could be ordered to garnish the offender's wages to pay the fine was the offender himself ordered to make a deposit – weekly or monthly – for the proportionate amount of his gross income from work, after submitting the supporting documents or, failing that, a sworn statement.

But, as Rusche and Kirchheimer (1939 [2003]: 171) put it, '[e]fforts to reduce commutation to a minimum by installment payments, and thus to make the fine system applicable to people in very reduced circumstances, can succeed only when the strata affected receive an income no matter how small'. In fact, '[e]ven with means-based fines, poverty and wealth remain difficult issues in the use of monetary penalties. Presumably a totally destitute person should not be sentenced to such a penalty' (Hillsman and Greene 1992: 139). No solution was found for people without any income at all (Von Liszt 1889a: 781; Bertola 1893: 549–550 and 1895: 5–6; Carfora 1928: 1430). If offenders completely lack financial resources, then punishing them through fines is a futile attempt to squeeze blood from the proverbial stone. Recognition that payment of fines by instalments was not possible for those who completely lacked means or employment led to the establishment of payment of the fine by working, with a minority asking unsuccessfully for the remission of the penalty (Stooβ 1907: 246).

Paying off the fine by working: community service for fine defaulters

The third mechanism used to enable payment of the fine without it turning into a substitutive custodial sentence was to allow the offender to work his debt off in the case of insolvency. In this regard, classical reformers, like Beccaria, 'almost always proposed public works as one of the best possible penalties' (Foucault 1977: 109), because for them work in prison or in public works projects could be 'an example for the public or a useful reparation for society' (Foucault 1977: 240). In fact, as we have seen, Beccaria (1764 [1872]: Chapter 22) recommended slavery, understood as appropriation of the offender's work. This proposal found recognition when concerns about the injustice and unfairness of imprisonment for defaulters grew. As Sevdiren (2011: 23) articulated, 'In this respect, it may be argued that the attempts to reduce the use of default detention also gave stimulus to alternative modes of punishment'. The conversion of the unpaid fine into work can have a double meaning (Padovani 1981: 162; Paliero 1986a: 154–155 and 1986b: 95). On the one hand, it can be considered an alternative sanction to the fine, with the work being equivalent to the fine gauged by the length of the subsidiary prison sentence that would otherwise be imposed; on the other hand, it can be used to enable the offender to procure the necessary means in order to pay the imposed fine, being an alternative mode of execution of the fine itself. In the first case, the conversion of the fine into work presupposes that the fine has remained unpaid; in the second case, on the contrary, conversion serves the purpose of avoiding the non-payment of the fine, offering the offender the opportunity to procure the money needed to pay the fine. Whereas free labour in favour of the state or public institutions is a typical example of the second solution, compulsory work, with or without the removal of liberty, with a temporary duration based on the term established for the subsidiary imprisonment in the case of non-payment – for example, two days of work for one day in prison in the 1889 Italian Zanardelli Penal Code, Article 19 – may be considered an example of the first option, although it was, on occasion, also structured as a means of obtaining payment of the fine in kind.[20] The fact is that these possibilities or variants do not exclude each other, but instead may exist within the very same legal system. Without depriving liberty, community service appears to be an acceptable substitute for short-term prison sentences imposed in cases of insolvency when the offender's consent is guaranteed. The fact that the validity of consent can be disputed in such circumstances, where the alternative is custody, worried nobody for a long time.

Next, I will analyse the consolidation process of free work as an alternative to imprisonment in cases of non-payment of the fine. I do not try to give a general view of the transformations in the use of penal labour (for this, see Kilcommins 2002: 277ff.). Instead I focus on understanding the relationship between community service and the payment of the penal fine.

At the end of the nineteenth century, the idea of establishing a punishment of free work, which did not involve deprivation of liberty, began to spread. This proposal, with interesting legislative precedents,[21] was very welcome in the context of criticisms of short-term prison sentences and of imprisonment for defaulters, almost always a short-term prison sentence itself, so work was established as an alternative or substitute punishment and, indirectly, it also became a substitute punishment for unpaid fines. In fact, distinguished representatives of the crusade against short-term imprisonment, like Von Liszt (1889b: 46–47; 1892: 221) and Carrara (1871: 464), expressed their agreement with the creation of a labour sanction that could be used as a substitute for custodial sentences in the case of unpaid fines. Other criminologists, German ones in particular, supported this proposal (Aschrott 1888: 45–46; Krohne 1889: 236; Lammasch 1889: 450; Fuld 1890: 457–458; Rosenfeld 1890: 354; Mittelstädt 1891: 66; Schmölder 1902: 22–25).[22] Community service for fine defaulters was massively supported by German literature during the 23rd German Jurists' Conference (*Juristentag*) in 1895 (Felisch 1895: 280ff.; Merkel 1895: 385ff.). It was also supported by the European one in the 7th International Penal and Penitentiary Congress held in Budapest in 1905 (Barrows 1907). The main reason for this support was that community service adopted a functionally significant element, the rehabilitative effects of working, from custodial sentences without all the negative effects of imprisonment.

However, support for community service was limited to its function as a punishment to replace imprisonment for fine defaulters (Bonneville de Marsangy

1864: 302–303; Merkel 1889: 281–282; Von Liszt 1905: 388; Galdo 1908: 50–51; Heilborn 1908: 55; Rauh 1912: 88–89; Vila Miquel 1917: 151ff.). There are two factors explaining this limited support. First, the idea at the time was to increase the role of the monetary sanction in the penal system, with the aim that it could replace short-term imprisonment. To do this it was necessary to find an appropriate measure to replace imprisonment for defaulters, which was seen as grossly unfair. This measure appeared to be forced labour without imprisonment. Second, the relationship between the fine and work seemed to be mediated by the value of the work the offender must undertake for the benefit of the community. It was considered doubtful that it would be possible to achieve results of a similar economic value as those achieved by a normal worker (Heilborn 1908: 57; Mohr 1913: 55). What gave meaning to the punishment was not simply the fact that the offender had to work for a certain amount of time on a specific activity, but that the fruits of his labour were given back to the community. From this perspective, implementing community service was a kind of reversal (implicit) turning imprisonment into a monetary sanction, replacing time with value, according to an idea that was extremely widespread at the end of the nineteenth century and the start of the twentieth (e.g., Bonneville de Marsangy 1864: 354–355). For example, the 1885 Michaux project, Article 4, explicitly allowed punishments for offenders sentenced to *emprisonnement* to be substituted with community work for a similar number of days, converting these work days into a fine equal to their assessment: '*de convertir ces journées de travail en une amende égale à leur évaluation*' (Rosenfeld 1890: 343).

At the same time, this close relationship between the fine and community service was seen clearly in the doctrinal debate about whether the work should be compulsory or free. A significant doctrinal sector was in favour of the work being undertaken without compulsion (Bonneville de Marsangy 1864: 293; Von Holtzendorff 1864: 654; Silvela 1874: 411; Stooß 1891: 347ff.; Goldschmidt 1908: 410; Heilborn 1908: 57–58; Rauh 1912: 88; Carfora 1928: 1440). Two arguments justified this proposal. First was the idea that the punishment imposed in substitution of the fine should remain as similar as possible to the nature of the monetary punishment. In fact, it was thought that there was no sanction more suitable to be turned into money than work (Bonneville de Marsangy 1864: 293; Silvela 1874: 411; Rosenfeld 1890: 316, 327), underscored by the idea that non-forced work was closely related to a monetary sanction, since 'this system resembles that of paying in installments' (7th International Penal and Penitentiary Congress held in Budapest in 1905, in Barrows 1907: 30). Von Liszt (1889a: 764) clearly stated that sentencing offenders to work was a monetary sanction, as the limitation of personal freedom was pushed almost completely into the background.[23] The offender's consent to perform community service was finally required in the first legal regulations, such as the 1889 Italian Zanardelli Penal Code. The main reason has a very practical nature: community service is thought to be ineffective in the case of a totally uncooperative offender, since the offender would be unlikely to complete his or her sentence satisfactorily. 'The requirement of consent thus bars some offenders who are unsuitable in any case' (Young 1979: 28). Added to this is the fact that since the work was undertaken 'freely', it was easier to overcome the resistance shown by employers and unions to the work of offenders (Baumann 1968: 75). The present-day version of a voluntarily undertaken obligation has also been shaped by an international consensus against forced labour crystalized in international instruments, such as the Convention concerning Forced or Compulsory Labour of the International Labour Organization (1930 Forced Labour Convention, no. 29), the Convention for the Protection of Human Rights and Fundamental Freedoms of the Council of Europe (The 1950 Convention of Rome), the Convention concerning the Abolition of Forced Labour of the ILO (The 1957 Abolition of Forced Labour Convention, no. 105), and the International Covenant on Civil and Political Rights (The 1966 New York Convention).

The second idea behind the proposal for voluntary work, as a protection for the wealthier classes, was that the work cannot be compulsory because 'it would be very strange indeed to force someone who has never done manual work to suddenly work on the construction of a public highway or a building intended for public use' (Carfora 1928: 1440). This observation was related to the concern to assign tasks to each person that were similar to the jobs he or she usually did outside the penal system; in short, middle- or upper-class people would not have to do manual work (Von Lilienthal 1892: 84–85). In fact, it was even stated that replacing the fine with work would be applicable only to labourers or, in general, to those who were able to do manual work. These proposals were fiercely opposed by those who, like Mittelstädt (1891: 66), thought that this involved the introduction of unjustifiable inequality. In the end, they contributed to the evolution of the work sentence into a manual labourers' penalty.

With some exceptions,[24] the first legal regulations for community service as a substitute punishment for unpaid fines emerged in legislation with a very specific purpose, reforestation: for example, the General Ordinance of the Kingdom of Saxony concerning procedures in forestry cases (*General-Verordnung betreffend das Verfahren in Forst-Untersuchungssachen*) of November 30, 1814, the French Forest Code (*Code forestier*) of May 21, 1827, or the Prussian Law on Forest Theft (*Gesetz betreffend den Forstdiebstahl*) of February 20, 1879. As there was the need for manpower for a specific task, offenders could be put to work, making this penalty extremely economical for the state (Bonneville de Marsangy 1864: 302). There were attempts to generalize this punishment beyond offences involving forestry issues, especially in Germany, where it was possible to find interesting legal precedents, as we have seen. By the end of the nineteenth century and the beginning of the twentieth century, community service as an alternative to a fine or its subsidiary punishment of deprivation of liberty was introduced in a number of Western European countries, such as Germany, Italy, Switzerland, and Norway. However, various problems emerged, both of a theoretical and practical nature. Those of a theoretical nature included the concern for the justice of a solution that forced the poor to work, while the rich could simply pay a sum of money. The observation was also made that work is not punishment; we are in fact fortunate to be able to work, and therefore linking a penalty and work together devalues the notion of work. Those of a practical nature pertain to the lack of alternatives for offenders who were unable to work, the (un)availability of suitable work for all insolvent offenders, mostly because of lack of organization, and the possible competition to free work. Let us analyse these problems in more detail.

The first theoretical problem relates, once again, to the way the equality principle is understood. On one hand, it is true that leaving it to the offender to choose whether he worked or paid the fine was beneficial to the wealthier classes. But, on the other hand, the possibility of avoiding a custodial sentence in the case of non-payment by carrying out public work meant that insolvent offenders who could not pay the fine even if they wanted to could avoid imprisonment (Von Holtzendorff 1864). This notion carried more weight with legislators, as evidenced by the Law Commission's justification of this novelty in the preamble of the project that would culminate in the 1928 Spanish Penal Code, in the following terms:

> the Commission thought it was time to implement, in our legislation, the radical reform required in the name of justice and criminal science, suppressing subsidiary imprisonment for insolvency, which divides offenders into two classes, the rich and the poor, imposing custodial sentences, with all they entail, on those lacking means, while, in contrast, others may redeem themselves by paying a fine even though they may have worse morals but they are fortunate enough to dispose of a sum of money to pay the sanction imposed on them for the offence they committed, with no personal sacrifice.

The fact that such a reform had not yet been passed was not due to a lack of proposals – including those stated in legislative drafts, like the Ugarte project (1906: 112), the first to establish the replacement of all custodial sentences shorter than six months with a fine for solvent offenders and neighbourhood work for offenders lacking financial means – but was rather due to the fact that organizing compulsory work without a custodial sentence 'involves, or rather demands, a state of progress in administrative bodies that we will take years to achieve' (Armengol y Cornet 1894: 56; see more optimistic Vila Miquel 1917: 151–152). In fact, it took nearly a century to achieve this.

Regarding the second theoretical objection, posed by those who considered that a work punishment devalued work itself (Von Thielau 1837, quoted by Rosenfeld 1890: 323ff.; Buchwald 1948: 213), this perspective was soon challenged as being incorrect, as the punishment was not having to work but rather having to work for no pay. It could therefore be said that this punishment was simply a fine enforced in a different manner (Rosenfeld 1890: 237). In short, the punishment indirectly reduced the offender's wealth (Brenn 1945: 61).

The problem of a lack of alternatives for offenders who were unable to work because of poor health prompted a fair amount of debate at a time when community work was physically very hard. Those who were unable to do such work seemed inevitably doomed to prison, thereby being unfavourably compared to those who, while capable, refused to work. This led to some authors (Felisch 1895: 366; Stooß 1907: 246) proposing alternatives, like conditional sentences or other ways of suspending punishment, or waiving any penal measure (Mittelstädt

1879: 87; Krohne 1889: 230). This sparked criticism, particularly from those who feared that non-existent illnesses would be feigned in an effort to gain milder penalties (Heilborn 1908: 59).

The unavailability of suitable work for all insolvent offenders remains unresolved in many countries today. At the end of the nineteenth century this issue was raised as an organizational one. The argument was that only salaried manual work could be imposed as a penalty to replace a fine. However, since anyone could perform such work, concerns were raised about the feasibility of properly controlling and assessing the quality of office work or craftwork (Von Liszt 1889b: 46–47, explaining that it would be applied only to the poor – i.e., to the working class who would otherwise be insolvent – with it being very simple to replace an unpaid fine with days of work based on a daily wage; Stooß 1891: 352). In more general terms, it was also noted that the lack of organizational means meant it was necessary to limit the application of this penalty to cases of replacing an unpaid fine, and it was not advisable to extend this use further (Von Liszt 1889b: 46–47, 1889a: 779–781; Rosenfeld 1890: 343), to rural zones (Rosenfeld 1890: 349) or to minor offences (Lammasch 1889: 479).

In effect, it requires considerable organizational effort to create enough jobs for all those sentenced to this penalty. Community service is developed only within a framework of close cooperation with the community, which not only is the beneficiary of the activity but also is involved in the execution of the penalty. This community involvement is linked to a way of thinking in which the community takes a role in resolving criminal problems which the state is unable to find a solution for on its own. But the conditions of expansion of community service can be seen only with the emergence of the welfare state (Kilcommins 2002). Success depends to a large extent upon a good infrastructure. In 1910 Italy, the scarce use of compulsory work as a replacement for imprisonment for unpaid fines was lamented (Conti 1910: 502). In 1925 it was still evident that the state lacked the organizational ability necessary to implement community service as a substitute for short-term imprisonment (De Marsico 1925: 280). In Germany, the only available statistical data regarding community service are for the Free State of Thuringia. According to the Imperial Statistics (Reichsstatistik 1930: 45), only 5.8 per cent of the fined offenders paid their fines through community service. In 1939 Rusche and Kirchheimer (1939 [2003]: 176) could still say, 'The apparatus for the administration of criminal justice is not adjusted to such positive activity, nor is it expected to be so adjusted under the prevailing conceptions'. The possible competition to free work is still cited today as an argument against community service. Negative effects in terms of stress on labour opportunities for the general population are feared (Pfohl 1983: 33; Paliero 1986a: 165). The same happened regarding prison labour. Beginning in mid-nineteenth-century France, workers periodically objected to the unfair competition presented by the reduced wages of the prisoners and demanded a stop to prison productions (O'Brien 1995: 204). The issue was clearly expressed in its day by Felisch (1895: 334ff.): the wages to be paid for community service would have to be lower than those paid for free work, which would lead the state and employers to employ convicts rather than labourers. From the point of view of the working class, the state should first consider the need for work of those who have not committed offences. From the point of view of the ruling class, suspicion was rife about the potential contact between convicts and free workers, as it was feared that this would lead to an increase in social unrest, and in particular in the proclamation of a right to work in a social democratic or socialist sense. Businessmen and manufacturers also protested over low labour costs of convicts from another perspective: they feared that the state's unfair advantage of a captive work force with minimal costs would undercut prices and destroy their businesses (O'Brien 1995: 204). Opposition from unions and worker associations and the lack of interest from employers, which was mirrored by similar disinterest from the government in terms of producing the necessary governing regulations, were two of the most significant factors that led to the failure of free work as a substitute for unpaid fines as established in German legislation in the 1920s (Pfohl 1983: 30; Pritikin 2010: 365–367). In other countries, legal limitations were introduced: for example, Italian regulation prohibited regular employees as well as positions required by law from being staffed by community service workers (Italian Law no. 689 of November 24, 1981, amending the criminal justice system – *di modifiche al sistema penale*).

The truth is that the consolidation of an alternative like the one analysed was not possible until minimum standards of dignified and humane working conditions were achieved. According to the principle of less eligibility,[25] it was difficult for social actors and legal scholars to accept the generalized implementation of a work penalty that left offenders free when at the time many sections of the 'free' population were working in almost inhuman conditions, as occurred with the first industrial proletariat (Rusche and Kirchheimer 1939 [2003]; Kilcommins 2002: 222ff.).

Along with this 'dignifying' of work, the notion of community service was also strengthened when civil society started to become structured around free time and leisure, understood as collective commodities and rights. In effect, if free time is not seen as a desirable commodity, a lack of it cannot be seen as the basic element of a criminal sanction. Leisure in its modern sense is a recent phenomenon and a product of modern industry (Sayers 1989: 46). The growing commodification of leisure has led to a gradual increase in the need to earn more money by working more, which has given added value to free time (Cross 1993). Community service continued to evolve so that, in the case of convicts who had their own jobs, it took up only free time (Radzinowicz and King 1977: 302; Cartledge 1986: 19), which would otherwise be given to leisure. From early on it was clear to see how important it was for the convict to retain his main job, meaning that the penalty took up only his leisure time (e.g., Vila Miquel 1917: 151). This clashed with labour laws, which established mandatory periods of rest between two jobs, as well as annual holidays, weekly rest days, and so forth (Best 1932: 19). However, this problem was relativized by the fact that community service tended to be imposed on those who were unemployed and insolvent. Thus they encountered no scheduling conflicts, whereas convicts who had a job and were able to pay the fine were expected to do so. Some legal systems also stated that the offender must not work less than a very short minimum term (one day per week), thus granting him or her the opportunity to maintain a regular job (e.g., the Italian law no. 689 of 1981).

Only after these aspects had been resolved could community service become a generalized sanction used as a substitute for unpaid fines. This explains, at least in part, why various regulations considered in their day to be the most forward-thinking actually deserve to be classified as failures. Then the practical application of the 1875 Swiss regulations of the canton of Waadt received a negative appraisal in the report produced to prepare a draft project of the Swiss Penal Code of 1904, so the option of settling an unpaid fine by working was omitted from subsequent legislation (Brenn 1945: 61–62), only to be reintroduced in the 1937 Penal Code, Article 49.1. This regulation did not achieve much success in this regard. The 1912 Austrian Bill for a Penal Code, Section 28, which made provision for default detention to be worked off by doing unpaid labour, was considered an excellent but unattainable idea in Austria for organizational reasons. For its part, the German legislation on fines in the years 1921, 1923, and 1924, which established work penalty without imprisonment (*Arbeitsstrafe ohne Einsperrung*) as a substitute for an unpaid fine, failed in practice (Best 1932: 19; Grünhut 1944: 14; Grebing 1978: 151; Pfohl 1983: 29–30), like the precedent regulation in the 1871 German Imperial Penal Code did.[26] Work as a substitute or accumulative measure of the fine also failed in the 1928 Spanish Penal Code (Quintero Olivares 1977: 118), considered at that time as an 'almost unprecedented legislation in a Penal Code' (Cuello Calón 1929: 202–203). Failure of this legislation seems to have been due to lack of clarity (Roldán Barbero 1983: 51) and infrastructure (Jaramillo García 1928: 391–392). In Italy it was introduced in the 1889 Zanardelli Penal Code,[27] where it was applied in two forms: as a substitute of imprisonment for fine default in the case of insolvency, and as a sanction for two minor offences (begging, Article 455, and public drunkenness, Article 488), substituting *arresto*. Its first form had almost no practical incidence (Padovani 1981: 167, regarding its implementation as 'sporadic'; Paliero 1986a: 152; 1986b: 89–90). Between 1895 and 1899 it was applied as a substitute for default imprisonment or detention in only 39 cases, while there were over 180,000 prison sentences annually and the conversion of fines into a subsidiary prison sentence amounted to more than 80,000 *a year* during the same period. The same can be said about the second role of community service as a principal penalty: between 1895 and 1899 it was imposed as such only in 26 cases (Lucchini 1904: 528–529). As in the German case, the government did not adopt the necessary implementing regulation (Lucchini 1904: 523–524 and 529–530; Paliero 1986a: 152). The mere existence of community service was ignored by many judges and rejected by the vast majority of those who knew, because of the patchy infrastructure due to lack of commitment from the government (Lucchini 1904: 530; Paliero 1986a: 152). As a result, community service was excluded from the 1930 Rocco Code. The explanatory notes stated that 'there was little point in maintaining an institution that had ceased to be used, was rarely applied and furthermore, was ineffective' (Ministero della giustizia e degli affari di culto 1929: 36).

England was the first European country to successfully use community service work as a penal measure in itself (Young 1979: xi). Only after passing the 1972 Criminal Justice Act, which introduced this penal measure for any offender aged 17 and over convicted of any offence – other than murder – punishable by imprisonment, was its development rapid enough to ensure continuance of the scheme. The expansion was most prominent in Western Europe, with France offering a good example of implementation, after a less than encouraging beginning.[28] It must be pointed out, however, that in some countries, like Italy, Portugal, Switzerland, and West Germany, the renewed interest in community service in the 1970s and early 1980s did not achieve much more success than their nineteenth-century precedents,[29] despite the new cultural framework inspired by the postulates of the International Movement of Penal Law Reform. In countries like Finland or Spain, community service was not introduced in the Penal Code until much later in the 1990s.[30] Finland quickly achieved good annual numbers of community service orders and was able to avoid a substantial percentage of short-term prison sentences (Lappi-Seppälä 2001: 117; 2012: 89–90), whereas Spain was not able to implement it on a full scale until 2008, after community service had been established as a cumulative penalty for driving offences (Brandariz García 2013: 371–372; Blay and Larrauri 2016).

In any case, community service as a substitute for unpaid fines did not eliminate the possibility of defaulters being imprisoned: there is always the possibility that fine defaulters will further swell the prison population. Those who do not respect labour discipline and breach the terms of community service end up going to prison.

First doctrinal formulations of the day-fine system

The need to consider the offender's financial situation to determine the end amount of the fine concurred with other factors that should also be taken into account, in particular the seriousness of the offence and the blameworthiness of the perpetrator. The day-fine system is the sole system which considers only the offender's ability to pay the fine when setting the monetary value for the fine units – each one of them is a 'day' – while the number of these units is selected according to the degree of punishment appropriate for the specific criminal behaviour. In particular, 'the basis of the day-fine system is the two-stage breakdown of the determination method' (Roldán Barbero 1983: 45). In fact, the need to take the offender's financial situation into account does not, per se, define the day-fine system; rather it is one of the methods of the so-called total amount fine system (*Gesamtsummensystem*), under the terms of which the judge imposes a specific amount basically resulting from the combination of two coordinates, the seriousness of the offence and the offender's financial situation (Beristain Ipiña 1976: 31, Hillsman 1990: 76–77, Albrecht 2001: 307; see, e.g., Zürcher 1891: 268–269, or Glauning 1905: 283), which eventually became three when the blameworthiness of the perpetrator was added to the seriousness of the offence – once it was accepted that it is an imperative of justice to express the offender's level of culpability in the sentence (Mittelbach 1957: 1139). Although Garofalo (1887: 106–107) proposed in 1887 Italy that 'a previously determined amount, proportionate to his alleged earnings' should be imposed on the offender as a fine, and in 1893 Getz (1893: § 22) introduced in his second draft for a Norwegian penal code a tariff system modulated by the need to consider the offender's daily income, there was still a long way to go to establish the day-fine system.

The first doctrinal formulations of the day-fine system, defined in terms of the need to break the determination process of the fine down into two elements, are found at the end of the nineteenth century, almost simultaneously in Austria (Friedmann 1892: 148, followed by Merkel 1893: 351ff.) and Italy (Bertola 1895: 10, 12). They shared the idea of adopting a term of imprisonment as the basis for calculating the amount of the fine – in other words, as a means of determining the penalty – then using a conversion method based on the offender's financial situation, replacing each day of the penalty with a specific amount of money. This proposal, although based on a term of imprisonment, which, to a certain extent, blurred the autonomy of the fine (Brenn 1945: 28; Grebing 1978: 75), should be considered as the first doctrinal formulation of the day-fine system (Driendl 1978: 19, 39; Roldán Barbero 1983: 44–45), since this occurred several years prior to the proposal made by Thyrén (1910: 75), who many mistakenly took to be the creator of this system (see, e.g., Florian 1934: 807, Mittermaier 1936: 647, Schuchbauer 1948: 31–32, Thornstedt 1974: 595, and Strahl 1951: 60). Thyrén's work was undoubtedly the inspiration of the regulation adopted first in Finland in 1921, Sweden in 1931, and Denmark in 1939 – the reason why the day-fine system is also known as the 'Scandinavian system', although after Finland two American countries, Peru in 1924 and Mexico in 1929, were the first adopters of the new system.

Once the determination of the day-fine penalty called for a distinction between the duration of the penalty, which depended on the seriousness of the offence and the offender's blameworthiness, and the amount of the penalty, which depended on the offender's financial situation, the penal codes regained a certain complexity in the description of the methods used to determine this financial capacity.[31] This was in part thanks to the emergence of the protection of tax information under privacy provisions and the extension of information technology, which allowed judges and courts to access the financial details of the offender.

In any case, by using the day-fine system the fine obtained is proportionate to the offence – with this proportion expressed in temporal units, days or months – and reflective of the offender's means – with this reflection expressed in money, a certain sum to pay every day. Thus, the system does not offend the principle of proportionality between crime and punishment, or the equality principle between rich and poor offenders. Furthermore, it offers a calculation procedure from which both the offender and the community can discern the reasons underlying the amount of the fine, 'so that the outcome is more visible as well as more rational' (Hillsman 1990: 76).

But again, the day-fine system is no solution for people with no means at all. On the one hand, even a light fine with prison in default imposed upon a bankrupt person is really a sentence of imprisonment. On the other hand, there is a continuing debate about whether lower limits are too low to be taken seriously. In cases where the offender is dependent on social care, so that the state provides resources thought to represent a minimum level of maintenance, it is illogical to push him or her below that level with a day fine. Alternatives for this group of offenders are needed.

The opposite problem also arises. It is possible – and quite usual – to put a maximum limit both on the duration and the amount of the fine. The problem here is not that poor people cannot pay fines due to a lack of means, but rather that affluent people are so rich that fines, even hefty ones, pose only a minor annoyance (Baumann 1968: 29–30).

> For the very wealthy, inequities may also remain with a means-based system, although they will be significantly smaller than under a fixed-fine system [. . .] For more specialized and less frequent cases, however, further consideration of ways to take account of very high incomes and capital assets would be useful.
>
> (Hillsman and Greene 1992: 139)

Even for very rich offenders, establishing a maximum limit on the duration and the amount of the fine prevents the penalty from being adapted to suit their real economic capacity. As a matter of fact, some thinkers unsuccessfully campaigned for the elimination of upper limits (Stooß 1917: 105). The proposal failed because imposing a very large fine on a rich offender would not be seen as proportional to the severity of the offence while appearing preposterous for a minor transgression (Brenn 1945: 31; Warner 2012: 235). As we will see in Chapter 6, the abandonment of the unit-fine system in England and Wales in 1993 is a good example of this. The maximum unit amount was quite high, even higher than the maximum in the successful pilot projects. After implementing the new system, media coverage of fines considered too high for minor offences without correctly explaining the reason ultimately undermined its legitimacy. It was considered illegitimate to increase fines in correlation to offenders' wealth because such fines were viewed as disproportionate to the limited seriousness of the offence. Courts were reluctant to impose fines that appeared derisory to them and public opinion. As a result, fines were not increased for the rich, somewhat blunting the principle of equal impact in practice.

And obviously, the question as to whether people can effectively hide their financial status is always open to discussion, particularly if one takes into account the ability of the wealthy to hide financial circumstances and the difficulty of assessing the wealth of those who earn their income through illicit activities (Levitt 1997: 181; Pritikin 2010: 357; Warner 2012: 242).[32] This is crucial, since virtually all advantages attributed to the day-fine system depend on reliable and valid information about the offender's financial situation (Albrecht 2001: 309).

The important question of how to translate day fines into prison terms for fine defaulters is answered without creating differences between diverse income groups, as feared by Mittelbach (1957: 1139). It is addressed with an effective system: one, two, or three temporal units of the fine for one day in prison. This approach nullifies differences between income groups of criminals, because the number of days in the day-fine system is fixed according to the seriousness of crime, and not keyed to the amount of the unpaid fine. Thus, the system does not offend the principle of proportionality between crime and punishment, or the equality principle between rich and poor offenders.

The last step towards consideration of the offender's financial situation constitutes distinguishing between cases of impoverishment after the sentence and before paying the fine and subsequently treating them differently. The possibility of revising the amount of the fine imposed was suggested. This solution appears in current penal codes (e.g., 1995 Spanish Penal Code, Article 51, 1889 Finnish Penal Code, Section 2 of Chapter 2[a]).

First European implementations of the day-fine system

The day-fine system was first adopted in Finland in 1921. Serlachius introduced Thyrén's formulation in his 1921 draft penal code, with only a minimal change regarding the maximum number of days. The Finnish Law no. 130 of May 21, 1921, reforming the Penal Law (*Lag Nr.130 angaende ändrad lydelse av 4, 5 och 16 §§ 2 Kapitlet strafflagen*), adopted it as § 4 of the Chapter 2 of the Penal Law. The primary reason for this reform, however, was not to equalize the impact of the penal fine. Instead it was the rapidly declining value of money. Compared to summary fines, day fines could easily be adjusted to changes in the value of money brought about by inflation or recession, since the amount to be paid was tied to the level of income (Ermgassen 1977: 901; Albrecht 2001: 306).

Other Nordic countries followed suit. The Swedish minister of justice Thyrén proposed the introduction of the day-fine system in his draft law on fines of February 24, 1927. It was rejected because it was believed that the need to investigate the offender's financial circumstances would disproportionately increase the work of the courts, lengthening the whole process (Ermgassen 1977: 902). But it was not long before changes were made. The law amending some parts of the Penal Law, no. 327 of September 24, 1931 (*Lag nr.327 om ändring i vissa delar av strafflagen*), adopted the day-fine system. The court was not required to discover the information. It was merely limited to requesting it, determining the offender's financial situation based on the details obtained. In turn, the law on special fines, no. 328 of the same date (*Lag nr.328 angăende dagsböter utom strafflagens område [särskilt böteslag]*), regulated the implementation of the day-fine system in the secondary Criminal Law (more details in Schuchbauer 1948: 59ff.). The main aim of both legal norms was to depopulate the prisons, stating that primarily fine defaulters should not be sentenced to imprisonment. And in fact, the reform, although heavily criticized (Mittermaier 1936: 650ff.), took circa 10,000 prisoners out of prison in the following ten years (Bondeson 2009: 417). In 1937, another statute required a second examination of the case before commutation of unpaid fines into imprisonment, opening up the possibility of remission of sentence for offenders unable to pay the fine through no fault of their own, unless commutation was considered necessary for their reform. This regulation 'has its basis in the danger of insecurity which might arise if fines inflicted upon paupers could not be commuted even in cases of recidivism' (according to the official commentary on the statute reported by Heüman 1938: 549–551).

During negotiations on the 1930 Danish draft penal law, a majority proposed the introduction of the day-fine system. Nevertheless, the minority, led by Oluf Krabbe, could impose its opinion: § 51 of the Danish Penal Law of April 15, 1930, stated that fines would have a minimum limit of four kroner, without setting a maximum limit, and when setting the amount of the fine, the type and severity of the offence should be considered, along with the perpetrator's circumstances, his reasons, and his behaviour before and after the offence, with special attention paid to the offender's ability to pay. This ruling, like so many others at the time, was not implemented in practice. For one thing there was some concern that the general preventive effect would be lost if a small fine were to be imposed on the perpetrator of a serious offence, which led to excessively high fines being imposed on people who were unable to pay them. Furthermore, the courts were reluctant to increase the amount of a fine for wealthy people convicted of minor offences (Ermgassen 1977: 903). Law no. 87 of March 15, 1939, on amendments and additions to the 1930 Civil Penal Code (*Lov Nr.87 af 15. Marts 1939 om Ændringer og Tilføgelser til Borgerlig Straffelov af 15. april 1939*), introduced the day-fine system, albeit 'in a half-hearted way against strong opposition', the common opinion being that it never worked well in Denmark (Thornstedt 1975: 307).

Finland, Sweden, and Denmark were the only European countries to introduce the day-fine system during the first half of the twentieth century. As Albrecht (2001: 306) pointed out, 'the concept generated substantial controversy in all three Scandinavian countries, and was far from being unanimously supported'. Other countries, such as Austria, England, Germany, or Switzerland, made substantial revisions regarding fines during the 1920s and 1930s, in some case with excellent results in terms of reducing short-term prison sentences (see the German example in Chapter 5), but did not adopt the day-fine system.

The day-fine system, establishing similarities with the penalty of imprisonment, resulted in increasing the possibility of substitution between both punishments. Since the seriousness of the offence is the basic determinant of the number of temporal units, this number can be readily indexed to the length of time in prison. At the same time, by reducing the possibility of imprisonment for defaulters, the process of taking into account the offender's means, giving time to pay, and substituting imprisonment for defaulters with non-custodial alternatives made the fine a more palatable substitute for this sort of custodial sentence. This held true even in countries, like Switzerland, where the day-fine system was not implemented in legislation but the need to assess the offender's financial capacity when imposing a fine was. On the other hand, the complete failure of fines as a substitutive penalty for short-term prison sentences in other countries like Italy stemmed from refusing to adapt the fine to the offender's financial circumstances, which ultimately strongly undermined its use.

Nevertheless, many questions about fines remain open. Some of them will be explored in Chapter 6. Does the day-fine system per se reduce the use of short-term prison sentences? Does it reduce the use of imprisonment for defaulters? Is this form of calculating the fine always fairer than a fixed-fine system? Should very high fines be imposed on rich offenders even for a minor infraction for the sake of equal impact? Is a functioning fine system possible without a strong subsidiary penalty? Does imprisonment for defaulters violate constitutional principles? The contrasting experiences of England and Wales, Finland, Germany, Italy, Spain, and Sweden with fines offer surprising answers and new insights. But first we will take a look at the position of fines in the twentieth-century criminal justice systems. Changes include transition from short-term prison sentences as the standard punishment to alternatives such as the fine, community service, probation, and suspended sentences. As will be shown in Chapter 5, these enormous changes in the criminal justice system demonstrate in part shifts in underlying philosophies and in part merely financial concerns about the sustainability of the prison system.

Notes

1 With a few exceptions. See Bonneville de Marsangy (1864: 263–264), Schmölder (1902: 11), and Vila Miquel (1917: 120ff.), for example.

2 As said by Aurioles Montero (1849: 63). He forgot that during the *ancien régime* it was possible to order an offender to remain in prison until the fine was paid. This fact could threaten a poor man with life imprisonment (extensively, Fox 1927: 119; Alonso Romero 1985: 52–54). The same could happen in seventeenth- and eighteenth-century England, according to Beattie (1986: 459). This system, known as *contrainte par corps*, was adopted by the 1810 Napoleon Penal Code (Articles 52, 53, and 467), with some restrictions in case of proven insolvency. It is still in use in France – now limited to debts owed to the state. The difference with imprisonment for default is that the *contrainte par corps* was not a subsidiary punishment in case of default but a way of constraining the payment of the fine: a form of prison for debtors, meaning that the prison term did not alleviate a person's debt, since he or she was typically required to repay the debt in full before being released (Adams 1912: 45–46). Viewed solely as a means of collection, this sort of imprisonment of the poor is subject to several obvious criticisms (see Westen 1969: 777 ff.).

3 The numbers of people in prison for the non-payment of fines were very different from one country to other. For example, in Spain it was argued that in 90 per cent of sentences the fine was misleading, because the offender then proceeded to declare himself insolvent (Armengol y Cornet 1894: 57). In Switzerland Stooβ (1907: 243; 1916: 2–3) stated that there were more people in prison for the non-payment of fines than people who had originally received a custodial sentence. Statistical data confirmed this observation. In Italy pecuniary punishments were imposed on the poor only pro forma, since in reality they turned into prison sentences as the fines inevitably remained unpaid (Florian 1934: 807). In Germany Von Liszt (1889a: 742) also stated that in the majority

of cases the fine became a short-term prison sentence due to non-payment. However, there are no data on this matter in the imperial statistics. It was simply stated in 1884 that the fines that became prison sentences made up a 'not insignificant' percentage (Reichs-Justizamt und Kaiserlichen Statistischen Amt 1898: 14). According to a study concerning the situation of the Grand Duchy of Württemberg between the years 1888 and 1892, approximately 34 per cent of the fines handed out turned into prison sentences or were recorded as bad debts, 41 per cent were paid, and 25 per cent were immediately substituted because of the offender's insolvency (Rettich 1894: 507).

4 For example, the 1925 English Rating and Evaluation Act, which stipulated that a defaulter who proved that his failure to pay was due to circumstances beyond his control should not be imprisoned, had no effect at all (Thoday 1937: 389). Something similar happened with the Swedish statute no. 119 of April 9, 1937, and the 1937 Swiss Penal Code, Article 49.

5 As it was acknowledged in some of the first enlightened criminal legislation. For example, in the Spanish *Novísima Recopilación*, introduced by Carlos IV on July 16, 1803, and in force until the 1848 Spanish Penal Code came into effect, it was stated that 'pecuniary penalties will be imposed on wealthy people in place of the punishment of imprisonment or detention and others of a similar nature for minor offences; and the higher courts may also swap custodial sentences for pecuniary penalties, should the type of crime permit it' (Book 12, Section 41, Law 20), justifying this by stating that 'the useful increase in funds required for the administration of justice would cause fewer penalties and less severe consequences for many families'. See also the 1794 Prussian *Allgemeines Landrecht*, § 85, which stipulated that 'fines cannot be imposed on persons without means of the lower classes', and which legally stated that they should be replaced with a proportionate prison or labour sentence. As Neumaier (1947: 48–49) points out, it was a paradoxical privilege for the rich, proving that this legal text still did not fulfil the equality principle as described in the Enlightened philosophy. In fact, some of the subsequent codes on this matter, of German influence, like the 1813 Penal Law Code for the Kingdom of Bavaria (Article 34), explicitly stated that 'none of the punishments of deprivation of liberty or corporal punishments established in law may be replaced with a fine', admitting the conversion of a fine into imprisonment only in the case of offenders under 16 years old, persons under guardianship, and the poor. It is interesting to note that the project added a fourth case to these three cases, consisting of those who were so wealthy that the loss of the sum legally established would not be a punishment for them (Neumaier 1947: 55). As a means of avoiding 'mortifying' financial investigations, this category disappeared from the final approved text. The 1838 Criminal Code for the Kingdom of Saxony, as a reaction against the fine being used to buy freedom and personal indemnity by the rich, also stated that 'fines are only admissible in cases in which this Code or subsequent laws or ordinances impose them as the exclusive punishment, or as an alternative or accumulatively with other punishments' (Article 15). Other similar rulings existed in, among others, the 1839 Penal Code for the Kingdom of Wurttemberg, Article 46, or the 1840 Penal Code for the Kingdom of Hannover, Article 29.

6 For example, two months for regulatory offences in the 1853 Penal Code of Tuscany – which did not allow substitution for imprisonment in case of criminal offences – two years for criminal offences in the 1822 and 1848 Spanish Penal Codes and the 1859 Sardinian Penal Code, four years in the 1851 Prussian Penal Code, one year for crimes and six weeks for misdemeanours in the 1871 German Imperial Penal Code, and four years of *reclusione* or three of *arresto* in the 1930 Italian Rocco Code.

7 For example, in Spain, Law 1, Title 1, Book 12 of the *Fuero Juzgo*, a codex of Spanish laws enacted by Fernando III of Castile in 1241; and more recently, Law 8, Title 31, Partida 7 of the *Siete Partidas* or Seven-Part Code, a Castilian statutory code first compiled in 1348, during the reign of Alfonso X of Castile.

8 See, for example, the 1803 and 1852 Austrian Penal Codes, §§ 23 and 260, the 1839 Penal Code for the Kingdom of Wurttemberg, Article 32, the 1840 Criminal Code for the Kingdom of Hanover, Article 28, or the elaborated proposal of the 1852 Portuguese

Penal Code, Article 41, strongly influenced by the 1830 Criminal Code of the Empire of Brazil, Article 55, by many considered to be the first exponent of the day-fine system (e.g., Figueiredo Dias 1989: 292–293).

9 This approach is very clear in Blackstone (1769: Book 4, Chapter 29):

> The *quantum* [. . .] of pecuniary fines neither can, nor ought to be ascertained by invariable law. The value of money itself changes from a thousand causes; and, at all events, what is ruin to one man's fortune may be matter of indifference to another's. [. . .] no man shall have a larger amercement imposed upon him than his circumstances or personal estate will bear. [. . .] the penalty must otherwise fall upon a man's person, unless it be redeemed or ransomed by a pecuniary fine: according to an ancient maxim, qui non habet in crumena luat in corpore [let him who has nothing in purse pay in person].

Also Filangieri upheld the idea that instead of a fine, a corporal punishment should be imposed when the fortune of the offender fell short of a certain amount, as 'without this rule, the proposed method could often lead to the punishment for an offence being reduced to the loss of a few grains'. The same approach can be seen in Ørsted. There was still no move away from the equation that the money of the upper classes was equal to the time of the lower classes, typical of the *ancien régime*.

10 See the 1803 Austrian Criminal Code; the 1813 Penal Law Code for the Kingdom of Bavaria, Article 33; the 1812 Spanish Cadiz Constitution, Article 304; and the 1814 French *Charte Constitutionnelle*, Article 66. In Italy it was suppressed by Carlo Alberto in 1831 – Article 5 of the *Regie patenti* May 19, 1831, following the precedents of the 1819 Penal Codes of the Kingdom of the Two Sicilies and 1820 of the Kingdom of Parma, in which it no longer appeared.

11 So, for example, in Spain, with regard to the general demand to not make distinctions when imposing penalties, Calatrava, one of the main authors of the 1822 Spanish Penal Code, said during the pre-legislative discussions,

> For me legal equality means that a Spaniard of any class, who commits an offence the same as one committed by another Spaniard of a different class, is subject to the same punishment [. . .] This is the equality of the Constitution, and I believe that it is also in line with the principles of good legislation.
>
> (*Diario de las Sesiones de Cortes*, *Congreso*, legislature of September 22, 1821, to February 14, 1822, no. 60, 926)

In Germany, in turn, there was also some resistance to measuring wealth in order to determine the amount of the fine, based on the grounds that

> to justify this we need a new definition of the concept of 'Justice'; otherwise we run the risk of confusing this concept with the levelling activity that believes it right to impose as many charges as possible on the rich until they are all at the same level as the have-nots.
>
> (Von Stenglein 1892: 273; see also Appelius 1891: 52, Berolzheimer 1907: 255, and Heilborn 1908: 53–54)

All of them had forgotten Bentham's opinion:

> The *same punishments* for the *same offences*, is often said. This adage has an appearance of justice and impartiality, which seduces superficial minds. To give it a reasonable meaning, it would be necessary to determine beforehand what is meant by the same punishments and the same offences. An inflexible law – a law which should regard neither sex, nor age, nor fortune, nor rank, nor education, nor the moral nor religious prejudices of individuals – would be doubly vicious, as inefficacious, or as tyrannical. Too severe for some, too lenient for others; always sinning by excess or defect; under an appearance of equality, it would hide the most monstrous inequality.
>
> (1830: Book 3, Chapter 4, italics in the original)

12 Interestingly, the argument has again been upheld in recent years by Hudson (1995: 65 ff., 1998, 2000), albeit in a different form: she argued that economic duress should be admissible as a 'relevant criterion' in establishing blameworthiness because of the constraint that poverty places upon choice.

13 See, for example, the conclusions of the 9th Prison Congress held in London in 1925, where, to the question regarding the measures that could be taken, instead of imprisonment, with regard to offenders who have committed a petty offence or an offence which does not constitute a danger to public security, the answer was to extend the system of probation, but also the power of the court to impose fines instead of imprisonment, once imprisonment in default of payment is eliminated (Van der Aa 1927).

14 In Austria Wahlberg (1877: 236); in Germany Friedmann (1892: 140), Heilborn (1908: 52–53), and Goldschmidt (1908: 403); in Italy Rossi (1853: 494 ff.) and Bertola (1893: 550), for whom, however, 'it is equally distressing for everyone to reduce the source of their own satisfaction, whatever the nature of this may be'; in Spain García Goyena and Aguirre (1852: 164–165). See in general the conclusions of the 7th International Penal and Penitentiary Congress held in Budapest in 1905 (Barrows 1907).

15 According to the 1893 second draft for a penal code, § 22:

> For crimes a fine of 3 to 20,000 kroner may be imposed and for misdemeanours this is reduced to between 1 and 10,000 kroner. As a general rule, the fine must be set within these limits, so that the minimum limit of a fine given for a crime is not lower than the presumed income of the offender earned over a 3-day period and the maximum limit does not exceed the presumed income earned over a 3-month period; and the minimum limit of a fine given for a misdemeanour is not lower than the offender's income earned over half a day and the maximum limit does not exceed his income earned over a month and a half. If the offender does not have an income that can be used as the basis for this calculation his alleged average amount of spending will be used instead. Due consideration should be given to financial position of the convicted person and to what he can presumably afford to pay in his circumstances.

Although Getz's draft became a law and went into effect on January 1, 1905, his detailed proposal regarding fines was not embodied in the 1902 Norwegian General Civil Penal Code, Section 27, which simply stated,

> When a fine is imposed, due consideration should be given not only to the nature of the offence but also especially to the financial position of the convicted person and to what he can presumably afford to pay in his circumstances.

16 Thus, the 1848 Spanish Penal Code stated,

> When applying fines, the courts could make use of the full scope of the law when imposing this penalty, consulting, to determine the amount in each case, not only the mitigating and aggravating circumstances of the offence, but also the wealth or affluence of the offender.
>
> (Article 75; identical to Article 84 of the 1870 Spanish Penal Code and 69 of the 1932 Spanish Penal Code)

This redaction was probably due to the fact that the Spanish legislator was aware of the limitations existing in reality and tried to compensate for them by giving more possibilities of appreciation of the individual particularities to the judge (Pacheco 1848: 430; Vila Miquel 1917: 145ff.). However, more optimistically, the 1928 Spanish Penal Code established that

> [the] courts would set the amount of the fine at their discretion, within the limits indicated for each case, based on the modifying circumstances of responsibility concurrent for the offence, or the offender, and more particularly, taking into

> account his livelihood or wealth, income, assets or wages he receives, and, in general, his position and financial possibilities.
>
> (Article 160)

The 1944 Spanish Penal Code went back to the 1848 formulation (Article 63).

17 The 1930 Italian Rocco Code was left out of this development. The refusal to take into account the offender's financial situation is based on two arguments: the first one is that a system that takes these conditions into account when they are bad 'would logically lead to not applying pecuniary penalties to those who had nothing' (see *Lavori preparatori del codice penale e del codice di procedura penale*, vol. 5, Rome, 1929: 72); the second one is that this financial situation is an incidental characteristic, unrelated to the offence, variable and hardly ideal for achieving the aims of general prevention.

18 By 1947 almost four-fifths of convictions were fine sentences, and of the half-million fines imposed, less than 3,000 eventually led to prison (Briggs et al. 1996: 239). Not for very long. The growing employment of the fine in the 1960s was eventually accompanied by a new upturn in the numbers imprisoned for default.

19 By contrast, the 1944 Spanish Penal Code, Article 90, already established as a requisite for payment periods to be granted that 'the fined individual lacks resources', an expression that was understood not as a total lack of funds but as a way of preventing, as far as possible, the offender from being forced to endure personal subsidiary liability for non-payment (Beristain Ipiña 1979: 707). Therefore, the instalment system could also be granted to solvent people who could find themselves struggling if full payment was demanded immediately. This was due to the fact that the most modern justification of the payment of fines by instalments lay in structuring the fine as a penalty used to limit a person's socio-economic standard, 'reducing, for a period of time, the offender's money, which signified his objective freedom, a sign of his social level and the possibility of buying the things he wants' (Beristain Ipiña 1976: 27–28). For the general and special prevention to be achieved, it was deemed necessary that this decline in the offender's socio-economic standing lasted for a certain amount of time, as with custodial sentences (in Germany, already Glauning 1905: 288–289, and Baumann 1968; in Spain, Beristain Ipiña 1976: 28).

20 See, for example, the 1859 French Forestry Code (*Code forestier*), Article 210, according to which 'the Forestry Commission may allow insolvent convicts to be released from fines, damages, and civil costs, by providing services in kind, consisting of forestry conservation work or working on local roads'.

21 The first legislative reference commonly cited is an ordinance of 1698 by Frederick Augustus of Saxony and Thuringia, in which he established the possibility of allowing punishments sentencing the offender to imprisonment or alternatively to a fine to be served by carrying out manual work with the offender remaining at liberty, substituting the custodial sentence with three days of work for each day in prison, which meant that it was used as a way of applying subsidiary prison sentences for unpaid fines (Rosenfeld 1890: 314–316). The equation of three days of work for one day in prison was changed to one day of work for one day in prison by an ordinance of April 30, 1783, § 15.

22 This proposal also spread to cases other than being used to replace unpaid fines (Lammasch 1889: 449; Aschaffenburg 1903: 216). But it came up against a strong opposition (see, e.g., Berolzheimer 1903: 456; Gennat 1905: 50).

23 There was no shortage of opposition to this idea. There were those who thought

> [t]he pressure of having to work for the State for a certain amount of time with other convicts under official supervision, has a major impact on the offender's freedom. Such a punishment is, by its very nature, predominantly a custodial sentence.
>
> (Stooß 1891: 349–350)

24 The 1838 Criminal Code for the Kingdom of Saxony, Articles 14 ff., established that for fines replaced with custodial sentences shorter than three months, the prison

sentence could be replaced with unpaid manual work for a maximum of four weeks working a maximum of three days a week. This was dependent on the offender, 'in line with his social status', already carrying out such activity previously. Similar provisions, although with reduced scope, were established in the 1855 Penal Code for the Kingdom of Saxony, and in its 1868 revision. They were also included in the 1850 Penal Code of Thuringia, Articles 14–16 (Rosenfeld 1890: 333–334; these provisions were echoed in Italy – see Lecci 1891: 135–136). In Switzerland, in the middle of the nineteenth century the principle was stated that compulsory work without confinement (*Zwangsarbeit ohne Einsperrung*) could replace an unpaid monetary sanction, to be used at first only in cases of offences contravening federal financial, customs, or police legislation, although it slowly spread to other cases in the cantonal penal codes (Rosenfeld 1890: 239–240; Von Liszt 1905: 373–374).

25 First formulated as one of the principles of the new regime of poor relief that was introduced by the 1834 Poor Law Amendment Act, the principle of less eligibility was defined as follows: that the situation of the able-bodied recipient of poor relief 'on the whole shall not be made really or apparently as eligible as the independent labourer of the lowest class'. By this, it was meant that the condition of a pauper in the workhouse should not be as attractive as that of the poorest labourer outside the workhouse. Effectively, a person who was able-bodied had to be destitute in order to qualify for poor relief. Often, the phrase has been taken to mean that the workhouse inmates were to be made to endure conditions worse than those outside, but it was not intended in this way; neither was it intended that workhouse conditions be untenable. Ferri (1900: 393) is a clear example of this other way of interpretation. He expressed strong opposition to

> this upheaval of every principle of social justice which would have prisons more convenient and more comfortable than dwellings of poor and honest folk, who may, so long as they remain honest, die there of acute or chronic starvation since society assures them food and lodging only when they commit culpable acts.

26 This failure was due largely to the negligence of the authorities, who did not draft the provisions for enforcement prescribed by law, with the only exception of the Free State of Thuringia (Heinitz 1953: 41). In turn, this lack of interest stemmed from the economic and social situation prevailing over interwar Germany, shaken by a severe recession which, in a context of increasing unemployment, made the possibility of offering the alternative of community service unrealistic.

27 With very little enthusiasm from Zanardelli, who, despite being aware of the practical difficulties of its implementation, claimed that free work could be found in every previous project from 1879; and that was the only reason why he maintained it in his own project, trusting that well-thought-out execution regulation would promote the right approach to application (see Camera dei Deputati 1887: 118–119).

28 In France, community service was introduced in the Penal Code only in 1983, although it already existed in the 1859 *Code forestier*, Article 210 (on its practical application, see Boullaire 1893: 1033 ff.). Initially, it was not used to any significant degree, to the point that in 1985 only 2 per cent of those sentenced received such a sanction. Today, 'community service orders represent more than 16 percent of the noninstitutional sanctions' (Terrill 2016: 206).

29 In Italy, community service was conceived as a substitute for default imprisonment. Article 49 of the Law no. 354 of July 26, 1975, regarding regulations on the penitentiary system and the execution of imprisonment and freedom restricting measures (*Norme sull'ordinamento penitenziario e sulla esecuzione delle misure privative e limitative della libertà*) reproduced exactly Article 19 of the Zanardelli Code. It was implicitly derogated by the Constitutional Court Judgement no. 131 of 1979 (Di Gennaro et al. 1980: 240), and explicitly by Law no. 689 of November 24, 1981, amending the criminal justice system (*modifiche al sistema penale*) (Paliero 1986b: 91). But even before that it was considered 'inoperative' (Di Gennaro et al. 1976: 229).

In Portugal, community service was introduced as a substitute for a prison sentence of no more than one year (Articles 58 and 59 of the 1982 Penal Code), without achieving 'statistical expression' (Paliero 1986b: 99; Pereira 2002: 470). It developed in full only after a legal reform enacted in 2007. Article 47 of the 1982 Penal Code also enabled substituting non-payment of fines due to insolvency with labour. A very low level of implementation was reported (Pereira 1986: 146, and 2002: 469; Tak 1986: 12), once again until the 2007 reform.

In Switzerland, free work was conceived as an alternative to the payment of the fine. Article 49 of the 1937 Swiss Penal Code was defined as a 'norm that sadly only exists on paper' (Schultz 1977: 112, confirmed by Beckmann and Wagensonner 1983: 911, and Killias 2002: 535, the latter explaining that 'this option was not often used, mainly because of the rather modest size of fines in the Swiss sentencing system'). Community service did not presuppose the offender's insolvency. Obviously, it was remunerated, since its purpose was to provide the means to pay the fine. Only in 1990 community service was introduced as another form of custodial sentences not exceeding one month, and since 1996 prison terms of up to three months could be executed through it. These reforms increased its use (Killias 2002: 545).

In West Germany community service as a penalty in itself was considered and rejected during the 1969–1974 reforms, mainly because of doubts regarding whether it could be put into practice (Van Kalmthout and Task 1992: 438). It could be imposed only as a condition of dismissal (§ 153a [1] of the Code of Penal Procedure) or of probation (§ 56b [2] of the Penal Code), and as a substitute of imprisonment for fine defaulters. Weigend (2001: 200) wrote that at the turn of the century the practical relevance of community service was quite limited:

> As a condition of probation or of conditional dismissal, community service is imposed in less than 1 percent of the relevant cases [. . .]. Programs that seek to replace jail for fine-defaulters by community service have so far managed to reach only 6 percent of defaulters.

This observation has been confirmed by other authors (Pfohl 1983; Feuerhelm 1991: 76, and 1997; Eisenberg 1995: 368). The situation was a 'bitter disillusionment' for some (Stöckel 2002: 334). Today the practice and enforcement frequency of community service are still portrayed as less than satisfactory (Sevdiren 2011: 171 ff.). Nevertheless, the number of offenders who work for the community as a substitute for unpaid fines increased substantially between 1991 and 2010 (Heinz 2012: 72).

30 Community service in Finland began on an experimental basis in 1991 in four regions. The experimental phase lasted five years. On January 1, 1997, community service was nationally adopted as an alternative to sentences less than or equal to eight months (Utriainen 2002: 201–202), in order to avoid net widening and to ensure that it really would be used in cases where the offender would otherwise have received an unconditional prison sentence (Lappi-Seppälä 2001: 116).

In Spain extensive discussion on community service took place during debates on the draft for a new penal code presented in 1980. In the end, it was not included as an alternative sanction until the enactment of the 1995 Penal Code because of a lack of infrastructure and high levels of unemployment (Brandariz García 2002: 108).

31 For example, the 1995 Spanish Penal Code states that in order to set a monetary value for these fine units 'the offender's financial situation, deduced from his assets, income, obligations and family duties and other personal circumstances' will be exclusively taken into account (Article 50.5). More detailed, the 1889 Finnish Penal Code states, 'one sixtieth of the average monthly income of the person fined, less the taxes and fees defined by a Decree and a fixed deduction for basic consumption, is deemed to be a reasonable amount of a day fine', adding:

> the maintenance liability of the person fined may decrease the day fine. The primary basis for the calculation of the monthly income is the income of the person fined as

indicated in the most recent taxation. If the income of the person fined cannot be reliably ascertained from the tax records or it has essentially changed since the most recent taxation, it may be assessed also on the basis of other information.

(Section 2 of Chapter 2[a])

32 However, most European systems do not raise issues of morality regarding the source of the income, as a basis for excluding income of illicit origin from consideration. Thus, for example, as Albrecht (2001: 312–313) indicates, income derived from criminal activities, whether full-time or supplemental, may serve as a basis for fixing the level of the day-fine unit, although there is a trend towards confiscation of such earnings, which would preclude their inclusion when determining the amount.

References

Adams, F. (1912) *Die geschichtliche Entwicklung der subsidiären Freiheitsstrafe*. Breslau: Schletter.

Albrecht, H.-J. (2001) 'Post-Adjudication Dispositions in Comparative Perspective'. In Tonry, M. and R. S. Frase (eds.) *Sentencing and Sanctions in Western Countries*. New York: Oxford University Press, 293–330.

Alonso Romero, M. P. (1985) 'Aproximación al estudio de las penas pecuniarias en Castilla (siglos XIII–XVIII)'. *Anuario de Historia del Derecho Español* 55: 9–94.

Appelius, U. (1891) *Die bedingte Verurteilung und die anderen Ersatzmittel für kurzzeitige Freiheitstrafen*. 4th ed. Kassel: Keßler.

Arenal, C. (1890) 'Informe al Congreso penitenciario internacional de San Petersburgo. 2ª parte: ¿Cómo se disminuiría el número de incorregibles?' *Revista General de Legislación y Jurisprudencia* 77: 309–330.

Armengol y Cornet, P. (1894) *Ensayo de estudio de Derecho penal*. Barcelona: Establecimiento Tipográfico de Jaime Jepús Roviralta.

Aschaffenburg, G. (1903) *Das Verbrechen und seine Bekämpfung: Kriminalpsychologie für Mediziner, Juristen und Soziologen, ein Beitrag zur Reform der Strafgesetzgebung*. Heidelberg: Carl Winter's Universitätsbuchhandlung.

Aschrott, P. F. (1888) 'Zur Reform des deutschen Strafen- und Gefängniswesen'. *Zeitschrift für die gesamte Strafrechtswissenschaft* 8: 1–50.

Aurioles Montero, I. (1849) *Instituciones del Derecho penal de España, escritas con arreglo al nuevo Código*. Madrid: Establecimiento Tipográfico de D. Ramón Rodríguez de Rivera.

Barrows, S. J. (1907) *Report of Proceedings of the Seventh International Prison Congress, Budapest, Hungary, September, 1905, by Samuel J. Barrows, Commissioner for the United States on the International Prison Commission*. Washington, DC: Govt. Print. Off.

Baumann, J. (1968) *Beschränkung des Lebensstandards anstatt kurzfristiger Freiheitsstrafe*. Neuwied: Luchterhand.

Beattie, J. M. (1986) *Crime and the Courts in England. 1660–1800*. Princeton, NJ: Princeton University Press.

Beccaria, C. Bonesana di (1764 [1872]) *An Essay on Crimes and Punishments: By the Marquis Beccaria of Milan. With a Commentary by M. de Voltaire. A New Edition Corrected*. Albany: W. C. Little.

Beckmann, W. and A. Wagensonner (1983) 'Die Freiheitsstrafe und ihre Surrogate in der Schweiz'. In Jescheck, H.-H. and G. Grebing (eds.) *Die Freiheitsstrafe und ihre Surrogate im deutschen und ausländischen Recht. Band 1*. Baden-Baden: Nomos, 861–927.

Bentham, J. (1789) *An Introduction to the Principles of Morals and Legislation*. London: Payne.

Beristain Ipiña, A. (1976) 'La multa penal y la administrativa en relación con las sanciones privativas de libertad'. In AA.VV (ed.) *III Jornadas de Profesores de Derecho Penal*. Madrid: Universidad de Santiago de Compostela, 11–56.

Beristain Ipiña, A. (1979) 'Voz Multa penal'. In Pellisé Prats, B. (ed.) *Nueva Enciclopedia Jurídica. Volume 16*. Barcelona: Seix, 699–716.

Bernaldo de Quirós, C. (1898) *Las nuevas teorías de la criminalidad*. Madrid: Imprenta de la Revista de Legislación.

Bernaldo de Quirós, C. and A. Navarro de Palencia (1911) *Teoría del Código Penal: Parte general*. Alcalá de Henares: Imprenta del Reformatorio de Jóvenes Delincuentes.

Berolzheimer, F. (1903) *Die Entgeltung im Strafrecht*. Munich: Beck.

Berolzheimer, F. (1907) *System der Rechts- und Wirtschaftsphilosophie. 5. Strafrechtsphilosophie und Strafrechtsreform*. Munich: Beck.

Bertola, E. (1893) 'Della pena pecuniaria'. *Rivista Penale* 1: 548–553.

Bertola, E. (1895) 'Ancora della pena pecuniaria'. *Rivista Penale* 2: 5–15.

Best, E. (1932) *Studien über die Anwendung der fakultativ angedrohten Geldstrafen im Deutschen Reiche*. Gießen: Univ. Diss.

Birkmeyer, K. (1901) 'Das Strafrecht'. In Birkmeyer, K. (ed.) *Enzyklopädie der Rechtswissenschaft in systematischer und alphabetischer Bearbeitung*. Berlin: D. Häring, 1025–1092.

Blackstone, W. (1769) *Commentaries on the Laws of England. Book 4*. Oxford: A. Strahan, for T. Cadell and J. Butterworth and Son.

Blay, E. and E. Larrauri (2016) 'Community Punishments in Spain: A Tale of Two Administrations'. In Robinson, G. and F. McNeill (eds.) *Community Punishments: European Perspectives*. London: Routledge, 191–208.

Bondeson, U. V. (2009) 'Crime and Justice in Scandinavia'. In Schneider, H. J. (ed.) *Internationales Handbuch der Kriminologie. Band 2: Besondere Probleme der Kriminologie*. Berlin: Walter de Gruyter, 413–434.

Bonneville de Marsangy, A. (1864) *De l'amélioration de la loi criminelle en vue d'une justice plus prompte, plus efficace, plus généreuse et plus moralisante. Volume. II*. Paris: Cosse et Marchal.

Bottoms, A. E. (1983) 'Some Neglected Features of Contemporary Penal Systems'. In Garland, D. and P. Young (eds.) *The Power to Punish*. London: Heinemann, 166–202.

Boullaire, J. (1893) 'Rapport sur les peines qui pourraient, dans certains cas, être substituées à l'emprisonnement'. *Revue pénitentiaire et de droit pénal* 17: 706–722, discussion 722–736, 862–889, 1026–1265.

Brandariz García, J. A. (2002) *El trabajo en beneficio de la comunidad como sanción penal*. Valencia: Tirant lo Blanch.

Brandariz García, J. A. (2013) 'La pena de trabajos en beneficio de la comunidad'. In Faraldo-Cabana, P. and L. M. Puente Aba (eds.) *Las penas privativas de derechos y otras alternativas a la privación de libertad*. Valencia: Tirant lo Blanch, 345–372.

Brenn, A. (1945) *Die Busse und ihr Vollzug nach dem Schweizerischen Strafgesetzbuch*. Affoltern am Albis: Dr. J. Weiss.

Briggs, J., Harrison, C., McInnes, A. and D. Vincent (1996) *Crime and Punishment in England: An Introductory History*. New York: St. Martin's Press.

Buchwald, F. (1948) 'Zum Problem der kurzfristigen Freiheitsstrafe'. *Süddeutsche Juristen-Zeitung* 3: 211–212.

Camera dei Deputati (1887) *Progetto del Codice Penale del Regno d'Italia. Volume I. Relazione Ministeriale*. Rome: Stamperia Reale Ripamonti.

Carfora, F. (1928) 'Pene (in genere ed in specie)'. In Lucchini, L. (ed.) *Il Digesto italiano. Enciclopedia metodica e alfabetica di legislazione, dottrina e giurisprudenza. Volume XVIII, parte prima*. Turin: Unione Tipografico-Editrice Torinese, 1420–1468.

Carrara, F. (1871) *Programa del Corso di Diritto Criminale dettato nella R. Università di Pisa. Parte Generale*. 4th ed. Lucca: Tipografia Giusti.

Cartledge, G. C. (1986) 'Community Service in England/Wales – Organization and Implementation of Community Service: An Evaluation and Assessment of Its Outcomes'. In Albrecht, H.-J. and W. Schädler (eds.) *Community Service: A New Option in Punishing Offenders in Europe*. Freiburg: Max Planck Institute for Foreign and International Penal Law, 15–38.

Castro y Orozco, J. and M. Ortiz de Zúñiga (1848) *Código penal explicado para la común inteligencia y fácil aplicación de sus disposiciones. Tomo I*. Granada: Imprenta y Librería de Don Manuel Sanz.

Ciccarelli, A. (1897) 'Per l'abolizione della pena pecuniaria'. *La Scuola Positiva* 7: 577–598.

The Commission on Criminal Law (1843) *Seventh Report of Her Majesty's Commissioners on Criminal Law: Dated the 11th Day of March 1843. Presented to Both Houses of Parliament by Command of Her Majesty*. London: W. Clowes and Sons.

Conti, U. (1910) 'La pena e il sistema penale del codice italiano'. In Pessina, E. (ed.) *Enciclopedia del diritto penale italiano. Volume IV*. Milan: Società Editrice Libraria, 1–970.

Cross, G. (1993) *Time and Money: The Making of Consumer Culture*. London: Routledge.

Cuello Calón, E. (1929) *Las faltas en el nuevo Código Penal (su exposición y comentario)*. Madrid: Librería General de Victoriano Suárez.

Dodd, N. (1994) *The Sociology of Money: Economics, Reason and Contemporary Society*. Cambridge: Polity Press.

Driendl, J. (1978) *Die Reform der Geldstrafe in Österreich*. Baden-Baden: Nomos.

Eisenberg, U. (1995) *Kriminologie*. 4th ed. Cologne: Heymanns.

Ermgassen, O. (1977) *Die Geldstrafe in den nordischen Ländern (Dänemark, Norwegen, Schweden, Finnland)*. Freiburg im Br.: Univ. Diss.

Felisch (1895) 'Empfiehlt sich hinsichtlich der Geldstrafen: a) Die Zulassung und Begünstigung des freiwilligen Abverdienens derselben?, b) Die Androhung des erzwungenen Abverdienens in einer Anstalt (Arbeitshaus) für den Fall, dass der Mangel guten Willens zur Tilgung der Strafe festgestellt ist?'. In Deutscher Juristentag (ed.) *23. Verhandlungen des Deutschen Juristentages. Erster Band*. Berlin: Guttentag, 277–366.

Ferri, E. (1900) *Sociologia Criminale*. 4th ed. Turin: Fratelli Bocca Editori.

Feuerhelm, W. (1991) *Gemeinnützige Arbeit als Alternative in der Geldstrafenvollstreckung*. Wiesbaden: Eigenverlag Kriminologische Zentralstelle.

Feuerhelm, W. (1997) *Stellung und Ausgestaltung der Gemeinnützigen Arbeit im Strafrecht*. Wiesbaden: Kriminologische Zentralstelle.

Figueiredo Dias, J. de (1989) 'Problemas de igualdade na estruturaçâo e aplicaçâo da pena de multa'. In AA.VV. *Estudios Penales en Memoria del Profesor Agustín Fernández-Albor*. Santiago de Compostela: Servicio de Publicaciones de la Universidad de Santiago de Compostela, 289–305.

Filangieri, G. (1788) *La scienza della legislazione*. Catania: Pastore.

Florian, E. (1934) *Parte generale del Diritto penale. II*. 4th ed. Milan: Casa Editrice Dottor Francesco Vallardi.

Foucault, M. (1977) *Discipline and Punish*. New York: Pantheon Books.

Fox, J. C. (1927) *The History of Contempt of Court*. Oxford: Clarendon Press.
Fox, L. W. (1936) *The Modern English Prison*. London: Routledge.
Friedmann, O. (1892) 'Sind Änderungen des geltendes Recht erwünscht in Betreff des Verhältnisses zwischen Geld- und Freiheitsstrafen?' In Deutscher Juristentag (ed.) *Verhandlungen des Zweiundzwanzigsten Deutschen Juristentages. Zweiter Band*. Berlin: Guttentag, 95–183.
Fuld, L. (1890) 'Die kurzzeitigen Freiheitsstrafen und ihr Ersatz'. *Der Gerichtssaal* 43: 444–480.
Galdo, G. (1908) 'La pena pecuniaria'. *Rivista di diritto penale e sociologia criminale* 9: 42–56.
García Goyena, F. and J. Aguirre (1852) *Febrero ó librería de Jueces, Abogados y Escribanos, comprensiva de los Códigos civil, criminal y administrativo, tanto en la parte teórica como en la práctica, con arreglo en un todo a la legislación hoy vigente. Tomo V*. 4th ed. Madrid: Imprenta y librería de Gaspar y Roig.
Garland, D. (1985) *Punishment and Welfare*. Aldershot: Gower.
Garofalo, R. (1887 [2002]) *Indemnización a las víctimas del delito: Traducción y estudio crítico*. Pamplona: Analecta (*Riparazione alle vittime del delitto*. Turin: Bocca, 1887).
Gennaro, G. di, Bonomo, M. and R. Breda (1976) *Ordinamento penitenziario e misure alternative alla detenzione*. Milan: Giuffrè.
Gennaro, G. di, Bonomo, M. and R. Breda (1980) *Ordinamento penitenziario e misure alternative alla detenzione*. 2nd ed. Milan: Giuffrè.
Gennat, G. (1905) *Das Strafensystem und seine Reform*. Hamburg: Mauke.
Getz, B. (1893) *Udkast til Almindelig borgerlig Straffelov for Kongeriget Norge. Motiver*. Kristiania: Steenske Bogtr.
Glauning, D. (1905) 'Zur "Reform der Geldstrafe" '. *Blätter für Gefängnisskunde* 39: 277–289.
Goisis, L. (2008) *La pena pecuniaria: Un'indagine storica e comparata. Profili di effettività della sanzione*. Milan: Giuffrè.
Goldschmidt, J. (1908) 'Die Geldstrafe'. *Vergleichende Darstellung des deutschen und ausländischen Strafrechts* 4: 398–411.
Grebing, G. (1978) 'Die Geldstrafe im deutschen Recht nach Einführung des Tagessatzsystems'. In Jescheck, H.-H. and G. Grebing (eds.) *Die Geldstrafe im deutschen und ausländischen Recht*. Baden-Baden: Nomos, 1–184.
Grebing, G. (1982) *The Fine in Comparative Law: A Survey of 21 Countries*. Cambridge: Institute of Criminology Occasional Papers n° 9.
Groß, H. (1894) 'Zum Stooβ'chen Vorentwurf für ein "Schweizerisches Strafgesetzbuch" '. *Allgemeine österreichische Gerichtszeitung* 45: 325–329.
Grünhut, M. (1944) *The Development of the German Penal System 1920–1932*. Toronto: The Canadian Bar Association.
Grünhut, M. (1948) *Penal Reform: A Comparative Study*. Oxford: Clarendon Press.
Gutmann, H. (1909) *Die Natur der Geldstrafe und ihre Verwendung im heutigen Reichsstrafrecht*. Leipzig: Druck von J. B. Hirschfeld.
Heilborn, P. (1908) *Die kurze Freiheitsstrafe*. Leipzig: Engelmann.
Heinitz, E. (1953) 'Der Ausbau des Strafensystems'. *Zeitschrift für die gesamte Strafrechtswissenschaften* 65: 26–52.
Heinz, W. (2012) *Das strafrechtliche Sanktionensystem und die Sanktionierungspraxis in Deutschland 1882–2012*. Stand: Berichtsjahr. Available at www.ki.uni-konstanz.de/kis
Hellwig, A. (1924) *Das Geldstrafengesetz: Die Verordnung über Vermögenstrafen und Bussen vom 6. Februar 1924 mit der Begründung und den Ausführungsbestimmungen*. 3rd ed. Munich: Müller.

Henry, J. F. (2004) 'The Social Origins of Money: The Case of Egypt'. In Wray, L. R. (ed.) *Credit and State Theories of Money: The Contributions of A. Mitchell Innes*. Cheltenham: Edward Elgar, 79–98.

Heüman, M. (1938) 'Schweden'. *Zeitschrift für die gesamte Strafrechtswissenschaft* 57: 538–553.

Hillsman, S. T. (1990) 'Fines and Day Fines'. In Tonry, M. (ed.) *Crime and Justice: A Review of Research. Volume 12*. Chicago: University of Chicago Press, 50–98.

Hillsman, S. T. and J. A. Greene (1992) 'The Use of Fines as an Intermediate Sanction'. In Byrne, J. M., Lurigio, A. J. and J. Petersilia (ed.) *Smart Sentencing: The Emergence of Intermediate Sanctions*. London: SAGE, 123–141.

Home Department (1937) *Report of the Commissioners of Prisons and Directors of Convict Prisons for the Year 1935*. London: His Majesty's Stationery Office.

Hudson, B. (1995) 'Beyond Proportionate Punishment: Difficult Cases and the 1991 Criminal Justice Act'. *Crime, Law and Social Change* 22: 59–78.

Hudson, B. (1998) 'Doing Justice to Difference'. In Ashworth, A. and M. Wasik (eds.) *Fundamentals of Sentencing Theory: Essays in honour of Andrew von Hirsch*. Oxford: Clarendon Press, 223–250

Hudson, B. (2000) 'Punishing the Poor: Dilemmas of Justice and Difference'. In Heffernan, W. C. and J. Kleinig (eds.) *From Social Justice to Criminal Justice: Poverty and the Administration of Criminal Law*. New York: Oxford University Press, 189–216.

Ingham, G. (2000) 'Class Inequality and the Social Production of Money'. In Crompton, R., Devine, F., Savage, M. and J. Scott (eds.) *Renewing Class Analysis*. Oxford: Blackwell, 66–86.

Jaramillo García, A. (1928) *Novísimo Código Penal comentado y cotejado con el de 1870. Volumen I*. Salamanca: Imprenta de Silvestre Ferreira.

Jordão, L. M. (1853) *Commentario ao Codigo Penal Portuguez. Tomo I*. Lisbon: Typographia de José Baptista Morando.

Kilcommins, S. (2002) *The Introduction of Community Service Orders: An Historical Interpretation*. Chichester: Barry Rose Law.

Killias, M. (2002) 'Community Service in Switzerland: Implementation, Recidivism and Net-Widening. Experimental Evidence as an Alternative to Speculation'. In Albrecht, H.-J. and A. van Kalmthout (eds.) *Community Sanctions and Measures in Europe and North America*. Freiburg: iuscrim, 535–549.

Krohne, K. (1889) *Lehrbuch der Gefängniskunde unter Berücksichtigung der Kriminalstatistik und Kriminalpolitik*. Stuttgart: Verlag von Ferdinand Enke.

Lammasch, H. (1889) 'Über Zweck und Mittel der Strafe'. *Zeitschrift für die gesamte Strafrechtswissenschaft* 9: 423–451.

Lammasch, H. (1891) 'Criminalpolitische Studien'. *Der Gerichtssaal* 44: 147–248.

Lappi-Seppälä, T. (2001) 'Sentencing and Punishment in Finland: The Decline of the Repressive Ideal'. In Tonry, M. and R. S. Frase (eds.) *Sentencing and Sanctions in Western Countries*. Oxford: Oxford University Press, 92–150.

Lappi-Seppälä, T. (2012) 'Penal Policies in the Nordic Countries 1960–2010'. *Journal of Scandinavian Studies in Criminology and Crime Prevention* 13(1): 85–111.

Lecci, A. (1891) *Il sistema delle pene nel codice italiano*. Rome: Unione Tipografico-Editrice Torinese.

Levitt, S. (1997) 'Incentive Compatibility Constraints as an Explanation for the Use of Prison Sentences Instead of Fines'. *International Review of Law and Economics* 17(2): 179–192.

Lucchini, L. (1904) 'Su alcuni istituti complementari del Codice penale'. In Direzione Generale della Statistica (ed.) *Annali di Statistica: Atti della Commissione per la Statistica Giudiziaria e Notarile. Sessione del gennaio 1904*. Rome: Tipografia Nazionale di G. Bertero e C., 501–539.

Maffei, N. (1875) 'Intorno al progetto 24 febbraio 1874 di un nuovo codice penale italiano'. *Rivista Penale* 1: 399–416.

Manchester, A. H. (1980) *A Modern Legal History of England and Wales 1750–1950*. London: Butterworths.

Marcos Gutiérrez, J. (1826) *Práctica criminal de España. Tomo III*. 4th ed. Madrid: Imprenta de Don Fermín Villalpando.

Marsico, A. de (1925) 'Relazione della Commissione della Camera dei deputati per la riforma del cod. pen'. *La Scuola Positiva* 5: 277–305.

Martin, F. (2013) *Money: The Unauthorised Biography*. London: The Bodley Head.

Merkel, A. (1889) *Lehrbuch des Deutschen Strafrechts*. Stuttgart: Verlag von Ferdinand Ente.

Merkel, A. (1893) 'Sind Aenderungen des geltenden Rechts erwünscht in Betreff des Verhältnisses zwischen Geld- und Freiheitsstrafen?' In Deutscher Juristentag (ed.) *Verhandlungen des Zweiundzwanzigsten Deutschen Juristentages. Vierter Band*. Berlin: Guttentag, 336–360.

Merkel, A. (1895) 'Empfiehlt sich die Einführung von Verschärfungen der Freiheitsstrafen im Sinne des österreichischen Entwurfs?' In Deutscher Juristentag (ed.) *23. Verhandlungen des Deutschen Juristentages. Zweiter Band*. Berlin: Guttentag, 350–425.

Michaux, E. H. (1872) *Étude sur la question des peines*. Paris: Challamel.

Miedico, M. (2008) *La pena pecuniaria: Disciplina, prassi e prospettive di riforma*. Milan: Egea.

Ministero della giustizia e degli affari di culto (1929) *Lavori preparatori del codice penale e del codice di procedura penale. Volume IV. Atti della Commissione ministeriale incaricata di dare parere sul progetto preliminare di un nuovo Codice penale. Parte prima*. Rome: Tipografia del Senato.

Mittelbach, H. H. (1957) 'Ersatzfreiheitsstrafe (§ 29 StGB)'. *Neue Juristische Wochenschrift* 10: 1138–1139.

Mittelstädt, O. (1879) *Gegen die Freiheitsstrafe: Ein Beitrag zur Kritik des heutigen Strafensystems*. Leipzig: Hirzel.

Mittelstädt, O. (1891) 'Sind Änderungen des geltenden Rechts erwünscht in Betreff des Verhältnisses zwischen Geld- und Freiheitsstrafe?' In Deutscher Juristentag (ed.) *Verhandlungen des Einundzwanzigsten Deutschen Juristentages. Zweiter Band*. Berlin: Guttentag, 49–69.

Mittermaier, W. (1936) 'Das Tagesbussensystem in Skandinavien'. *Zeitschrift für die gesamte Strafrechtswissenschaft* 55: 646–676.

Mohr, K. (1913) *Die Bemessung der Geldstrafe*. Breslau: Schletter.

Molinari-Tosatti, G. (1888) 'Le brevi pene e la condanna condizionale'. *Rivista Penale* 40: 24–54, 113–161.

Montesquieu, Charles de Secondat, Baron de (1748) *De l'esprit des lois*. Geneva: chez Barrilot & fils.

Navarro de Paiva, José da Cunha (1915) *Estudos de Direito Penal*. Lisbon: Liv. Aillaud e Bertrand.

Neumaier, R. (1947) *Die geschichtliche Entwicklung der Geldstrafe vom 15*. Jahrhundert bis zum StGB. Tübingen: Univ. Diss.

O'Brien, P. (1995) 'The Prison on the Continent. Europe, 1865–1965'. In Morris, N. and D. J. Rothman (eds.) *The Oxford History of the Prison. The Practice of Punishment in Western Society*. New York: Oxford University Press, 199–225.

O'Malley, P. (2009) *The Currency of Justice: Fines and Damages in Consumer Societies*. New York: Routledge-Cavendish.

O'Malley, P. (2013) 'Monetized Justice: Money and Punishment in Consumer Societies'. In Simon, J. and R. Sparks (ed.) *The SAGE Handbook of Punishment and Society*. London: SAGE, 375–392.

Ørsted, A. (1818) *Ueber die Grundregeln der Strafgesetzgebung. Band 1*. Copenhagen: Gyldendal.

Ortolan, J.L.E. (1874) *Éléments de droit pénal*. 4th ed. Paris: Plon.

Pacheco, J. F. (1848) *El Código penal: Concordado y comentado. Tomo I*. Madrid: Imprenta de don Santiago Saunaque.

Pacheco, J. F. (1856) *El Código penal: Concordado y comentado. Tomo I*. 2nd ed. Madrid: Imprenta de la Viuda de Perinat y Compañía.

Padovani, T. (1981) *L'utopia punitiva*. Milan: Giuffrè.

Paliero, C. E. (1986a) 'Community Service in Italy – Legislation and Practice'. In Albrecht, H. J. and W. Schädler (eds.) *Community Service: A New Option in Punishing Offenders in Europe*. Freiburg: Max Planck Institute for Foreign and International Penal Law, 151–172.

Paliero, C. E. (1986b) 'Il "Lavoro libero" nella prassi sanzionatoria italiana: cronaca di un fallimento annunciato'. *Rivista Italiana di Diritto e Procedura Penale* 32: 88–117.

Pastoret, C.E.J.P. de (1790) *Des loix pénales. Tome Premier*. Paris: Chez. Buisson.

Pereira, L. M. Oliveira de Miranda (1986) 'Community Service in Portugal: How Did Community Service Perform since Its Implementation in the 1982 Amendment of the Penal Code?' In Albrecht, H. J. and W. Schädler (eds.) *Community Service: A New Option in Punishing Offenders in Europe*. Freiburg: iuscrim, 139–149.

Pereira, L. M. Oliveira de Miranda (2002) 'Community Sanctions and Measures in Portugal'. In Albrecht, H.-J. and A. van Kalmthout (eds.) *Community Sanctions and Measures in Europe and North America*. Freiburg: iuscrim, 453–475.

Pessina, E. (1906) 'Il diritto penale in Italia da Cesare Beccaria sino alla promulgazione del codice penale vigente (1764–1890)'. In Pessina, E. (ed.) *Enciclopedia del diritto penale italiano. Volume II*. Milan: Società Editrice Libraria, 541–769.

Pfohl, M. (1983) *Gemeinnützige Arbeit als strafrechtliche Sanktion*. Berlin: Duncker & Humblot.

Pritikin, M. H. (2010) 'Fine-Labor: The Symbiosis between Monetary and Work Sanctions'. *University of Colorado Law Review* 81: 343–424.

Puccioni, G. (1855) *Il Codice penale toscano illustrato sulla scorta delle fonti, del diritto e della giurisprudenza. Tomo I*. Pistoia: Tipografia Cino.

Quintero Olivares, G. (1977) 'El arresto sustitutorio'. *Cuadernos de Política Criminal* 2: 111–141.

Radzinowicz, L. and R. Hood (1986) *A History of English Criminal Law and Its Administration from 1750. Volume 5: The Emergence of Penal Policy*. London: Stevens & Sons.

Radzinowicz, L. and J. King (1977) *The Growth of Crime: The International Experience*. London: Hamish Hamilton.

Rauh, M. F. (1912) *Die Vermögensstrafen des Reichsstrafrechts und ihre Reform*. Breslau: Schlatter.

Rettich, H. (1894) 'Die württembergische Kriminalität. Ein Beitrag zur Landeskunde auf Grundlage der Reichstatistik'. In Statistisch-Topographisches Bureau (ed.) *Württembergische Jahrbücher für Statistik und Landeskunde: Heft I*. Württemberg: Statistisches Landesamt, 329–519.

Roldán Barbero, H. (1983) *El dinero, objeto fundamental de la sanción penal*. Madrid: Akal.

Rosenfeld, E. (1890) 'Welche Strafmittel können an die Stelle der kurzzeitigen Freiheitstrafe gesetzt werden?' In Von Liszt, F. (ed.) *Abhandlungen des kriminalistisches Seminars zu Halle. Zweiter Band, 2. Heft*. Berlin: Guttentag, 110–355.

Rosenfeld, E. (1892) 'Die Regelung der Geldstrafe'. *Mitteilungen der Internationalen Kriminalistischen Vereinigung. Bulletin de l'Union internationale de droit pénal* 3: 135–221.

Rossi, P.L.O. (1853) *Trattato di diritto penale*. Turin: Società Editrice.

Runkel-Langsdorff, G. (1908) 'Die Bemessung der Geldstrafe im Entwurf des schweizerischen Strafgesetzbuches'. *Zeitschrift für Schweizer Strafrecht* 21: 43–49.

Rusche, G. and O. Kirchheimer (1939 [2003]) *Punishment and Social Structure*. New Brunswick: Transaction.

Saleilles, R. (1911) *The Individualization of Punishment*. Boston: Little, Brown.

Sayers, S. (1989) 'Work, Leisure and Human Needs'. In Winnifrith, T. and C. Barrett (eds.) *The Philosophy of Leisure*. Basingstoke: Macmillan, 34–53.

Schmölder, R. (1902) *Die Geldstrafe: Vortrag, gehalten auf der 74. Jahresversammlung der Rheinisch-westfälischen Gefängnissgesellschaft in Düsseldorf am 15. Oktober 1902*. Hamm: Griebsch.

Schuchbauer, A. (1948) *Die Geldstrafe im deutschen und schwedischen Strafrecht*. Würzburg: Univ. Diss.

Schultz, H. (1977) *Einführung in den allgemeinen Teil des Strafrechts. Zweiter Band. Die kriminalrechtlichen Sanktionen. Das Jugendstrafrecht*. 3rd ed. Bern: Stämpfli.

Seagle, W. (1948) 'Fines'. In Seligman, E. and A. Johnson (ed.) *Encyclopaedia of the Social Sciences. Volume 6*. New York: Macmillan, 249–252.

Seidler, E. (1890) 'Die Geldstrafe vom volkswirtschaftlichen und soziologischen Gesichtspunkte'. *Jahrbücher für Nationalökonomie und Statistik* 20(3): 241–258.

Seligman, E.R.A. (1927) *The Economics of Instalment Selling*. New York: Harper & Brothers.

Semenova, A. and L. R. Wray (2015) *The Rise of Money and Class Society: The Contributions of John F. Henry*. New York: Levy Economics Institute.

Sevdiren, O. (2011) *Alternatives to Imprisonment in England and Wales, Germany and Turkey*. Berlin: Springer.

Silvela, L. (1874) *El derecho penal estudiado en principios y en la legislación vigente en España*. Madrid: Imprenta de M. G. Hernández.

Simmel, G. (1907 [1990]) *The Philosophy of Money*. New York: Routledge.

Stöckel, H. (2002) 'Strafen mit Fantasie: Zur Frage neuer Sanktionen im Strafrecht'. In Dölling, D. and V. Ebb (eds.) *Festschrift für Karl Heinz Gössel zum 70. Geburtstag am 16. Oktober 2002*. Heidelberg: Müller, 329–344.

Stooß, C. (1891) 'Das sogenannte Abverdienen von Geldstrafen'. *Zeitschrift für Schweizer Strafrecht* 4: 344–352.

Stooß, C. (1907) 'Die Geldstrafe im schweizerischen Strafgesetzentwurfe'. *Zeitschrift für Schweizer Strafrecht* 20: 242–249.

Stooß, C. (1916) 'Geldstrafe und Bußenabdiener'. *Zeitschrift für Schweizer Strafrecht* 29: 1–36.

Stooß, C. (1917) 'Zur Reform der Geldstrafe'. *Zeitschrift für Schweizer Strafrecht* 30: 87–107.

Strahl, I. (1951) 'Les jours amendes dans les pays nordiques'. *Revue de Science Criminelle et de Droit Pénal Comparé* 6: 59–67.

Sutherland, E. H. (1934) 'The Decreasing Prison Population of England'. *Journal of Criminal Law and Criminology* 24(5): 880–900.

Tak, P.J.P. (1986) 'Community Service Orders in Western Europe: A Comparative Survey'. In Albrecht, H.-J. and W. Schädler (eds.) *Community Service*. Freiburg: iuscrim, 1–14.
Terrill, R. J. (2016) *World Criminal Justice Systems: A Comparative Survey*. 9th ed. New York: Routledge.
Teruel Carralero, D. (1956) *Las faltas*. Barcelona: Bosch.
Thoday, W. (1934) 'Imprisonment for Debt'. *The Howard Journal of Criminal Justice* 4(1): 29–34.
Thoday, W. (1937) 'The Money Payments Act at Work'. *The Howard Journal of Criminal Justice* 4(4): 387–390.
Thornstedt, H. (1974) 'Skandinavische Erfahrungen mit dem Tagesbuβensystem'. *Zeitschrift für die gesamte Strafrechtswissenschaft* 86: 595–613.
Thornstedt, H. (1975) 'The Day-Fine System in Sweden'. *The Criminal Law Review*, June: 307–312.
Thyrén, J. (1910) *Prinzipien einer Strafgesetzreform. Band 1: Die soziale Aufgabe der Strafe*. Berlin: Guttentag.
Tittmann, C. A. (1822) *Handbuch der Strafrechtswissenschaft und Strafgesetzkunde*. Halle: Hemmerde und Schwetschke.
Ugarte y Pagés, F. J. de (1906) *Reformas en la administración de justicia: Apuntes para su estudio*. Madrid: Suárez.
Utriainen, T. (2002) 'Community Sanctions in Finland'. In Albrecht, H.-J. and A. van Kalmthout (eds.) *Community Sanctions and Measures in Europe and North America*. Freiburg: iuscrim, 193–207.
Van der Aa, J. S. (1927) *Proceedings of the IXth International Penitentiary Congress Held in London, August 1925*. Bern: Bureau of the International Prison Commission.
Van Kalmthout, A. M. and P.J.P. Tak (1992) *Sanctions-Systems in the Member States of the Council of Europe. Part II: Deprivation of Liberty, Community Service and Other Substitutes*. Deventer: Kluwer.
Vargha, J. (1896) *Die Abschaffung der Strafknechtschaft*. Graz: Leuschner & Lubensky.
Viada y Vilaseca, S. (1890) *Código Penal de 1870. Tomo I*. Madrid: Fernando Fe.
Vida, F. (1885) *El Proyecto de Código penal*. Apuntes críticos. Madrid: Imprenta de El Progreso.
Vila Miquel, E. (1917) *De la necesidad y medios de sustituir las penas cortas de privación de libertad*. Madrid: Imprenta de Juan Pueyo.
Vizmanos, T. M. de, and C. Álvarez Martínez (1848) *Comentarios al Código penal. Tomo I*. Madrid: Establecimiento Tipográfico de J. González y A. Vicente.
Von Buri, M. (1878) 'Zur Natur der Vermögensstrafen'. *Der Gerichtssaal* 30: 1–8.
Von Feuerbach, A. (1804) *Kritik des Kleinschrodischen Entwurfs zu einem peinlichen Gesetzbuche für die Chur-Pfalz-Bayrischen Staaten*. Giesen: Tasché & Müller.
Von Holtzendorff, F. (1864) 'Die Strafrechtreformvorschläge von Bonneville de Marsangy'. *Allgemeine Deutsche Strafrechtszeitung* 4: 642–658.
Von Ihering, R. (1877 [1904]) *Der Zweck im Recht*. Leipzig: Breitkopf & Haertel.
Von Lilienthal, K. (1892) 'Sind Aenderungen des geltenden Rechts erwünscht in Betreff des Verhältnisses zwischen Geld- und Freiheitsstrafe?' In Deutscher Juristentag (ed.) *Verhandlungen des Zweiundzwanzigsten Deutschen Juristentages. Zweiter Band*. Berlin: Guttentag, 63–94.
Von Liszt, F. (1883) 'Der Zweckgedanke im Strafrecht'. *Zeitschrift für die gesamte Strafrechtswissenschaft* 3: 1–47.
Von Liszt, F. (1889a) 'Kriminalpolitische Aufgaben'. *Zeitschrift für die gesamte Strafrechtswissenschaft* 9: 454–498, 737–782.

Von Liszt, F. (1889b) 'Welche Maßregeln können dem Gesetzgeber zur Einschränkung der kurzzeitigen Freiheitsstrafe empfohlen werden?' International Union of Penal Law/ Deutsche Landesgruppe (ed.) *Mitteilungen der Internationalen Kriminalistischen Vereinigung: Bulletin de l'Union internationale de droit pénal*. Berlin: Guttentag, 44–51.

Von Liszt, F. (1892) 'Anträge zur Frage der Regelung der Geldstrafe'. In International Union of Penal Law/ Deutsche Landesgruppe (ed.) *Mitteilungen der Internationalen Kriminalistischen Vereinigung. Bulletin de l'Union internationale de droit pénal*. Berlin: Guttentag, 220–221.

Von Liszt, F. (1905) 'Kriminalpolitische Aufgaben (1889–1892)'. In Von Liszt, F. (ed.) *Strafrechtliche Aufsätze und Vorträge. Band I*. Berlin: Guttentag, 290–467.

Von Stenglein, M. (1892) 'Die Regelung der Geldstrafe nach den Berathungen der internationalen kriminalistischen Vereinigung'. *Der Gerichtssaal* 47: 264–281.

Von Thielau in AA.VV. (1837) *Mittheilungen des sächsischen Landtags. 22.4.1837, 63. Sitzung am 15.4.1837*. Dresden: Zenbuer.

Wahlberg, W. E. (1869) *Das Princip der Individualisierung in der Strafrechtspflege*. Vienna: Gerold.

Wahlberg. W. E. (1872) *Criminalistische und nationalökonomische Gesichtspunkte mit Rücksicht auf das deutsche Reichsstrafrecht*. Vienna: Gerold.

Wahlberg, W. E. (1877) 'Nationalökonomische Gesichtspunkte im Strafrecht mit besonderer Rücksicht auf die Geldstrafe'. In Wahlberg, W. E. (ed.) *Gesammelte kleinere Schriften und Bruchstücke über Strafrecht, Strafprozess, Gefängnisskunde, Literatur und Dogmengeschichte der Rechtslehre in Oesterreich*. Vienna: Alfred Hölder, 231–264.

Warner, K. (2012) 'Equality before the Law and Equal Impact of Sanctions: Doing Justice to Differences in Wealth and Employment Status'. In Zedner, L. (ed.) *Principles and Values in Criminal Law and Criminal Justice: Essays in Honour of Andrew Ashworth*. Oxford: Oxford University Press, 225–244

Weigend, T. (2001) 'Sentencing and Punishment in Germany'. In Tonry, M. and R. S. Frase (eds.) *Sentencing and Sanctions in Western Countries*. New York: Oxford University Press, 188–221.

Westen, D. A. (1969) 'Fines, Imprisonment, and the Poor: Thirty Dollars or Thirty Days'. *California Law Review* 57(3): 778–820.

Young, W. (1979) *Community Service Orders: The Development and Use of a New Penal Measure*. London: Heinemann.

Zürcher, E. (1891) 'Thesen zu den Fragen betreffend die Geldstrafe'. *Zeitschrift für Schweizer Strafrecht* 4: 268–270.

5 The expansion of the fine in the twentieth century

Old wine in new bottles: continuity of the debate on fines at the beginning of the twentieth century

It has been said that while the fine was well understood in principle by classical thinkers, such as Bentham and Beccaria, fines could not be deployed to any degree before the end of the nineteenth century because of the extent of unemployment and poverty. 'The poorer the population of the country, the less frequent is the use of fines for offences characteristic of the great mass of the people' (Rusche and Kirchheimer 1939 [2003]: 172). For Rusche and Kirchheimer (1939 [2003]: 168), only an increase in employment and living standards in the twentieth century could provide the conditions under which fundamental change could happen and render the fine a more generally applied sanction:[1] 'The decline in unemployment and the rising living standard in the second half of the century, however, introduced a fundamental change. Many of the earlier difficulties lying in the way of a fine system lost their force'. It seems that all obstacles to fines would have disappeared by themselves if the material conditions of the poor had only improved. Reality, though, was very different. The period preceding the outbreak of World War I witnessed a lively discussion on the aims and practical results of different modes of punishment. Once the Great War was over, the decline in the intensity of the controversy about short-term imprisonment was sharp and sudden: the debates were far less frequent and the arguments became solid, without any new opposing developments being introduced (Padovani 1981: 193). The problem stopped being the symptom of a more general discomfort with the structure and functions of the punitive system and became a relatively marginal question, the solution for which could be found simply by resorting to the instruments that had already been designed in the preceding era, which were now starting to gain legislative recognition – that is, conditional suspension, probation, and community service (Bamberger 1917; De Ryckere 1922: 825–826 and 937–938; Lucchini 1926: 205–206; Neymark 1928: 929–930).

The fact that the offender's economic means were finally taken into account meant it could be stated that the fine, although 'it should always cause the offender some distress [. . .,] is in essence flexible so that it can be perfectly adapted to the offender's economic situation' (Cuello Calón 1929: 202). Thanks to the adoption of the day-fine system in some countries and to the obligation to take the offender's economic situation into account in many countries that did not adopt it, the objections to the inequality of impact of the fine on offenders with different economic situations could at last be circumvented, if not completely solved.[2]

In sum, more widespread use of fines became possible when the subsidiary punishment of a prison sentence was applied only in truly exceptional cases, following the general tendency to avoid committing offenders to prison whenever possible. This happened only when the amount of the fine was set with the offender's financial situation in mind and practical alternatives to imprisonment for defaulters were designed, thereby weakening the arguments used against fines. Only after the problem of default had been successfully addressed was the literature able to display the positive effects of fines (Von Holtzendorff 1864: 651–652; Tallack 1889: 280–281; Seidler 1890: 241ff.; Schmölder 1902: 50–51), such as

- their capacity to be adjusted in line with the seriousness of offences and the offenders' financial situation using criteria of proportionality and equality (Rosenfeld 1890: 310; Schuchbauer 1948: 77);
- their impact on a commodity appreciated by all (Bonneville de Marsangy 1864: 252);
- their economical enforcement (Ferri 1900: 454; Vila Miquel 1917: 168–169; Cuello Calón 1929: 202), not so much in revenue earned by the state – which 'would be unseemly' (Montes 1929: 389) and could produce abuses for fiscal reasons (Seidler 1890: 247; Friedmann 1892: 118ff.), so that it should be better considered a mere 'reflex' of the impoverishment of the offender (Stooß 1878: 24) – but rather in reducing the costs involved in other punishments;
- the facility of their reparation for an unjust sentence, because as they affect a 'non-personal' commodity it is easy to return the offender to the situation he or she was in before experiencing the punishment (Valdés Rubio 1909: 742; Navarro de Paiva 1915: 193; Donnedieu de Vabres 1937: 386);
- their contribution to repairing the damage suffered by the victim (Ferri 1900: 454); and
- the advantage of not withdrawing manpower from the economic system (Rusche and Kirchheimer 1939 [2003]: 169).

They were largely the same advantages already highlighted by Bentham in his work *The Rationale of Punishment* (1830: Book 3, Chapter 4) almost a century earlier, as Schuchbauer (1948: 78) pointed out, but boosted by public demand for a general restriction of short-term imprisonment. Both reform movements of the 1920s and 1970s were built on this nineteenth-century ideological foundation and expressions of this continuity will be shown on the following pages.[3] For now, it is enough to point out that because of this continuity new legislation met little opposition.

Two new arguments in favour of monetary punishments were added to the more classical ones: first, the lack of dissocializing effects of the fine, compared to imprisonment; second, the growing importance of money, with the corresponding increase in the deterrent efficacy of the fine. Both are connected. The first one stems from the comparison between the decidedly detrimental effects of short-term imprisonment and the simple lack of reformative value of the fine. This comparison led to a view that the fine, while not exactly re-socializing – it was generally acknowledged that 'it has little significance in terms of educational importance' (Merkel 1889: 227), being not reformative at all – was at least more positive on the grounds that it involves less stigmatization than imprisonment: '[the fine] does not degrade the offender, nor does it create an obstacle for his social rehabilitation or dishonour his family unlike imprisonment that causes such serious harm' (Cuello Calón 1929: 202). Comparison with imprisonment allows one to conclude that

> as an abstract position, it seems to be generally true that restraint by the infliction of just and moderate pecuniary fines is, as regards the mode of punishment, advantageous to society. For it is better to attain to the same object by moderate privation of property than by subjecting offenders to imprisonment or bodily suffering, which cannot be inflicted without risk of moral taint or personal degradation and disgrace.
>
> (Commission on Criminal Law 1843: 1–2)

In this way, the criticism of the fine's lack of rehabilitative effects was gradually substituted by the acknowledgement that at least it does not dissocialize. As we will see later on in this chapter, this argument will be picked up again during the 1970s, transformed into two positive assertions: first, fines do have a preventive effect and can contribute to rehabilitate offenders; and second, their efficacy as a general deterrent is much greater than many would credit.

The second argument is connected to the emergence of a consumer society and the generalization of the use of money. In effect, the fine's capability to act as a deterrent had long been doubted. However, starting in the 1930s, the fine was finally attributed a general deterrent effect simply based on the increased importance of money in consumer societies and the premise that an increase in value leads to a fear of its loss (Rusche and Kirchheimer 1939 [2003]: 168–169). Discussion focuses on 'the intimidating strength of the loss of economic means in a society such as the current one, so centred around money' (Beristain Ipiña 1976: 19; also Hassan 1959: 38–39; Musco 1984: 69ff.). In a world where so much depends on money the fine is one of the most satisfactory sentences. As indicated by Thornstedt (1975: 312), 'The high standard of living makes people more reluctant than formerly to pay out money for offences and thus deprive themselves of opportunities to buy TV sets, cars, etc., or to be forced to postpone holiday trips'. These two arguments added to the clear continuity in the academic and political debate on alternatives to imprisonment. Along with the conditional suspension of sentences, with or without probation,[4] the use of fines as an alternative or substitute for short-term imprisonment gradually increased since they were considered the most effective instrument for achieving the objective of limiting the use of short-term imprisonment (Bamberger 1917: 11–12; 9th Prison Congress held in London in 1925). This led to the phenomenon of short prison sentences being restricted to rather more modest limits than those seen at the end of the nineteenth century.

Yet with all of these ideological similarities, it is remarkable how many differences surfaced among Western European countries. The massive expansion of the fine over the first half of the twentieth century in some countries but not in others, and the discontinuities in the same country, must be viewed partially in relationship to changes in ideologies sustaining political regimes and partially in the timely divergent emergence of new regulatory demands. To illustrate the situation at the beginning of the twentieth century the development of Germany is particularly interesting, not only because of the period of inflation followed by depression and a profound change in dominant political regimes and accompanying ideology, but also due to its subsequent influence on other countries in terms of technical achievements. In other words, in spite of the great divide that triggered World War II and the eventual fall of the Nazi regime, numerous statutory amendments, legislative draft codes, critical considerations, and counter-proposals stemming from pre–World War II Germany led to the accumulation of invaluable expertise that would be of use when questions regarding the increase of crime and prison population rose again in the 1960s. Furthermore, the German experience shows that it is possible to implement the fine in such a way that it substantially reduces the use of short-term imprisonment, simply by introducing the obligation to set the amount of the fine in line with the financial means of the offender and by giving him or her time to pay in instalments. It also suggests the possibility that, in absence of legally imposed changes, courts' sentencing behaviour can be strongly influenced by a new ideologically based juridical reasoning. Before addressing the current state of affairs, the re-proposition of the debate regarding intermediate punishments in the second half of the twentieth century will be explained, because it is fundamental in understanding the preference for fines in current Western European criminal policy.

War, depression, and dictatorship: the German case

It has been argued that during periods of depression the fine becomes less feasible, and consequently short terms of imprisonment become more prevalent (Rusche and Kirchheimer 1939 [2003]: 166ff.). A good way of confirming this thesis is to analyse what happened in Germany during the severe depression of the 1870s and the inflationary period in the 1920s, which was followed by the Great Depression of 1929. Not only was there good statistical data, but also there was widespread belief in literature and jurisprudence that it was necessary to reduce the use of short-term imprisonment. In order to properly assess what happened in Germany during this period we need to first understand the situation at the turn of the century, as well as the changes in crime and punishment resulting from World War I and the legislative attempts to maintain the level of fines during the inflationary interwar period. I will analyse the development of the fine under the Nazi regime in order to demonstrate the influence that a radical change in ideology can have on the practical application of laws whose wording did not change much.

German criminal law until the Great War

The German penal system during the first third of the twentieth century developed out of the German criminal law shaped by the codification movement of the nineteenth century. The 1871 German Imperial Penal Code, strongly influenced by the 1851 Prussian Penal Code – in essence, the Imperial Penal Code was a mere revision of the Prussian one, first enacted as law for the North German Union – was essentially a product of the classical school (Grünhut 1944: 3; Hoefer 1945: 385). The penalties were the death penalty – for murder only –, deprivation of liberty – in four forms: penal servitude, imprisonment, confinement to a fortress, and detention, which differed partly in the length of the term to be served and partly in the prison regime – and fines. On the whole, deprivation of liberty characterized the criminal justice system, with 'imprisonment as the normal form of legal punishment' (Grünhut 1944: 4). Fines played a less important role (Vormbaum 2014: 105). They were used for a relatively small number of offences compared to other European countries (Schmölder 1902: 8): in the German Imperial Penal Code 77 offences were mandated as punishable by fine, with only 3 such offences solely punishable by fine, while imprisonment was mandated for 334 offences (Meemar 2009: 18). Fines were not used for serious crimes, and for petty crimes they were usually an alternative to imprisonment. The German system did not follow on from the preceding code of 1851, which saw a significant increase in the use of the fine as a form of punishment (Neumaier 1947: 92–93). The 1871 German Imperial Penal Code did not include any rules for determining punishments to guide judges, as it adopted the stance that the judge should have the broadest scope possible, considering the requirements of general intimidatory deterrence, acknowledged as being the fundamental aim of the punishment thanks to the influence of Von Feuerbach (Schmidt 1946: 205). It made no mention of the consideration of the offender's financial circumstances. Fine defaulters were subject to a prison sentence or a detention sentence depending on the classification of the offence.

Between 1882 – the first year in which statistics were collected – and 1914 a dramatic growth in the proportion of offenders fined in Germany can be observed, in spite of the severe and long depression triggered by the bank and stock exchange crash of 1873, whose consequences lasted well into the 1890s. The percentage of issued fines doubled during the period. If we take into account convictions for offences against the Penal Code as well as against criminal supplementary laws, the numbers are as shown in Table 5.1.

As can be observed, between 1882 and 1889 prison sentences constituted approximately 70 per cent of all sentences. Prison sentences under three months constituted more than 50 per cent of all sentences. These short sentences of less than three months became less common as the use of the fine increased. In the beginning there was a slight increase in the amount of prison sentences of over three months, probably to cover those cases that were considered too serious to be punished with just a fine, but for which the criticized punishment of short-term imprisonment was no longer deemed suitable. After a while these sentences also

Table 5.1 Prison and fine sentences (percentages), German Empire: 1882–1913

Year	*Convictions per 100,000 population above the age of discretion*	*Penal servitude (Zuchthaus)*	*Prison sentences*			*Fines*
			Prison of one year or over	*Prison from three months to one year*	*Prison under three months*	
1882/84	1,002	4.0	1.9	10.1	59.1	23.3
1885/89	1,012	3.4	2.9	11.3	53.5	27.1
1890/94	1,125	2.9	3.0	11.2	49.2	31.5
1895/99	1,204	2.3	2.9	10.7	44.0	37.7
1900/04	1,212	2.0	2.8	10.4	40.3	41.7
1905/09	1,215	1.5	2.4	9.1	36.8	47.0
1910/13	1,190	1.4	2.6	9.0	33.8	50.5

Source: Adapted from Rabl (1936: 8). Only sentences for offences against the Reich are included.

became less common, albeit in a much more gradual fashion. Shortly before the outbreak of World War I the fine already constituted more than 50 per cent of all convictions in Germany.

Figure 5.1 Prison and fine sentences (percentages), German Empire: 1882–1913

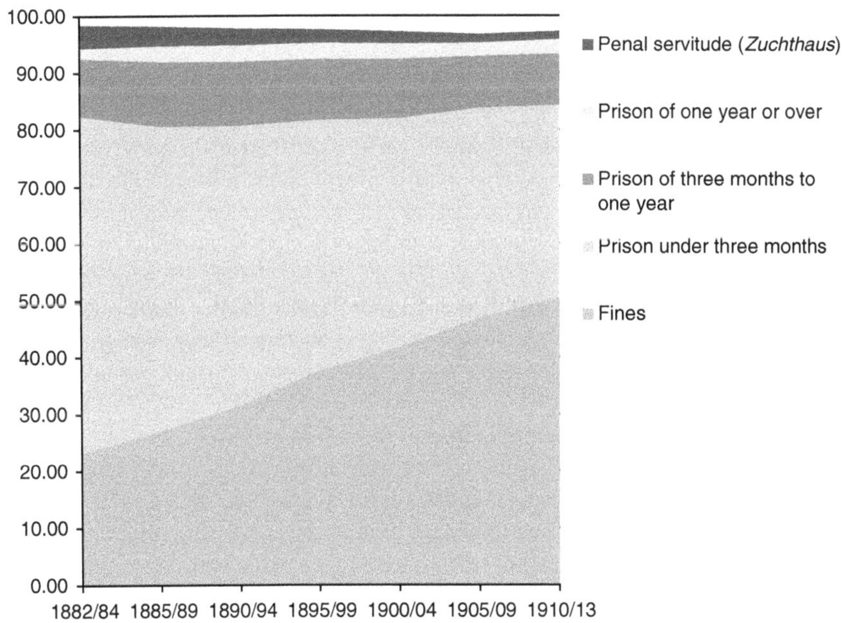

Source: Adapted from Rabl (1936: 8). Only sentences for offences against the Reich are included.

This significant increase in the use of fines has been explained by the influence of the academic debate on the adverse effects of short-term imprisonment (Bamberger 1917: 20; Pischel 1929: 8; Roldán Barbero 1983: 53–55; Kubink 2002: 183; Wilde 2016: 41), with a similar tendency in the practice of the courts, where a steady trend to pronounce milder sentences can be observed (Grünhut 1944: 14). The increase in the use of the fine supposedly had nothing to do with legal innovations.

There is no question that the courts became much more inclined to hand out fines for those cases where it could be combined alternatively with a custodial sentence. As indicated in the German imperial criminal statistics (Reichskriminalstatistik 1898/1899: I.48; see also Exner 1931: 18–19; Rabl 1936: 12; Heinz 2011: 2; Wilde 2016: 56), the fundamental reason for this change was unquestionably rooted in the growing opposition to short-term imprisonment, which attempted to limit its use. As already shown, since the last third of the nineteenth century in German-speaking countries the majority of scholars and practitioners were in favour of the possibility of replacing short-term imprisonment with a fine (Mittelstädt 1879; Von Liszt 1889; Schmölder 1902; Glauning 1905). Von Ihering (1877 [1904]: 292–293), a representative of social finalism, stated,

> When the fine is sufficient, there shall be no custodial sentence; when a custodial sentence is enough, there shall be no death penalty. With a fine the harm is only suffered by the offender, not society; with imprisonment and the death penalty, society has to pay with its own losses, for the punishment imposed on the offender; all excess turns against it.

Framed within this trend, the first two reform projects of the 1871 Imperial Penal Code, the 1909 preliminary draft, written by a commission appointed by the Reich Justice Office, and the 1911 alternative draft, published by a body of private experts, pointed towards an expansion of the legal applicability of the fine, also proposing that the financial circumstances of the offender be taken into account in determining the amount of the fine, and that offenders be permitted to pay the fine in instalments and to do public work in the case of default (Büdemann 1912; Rauh 1912: 93ff.; Georgi 1914). Although these drafts did not come into effect, the advance of the fine and the corresponding reduction of custodial sentences, especially short-term imprisonment, are well documented in this period (Exner 1931: 20ff.; Stapenhorst 1993: 31–34; Heinz 2010: 55; Wilde 2016: 56). But was this change due simply to the preference of the courts?

It is certainly true that the socio-economic problems caused by the decolonization and industrialization processes and the political tensions that led to World War I did not provide an appropriate breeding ground for addressing important legal innovations. Of the more than 200 amendments made to the body of criminal laws up to the 2010s, a period of around 140 years, only 18 date from the 45-year period up to 1914 we are now considering (Vormbaum 2014: 135). But the low number of amendments to the Penal Code should not cause us to forget that a deluge of criminal laws was passed *beyond* the codified criminal law. Between 1871 and 1914 supplementary penal regulations (*Nebenstrafrecht*) were enacted in many areas related to public order and industry, such as copyright law, patent law, emigration, the press and associations, morals and the family, railways, shipping, communications, the financial system, the military, and colonies. Most of the regulations only threatened to issue fines for infringements of civil or administrative norms of special laws. These offences were called '*reine Geldstrafendelikte*' (offering data, see Troschiz 1907: 65–120). The imperial criminal statistics of 1882 show that 142 of such offences were included, whereas in 1913 they were already 550. There was a noticeable increase in this period in the number of fines imposed on offenders for these new offences as well as in their percentage of all fine convictions.

Table 5.2 Fine sentences imposed for new offences contained in the *Nebenstrafrecht*, German Empire: 1882–1911 (selected years)

Year	*Total number of convictions*	*Percentage of all fine sentences*
1882	116	0.2
1891	498	0.4
1901	11,293	5.8
1911	32,832	12.1

Source: *Reichskriminalstatistik* (1911: I.42).

This is undoubtedly due to the fact that for three-quarters of these cases the court had no other option but to impose a fine, as there were many offences that could be punished only with a fine (Stapenhorst 1993: 16). Added to this was the favourable judicial stance towards the fine, which was very pronounced for these new offences, while not quite so significant for the traditional offences included in the Penal Code: for traditional offences punishable by either imprisonment or a fine the fine was selected in 68.3 per cent of the cases, while for new offences with the same two options the fine was selected in 96.6 per cent of the cases (Stapenhorst 1993: 17; Reichskriminalstatistik 1911: I.43).

However, the seemingly unstoppable all-conquering march of the pecuniary punishment was abruptly interrupted between 1914 and 1918. In 1917 the percentage of imposed fines fell below 1886 levels, reaching 29.14 per cent (Pitschel 1929: 9). Stenner (1970: 22) gives the figure of 32 per cent of imposed fines one year later, in 1918. Since not one change was made to the German Imperial Penal Code during the war – following the outbreak of the war, work on the reform of the Penal Code had come to a standstill – Pitschel (1929: 10) and Exner (1931: 26) attributed the reduction in the use of the fine to a hardening in the attitude of the courts. This may be an important factor, but there is no doubt that the different types of crimes committed due to the war also had an impact. Statistics show an increase in theft, which was not sanctioned with a fine, and a considerable decrease in the number of offences for causing bodily harm, which were normally sanctioned with a fine (Liepmann 1930: 69: Blau 1952: 64). Moreover, it is worth noting that martial commercial criminal law was created as a supplementary penal provision, with the term 'commercial' interpreted rather loosely (Naucke 2000: 293). It continued the trend already visible since the end of the nineteenth century to use not the penal code but supplementary criminal laws to control the economy. The best example is the Decree of the Federal Council on the authorization of orders of summary punishment for misdemeanours against the economic measures (*Verordnung des Bundesrates über die Zulassung von Strafbefehlen bei Vergehen gegen Vorschriften über wirtschaftliche Maßnahmen*) of June 4, 1915. This new legislation favoured the imposition of fines for technical infractions of the vast array of supplementary criminal laws, because it created offences where the sanction of imprisonment was inappropriate in the first place.

The interwar period: inflation and depression

Once World War I was over, 1920s Germany witnessed a period of dominance of the social-democrat party and preponderance of radical reformist tendencies. The dominant literature of that time fully took on board the nineteenth-century criticisms against short-term imprisonment (Hellwig 1924; Schäfer 1934; Bumke 1926 and 1928; Pitschel 1929). Preliminary drafts were presented that were very favourable towards the fine. One example is a 1919 draft which intended to broaden the scope of the fine by making a greater number of offences punishable by fine and by requiring courts to ensure whether the purpose of the punishment could be fulfilled by a fine in cases where the law provided for the fine and imprisonment as alternatives (Oetker 1922: 161ff.). A second example is a 1922 draft, written by Radbruch – then minister of justice – which was described as 'by and large the zenith of the legislative reform work' beginning in the nineteenth century (Jescheck, quoted by Kubink 2002: 173), and as 'the most progressive ever submitted in the history of German criminal law' (Grünhut 1944: 27). This groundbreaking draft conceived the fine as the primary reaction against offences and placed it at the centre of the criminal justice system (Radbruch 1952: 55). It was never enacted.[5] The failure of the Penal Code reform projects led to laws being established for the fine that formed the basis of its recovery (Bumke 1928: 16–19, with statistical data; Reichstatistik 1930: 44ff.).

The four laws enacted between 1921 and 1924[6] established the following objectives:

- Set a maximum amount of the fine, which did not exist until then;
- Substitute imprisonment sentences of less than three months with a fine of up to 150,000 marks, 'whenever the purpose of punishment can be achieved just as well by a fine'.

In order to avoid the vicious circle of an offender being first fined instead of being sent to prison, and then subsequently, however, being imprisoned because he or she was unable to pay the fine, the first law of 1921

- obliged courts to take the financial circumstances of the offender into account in determining the amount of the fine;

- authorized courts to give the offender leave to pay the fine in instalments within an specified period of time if immediate payment of the total amount could not reasonably be expected; and
- provided for work (*freie Arbeit*) to be used as a way of dealing with fine defaulters, so that the offender could remain free and work off his or her fine.

The three other laws centred on the problem of inflation. The law of April 27, 1923, adjusted fines to the increasing inflation – the maximum limit grew from 150,000 to 10 million marks, an amount that could be increased when it was not 'enough' (§ 27c of the Imperial Penal Code). It had to be complemented only a few months later by the law of October 23, 1923, and the decree of November 23, 1923, both of which included new measures to fight the persistent problem of inflation (Alsberg 1924: 276–277).

These laws, particularly the first one, had the desired effect of increasing the percentage of fine sentences and reducing prison sentences, even if the possibility of allowing the offender to work his or her fine off in liberty remained a dead letter (Grünhut 1944: 14). In 1921 the percentage of prison sentences reached 56.9 per cent, but in 1922 it went down to 36.9 per cent. This decrease was also very significant regarding short-term imprisonment, which, over the same period, went down from 38.3 per cent in 1921 to 20.2 per cent in 1922. During the same period the percentage of imposed fines grew from 39.3 per cent to 59.5 per cent of all penalties (according to *Reichskriminalstatistik* 1930: 44), with literature elaborating on a 'strong effect of the Acts on Fines' (Pitschel 1929: 10). These laws brought a significant change in the sanctioning practice, a fact which can be described only as 'a turning point of German penal policy' (Heinz 1981: 159; Stapenhorst 1993: 45).

The enacted laws were, nevertheless, not without their ups and downs. The inflationary process that the German economy of the 1920s went through had an adverse effect on the fine. In fact, it was a decisive factor which rendered the fine ineffective despite the frequency with which it was imposed by the courts.[7] In essence, the constant depreciation of the value of money meant that the amount the judge set in the sentence bore little relation to the amount actually paid by the offender. If we also take into account that it was obligatory to grant an extension and instalment periods for payment in cases where the offender was unable to pay, the time that elapsed between the fine being set and it actually being paid made the real value of the fine have no connection whatsoever to the intention of the judge who originally imposed it (Kitzinger 1923: 599; Kronecker 1924: 578ff.). This led to a decrease in the use of the fine in 1924 and 1925, so that the percentages of 1913 and 1925 were practically the same (Pitschel 1929: 10). This hiatus was quickly overcome – that is, until the Great Depression of 1929 unleashed its effects.

In fact, the assertion that economic depressions have an adverse effect on the propensity to fine seems to find no strong statistical correlation. Regarding the Great Depression, Germany was the European country 'in which the crisis was most severe, and in which wage cuts and unemployment created the sharpest decline in the living standard of broad sections of the population' (Rusche and Kirchheimer 1939 [2003]: 177–178). During this period the proportion of unpaid fines increased, as expected. As indicated by the imperial criminal statistics (*Reichskriminalstatistik* 1930: 45), in 1928 77.7 per cent of fines were paid in full, but the percentage fell to 62.7 per cent in 1931. That is to say that the number of fines levied decreased because of the reduced possibilities of collecting the fine (Rusche and Kirchheimer 1939 [2003]: 171; Albrecht 1978: 174). Consequently, the number of defaults went up rapidly, and so did imprisonment for defaulters: the percentage of fines that were left unpaid and converted into a prison sentence increased from 6.7 in 1925 to 8.1 per cent in 1928 and almost doubled to 15.4 per cent in 1931 (Albrecht 1978: 188; Janssen 1994: 12). The proportion of sentences that *imposed* fines also declined, but clearly not as sharply as it should have according to Rusche and Kirchheimer's thesis.

Table 5.3 Prison and fine sentences (percentages), German Empire: 1882–1932 (in five-year periods)

Year	*Convictions per 100,000 population above the age of discretion*	*Penal servitude (Zuchthaus)*	*Prison*			*Fines*
			Prison of one year or over	*Prison from three months to one year*	*Prison under three months*	
1882/84	1,002	4.0	1.9	10.1	59.1	23.3
1885/89	1,012	3.4	2.9	11.3	53.5	27.1
1890/94	1,125	2.9	3.0	11.2	49.2	31.5
1895/99	1,204	2.3	2.9	10.7	44.0	37.7
1900/04	1,212	2.0	2.8	10.4	40.3	41.7
1905/09	1,215	1.5	2.4	9.1	36.8	47.0
1910/13	1,190	1.4	2.6	9.0	33.8	50.5
1920/21	1,319	1.3	4.4	13.8	38.6	38.7
1922/24	1,504	1.3	3.5	13.7	19.7	60.1
1925/29	1,215	1.1	2.1	9.9	18.8	66.9
1930/32	1,145	0.9	2.2	11.1	23.1	61.4

Source: Adapted from Rabl (1936: 8).

O'Malley (2009: 39) observed,

> Rusche and Kirchheimer (1939: 169–172) put stress on the proportions of fines that are not paid in full and that therefore result in imprisonment. But the proportion of *sentences* that are fines does not decline as it should, given the severity of the depression. They dip by only three per cent throughout the period. In short, people may be unable to pay, but the courts are only marginally changing their sentencing behaviour.
>
> (italics in the original)

O'Malley relates this slight decline to the possibility that courts do not sentence as a reflex of the state of the economy, but are influenced far more by other considerations. He takes into account only the data up to 1931, while the strongest decrease of fine sentences can be seen in 1932, just before the Nazis came to power. By then, fines were only 56.2 per cent of all convictions, while prison sentences under three months increased to 26 per cent and prison sentences between three months and one year increased to 12.9 per cent (Rabl 1936: 8).

Figure 5.2 Prison and fine sentences (percentages), German Empire: 1882–1932 (in five-year periods)

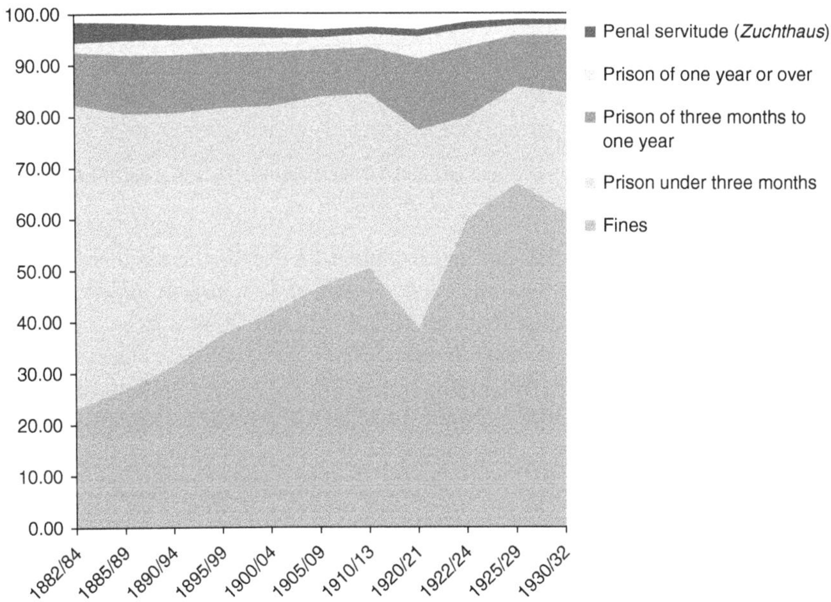

Source: Adapted from Rabl (1936: 8). Only sentences for offences against the Reich are included.

On the contrary, German literature agreed that 1929 put a stop to the growth in the proportion of sentences that were fines (Exner 1932: 749; Stapenhorst 1993: 45). The explanation given was that because many offenders could not pay their fines, due to their dire financial situation, courts went back to imposing custodial sentences (Stapenhorst 1993: 45). This would mean that there was a change in the attitude of judges.

Conversely, the available statistical data show that throughout the reporting period the proportion of offenders sentenced to terms of over three months of imprisonment remained fairly stable, with only negligible growth. Fines were substituted only by the shortest periods of imprisonment. This produced an increase in the total occupancy of prisons and a corresponding decrease in the daily average occupancy.

Table 5.4 Total and daily average occupancy, Free State of Prussia:* 1923–1932

Year	*Daily average occupancy*	*Total occupancy*
1923	70,035	473,351
1924	66,366	460,682
1925	54,253	394,899
1926	46,030	362,975
1927	36,692	281,156
1928	32,211	257,835
1929	30,155	263,422
1930	30,141	280,118
1931	32,525	317,294
1932	37,982	368,967

Source: Justizministerium Preußen (1926–1931) for the years 1923–1929, Schmidt (1934: 1023ff.) for the years 1930–1932.

* It was not possible to find data for the whole German Empire. Prussia was the major state of the German Empire during the existence of the Weimar Republic, comprising more than 60 per cent of its territory and population. It held about 60 per cent of all German inmates (Wachsmann 2014: 133), so these data can be considered representative of a general trend.

It is worth keeping in mind that imprisonment for defaulters was also a short-term prison sentence that increased the percentage of these prison sentences. The German legislation on fines in the years 1921, 1923, and 1924, which established work penalty without imprisonment (*Arbeitsstrafe ohne Einsperrung*) as a substitute for an unpaid fine, failed in practice (Best 1932: 19; Grünhut 1944: 14; Grebing 1978: 151; Pfohl 1983: 29–30), just like the precedent regulation in the German Imperial Penal Code 1871 did.

In sum, this means that the courts were not changing their sentencing behaviour due to the growing percentage of unpaid fines, but only applying the statute that provided imprisonment in case of default, due to the lack of alternatives. The available data also show that under conditions of poverty the fine can still operate as a mass sanction. As the German experience illustrates, the fine could be applied according to the economic circumstances of the time as well as to the offender's financial situation and the seriousness of the offence.

A new governing mentality: the Nazi dislike of fines

What happened when the Nazis came to power? As Sevdiren (2011: 129) pointed out, '[a]s far as the conceptualization of alternatives to imprisonment is concerned, prima facie it may appear that in the Third Reich era, there was continuity rather than discontinuity'. In fact there were no legislative changes concerning the fine after 1929. However, there was a clear change in trends that was reinforced in the middle of the 1930s. The use of fines strongly declined. What was the reason for this? It had nothing to do with changes in the system of production – with the change towards a monopolistic capitalism – nor with the economic crisis, but with a new governing mentality. The ascension of the Nazis to power in 1933, after years of enormous political and economic tension, opened a new political period.

It also marked the start of a new penal culture. Compared with the abolition of infamous punishments in the amended Radbruch's draft, adopted as the official draft in 1925, and considering the effort made to turn the fine into a fundamental cornerstone of the sanctioning system in the reforms of 1921, 1923, and 1924, the national-socialist penal law was based on *Gesinnung*, the need for the offender to feel the 'shame' of his or her unlawful act (Schaffstein 1934: 280). This meant redefining the punishment system: the punishments of proscription and confiscation reappeared, the applicability of the death penalty was widened, custodial sentences were linked to ulterior infamous consequences, and the opposition to short-term imprisonment gave way to more intense punitive content. There was a drastic restriction in the scope of the alternatives to imprisonment by limiting the number of eligible candidates for more lenient sentencing options, with a strong emphasis on deeply intrusive supervision measures (Sevdiren 2011: 129–130).

In this context, the decrease in the importance of the fine is easy to understand. If we add the problem of unemployment, which reached intolerably high levels due to a combination of factors – demobilization and the curtailment of arms production in the winter of 1918–1919, the Ruhr occupation in 1923, and the depression of 1929–1933 – it is no surprise that the *vexata quaestio* of whether the fine was a privilege of the wealthy was again reviewed (Mengele 1936: 57). But beyond the continuity of old debates we should note that penal fines were also considered undesirable under the Nazi regime due to ideological reasons (Rusche and Kirchheimer 1939 [2003]: 186). The rise in the use of fines during the Weimar Republic was seen as an unfortunate development that had to be halted. In the words of a member of the Criminal Law Commission, which was appointed by the Nazi government and tasked with a complete renewal of the penal law, the fine was 'an unpleasant and unworthy means of punishment' associated with a capitalist and decadent society (Rietzsch 1934: 100–101). It was seen as an ancillary penalty only in crimes of profit. In other cases it should be applicable only for petty offences, such as libels, minor bodily injuries, and insults.

In light of this new governing mentality two complementary trends regarding the penal fine began to emerge: first, to impose it much more sparingly than before; and second, to eliminate its 'plutocratic' character through the day-fine system, with the unpaid fine being worked off by labour (Rietzsch 1934: 100–101; Wolf 1935: 564ff.; Mengele 1936: 17ff.). Only the first one was implemented in legislation. The second one, proposed in the Gürtner Project 1936, was the first appearance of the day-fine system in the history of German penal codification (according to Grebing 1978: 35 and 78). It did not gain any traction and was steamrolled by preparations for war, hardly compatible with its technical refinement (Roldán Barbero 1983: 60), thus adding to Hitler's reluctance to pass basic laws after the war had broken out (Vormbaum 2014: 189). The spirit of the times focused on establishing 'community interest' as the fundamental principle of the system, at the expense of individual rights. To this end, the Nazi regime promoted community service not only as a substitute for an unpaid fine but also more tragically as a fundamental part of the confinement of offenders and other undesirable people (Stock 1933: 17 and 109; Schaffstein 1934: 618; Siegert 1934: 67). The resulting horrific exploitation of forced labourers in both concentration camps and industry needs not to be elaborated on.

As a result of this ideological aversion, the use of fines experienced a considerable reduction between 1933 and 1943, in percentage as well as in total numbers. In 1933 the prison sentence was used in 44.3 per cent of total convictions, while for the fine it was 52.3 per cent. In 1939 the ratio was 40.4 to 54.8 per cent. During the war, the rates of prison sentences remained steady, with an average of 41.3 per cent, while the use of fines declined by 17 per cent (Stapenhorst 1993: 66; Sevdiren 2011: 131).

Figure 5.3 Convictions to prison, fine, and other penalties (in percentages), German Empire: 1933–first semester 1943*

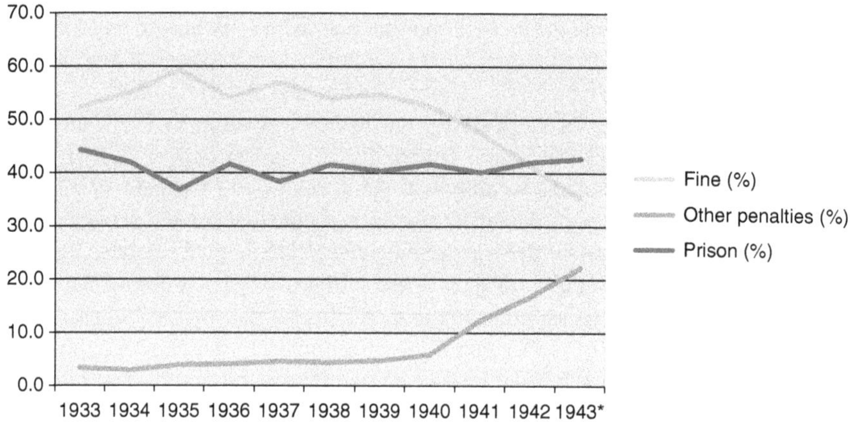

Source: Adapted from Stapenhorst (1993: 66), based on Statistik des Deutschen Reichs Band 478, 507, 577 for the period 1933–1936, *Wirtschaft und Statistik* (1940: 476, 557; 1941: 247) for the period 1939–first semester 1940; Blau (1952: 31–35) and Angermund (1990: 208) for the period 1941–first semester 1943.

* Only the first half of the year. There are no available statistical data for the last two and half years of World War II.

If we consider total numbers the picture is somehow different.

It is important to know that the reasons for the sharp reduction in the total number of prison sentences, without much influence on the percentage, are twofold. On the one hand, it was due to the wide use of amnesty laws by the Nazi regime – Amnesty Laws of August 7, 1934, of April 23, 1936, of April 30, 1938, and of September 9, 1939 (Stapenhorst 1993: 76), following earlier lines of similar developments in the Weimar Republic. The wide use of amnesty produced a significant reduction of the incarceration rate in the short term. On the other hand, the sharp reduction of prison sentences was also a result of changes in the territorial composition of the German Empire during the war (Blau 1952: 36). The decrease in total numbers and percentage of fine sentences during the war is mainly related to a change in criminality patterns, but also in sentencing. Heavily punished wartime crimes sharply increased between 1939 and the first half of 1943.[8]

Table 5.5 War crimes to overall crimes against the *Reich* (total numbers and percentages), German Empire: 1939–1943*

Year	*Crimes against the Reich (total number)*	*War crimes (total number)*	*Percentage of war crimes of overall crimes against the Reich*
1939	298,851	220	0.07
1940	266,223	8,700	3.3
1941	320,766	19,273	6.0
1942	345,150	42,153	12.2
1943*	177,332	29,649	16.7

Source: Blau (1952: 58).

* Only the first half of the year. There are no available statistical data for the last two and half years of World War II.

Figure 5.4 Convictions to prison, fine, and other penalties (total numbers), German Empire: 1933–first semester 1943*

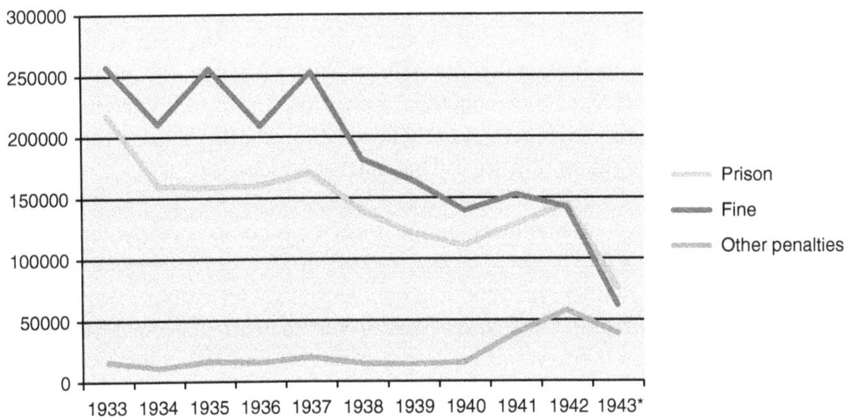

Source: Adapted from Stapenhorst (1993: 66), based on Statistik des Deutschen Reichs Band 478, 507, 577 for the period 1933–1936, *Wirtschaft und Statistik* (Statistisches Bundesamt 1940. 476, 557; 1941: 247) for the period 1939–first semester 1940; Blau (1952: 31–35) and Angermund (1990: 208) for the period 1941–first semester 1943.

* Only the first half of the year. There are no available statistical data for the last two and half years of World War II.

In general, a comparison of the legal penalties imposed in 1937 and 1943 shows a dramatic increase in the use of the death penalty (+2,502 per cent), juvenile detention (+10,883.6 per cent), and temporarily limited penal servitude (+45.8 per cent), while both prison sentences (−11.2 per cent) and fines (−50.7 per cent) experienced a significant decrease (Blau 1952: 72).

The Nazi example perfectly illustrates the relevance of governing mentalities on the place of sanctions. Continuity existed not just at a broader level of legal discourse but also in the influence by earlier, non-Nazi developments in the field of criminal law. However, there is clear evidence that ideology informed a new eugenic world view according to which criminals and other asocial elements are born, not made, and in which society can, and must, protect itself by taking proactive measures. In such a legal system the role of fines was deemed to be small.

Re-proposition of the debate regarding intermediate punishments in the second half of the twentieth century

A major terminological question arises when trying to define the subject matter of this section and delineate its boundaries. The term 'community sanctions and measures' as used in documents of the Council of Europe (e.g., Recommendation no.[2000]22 of the Ministers to Member States on Improving the Implementation of the European Rules on Community Sanctions and Measures) as well as in comparative studies usually covers the following types of sanctions: suspension of the enforcement of a sentence to imprisonment with imposed conditions, probation imposed without the pronouncement of a sentence of imprisonment, high-intensity supervision, community service, treatment orders, victim-offender mediation or victim compensation, and restriction of freedom of movement by means of, for example, curfew orders or electronic monitoring. The term 'community' refers clearly to the fact that not only are such sanctions executed outside the prison but also their execution encompasses various forms of involvement and assistance of community members in the reintegration of offenders into society – that is, in the administration of justice. The underlying idea is

> [t]he involvement of members of the local community greatly facilitates access to an extensive range of human and material resources and social support systems. Offenders are able to establish links with voluntary agencies, trade unions and staff associations, social and recreational clubs, religious groups, charitable bodies and other organisations and individuals with the capacity to provide them with assistance and support. The maintenance of links with the wider society is likely to enhance the prospects of an offender's social reintegration.
>
> (Rule 45 of the Recommendation no.[2000]22)

Such a community approach, although deeply embedded in the legal, cultural, and political context of England and Wales (Crawford 1997; Brownlee 1998: 56–59; Cavadino et al. 1999: 97–98; Worall and Hoy 2005: 57–70; Sevdiren 2011: 6–7), is not shared by other European countries. Furthermore, the question arises of whether the term extends to monetary sanctions (Sevdiren 2011: 7). For many, fines fell outside the scope of the concept of community sanctions, either because they do not include any sort of supervision in the community or because they do not restrict personal liberty. As Bottoms et al. (2004: 13) clearly stated,

> Court ordered punishments structurally located between custody, on the one hand, and financial or nominal penalties (fines, compensation, and discharge)

> on the other. What distinguishes community penalties from fines and compensation is that they are personally restrictive, involving some active contact with a penal agent; but, unlike custodial sanctions, this contact takes place in a community-based setting.

That is why it could be preferable to abandon the specific 'communal' element of the so-called community sanctions and simply use the term 'intermediate punishments', also widely used in literature (Morris and Tonry 1990; Byrne et al. 1992; Tonry and Hamilton 1995; Tonry and Lynch 1996: 99–144; Klein 1997). Here there is no doubt that fines must be included in any attempt to analyse the relationship between the use of non-custodial and custodial penalties, even if the term 'intermediate' is sometimes referring to disposals with a severity level above fines and below custody (Easton and Piper 2005: 390). The inclusion of fines is particularly important since, as we will see later on, fines played a crucial role in reducing the use of imprisonment in many countries during the last third of the twentieth century (Albrecht and Van Kalmthout 2002: 4; Sevdiren 2011: 7–8).

Certainly, I could also use other terms, such as 'alternatives to imprisonment' or 'non-custodial penalties'. The first one, alternatives to imprisonment, raises two problems. One is that it refers to an extremely wide variety of practices, ranging from programmes prior to court proceedings to early release arrangements. Since this section is primarily concerned with court-ordered alternatives to imprisonment, and not with pretrial diversionary measures, the term 'intermediate sanctions' simply seems more appropriate. It is worth noting that in many of the texts of the 1980s when the concept of 'alternatives to imprisonment' was discussed, fines received relatively little attention (e.g., Stanley and Baginsky 1984; Pointing 1986, or Vass 1990). Another problem is that the term 'alternatives to imprisonment' reinforces the popular but wrong idea that imprisonment is the dominant form of punishment in quantitative terms, the norm against which 'alternatives' should be considered (Robinson and McNeill 2016: 5). The second term, 'non-custodial penalties', often used interchangeably with the other term, describes a range of criminal sanctions short of immediate incarceration in a penal institution, an extended continuum ranging from community service to probation, intensive probation, and house arrest supervised by electronic monitoring. Although it usually includes fines, the issue is that these sanctions are defined only in opposition to imprisonment, as if they could not have their own meaning. The concept of 'non-custodial sentences' defines these sanctions 'not by reference to what they are, but by reference to what they are not' (Young 1999: 185). It gives again the impression that it is prison or nothing, which does not help with an understanding of how these types of punishments work and what they aim to achieve. We should also remember that some of the 'non-custodial sentences', like fines or some deprivations of rights, existed long before prison became the punishment par excellence. It is easy to understand why some authors, such as Cohen, claim that 'the prison is the paradigm for understanding the whole picture' (Cohen 1985: 15).

A further caveat is necessary with reference to the length and breadth of this section. It aims to take one step towards understanding the development of fines in the second half of the twentieth century. It does not intend to present a complete historical development of intermediate penalties, not even temporally limited to the second half of the twentieth century, but to suggest, using a comprehensive historical analysis from a comparative perspective, that what happened with other intermediate punishments, in particular their failure in reducing the use of prison, strongly influenced the development of fines during this period. The rise and fall of intermediate, non-monetary sanctions, together with the widespread disillusion with imprisonment, facilitate a greater understanding of where fines stood during this period.

Having clarified these conceptual aspects, it is time to approach the topic. As we have already seen, a common trend against short terms of imprisonment was evident in the nineteenth century. In Chapter 4 I paid particular attention to the criticisms against imprisonment for defaulters and how it also reflected on the fine, which, on the other hand, had its own problems, mostly related to its characteristics as an impersonal, unfair penalty lacking rehabilitative effects. In the first section of Chapter 5, we looked at how the first decades of the century were concerned with the consequences of the crusade against short-term prison sentences and the search for prison alternatives. During the first post-war period, the debate, which began in the Enlightenment, tended towards exhaustion and the following two decades saw a sharp decline in the intensity of debates concerning fines.

After World War II another period began, a period relatively void of debate in the years immediately after the war. Starting in the 1960s, the debate on fines was revived, fuelled by the unprecedented growth of crime and prison population during these decades. But despite common preoccupations, a uniform penal policy concerning intermediate punishments did not develop in Europe. There was no consensus as to what type of alternative to imprisonment should be favoured. Regarding the use of fines, the only thing we can do at this point is to identify some common traits that had a strong influence. The second wave of European countries adopting the day-fine system in the 1970s is strongly related to the disillusion with imprisonment, but also with other community-based, intermediate sanctions.

Disillusion with imprisonment

The widespread disillusion with imprisonment as a penal sanction in the 1960s was an important incentive to give more attention to the fine, particularly in the form of the day fine. In contrast with the completely accepted late nineteenth-century criticism against short-term imprisonment, the long-held assumption that a *long*-term imprisonment could be an instrument of individual deterrence or a reformative tool through long-term training also disappeared. The value of imprisonment as such was considered dubious. These doubts coincided with the beginning of a long period of prison overcrowding and highly fluctuating prison population whose consequences we are still dealing with today.

There has been a clear rise in the total number of prison convictions since the 1960s in all the countries considered in this book, despite the fact that the proportion of convicted offenders given imprisonment fell sharply in many jurisdictions over the same period (Bottoms 1983: 182–184). Upon closer examination, after considering the effects of the post-war baby boom, the growth in the absolute number of people imprisoned seems to be largely the product of a sharp increase in the number of registered crimes,[9] a fact which could have many explanations. It could be the result of a real increase in crime rates, of the willingness of the public to report crimes to the police, or even of an increased readiness on the part of the police to record reported crimes. Although other possibilities may have had an influence, many studies confirm the growth of crime since the 1960s. It was accompanied by a subsequent growth in prison populations, even where reception into custody remained relatively stable (Council of Europe 1987: 18).[10] The causes of the massive growth in custody over the 1970s and 1980s have been and are still much discussed today among academic experts. It seems quite clear that although the volume of officially discovered crime does not directly relate to imprisonment rates (Young 1986: 125–135; Young and Brown 1993: 1–49; Snacken and Beyens 1994: 92; Aebi and Kuhn 2000: 65–75), it usually leads to 'a public outcry for stiffer sentencing' (Junger-Tas 1994: 44), and that means imprisonment.

Anyway, it is not my intention to further explain the different positions regarding this debate, not even in general terms. My only purpose here is to analyse the importance of this argument on the development of fines, where it has been as decisive as on the development of other intermediate measures, such as probation or community service. It bears mentioning that all these measures were already being proposed more than a century ago, but received legislative attention only after the imprisonment crisis in the 1970s began. Obviously, pragmatic considerations partially tipped the balance in this matter. The decision to experiment with or to reintroduce alternative sanctions into the penal system was prompted not only by the desire to obviate the negative consequences of prison sentences, both in terms of the obsolescence of the rehabilitation paradigm[11] and the overcrowding of prisons,[12] but also by the financial impossibility of simply continuing countering growing criminality with increased prison capacity and the high costs embedded in maintaining such capacities (Advisory Council on the Penal System 1970; Cartledge 1986: 15; Maestracci 1986: 89; Tak 1986: 3–4; Janssen 1994: 18). With the search for cost-benefit efficient responses to crime, it was clear that imprisonment puts a heavy financial burden on the state.

In sum, high inmate density, combined with scepticism about the effectiveness of imprisonment as an instrument of treatment and reform or a means of deterrence, and information about the cost to society of prisoner maintenance and lost labour, which proliferated during these years, led to the conclusion that the use of imprisonment was expensive and criminogenic. Against this backdrop, quite a large number of experts saw intermediate sanctions, including the fine, as a panacea for Europe's troubled correctional systems. However, intermediate sanctions would soon pose their own problems.

Rise and fall of intermediate sanctions

As a result of disillusion with the prison system there was a re-proposition of the debate on the need to replace imprisonment, especially short-term prison sentences, with other penalties that did not deprive offenders of their freedom. Starting in the 1970s, a wide range of intermediate sanctions were introduced and put into practice in Europe. This policy of proliferating alternatives to incarceration was strongly promoted by the influential Council of Europe. Several recommendations and resolutions issued by the Council of Europe over the last 50 years encouraged the use of alternatives to imprisonment and provided for a supranational normative framework.[13] For example, the Report of the European Committee on Crime Problems in 1976, accompanied by Resolution (76) 10 'On Certain Alternative Penal Measures to Imprisonment', adopted by the Committee of Ministers, mentioned the fine as an important alternative to imprisonment. It recognized both the need to take the offender's means into account in order to avoid fines going unpaid and the convenience of abolishing or, at least, considerably reducing the use of imprisonment in case of default, which again meant adapting the amount of the fine to the offender's financial circumstances. 'Considering that alternatives to prison sentences can serve the rehabilitative objectives and are less costly than imprisonment', the Council of Europe recommended the member states

1 examine their legislation with a view to removing legal obstacles to imposing alternatives to imprisonment;
2 spare no effort in developing existing alternatives, and in particular

> ensure that fines can be used as sanctions on a broad basis and that there are methods making it possible to adjust such fines to the offender's financial resources, and that methods of enforcing payment are such as to avoid whenever possible recourse to imprisonment.

The ground in which this seed was planted was fertile, fed as it was by the intense controversy surrounding short-term prison sentences since the end of the nineteenth century. This development was boosted by the economic crisis of the 1970s, since inflation led to major cuts in public expenditure, including the criminal justice system. It was a period of social, economic, and political turmoil, with crime continuing to rise and prison numbers continuing to increase.

Intermediate sanctions have been linked to an era of 'penal welfarism' in England (Garland 1985; Bottoms et al. 2004), which ended with the decline of the 'rehabilitative ideal' (Allen 1981). It coupled with the 1973–1975 recession, a period of economic stagnation that put an end to the post–World War II economic boom both in the United States and Western Europe and cast doubt on the sustainability – in pure economic terms – of the continued growth in prison populations. This ideological and empirical critique contributed to the search for intermediate sanctions and gave birth to the 'alternatives to custody in the community' movement that constituted a new phase of penal welfarism.

This may have been the case in England and Wales. However, the birth and development of intermediate sanctions in other European countries cannot be understood against this background, even if, at face value, they may seem similar in practice. Intermediate sanctions must be situated within a wider cultural framework in different national contexts. For example, in stark contrast to England

and Wales, where 'appeals to community connect with, and are nourished by anti-statism' (Crawford 2000: 220), Germany is a country in which the overall reliance on the state is strong. There was not an approach emphasizing the role of the 'community' in the enforcement of non-custodial sanctions. Rather, the debate on alternatives to imprisonment, which was particularly focused on short-term imprisonment, followed the road already mapped at the end of the nineteenth century. Intermediate sanctions were thought to be the best alternative to imprisonment for less severe offences, prompted by the desire to obviate the negative consequences of short-term prison sentences. In France, the term 'community' is tinted with negative connotations (Herzog-Evans 2016: 51). Regarding certain measures community is directly linked to the role of the state (Crawford 2000: 219). For example, mediation in France is located within debates about the need of a *justice de proximité*, which does not involve something undermining the efficacy of the republican model to which French political discourse clings, but is intended as a way of achieving both greater geographic proximity between the law and the people and greater temporal proximity, as a faster and more timely form of justice, without forgetting the need for a greater human proximity, which seeks to give the victim a voice within the criminal justice system (Tak 1986: 3; Crawford 2000: 209–210). In Spain the introduction of alternatives to prison, such as suspended sentences, prohibition orders, and community service, had nothing to do with the English concept of community. Community punishment 'is not a concept used in Spanish policy, legal discourse or academic literature' (Blay and Larrauri 2016: 191). There is no community involvement in the enforcement of these alternatives, with only a small level of cooperation with private, semi-public, and public organizations and institutions in order to implement them.

As already shown, one of the principal arguments in favour of fines is economic – the avoidance of costly incarceration. But 'any realistic prospect [. . .] of saving money or prison beds requires that [the alternatives] be used mostly for offenders who otherwise would have served prison terms' (Tonry and Lynch 1996: 101). It did not happen. In terms of reducing imprisonment rates specific 'community' sanctions clearly failed to have the desired impact on the ever rising prison population, which continued an upward trend during the 1980s and 1990s. The explanation seems to be that community sanctions led in many cases to 'net widening' and 'mesh thinning' (Cohen 1979, 1985; Mathiesen 1980) – that is to say, the bringing of greater numbers of less serious offenders into the penal net than might otherwise have been the case, and the imposition upon them of more severe sanctions, known as the 'dispersal of discipline thesis'. For example, in England nearly half of the offenders who received a community punishment order were convicted of the least serious type of offence, and over half had been convicted for the first time. In several cases the new measures were added to or replaced a less repressive penalty, producing an increase in both costs and punitiveness. The increase in punitiveness took place largely at the expense of fines, which experienced a dramatic fall during the period (Mair 2004). This means that in many cases intermediate sanctions were substituting *fines*, not imprisonment. That was also the case in France. Since the 1970s the most obvious trend has been a wider use of the alternatives to prison, although they needed some time to be accepted. But, as Kensey (2002: 223) put forth, 'the increase in alternatives to imprisonment was not made at the expense of prison sentences as their designation would suggest, but at the expense of sentences such as fines and suspended sentences'. In fact, in the last 40 years, the relative use of non-suspended prison sentences changed only slightly, representing approximately one-fifth of all sentences: 17.8 per cent in 1975, 19.8 in 2010 (Robert 2013: 111). On the contrary, the use of fines strongly declined in favour of other non-custodial sentences. As Robert (2013: 112) explained, 'Contrary to what we may consider *prima facie*, this trend has been led by increased punitiveness: whilst more than half of offenders got away with a simple fine at the beginning of this period, only one-third can expect to do so today'. Spain, when implementing alternatives to imprisonment, continued to use short-term imprisonment, with the supposed 'alternatives' being not so much replacements for short prison sentences as an alternative to fines. The new 1995 Penal Code, which entered into force in May 1996, introduced new intermediate punishments, but it did not expand the use of fines – quite the opposite: it maintained a fairly stable use of prison sentences (56.12 per cent in 1995, 54.05 per cent in 1997) while substantially increasing the number of other non-custodial sentences (0.39 per cent in 1995, 10.28 per cent in 1997). As a result, the proportion of fines correspondingly decreased (from 42.54 per cent in 1995 to 29.82 per cent in 1997), since fines were substituted by other intermediate punishments, such as disqualifications, removal of professional status and other deprivations of rights, or community service.[14] This means that, once again, the increase in alternatives to imprisonment did not come at the expense of prison sentences, as their designation would suggest, but at the expense of fines.

However, there were exceptions. The rise of the fine in Germany, as well as the general increase in other penalties not involving supervision in the community, does not seem fully congruent with the 'dispersal of discipline' thesis, as already stated by Bottoms (1983: 180). Germany and – to a certain extent also Austria – pursued a policy of 'day fines instead of short prison sentences'. As we will see in Chapter 6, this produced a substantial decrease in the percentage of prison sentences of total convictions, but also an unexpected increase in imprisonment for fine defaulters, which, in turn, increased the interest in alternative measures, such as suspension and community service (Gerken and Henningsen 1987).

But even when there was no net widening, and the new intermediate sanctions were truly a substitute for imprisonment, it could be verified that the supposed savings were minimal or even non-existent. Because many offenders who were given alternative sanctions were drawn from the group of offenders who were given the least costly sentencing option – fines – intermediate sanctions often increased, rather than decreased, the cost of corrections. This increased the crisis of intermediate sanctions, since both public opinion and the literature had been taken in by the rhetoric of economy-oriented governments for whom the principal advantages and even the main justification of the reforms consisted of potential savings. The time of monetary punishments was once again upon us.

Rediscovering fines

During the debate on intermediate punishments the old arguments defending the positive characteristics of fines were still there: fines are flexible, deterrent, economical, and easy to repair in case of wrongful conviction (Zipf 1966: 46–47; Samuels 1970: 201; Beristain Ipiña 1976: 18–21; Molinari 1983: 31–32; Lewis 1988; Cole 1989; McDonald and Moody 1993). Gary Becker (1968 [1974]) and other representatives of the powerful law and economics movement (e.g., Posner 1972) concluded that social welfare would be increased if fines were used whenever feasible. Thanks to the day-fine system it was possible to overcome the classical objection of unfairness towards poor offenders (Zipf 1966: 39–40; Padovani 1981: 209–210; Molinari 1983: 24), although the problematic shift of the burden of the fine to innocents was still an issue (Westen 1969: 792). One aspect of fines which received more attention was the fact that reconviction rates are not worse than other alternatives to imprisonment. Furthermore, a new approach emerged, framed within the development of a more victim-centred criminal justice system, which viewed the fine as a way for the offender either to pay back to the community something in return for the damage he has done or to compensate victims for personal injuries and damage to or loss of property. Let us take a closer look at these two aspects.

In the last third of the twentieth century it was quite common to insist on the benefits of this form of sentencing, particularly on the fact that fines produce less reoffending (Samuels 1970: 201; Softley 1978: 7–9). The comparison with other penalties often allows for the conclusion that '[t]he fine is the most commonly used of all penalties available to the criminal courts as a whole and appears to be one of the most effective in relation to offenders of almost all age groups and criminal histories' (Advisory Council on the Penal System 1970: 5, also known as the Wootton Report). From the perspective of recidivism, the deterrent function of monetary punishments was recognized: the ability to effectively warn the offender and thus deter future criminal activities (Playfair and Sington 1965: 101–104; Ranieri 1966: 266ff.; Zipf 1966: 67–69; Baumann 1968: 38ff.; Bradbury 1969; Westen 1969: 810; Hood and Sparks 1970: 188–189; Lernell 1979: 487ff.; Plawski 1983: 354; Musco 1984: 72–73; Lewis 1988: 19), albeit with important limitations, as in the case of repeat offenders.[15] In terms of reconviction rates, it was claimed that the success rate 'is better than other forms of sentence' (Samuels 1970: 201). In reality, there was no definitive research available to demonstrate that probation, discharges, or custody was a more effective sentence than fines. On the contrary, data research of reconviction rates found that fines were more successful than other approaches to crime. Fines appeared to be among the most 'successful' penalties for almost all types of offenders (Walker 1968: 252–254; Hall Williams 1970: 287) and were even deemed by some to be 'an effective deterrent' (Westen 1969: 810) and 'penologically effective' (Morgan and Bowles 1981: 204). For example, in the second edition of *The Sentence of the Court* (Home Office 1969), a handbook for sentencers describing the various disposals available, '[t]he most important finding [. . .] is that fines and discharges are much more effective than either probation or imprisonment for first offenders and recidivists of all age groups' (Hood and Sparks 1970: 188–189). This was also one of the findings in Hammond and Chayen's study on *Persistent Criminals* (1963) and in Lowald and Stub's analysis of reactions of chronic drunkenness offenders to court sanctions (1968: 528). The idea that fines are generally followed by somewhat lower recidivism rates compared to other penalties began to take hold in literature.

The claim that fines are penologically more effective in terms of reconviction rate did not go undiscussed (McClean and Wood 1969: 82–83; Wilkins 1969: 54–56; Hood and Sparks 1970: 188–189; Bottoms 1973). It relies on recidivism as the sole measure of the success of a sentence, and reconviction rates as the only possible measure of recidivism. Such an approach has a number of methodological flaws that limit its usefulness. As a consequence of several serious methodological limitations – Lappi-Seppälä (2014: 1637) spoke about 'fairly meager' evidence – clear-cut conclusions, such as 'fines are reasonably effective when judged in terms of reconviction rates' (Harding and Koffman 1995: 333), or 'offenders receiving fines have the lowest recidivism rates' (Lappi-Seppälä 2014: 1644), must be questioned.

The truth is that there is too little systematic research on the effects of fines on recidivism (see some examples in Gordon and Glaser 1991; Turner and Petersilia 1996; Gendreu et al. 2000; Moffatt and Poynton 2007). Nevertheless, the debate encouraged arguments favouring fines because they are likely to be less harmful than custody and other intermediate punishments – they involve 'no social dislocation and less stigma than most other criminal sanctions', according to Samuels (1970: 201) – as well as more promising regarding their effect on recidivism (Plawski 1983: 354).

Regarding the victimological approach, Bentham originally proposed that fines be paid to victims;[16] thus this notion of a 'restorative' fine is not new (O'Malley 2009: 62). However, it is quite clear that the interest is not properly on fines but on compensation. Fines, intended as money taken from the offender and put towards public revenue, and damages, as money also taken from the offender in order to give it to the person harmed, share the same underlying essence: the payment of a sum of money because a crime has been committed. In fact, for long periods of time, both of them were regarded as 'punishments'.[17] However, there are substantial differences between one payment and the other, which are not limited to the recipient of the sum paid.

In the majority of Western European countries examined in this book a renewed interest for the victim took the form of prioritizing restitution or compensation to victims – sometimes including other concepts, such as compensation to the state for the costs incurred on behalf of the offender in the case, the costs of the victim's private prosecutor, and other legal costs, including those of the offender's defence – whenever the offender lacked the means to pay both fine and damages, if not previously so regulated.[18] In the United Kingdom, following ancient precedents that tended to disregard any differences between fines and damages,[19] legal discourse was much more centred on the idea that the fine 'involves the offender actually paying back to the community something in return for the damage he has done, rather than requiring society to spend even more money upon him so that he can repay that debt' (British Government White Paper *Crime, Justice and Protecting the Public* 1990, para. 5.1). In some countries, such as Spain, there were proposals to pay state compensation to victims of crime with the money collected from fines (Beristain Ipiña 1976: 19). They were never implemented in legislation. In other countries courts may order any fine to be paid to the victim rather than the state in order to compensate for any physical or psychological harm suffered (O'Malley 2009: 62; Lappi-Seppälä 2014: 1639). The underlying rationale is that making restitution produces a sort of cathartic effect on the offender, forced to acknowledge the victim and the harm that was inflicted. The benefits for the victim are clear, because compensation may enable a recovery of losses more quickly and easily than through other means. It is also possible to order that the fine be paid directly to state-funded compensation schemes for victims of crime, a sort of 'payback' in both a symbolic and literal sense, which satisfies both victims and the community (Pritikin 2010: 351).

These benefits of fines over other penal sanctions are generally well known, as can be seen in the late twentieth-century literature as well as in government papers and reports on fines. However, an important obstacle to the full acceptance of these advantages of the fine in some countries is the high level of imprisonment still arising out of the default in payment. We should take into account that fines began to be used not only to punish petty offences but also to substitute terms of prison that were no longer short. If these fines were to appear as a plausible alternative to a significant deprivation of liberty, they had to have a 'bite' (Lappi-Seppälä 2014: 1640). Fines had to experience a significant increase in their amount, because otherwise they would not be recognized as a truly repressive measure. As O'Malley (2009: 43) explained, 'fines could not be reduced to trifling levels – unlike in the eighteenth century – because these fines were to appear as a plausible alternative to a significant deprivation of liberty'. Heavier fines could serve more effectively as alternatives to the much discredited short prison sentences, but this development also resulted in the more frequent use of default imprisonment. These high levels of imprisonment for fine defaulters jeopardized the cost-effectiveness of the fine, as was evidenced by legislation in England and Wales. The 1948 Criminal Justice Act, which expanded the range of indictable offences subject to fines by stating that 'any court before which an offender is convicted on indictment of felony (not being a felony the sentence for which is fixed by law) shall have power to fine the offender' (Section 13), led to an increase in fine impositions. This 'paved the way for the spectacular post-war increase in the use of the fine' (Cavadino and Dignan 1997: 209), with the fine becoming the most common form of sentencing in the 1980s. This rise in fine impositions, however, was accompanied by the fact that 21 per cent of all receptions to prison under sentence in 1980 – 15,938 offenders (Mulligan 1982: 137) – were fine defaulters. 'Whatever may be said of imprisonment for nonpayment of fines as an effective deterrent, it is clear that it is extremely expensive' (Westen 1969: 788).

In fact, such a high level of imprisonment for defaulters was seen to reduce the cost-effectiveness of the fine for two reasons: first, and very important in a period of economic crisis, the economic cost of additional prison receptions should be added to the economic loss of the unpaid fine; second, the personal costs arising out of the stigmatization of incarceration have a translation in economic terms, since it became quite clear that the possibilities of maintaining a job or finding a new one were considerably reduced after the prison experience. On the contrary, as the Government White Paper *Crime, Justice and Protecting the Public* (1990: para. 5.1) indicated, 'A fine, if properly assessed, can punish the offender without damaging his opportunities for employment or his responsibilities towards his family' – of course, only if the fine does not end in imprisonment. Concerns about cost efficiency were widespread in England and Wales, where the driving force for reforming the criminal justice system in the last part of the twentieth century was an increased emphasis upon the effectiveness of the enforcement process. This new focus was based on two rationales: the incorporation of managerialism and concerns regarding credibility. Managerialism had a profound impact upon the practice of English criminal justice system. As Raine and Willson (1997: 82) put it, 'most of the criminal justice initiatives which the government took from the mid-1980s onwards appeared to contain, or were founded upon, elements of the public sector managerialist agenda'. The enforcement process was important in developing managerialism. Fine enforcement was no exception in this regard (Jones 1993: 195–196). On the contrary, the monetary form of the sanction makes it particularly adapted to these sorts of arguments based on economy, efficiency, and effectiveness – the 'three Es' – due to the predictability and calculability of outcomes. The drive towards managerial efficiency was accompanied by concerns about the credibility of the fine, placing further pressure upon the criminal justice system to raise collection rates. The White Paper on *Crime, Justice and Protecting the Public* (Home Office 1990: i) clearly stated, 'If the system of prosecution and punishment currently operating in England and Wales is to retain credibility, the financial penalties imposed on offenders must be enforced consistently and promptly'. The implementation of the day-fine system in many Western European countries opened new perspectives in the last third of the twentieth century. Its expansion can be described only as a turning point in European criminal policy. But not all expectations were met. We will explore possible explanations in Chapter 6.

Notes

1 This observation was quite widespread among the authors of the time. Therefore, at the end of the nineteenth century, Bertola (1893: 551–552) stated that the increase in the distribution of wealth, as it paved the way for many citizens to earn income via new means, justified an increase in the use of fines, even though some were unable to pay, perhaps through their own carelessness or ineptitude, and should therefore pay 'with the wealth of their freedom, as they had no other riches'.

2 The fact that there were still many offenders going to prison for not paying a fine showed that 'the problem of social class and equality has not been completely resolved' (Tiedemann 1980: 492). As indicated before, although giving time to pay and making

possible the substitution of unpaid fines by other non-custodial sentences strongly impacted in the number of imprisonments for default, the fine is not the proper punishment for people with no means at all.

3 The statement in the text refers to the fine. I am well aware that from the 1870s and 1880s, in some countries from the 1890s and the first decades of the twentieth century, the essential elements of the old penal rationality began to be definitively overturned. Beccaria's and Bentham's theories, which purport that punishment as an instrument *ad deterrendum* counterweights the interest in committing crimes, are considered false both theoretically and practically: theoretically, because criminal behaviour cannot be explained as the behaviour of *homo economicus*, since the criminal is not properly a Man; practically, because the numbers of crimes and criminals simply continue to rise. In fact, the new penal theory is more concerned with rendering the criminal incapable of harm – neutralization or *Unschädlichmachung* – than with dissuading the citizen from law breaking – deterrence or *Abschreckung*.

4 Norway introduced the suspended sentence in 1894, following the Belgian example. Denmark did it in 1905, being the first country to introduce the conditional suspension of the sentence *with* probation. In the United Kingdom, probation was first introduced by the Probation of Offenders Act 1907. It spread quickly to Spain in 1908, the Netherlands in 1915, Finland and Sweden in 1918, Austria in 1920, and so forth.

5 The general structure of the 1922 draft remained the basis for the first official draft of 1925, which, after many parliamentary deliberations, came 'to a fatal stand-still' in 1931, when the right-wing parties refused to continue their cooperation with the legislative efforts of the Weimar Republic (Grünhut 1944: 28).

6 Law on the Extension of the Application Field of the Fine and the Restriction of Short-Term Imprisonment (*Gesetz zur Erweiterung des Anwendungsgebiets der Geldstrafe und zur Einschränkung der kurzen Freiheitsstrafen*) of December 21, 1921; Law on Fines (*Geldstrafengesetz*) of April 27, 1923; Law on Monetary Penalties and Fines (*Gesetz über Vermögensstrafen und Bußen*) of October 13, 1923; Decree on Monetary Penalties and Fines (*Verordnung über Vermögensstrafen und Bußen*) of February 6, 1924.

7 It is interesting to point out that the percentage of fines actually paid is higher during this period when the fine imposed is lower. Data from 1926, contained in the annex of the 1927 penal code reform project, p. 46, show that 80.1 per cent of fines of less than 20 Reichsmarks were paid in full, 68.1 per cent of fines between 20 and 100 Reichsmarks, 56.4 per cent of fines between 100 and 300 Reichsmarks, 39.2 per cent of fines between 300 and 1,000 Reichsmarks, 22.7 per cent of fines between 1,000 and 10,000 Reichsmarks, and only 6.3 per cent of fines of over 10,000 Reichsmarks.

8 As wartime criminal laws are included here the five most frequently applied (Blau 1952: 58) are the decree on extraordinary radio measures (*Verordnung über außerordentliche Rundfunkmaßnahmen*) of September 1, 1939, the wartime economy order (*Kriegswirtschaftsverordnung*) of September 4, 1939, the decree on public parasites (*Verordnung gegen Volksschädlinge*) of September 5, 1939, the decree against violent criminals (*Verordnung über Gewaltverbrecher*) of December 5, 1939, and the order to protect the rationing of consumer goods (*Verbrauchsregelungs-Strafverordnung*) of November 26, 1941.

9 Let me mention just a few examples. By 1960 the rise in registered crime was evident in England and Wales: in 1950 there were 461,435 indictable offences known to the police; by 1960 the figure was 743,713, which meant an increase of 61 per cent (Mair and Burke 2012: 84–85). In West Germany the total number of convicted offenders increased from 275,182 in 1950 to 599,832 in 1980, with a peak of 614,252 in 1978 (Sevdiren 2011: 148). In Italy, recorded crimes increased by almost 130 per cent between 1968 and 1983 (Direzione generale per gli istituti di prevenzione e pena 1987: 26, 33, 43).

10 In England and Wales, prison numbers rose continuously in the 1960s. In 1960 the average prison population was 27,099, while by 1965 it had risen to 30,421, an increase

of 12 per cent. In 1970 the average prison population was 39,028, an increase of more than 25 per cent since 1965. A 1969 White Paper entitled *People in Prison* admitted that 'overcrowding is the worst feature of our prison system' (Home Office 1969: 104). In 1979 the population of prison department establishments reached 43,036.

In Italy there was also a large increase in the number of prison sentences: from 48,225 in 1968 to 63,313 in 1983, an increase of over 33 per cent (Direzione generale per gli istituti di prevenzione e pena 1987: 26, 33, 43). The average prison population increased from 30,998 to 40,225 between 1968 and 1983, again an increase of about 30 per cent (Van Kalmthout and Tak 1992: 523).

11 The growing disappointment with the rehabilitation paradigm and the treatment model strongly contributed to this development. From the classical work of Martinson (1974) onwards, the failure of the prison system to rehabilitate offenders was widely accepted. Curiously, it is the same period in which the solemn legislative recognition of the principle of re-socialization of custodial penalties was introduced in many European constitutions. That was the case in France (1972, 1975), Italy (1975), West Germany (1976), and Spain (1978). Certainly, it remained an official discourse rather than an operative principle of the criminal justice system. This contradiction may be explained by the different temporal frames of the crisis of rehabilitation in Anglo-Saxon and continental countries. The academic discussion first took place in Anglo-Saxon countries. They also were the first countries that implemented neo-liberal policies, which were those that contributed to the anti-rehabilitation speeches becoming law.

12 Prison overcrowding combined with highly fluctuating prison population due to the frequent use of short-term prison sentences for very frequent, yet less serious crimes, such as road traffic offences. It was felt that this stood in the way of making far-reaching improvements in prison organization.

13 As early as 1965 the Council of Europe published a resolution on suspended sentences, probation and other alternatives to imprisonment (65, 1), followed by a resolution in 1976 on certain alternative penal measures to imprisonment (76, 10). In 1992, the Council issued recommendations (Rec. R [92] 16) on the European rules on community sanctions and measures, which for the first time provided a complete set of rules on the application and implementation of community sanctions. Special recommendations deal then with conditional release (Rec. R [2003] 22 concerning conditional release). In 1999 the Council of Europe in a recommendation concerning prison overcrowding and prison population inflation (Rec. R [99] 22) reiterated its view that prison sentences should be a last resort and that community sanctions should be the punishment of choice, except in the case that the seriousness of the crime prohibits any penalty other than a prison sentence. In 2000 a follow-up to the 1992 community sanctions recommendations focused on improving the implementation of the European rules on community sanctions and measures (Rec. R [2000] 22).

14 Until 2007 community service functioned in Spain mainly as an alternative to imprisonment for defaulters, hardly as an alternative to the principal prison sentence. It had little impact on the prison stock.

15 See Samuels (1970: 202), asserting that '[t]he habitual offender has rarely been reformed by the oft repeated fine'. However, some argue that the fine is also suitable for repeat offenders, who could not get used to the fine but to the prison (Grosso 1966; Ranieri 1966: 266 ff.; Samuels 1970: 206; Nowakowski 1973: 34–40). Others point out that the deterrent effect of the fine varies markedly depending on the personality of the offender: 'Those who are already immersed in a life of crime will not feel the sting of the fine. In contrast, those who live in orderly conditions and with certain social prestige will' (Beristain Ipiña 1976: 20).

16 Bentham defines the concept of 'pecuniary forfeiture' as follows: 'A pecuniary forfeiture is incurred when a man is, by a judicial sentence, compelled to pay a sum of money to another, or, as it is in some cases called, a fine' (Bentham 1830: Book 3,

Chapter 4). In this first definition, as revealed by the distinction he makes later on, Bentham jointly alludes to the fine and to compensatory payments or damages. In the case of the fine, compulsive means are used to oblige the offender to produce the sum himself to be taken as soon as he *has* done the thing required, by threatening him with some future punishment, to be applied at such a time in case of his or her *not* having done the thing required by that time. However, these traits also apply to the damages, making it difficult to distinguish between them. In fact, Bentham regards both of them as a 'punishment', in which one party is compelled to pay a sum of money to another. The most important difference, however, is quickly discovered: with fines money is taken from the offender and added to the state's general revenue; with damages money is given to the harmed person. But the truth is that for Bentham

> a punishment of this kind is known in different cases by different names, which have nothing to do with the nature of the punishment (that is of the suffering) itself, nor essentially with the manner in which it is inflicted. They are taken only from the accidental circumstance of the manner in which the produce of the punishment is disposed of.
>
> (Bentham 1830: Book 3, Chapter 4)

As we can see, to Bentham fines and damages are considered equal punishments for they are 'all reducible to the *pain of privation* occasioned by the loss of so much money' (Bentham 1830: Book 3, Chapter 4). This combination of criminal elements per se with elements from other sectors of the legal system, mainly – but not exclusively – civil law, is a characteristic of the legal literature well into the nineteenth century.

17 This characterization had, of course, consequences, like the possibility of imposing subsidiary imprisonment in the case of non-payment of victim compensation and the application of the same procedural rules for enforcing the fine and damages.

18 In France, Italy, and Spain the importance of victim compensation was already recognized in the first penal codes. Priority of victim compensation was provided in the 1810 French Penal Code, in which Article 54 said that 'If fine or confiscation be awarded, concurrently with restitutions and damages, and the property of the convicted be insufficient, the restitutions and damages shall have precedence in payment before the law', while Article 468, for the offences of police, established that '[i]n case of insufficiency of effects, the restitutions and indemnifications, due to the offended person, shall be levied before the fine'. Under French influence, Article 101.3 of the 1852 Portuguese Penal Code also provided that restitution and damages should have precedence, and in other cases of concurrence between fines and other monetary debts civil regulation should be observed.

This also occurred in the Spanish codification. Since the first 1822 Penal Code in cases where the offender did not have the means to pay all his or her pecuniary liabilities, an order of priority payment was established, with restitution and compensation for damages at the top of the list, following the model of the 1810 French Penal Code. This regulation, still in place today, has, throughout the ages, been met with unanimous doctrinal applause (Vizmanos and Álvarez Martínez 1848: 269–270; Groizard 1903: 323), highlighting the break with the legislation in place until then. However, it was not a real break with the practice of the courts at the time. The 1822 Spanish Penal Code was in force for only a very short time, and was never effectively implemented. Therefore, the previous situation was maintained until the 1848 Penal Code was approved. In Article 48, the priority of paying damages is established only with regards to the payment of the fine, with paying the expenses incurred by the trial and legal costs coming last on the list. In the 1850 reform, influenced by literature (Pacheco 1848: 355; Vizmanos and Álvarez Martínez 1848: 269), the order of priority of the payment of pecuniary liabilities was changed, with the fine being placed last on the list (Article 12 of the royal decree of June 7, 1850), which was applauded by the scholars of the subject (Aramburu y Arregui 1860: 84). In subsequent codes the fine remained lower down the list, after not only victim compensation but also the other concepts mentioned earlier. This is the case of the 1870 and 1995 Spanish Penal Codes, Articles 49 and 126 respectively.

For its part, in Italy Article 620 of the Code of Criminal Procedure at the time of the 1930 Rocco Penal Code also relegated 'pecuniary penalties and any other amount owed to the public treasury' to last place on the list, after the expenditure incurred by a public health institution for the care and maintenance of the victim, the sums owed as damages and the procedural expenses incurred by the wronged party, the costs of their defence, and the legal costs and maintenance costs of the offender himself during his or her stay in a penal institution. This regulation was welcome by literature (Florian 1934: 1091–1092).

19 The proximity of the fine to the reparation of damage was brought about not just because of the conceptual lack of distinction within punitive law between criminal law and civil law in the United Kingdom, but also by certain old practices of the courts. For example, during the eighteenth century in England there are signs that, in order to promote an agreement between the defendant and the victim in assault cases, the courts used the fine as a way of persuading a recalcitrant offender to come to terms with the complainant: a larger fine might well result when such agreement was not forthcoming, along with the further threat that the non-payment of a large fine could result in a period of imprisonment (Beattie 1986: 457–458; King 1996: 49–50). Only towards the end of the eighteenth century was the transfer of assault cases from the private to the public sphere demanded by authoritative voices, alleging that '[f]or, although a private citizen may dispense with satisfaction for his private injury, he cannot remove the necessity of public example' (Blackstone 1769: Chapter 27).

References

Advisory Council on the Penal System (1970) *Non-Custodial and Semi-Custodial Penalties*. London: HMSO.

Aebi, M. F. and A. Kuhn (2000) 'Influences on the Prisoner Rate: Number of Entries into Prison, Length of Sentences and Crime Rate'. *European Journal on Criminal Policy and Research* 8(1): 65–75.

Albrecht, H.-J. (1978) 'Statistische Angaben über die Geldstrafe in der Bundesrepublik Deutschland'. In Jescheck, H.-H. and G. Grebing (eds.) *Die Geldstrafe im deutschen und ausländischen Recht*. Baden-Baden: Nomos, 165–191.

Albrecht, H.-J. and A. van Kalmthout (2002) 'Intermediate Penalties: European Developments in Conceptions and Use of Non-Custodial Criminal Sanctions'. In Albrecht, H.-J. and A. van Kalmthout (eds.) *Community Sanctions and Measures in Europe and North America*. Freiburg: iuscrim, 1–12.

Allen, F. A. (1981) *The Decline of the Rehabilitative Ideal: Penal Policy and Social Purposes*. New Haven, CT: Yale University Press.

Alsberg, M. (1924) 'Geldentwertung und Strafrechtspflege'. *Juristische Wochenschrift* 10(5): 276–277.

Aramburu y Arregui, J. D. (1860) *Instituciones de Derecho penal español, arregladas al código reformado en 30 de junio de 1850*. Oviedo: Imp. y lit. de D. Benito González.

Bamberger, G. (1917) *Geldstrafe anstatt Gefängnis*. Stuttgart: Enke.

Baumann, J. (1968) *Beschränkung des Lebensstandards anstatt kurzfristiger Freiheitsstrafe*. Neuwied: Luchterhand.

Beattie, J. M. (1986) *Crime and the Courts in England. 1660–1800*. Princeton, NJ: Princeton University Press.

Becker, G. (1968 [1974]) 'Crime and Punishment: An Economic Approach'. In Becker, G. and W. Landes (eds.) *Essays in the Economics of Crime and Punishment*. New York: Columbia University Press, 1–54.

Bentham, J. (1830) *The Rationale of Punishment*. London: Robert Heward.

Beristain Ipiña, A. (1976) 'La multa penal y la administrativa en relación con las sanciones privativas de libertad'. In AA.VV (ed.) *III Jornadas de Profesores de Derecho Penal*. Madrid: Universidad de Santiago de Compostela, 11–56.

Bertola, E. (1893) 'Della pena pecuniaria'. *Rivista Penale* 1: 548–553.

Best, E. (1932) *Studien über die Anwendung der fakultativ angedrohten Geldstrafen im Deutschen Reiche*. Gießen: Univ. Diss.

Blackstone, W. (1769) *Commentaries on the Laws of England. Book 4*. Oxford: A. Strahan, for T. Cadell and J. Butterworth and Son.

Blau, B. (1952) 'Die Kriminalität in Deutschland während des Zweiten Weltkrieges'. *Zeitschrift für die gesamte Strafrechtswissenschaften* 64: 31–81.

Blay, E. and E. Larrauri (2016) 'Community Punishments in Spain: A Tale of Two Administrations'. In Robinson, G. and F. McNeill (eds.) *Community Punishments: European Perspectives*. London: Routledge, 191–208.

Bonneville de Marsangy, A. (1864) *De l'amélioration de la loi criminelle en vue d'une justice plus prompte, plus efficace, plus généreuse et plus moralisante. Voume. II*. Paris: Cosse et Marchal.

Bottoms, A. E. (1973) 'The Efficacy of the Fine: The Case for Agnosticism'. *The Criminal Law Review*, September: 543–551.

Bottoms, A. E. (1983) 'Some Neglected Features of Contemporary Penal Systems'. In Garland, D. and P. Young (eds.) *The Power to Punish*. London: Heinemann, 166–202.

Bottoms, A. E., Rex, S. and G. Robinson (2004) *Alternatives to Prison: Options for an Insecure Society*. Cullompton: Willan.

Bradbury, P. L. (1969) 'Fines – Are They a Deterrent?'. *The New Law Journal* 119: 466–467.

Brownlee, I. (1998) *Community Punishment: A Critical Introduction*. London: Longman.

Büddemann, H. (1912) *Die Geldstrafe: nach dem Vorentwurf zu einem Deutschen Strafgesetzbuch und dem Gegenentwurf von Kahl, v. Lilienthal, v. Liszt, Goldschmidt*. Erlangen: Univ. Diss.

Bumke, E. (1926) 'Wandlung der Strafen'. *Monatsschrift für Kriminalpsychologie und Strafrechtsreform* 17: 359–365.

Bumke, E. (1928) 'Die Freiheitsstrafe als Problem der Gesetzgebung'. In Bumke, E. (ed.) *Deutsches Gefängniswesen. Ein Handbuch*. Berlin: Verlag von Franz Vahlen, 16–32.

Byrne, J. M., Lurigio, A. J. and J. Petersilia (1992) *Smart Sentencing: The Emergence of Intermediate Sanctions*. Newbury Park: SAGE.

Cartledge, G. C. (1986) 'Community Service in England/ Wales – Organization and Implementation of Community Service: An Evaluation and Assessment of Its Outcomes'. In Albrecht, H.-J. and W. Schädler (eds.) *Community Service: A New Option in Punishing Offenders in Europe*. Freiburg: Max Planck Institute for Foreign and International Penal Law, 15–38.

Cavadino, M. and J. Dignan (1997) *The Penal System: An Introduction*. 2nd ed. London: SAGE.

Cavadino, M., Crow, I. and J. Dignan (1999) *Criminal Justice 2000: Strategies for a New Century*. Winchester: Waterside Press.

Cohen, S. (1979) 'The Punitive City: Notes on the Dispersal of Social Control'. *Contemporary Crises* 3: 339–363.

Cohen, S. (1985) *Visions of Social Control*. Cambridge: Polity Press.

Cole, G. F. (1989) 'Fines Can Be Fine – and Collected'. *Judges' Journal* 28(1): 5–9.

The Commission on Criminal Law (1843) *Seventh Report of Her Majesty's Commissioners on Criminal Law: Dated the 11th Day of March 1843. Presented to Both Houses of Parliament by Command of Her Majesty*. London: W. Clowes and Sons.

Council of Europe (1987) 'Statistics on Prison Populations in the Member States of the Council of Europe'. *Prison Information Bulletin* 9: 16–26.

Crawford, A. (1997) *The Local Governance of Crime: Appeals to Community and Partnerships*. Oxford: Clarendon Press.

Crawford, A. (2000) 'Contrasts in Victim Offender Mediation and Appeals to Community in France and England'. In Nelken, D. (ed.) *Contrasting Criminal Justice*. Aldershot: Ashgate, 205–229.

Cuello Calón, E. (1929) *El nuevo Código penal español (Exposición y comentario)*. Barcelona: Bosch.

Direzione generale per gli istituti di prevenzione e pena (1987) *Libro bianco*. Rome: Ministero di grazia e giustizia.

Donnedieu de Vabres, H. (1937) *Traité élémentaire de droit criminel et de législation pénale comparée*. Paris: Sirey.

Easton, S. and C. Piper (2005) *Sentencing and Punishment: The Quest for Justice*. Oxford: Oxford University Press.

Exner, F. (1931) *Studien über die Strafzumessungspraxis der deutschen Gerichte*. Leipzig: Ernst Wiegandt.

Exner, F. (1932) 'Kurze Mitteilungen. Die Reichskriminalstatistk für die Jahre 1928 und 1929'. *Monatsschrift für Kriminalpsychologie und Strafrechtsreform* 23: 747.

Ferri, E. (1900) *Sociologia Criminale*. 4th ed. Turin: Fratelli Bocca Editori.

Florian, E. (1934) *Parte generale del Diritto penale. II*. 4th ed. Milan: Casa Editrice Dottor Francesco Vallardi.

Friedmann, O. (1892) 'Sind Änderungen des geltendes Recht erwünscht in Betreff des Verhältnisses zwischen Geld- und Freiheitsstrafen?' In Deutscher Juristentag (ed.) *Verhandlungen des Zweiundzwanzigsten Deutschen Juristentages. Zweiter Band*. Berlin: Guttentag, 95–183.

Garland, D. (1985) *Punishment and Welfare*. Aldershot: Gower.

Gendreu, P., Goggin, C., Cullen, F. T. and D. A. Andrews (2000) 'Effects of Community Sanctions and Incarceration on Recidivism'. *Forum on Corrections Research* 12(2): 10–13.

Georgi, P. G. (1914) *Die Reform der Geldstrafe im Vorentwurf zu einem Deutschen Strafgesetzbuch und im Gegenentwurf zu diesem Vorentwurf unter Berücksichtigung der veröffentlichten Beschlüsse der Strafrechtskommission*. Leipzig: Univ. Diss.

Gerken, U. and J. Henningsen (1987) 'Ersetzung der Ersatzfreiheitsstrafe durch freie Arbeit'. *Zeitschrift für Rechtspolitik* 20(11): 386–390.

Glauning, D. (1905) 'Zur "Reform der Geldstrafe"'. *Blätter für Gefängnisskunde* 39: 277–289.

Gordon, M. A. and D. Glaser (1991) 'The Use and Effects of Financial Penalties in Municipal Courts'. *Criminology* 29: 651–676.

Grebing, G. (1978) 'Die Geldstrafe im deutschen Recht nach Einführung des Tagessatzsystems'. In Jescheck, H.-H. and G. Grebing (eds.) *Die Geldstrafe im deutschen und ausländischen Recht*. Baden-Baden: Nomos, 1–184.

Groizard y Gómez de la Serna, A. (1903) *El Código penal de 1870 concordado y comentado. Tomo II*. 2nd ed. Madrid: García.

Grosso, C. F. (1966) 'Le pene pecuniarie di fronte all'art. 27 comma 3° della Costituzione'. *Rivista Italiana di Diritto e Procedura Penale* 9: 999–1008.

Grünhut, M. (1944) *The Development of the German Penal System 1920–1932*. Toronto: The Canadian Bar Association.

Hall Williams, J. E. (1970) *The English Penal System in Transition*. London: Butterworths.

Hammond, W. H. and E. Chayen (1963) *Persistent Criminals: A Study of all Offenders Liable to Preventive Detention in 1956*. London: HMSO.

Harding, C. and L. Koffman (1995) *Sentencing and the Penal System: Text and Materials*. 2nd ed. London: Sweet & Maxwell.

Hassan, M. A. (1959) *L'amende pénale dans les droits modernes et spécialement dans le Code Pénal Suisse*. Paris: Librairie Générale de Droit et de Jurisprudence.

Heinz, W. (1981) 'Entwicklung, Stand und Struktur der Strafzumessungspraxis: Eine Übersicht über die nach allgemeinem Strafrecht verhängten Hauptstrafen von 1882–1979'. *Monatsschrift für Kriminologie und Strafrechtsreform* 64: 148–173.

Heinz, W. (2010) *Das strafrechtliche Sanktionensystem und die Sanktionierungspraxis in Deutschland 1882–2008*. Stand: Berichtsjahr. Available at www.ki.uni-konstanz.de/kis

Heinz, W. (2011) 'Punitiveness in German Sanctioning Practice – Myth or Reality?' In Kury, H. and E. Shea (eds.) *Punitivity – International Developments, Volume 3: Punitiveness and Punishment*. Bochum: Brockmeyer, 133–177.

Hellwig, A. (1924) *Das Geldstrafengesetz: Die Verordnung über Vermögensstrafen und Bussen vom 6. Februar 1924 mit der Begründung und den Ausführungsbestimmungen*. 3rd ed. Munich: Müller.

Herzog-Evans, M. (2016) 'France: Legal Architecture, Political Posturing, 'Prison Probation' and Adieu Social Work'. In Robinson, G. and F. McNeill (eds.) *Community Punishments: European Perspectives*. London: Routledge, 51–71.

Hoefer, F. (1945) 'The Nazi Penal System I'. *Journal of Criminal Law and Criminology* 35(6): 385–393.

Home Office (1969) *Penal Practice in a Changing Society: Aspects of Future Development*. London: Her Majesty Stationery Office.

Home Office (1990) *Crime, Justice and Protecting the Public*. London: Her Majesty Stationery Office.

Hood, R. and R. Sparks (1970) *Key Issues in Criminology*. London: World University Library.

Janssen, H. (1994) *Die Praxis der Geldstrafenvollstreckung*. Frankfurt: Peter Lang.

Jones, C. (1993) 'Auditing Criminal Justice'. *British Journal of Criminology* 33(2): 187–202.

Junger-Tas, J. (1994) *Alternatives to Prison Sentences: Experiences and Developments*. Amsterdam: Kluger.

Kensey, A. (2002) 'Community Sanctions and Measures in France'. In Albrecht, H.-J. and A. van Kalmthout (eds.) *Community Sanctions and Measures in Europe and North America*. Freiburg: iuscrim, 209–242.

King, P. (1996) 'Punishing Assault: The Transformation of Attitudes in the English Courts'. *Journal of Interdisciplinary History* 27(1): 43–74.

Kitzinger, F. (1923) 'Wertbeständige Geldstrafen!' *Deutsche Juristen-Zeitung* 28: 599–602.

Klein, A. R. (1997) *Alternative Sentencing, Intermediate Sanctions and Probation*. 2nd ed. Cincinnati: Anderson.

Kronecker (1924) 'Neuere Bestimmungen über Geldstrafen'. *Zeitschrift für die gesamte Strafrechtswissenschaft* 44: 578–647.

Kubink, M. (2002) *Strafen und ihre Alternativen im zeitlichen Wandel*. Berlin: Duncker & Humblot.

Lappi-Seppälä, T. (2014) 'Fines in Europe'. In Bruinsma, G. and D. Weisburd (eds.) *Encyclopaedia of Criminology and Criminal Justice*. Heidelberg: Springer, 1637–1648.

Lernell, L. (1979) 'Certain Aspects Philosophiques et sociologiques du problème des peines pécuniaires'. *Revue de Science Criminelle et de Droit Pénal Comparé* 3: 487–495.

Lewis, D. E. (1988) 'A Linear Model of Fine Enforcement with Application to England and Wales'. *Journal of Quantitative Criminology* 4(1): 19–37.

Liepmann, M. (1930) *Krieg und Kriminalität in Deutschland.* Stuttgart: Deutsche Verl.-Anst.

Lowald, K. and H. R. Stub (1968) 'The Revolving Door: Reactions of Chronic Drunkenness Offenders to Court Sanctions'. *Journal of Criminal Law, Criminology and Police Science* 59(4): 525–530.

Lucchini, L. (1926) 'Le brevi pene carcerarie'. *Rivista Penale*, 205–207.

Maestracci, N. (1986) 'Le Travail d'Intérêt Général: The French Option in Substituting Short-Term Imprisonment'. In Albrecht, H.-J. and W. Schädler (eds.) *Community Service*. Freiburg: Max Planck Institute for Foreign and International Criminal Law, 89–108.

Mair, G. (2004) 'Diversionary and Non-Supervisory Approaches to Dealing with Offenders'. In Bottoms, A. E., Rex S. and G. Robinson (eds.) *Alternatives to Prison: Options for an Insecure Society*. Cullompton: Willan, 135–161.

Mair, G. and L. Burke (2012) *Redemption, Rehabilitation and Risk Management: A History of Probation*. Abingdon: Routledge.

Martinson, R. (1974) 'What Works? Questions and Answers about Prison Reform'. *The Public Interest* 35: 22–54.

Mathiesen, T. (1980) *Law, Society and Political Action: Towards a Strategy under Late Capitalism*. London: Academic Press.

McClean, J. D. and J. C. Wood (1969) *Criminal Justice and the Treatment of Offenders*. London: Sweet and Maxwell.

McDonald, T. and C. Moody (1993) *Day Fines in American Courts: The Staten Island and Milwaukee Experiments*. Washington, DC: National Institute of Justice.

Meemar, A. F. (2009) *Die Strafanpassung im Rahmen der Tagessatzgeldstrafe: Der Versuch eines Ausgleichs zwischen Verfahrensökonomie und Opfergleichheit unter Berücksichtigung des Steuerrechts*. Berlin: Duncker & Humblot.

Mengele, K. (1936) *Die Ersatzgeldstrafe (§ 27b) und ihre Stellung im Strafrecht und Strafprozeß*. Günzburg: Univ. Diss.

Merkel, A. (1889) *Lehrbuch des Deutschen Strafrechts*. Stuttgart: Verlag von Ferdinand Ente.

Mittelstädt, O. (1879) *Gegen die Freiheitsstrafe: Ein Beitrag zur Kritik des heutigen Strafensystems*. Leipzig: Hirzel.

Moffatt, S. and S. Poynton (2007) 'The Deterrent Effect of Higher Fines on Recidivism: Driving Offences'. *Crime and Justice Bulletin* 106: 1–15.

Molinari, F. (1983) *La pena pecuniaria*. Verona: Team.

Montes, P. (1929) *Derecho Penal Español*. 2nd ed. San Lorenzo del Escorial: Imprenta del Real Monasterio.

Morgan, R. and R. Bowles (1981) 'Fines: The Case for Review'. *The Criminal Law Review*, April: 203–214.

Morris, N. and M. Tonry (1990) *Between Prison and Probation: Intermediate Punishments in a Rational Sentencing System*. New York: Oxford University Press.

Mulligan, G. (1982) 'Fines and Fine Enforcement in Northern Ireland'. *The Howard Journal of Criminal Justice* 21: 137–144.

Musco, E. (1984) *La pena pecuniaria*. Catania: C.U.L.C.
Naucke, W. (2000) *Über die Zerbrechlichkeit des rechtsstaatlichen Strafrechts: Materialien zur neueren Strafrechtsgeschichte*. Baden-Baden: Nomos.
Navarro de Paiva, José da Cunha (1915) *Estudos de Direito Penal*. Lisbon: Liv. Aillaud e Bertrand.
Neumaier, R. (1947) *Die geschichtliche Entwicklung der Geldstrafe vom 15: Jahrhundert bis zum StGB*. Tübingen: Univ. Diss.
Neymark, E. (1928) 'La peine d'amende'. *Revue de droit pénal et criminologie* 8: 929–962.
Nowakowski, F. (1973) 'Die Zurückdrängung der kurzen Freiheitsstrafe in der RV 1971'. *Österreichische Juristen-Zeitung* 28: 1–4.
Oetker, F. (1922) 'Die Geldstrafe nach dem Strafgesetzentwurf von 1919'. *Der Gerichtssaal* 88: 161–268.
O'Malley, P. (2009) *The Currency of Justice: Fines and Damages in Consumer Societies*. New York: Routledge-Cavendish.
Pacheco, J. F. (1848) *El Código penal: Concordado y comentado. Tomo I*. Madrid: Imprenta de don Santiago Saunaque.
Padovani, T. (1981) *L'utopia punitiva*. Milan: Giuffrè.
Pfohl, M. (1983) *Gemeinnützige Arbeit als strafrechtliche Sanktion*. Berlin: Duncker & Humblot.
Pitschel, W. (1929) *Die Praxis in der Wahl der Geldstrafe*. Leipzig: Wiegandt.
Plawski, S. (1983) 'Les jours-amendes'. *Revue pénitentiaire et de droit pénal* 107: 353–366.
Playfair, G. and D. Sington (1965) *Crime, Punishment and Cure*. London: Secker & Warburg.
Pointing, J. (ed.) (1986) *Alternatives to Custody*. Oxford: Basil Blackwell.
Posner, R. A. (1972) *Economic Analysis of Law*. Boston and Toronto: Little, Brown.
Pritikin, M. H. (2010) 'Fine-Labor: The Symbiosis between Monetary and Work Sanctions'. *University of Colorado Law Review* 81: 343–424.
Rabl, R. (1936) *Strafzumessungspraxis und Kriminalitätsbewegung*. Leipzig: Dr. Ernst Wiegandt.
Radbruch, G. (1952) *Entwurf eines allgemeinen deutschen Strafgesetzbuches (1922)*. Tübingen: J.C.B. Mohr (Paul Siebeck).
Raine, J. W. and M. J. Willson (1997) 'Beyond Managerialism in Criminal Justice'. *The Howard Journal of Criminal Justice* 36(1): 80–95.
Ranieri, S. (1966) 'Pene pecuniarie e rieducazione del condannato'. *La Scuola Positiva* 70: 265–268.
Rauh, M. F. (1912) *Die Vermögensstrafen des Reichsstrafrechts und ihre Reform*. Breslau: Schlatter.
Rietzsch, O. (1934) 'Strafsystem'. In Gürtner, F. (ed.) *Das kommende deutsche Strafrecht*. Berlin: Vahlen, 85–105.
Robert, P. (2013) 'The French Criminal Justice System'. In Ruggiero, V. and M. Ryan (eds.) *Punishment in Europe: A Critical Anatomy of Penal Systems*. Basingstoke: Palgrave Macmillan, 111–131.
Robinson, G. and F. McNeill (2016) 'Studying the Evolution of 'Community Punishment' in Comparative Context'. In Robinson, G. and F. McNeill (eds.) *Community Punishment: European Perspectives*. London: Routledge, 1–12.
Roldán Barbero, H. (1983) *El dinero, objeto fundamental de la sanción penal*. Madrid: Akal.
Rosenfeld, E. (1890) 'Welche Strafmittel können an die Stelle der kurzzeitigen Freiheitstrafe gesetzt werden?' In Von Liszt, F. (ed.) *Abhandlungen des kriminalistisches Seminars zu Halle. Zweiter Band, 2. Heft*. Berlin: Guttentag, 110–355.

Rusche, G. and O. Kirchheimer (1939 [2003]) *Punishment and Social Structure*. New Brunswick: Transaction.

Ryckere, R. de (1922) *De la suppression des courtes peines d'emprisonnement*. Brussels: Ferdinand Larcier.

Samuels, A. (1970) 'The Fine: The Principles'. *The Criminal Law Review*, May: 201–210, 268–272.

Schäfer, L. (1934). 'Strafbemessung'. In Gürtner, F. (ed.) *Das kommende deutsche Strafrecht*. Berlin: Vahlen, 106–116.

Schaffstein, F. (1934) 'Nationalsozialistisches Strafrecht: Gedanken zur Denkschrift des Preußischen Justizminister'. *Zeitschrift für die gesamte Strafrechtswissenschaft* 53: 603–628.

Schmidt, E. (1934) 'Aus der Statistik der preuβischen Gefangenenanstalten'. *Deutsche Justiz. Rechtspflege und Rechtspolitik* 96: 1023ff.

Schmidt, E. (1946) 'Probleme staatlichen Strafens in der Gegenwart'. *Süddeutsche Juristenzeitung* 1: 204–209.

Schmölder, R. (1902) *Die Geldstrafe: Vortrag, gehalten auf der 74. Jahresversammlung der Rheinisch-westfälischen Gefängnissgesellschaft in Düsseldorf am 15. Oktober 1902*. Hamm: Griebsch.

Schuchbauer, A. (1948) *Die Geldstrafe im deutschen und schwedischen Strafrecht*. Würzburg: Univ. Diss.

Seidler, E. (1890) 'Die Geldstrafe vom volkswirtschaftlichen und soziologischen Gesichtspunkte'. *Jahrbücher für Nationalökonomie und Statistik* 20(3): 241–258.

Sevdiren, O. (2011) *Alternatives to Imprisonment in England and Wales, Germany and Turkey*. Berlin: Springer.

Siegert, K. (1934) *Grundzüge des Strafrechts im neuen Staate*. Tübingen: Mohr.

Snacken, S. and K. Beyens (1994) 'Sentencing and Prison Overcrowding'. *European Journal on Criminal Policy and Research* 2(1): 84–99.

Softley, P. (1978) *Fines in Magistrates' Courts*. Home Office Research Study No. 45. London: HMSO.

Stanley, S. and M. Baginsky (1984) *Alternatives to Prison: An Examination of Non-Custodial Sentencing of Offenders*. London: Peter Owen.

Stapenhorst, H. (1993) *Die Entwicklung des Verhältnisses von Geldstrafe zu Freiheitsstrafe seit 1882*. Berlin: Duncker & Humblot.

Statistisches Bundesamt (1940) *Wirtschaft und Statistik*. Berlin: Paul Schmidt.

Statistisches Bundesamt (1941) *Wirtschaft und Statistik*. Berlin: Paul Schmidt.

Stenner, D. (1970) *Die kurzfristige Freiheitsstrafe und die Möglichkeiten zu ihrem Ersatz durch andere Sanktionen*. Hamburg: Kriminalistik-Verlag.

Stock, U. (1933) *Die Strafe als Dienst am Volke. Der Ausgleichungsgedanke in seiner Bedeutung für das Strafrechtssystem*. Tübingen: Mohr.

Stooβ, C. (1878) *Zur Natur der Vermögensstrafen*. Bern: M. Fiala.

Tak, P.J.P. (1986) 'Community Service Orders in Western Europe: A Comparative Survey'. In Albrecht, H.-J. and W. Schädler (eds.) *Community Service*. Freiburg: Max Planck Institute for Foreign and International Criminal Law, 1–14.

Tallack, W. (1889) *Penological and Preventive Principles*. London: Wertheimer.

Thornstedt, H. (1975) 'The Day-Fine System in Sweden'. *The Criminal Law Review*, June: 307–312.

Tiedemann, K. (1980) 'Stand und Tendenzen von Strafrechtswissenschaft und Kriminologie in der Bundesrepublik Deutschland'. *Juristen-Zeitung* 36: 489–495.

Tonry, M. and K. Hamilton (eds.) (1995) *Intermediate Sanctions in Overcrowded Times*. Boston: Northeastern University Press.

Tonry, M. and M. Lynch (1996) 'Intermediate Sanctions'. In Tonry, M. (ed.) *Crime and Justice: A Review of Research. Volume 20*. Chicago: University of Chicago Press, 99–144.

Troschitz, P. (1907) *Die Verwendung der Geldstrafe im geltenden Reichsstrafrecht*. Leipzig: C. Marquart.

Turner, S. and J. Petersilia (1996) *Evaluation of Day Fines in Maricopa County, Arizona, 1991–1993*. Santa Monica: RAND.

Valdés Rubio, J. M. (1909) *Derecho Penal*. Madrid: Imprenta del Asilo de huérfanos del S.C. de Jesús.

Van Kalmthout, A. M. and P.J.P. Tak (1992) *Sanctions-Systems in the Member States of the Council of Europe. Part II: Deprivation of Liberty, Community Service and Other Substitutes*. Deventer: Kluwer.

Vass, A. A. (1990) *Alternatives to Prison: Punishment, Custody and the Community*. London: SAGE.

Vila Miquel, E. (1917) *De la necesidad y medios de sustituir las penas cortas de privación de libertad*. Madrid: Imprenta de Juan Pueyo.

Vizmanos, T. M. de and C. Álvarez Martínez (1848) *Comentarios al Código penal. Tomo I*. Madrid: Establecimiento Tipográfico de J. González y A. Vicente.

Von Holtzendorff, F. (1864) 'Die Strafrechtreformvorschläge von Bonneville de Marsangy'. *Allgemeine Deutsche Strafrechtszeitung* 4: 642–658.

Von Ihering, R. (1877 [1904]) *Der Zweck im Recht*. Leipzig: Breitkopf & Haertel.

Von Liszt, F. (1889) 'Welche Maßregeln können dem Gesetzgeber zur Einschränkung der kurzzeitigen Freiheitsstrafe empfohlen werden?' In International Union of Penal Law/Deutsche Landesgruppe (ed.) *Mitteilungen der Internationalen Kriminalistischen Vereinigung: Bulletin de l'Union internationale de droit pénal*. Berlin:Guttentag, 44–51.

Vormbaum, T. (2014) *A Modern History of German Criminal Law*, ed. by M. Bohlander. New York: Springer.

Wachsmann, N. (2014) 'Between Reform and Repression: Imprisonment in Weimar Germany'. In Wetzell, R. F. (ed.) *Crime and Criminal Justice in Modern Germany*. New York: Berghahn Books, 115–136.

Walker, N. (1968) *Crime and Punishment in Britain: The Penal System in Theory, Law, and Practice*. 2nd ed. New Brunswick: Aldine Transaction.

Westen, D. A. (1969) 'Fines, Imprisonment, and the Poor: Thirty Dollars or Thirty Days'. *California Law Review* 57(3): 778–820.

Wilde, F. (2016) *Armut und Strafe: zur strafverschärfenden Wirkung von Armut im deutschen Strafrecht*. Wiesbaden: Springer.

Wilkins, L. T. (1969) *Evaluation of Penal Measures*. New York: Random House.

Wolf, E. (1935) 'Das künftige Strafensystem und die Zumessungsgrundsätze'. *Zeitschrift für die gesamte Strafrechtswissenschaft* 54: 544–574.

Worall, A. and C. Hoy (2005) *Punishment in the Community: Managing Offenders and Making Choices*. London: SAGE.

Young, P. (1999) 'The Fine as an Auto-Punishment: Power, Money and Discipline'. In Duff, P. and N. Hutton (eds.) *Criminal Justice in Scotland*. Aldershot: Darmouth, 182–197.

Young, W. (1986) 'Influences upon the Use of Imprisonment: A Review of Literature'. *The Howard Journal of Criminal Justice* 25(2): 125–136.

Young, W. and Brown, M. (1993) 'Cross National Comparisons of Imprisonment'. In Tonry, M. (ed.) *Crime and Justice: A Review of Research. Volume 17*. Chicago: University of Chicago Press, 1–49.

Zipf, H. (1966) *Die Geldstrafe in ihrer Funktion zur Eindämmung der kurzen Freiheitsstrafe*. Berlin: Luchterhand.

6 The triumph of the day-fine system? National perspectives and comparative approaches

'A turning point in European criminal policy'

In the last third of the twentieth century the legislative fruits of the bicentennial debate on the need to replace short prison sentences began to consolidate, rendering possible the equalization of impact of the penal fine through the implementation of the day-fine system in many European countries. With the day-fine system one of the most suitable sanctioning techniques for replacing custodial sentences was recognized, especially when it was implemented by applying payment instalments, which minimized the risk of non-payment, while also causing a reduction in the offender's living standards that was structurally akin to a loss of freedom, without the negative factors. In the geographical area we are considering, the Federal Republic of Germany and Austria introduced the day-fine system in 1975, followed by France and Portugal in 1983, England and Wales in 1992 – though briefly – and Spain in 1995. Conversely, Italy has a day-fine system for corporate offenders in regulatory law, but it has not incorporated day fines into its criminal justice system and is not considering abolishing summary fines. This wave of national implementations essentially marked a turning point in European criminal policy, similar to the one in the eighteenth century, which led to the abandonment of corporal penalties and their substitution with imprisonment (Kaiser 1973: 29; Jescheck 1977: 258; Heinz 1982: 638; Figueiredo Dias 1989: 292).

However, statutory changes and reform processes in Western European countries convey the message that change is rather slow and unpredictable. Although common issues and trends are visible, some outcomes and failures were clearly unexpected, thus making the path towards a general implementation of the day-fine system in Europe a bumpy one. Instead of detailing each national criminal justice system, the next sections aim to answer some key questions about fines based on examples from several national experiences. First, I will test the fine's impact on the reliance on imprisonment by contrasting the West German and Finnish experience. Second, I will compare Germany and Sweden to analyse the fine's potential in terms of decreasing the use of imprisonment for defaulters. Third, I will dissect the general assumption that the day-fine system better meets the principle of equality before the law by examining the English abandonment of the unit-fine system and the German disillusion with the fairness of the day-fine system.[1] Fourth, I will investigate the compatibility of imprisonment for defaulters and constitutional values by comparing decisions handed down by the Italian and Spanish constitutional courts. I will end this chapter by explaining the complete collapse of the Italian fixed-fine system, which was caused by the declared unconstitutionality of both the imprisonment for defaulters and part of the fine collection procedure.

A study of this type raises many technical and methodological challenges. It must be understood that I want only to present some aspects which I find particularly interesting. Despite their limited scope, the questions posed in this chapter will help us in Chapter 7 to outline the framework of a successful fine system which (1) reduces the use of prison, (2) eliminates the conversion of unpaid fines into imprisonment for defaulters, (3) equalizes the impact of fines for poor and wealthy offenders alike, and (4) can be effectively enforced and carried out.

Does the day-fine system reduce the use of prison? Contrasting West Germany and Finland

Does the day-fine system always reduce the use of prison? West Germany opted for statutory restrictions of short-term imprisonment in the 1960s and 1970s and filled the vacuum with the fine (Grebing 1982: 11). The adoption of the day-fine system produced a substantial reduction in the use of short prison sentences. On the contrary, Finland, the first country in the world to adopt the day-fine system, did it without enacting a preference for the fine in the selection of penalties. Thirty years later its imprisonment rate was one of the highest in Europe. Nevertheless, in the following decades Finland was able to reduce the use of prison by substituting short-term prison sentences with fines, once again without introducing a statutory preference for fines.

In the post–World War II period, the reform of the 1871 German Imperial Penal Code, still in force, was once again on the German agenda (Stammberger 1963: 11–29). Short prison terms still constituted a significant percentage of all prison sentences. Their use, especially of sentences of up to three months, increased by 7 per cent annually in the 1950s (Nüßlein 1969: 21). The arguments against short prison sentences were more or less the same as those at the turn of the century, with frequent references to their ineffectiveness for rehabilitative purposes (Schmidt 1952: 1ff.; Hall 1954: 77ff.). However, as will be shown, there was a strong resistance to their complete abolishment. In fact, it was not until 1953, when suspended sentences (*Strafaussetzung zur Bewährung*, suspension being the German equivalent of probation) proved to be a dismal failure in reducing the numbers of short-term prison sentences, that more compelling measures began to be explored and adopted.

The West German government formed a Grand Commission (*Grosse Strafrechtskommission*) in 1954 to revise the Imperial Penal Code. The Commission issued draft penal code E 1962 (*Entwurf eines Strafgesetzbuches*), which included provisions allowing fines to replace short-term imprisonment, without completely eliminating it. The day-fine system was also considered the best solution to the high numbers of fine defaults. Draft penal code E 1962 was severely criticized because of both its failure to eliminate the short-term prison sentence and its shortcomings as a modern criminal political conception (Roxin 1969; Baumann 1969b). The influential alternative draft code published in 1966 (*Alternativ-Entwurf eines Strafgesetzbuches, Allgemeiner Teil*) by certain German and Swiss criminal law scholars set six months as the minimum prison term, with fines replacing short-term prison sentences of up to two years. The main idea was that the fine was supposed to impact the living standard of the offender over a period of time. This was implemented by deducting a certain amount from the weekly wages or salary of the offender as specified by the court, with community service acting as the subsidiary penalty in case of insolvency (for a detailed analysis of the alternative draft's conception of the fine, see Stenner 1970: 102–110). Prompted by practical and constitutional problems caused by prison overcrowding, West Germany found a compromise between draft penal code E 1962 and the alternative draft 1966 through two reforms enacted in 1969 that introduced far-reaching changes to the sanctions system and revitalized the fine as a criminal sanction.[2]

The enactment of the First Criminal Law Reform Act (*Erstes Gesetz zur Reform des Strafrechts*) of June 25, 1969, was followed by the Second Criminal Law Reform Act (*Zweites Gesetz zur Reform des Strafrechts*) of July 4, 1969, which did not go into effect in its final version until January 1, 1975. Both laws were designed to limit imprisonment strictly to cases so serious that a custodial sentence appeared unavoidable. To achieve this goal, the reform acts combined several measures (Friedman 1983; Van Kalmthout and Tak 1992: 431–432; Weigend 2001: 192):

- First, prison sentences of less than one month were abolished altogether. Fines were considered enough in such petty offences.
- Second, short imprisonment – between one and six months – was declared to be ultima ratio. The reform acts mandated that the fine be the primary sanction for crimes formerly punishable by a prison term of six months or less.[3] The fine was given statutory priority by requiring the court to give specific reasons for imposing short-term prison sentences (§ 14 of the Penal Code, pre-1975 version; § 47 of the amended Penal Code). Furthermore, it was established that a short term of imprisonment, already an exceptional penalty, should be in principle always suspended. The court should give additional justification if it refrained from suspending a sentence of less than one year.
- Third, many petty offences – mostly traffic offences, but also a host of typical offences against public order – were directly decriminalized and turned into regulatory infractions (*Ordnungswidrigkeiten*) punishable by fines only.
- Fourth, the method of calculating the fine amount changed. Under the new method, modelled on the Scandinavian day-fine system, the fine for any particular crime was not a fixed sum but a variable figure adjusted to the offender's income, designed to have a proportionate impact across all economic strata. Judicial discretion was restricted by establishing formal rules for fine calculation. The law provided an upper limit for the daily amount. Nothing was said about whether the court could further increase the amount of the day fine for an offender with large personal wealth not represented in his or her income (Friedman 1983: 296).
- And fifth, since 1975 – through the Act introducing the Penal Code (*Einführungsgesetz zum Strafgesetzbuch*) of March 2, 1974 – the public prosecution service was given a leading role in out-of-court settlements. In particular, in misdemeanour cases the prosecutor can require the suspect to make restitution to the victim or a payment to charity or to the state in exchange for dropping

criminal charges (§ 153a of the German Code of Criminal Procedure, *Strafprozessordnung*). The amount of money to be paid is roughly equivalent to the fine that might be imposed if the suspect were convicted. The reasoning behind this provision is that the suspect, by making such a payment, eliminates the public interest in prosecuting the minor offence (Weigend 1995a: 45 and 1995b). Obviously this practice accelerates and eases the caseload of the courts because the adopted measures do not differ in concrete terms from some of the sanctions in the Penal Code which previously only trial judges could impose (Van Kalmthout and Tak 1992: 433), except in two important respects: first, the amount is not based on the statutory criteria governing the day-fine system; second, imprisonment for defaulters does not apply to it (Grebing 1978: 84–85). In 1988 these informal sanctions involving payment of a sum of money made up about 51 per cent of all sanctions imposed under general criminal law (Statistisches Bundesamt 1988: 18).

The First Criminal Law Reform Act reduced West Germany's reliance on short-term prison sentences (Gillespie 1980: 20–21; Heinz 1982: 639–642 and 1989; Friedman 1983: 293), even though the prison population grew intermittently but consistently during the 1970s.[4] While there was an immediate sharp reduction of prison terms after the reform of 1969 on sentencing law, it is interesting to note that the decrease of custodial sentences in the 1970s almost exclusively applied to sentences of less than nine months, and more precisely to ones of less than six months. Heinz (1989: 199) spoke about 'a disproportionate drop in short sentences'. A total of 113,273 prison sentences (20 per cent of all convictions, 86 per cent of all prison sentences) in 1968 were for a period of six months or less, but in 1970, the first year after the reform acts, the number of non-suspended prison sentences for a period of up to six months dropped to 23,664 (Gillespie 1980: 21), only 4 per cent of all convictions. In 1975, non-suspended prison sentences of less than six months constituted only about 2 per cent of all convictions imposed in West Germany.

Table 6.1 Total convictions under general criminal law, non-suspended prison sentences of less than six months and fines (total numbers and percentages), West Germany: 1968–1975

Year	*Total convictions*	*Prison sentences of less than 6 months*	*Fines*	*% prison sentences of less than 6 months to total convictions*	*% fines to total convictions*
1968	572,629	113,273	361,074	19.8	63.1
1969	530,947	64,073	371,918	12.1	70.0
1970	553,692	23,664	464,818	4.3	83.9
1971	571,423	22,207	476,785	3.9	83.4
1972	591,719	20,045	494,399	3.4	83.6
1973	601,419	17,747	504,266	3.0	83.8
1974	599,368	18,033	494,266	3.0	82.5
1975	567,605	11,350	472,577	2.0	83.3

Source: Adapted from Gillespie (1980: 21).

It seems quite clear that the decrease in short-term prison sentences was absorbed by the increase in fines (Janssen 1994: 17).

Figure 6.1 Non-suspended prison sentences of less than six months and fines (percentages), West Germany: 1968–1975

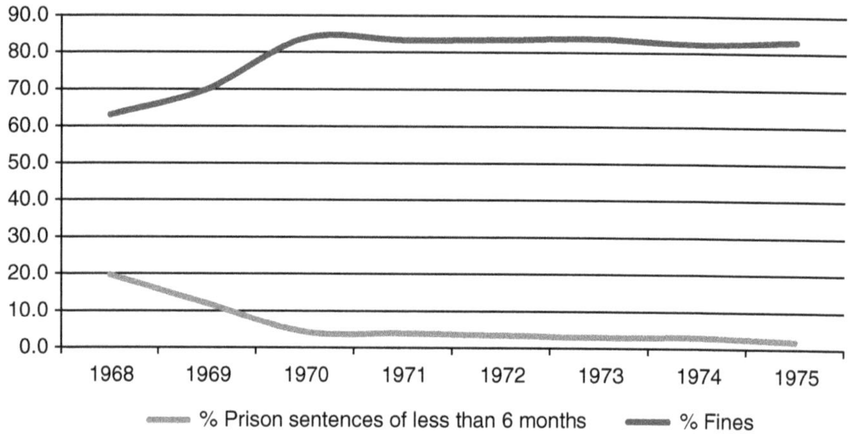

Source: Adapted from Gillespie (1980: 21), based on Drucksache 7/1089, Deutscher Bundestag 7. Wahlperiode 17.10.73 and Federal Ministry of Justice.

The number of prison sentences exceeding nine months diminished steadily between 1976 and 1996, while the number of prison sentences exceeding two years rose notably, as did the share of lengthy sentences (2–15 years) among all non-suspended prison sentences.

Table 6.2 Non-suspended prison sentences (total numbers and percentages), West Germany: 1968–1996 (selected yearly average)

Year	*Total convictions*	*Non-suspended prison sentences between 9 months and 2 years (and percentage to total convictions)*	*Non-suspended prison sentences between 2 and 15 years (and percentage to total convictions)*	*Percentage of non-suspended prison sentences of 9 months or more to total convictions*
1968	526,813	17,116*		3.24
1976	543,059	11,987 (2.20%)	4,744 (0.87%)	3.08
1980	553,212	11,559 (2.08%)	5,102 (0.92%)	3
1990	590,707	8,887 (1.50%)	5,776 (0.98%)	2.47
1996	656,895	9,816 (1.49%)	8,927 (1.36%)	2.84

Source: Bundeskriminalamt (1997: 259); Statistisches Bundesamt Reihe 9 (1970: 13); Statistisches Bundesamt Reihe 1 (1996: 24–25, 1997: 24–25).

* Statistics did not provide breakdown of sentences between nine months and five years.

Figure 6.2 Non-suspended prison sentences between 9 months and 2 years and 2 and 15 years (total numbers), West Germany*: 1976–1996 (selected years)

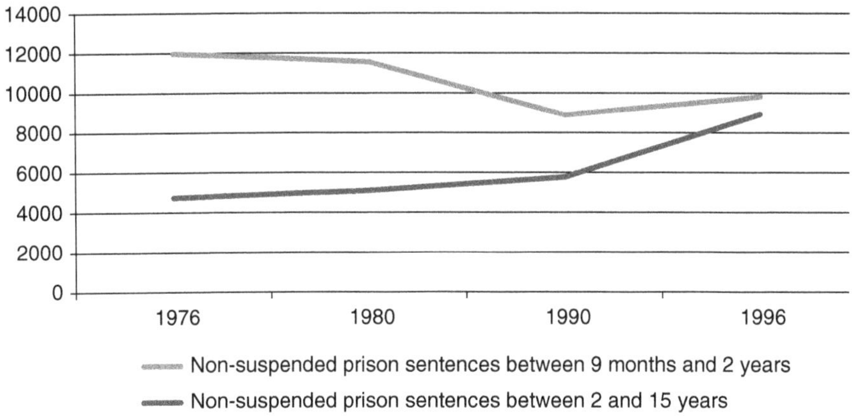

Source: Bundeskriminalamt (1997: 259); Statistisches Bundesamt Reihe 1 (1996), pp. 24–25; (1997), pp. 24–25.

* Since 1991 including East Germany.

Due to changes in the statistical categories only a partial comparison for the years pre-1970 is possible, yet even so it is quite clear that medium- and long-term prison sentences increased during the considered period.

The reduction in the number of sentences in the nine months to two year range between 1976 and 1996 was due to the fact that courts made increasing use of suspended sentences (Heinz 1989: 199–200; Weigend 1995a and 2001: 195–197; Morgenstern 2016: 76ff.), not of fines. In fact, during this period the percentage of cases resulting in imposed fines negligibly shifted from 83.79 per cent in 1976 to 82.19 per cent in 1996. What changed was the interpretation of the clause in Paragraph 56(2) of the German Penal Code which authorized courts to suspend a sentence between one and two years only if the court found 'special circumstances' in the offence or the personality of the offender, especially if the offender had made restitution to the victim. Originally understood as an exceptional art of clemency – there were only 878 suspended prison sentences between one and two years in 1976 – it became routine in the next 20 years – 4,824 suspended prison sentences in 1986, 10,735 in 1996. In light of the fact that convictions for offences of medium seriousness more than doubled during this 20-year period, substantial increases in suspended prison sentences actually prevented prisons from being overburdened (Weigend 2001: 196).

Fines were used for less serious offences, as the number of imposed daily units shows.

Figure 6.3 Fine sentences according to the number of daily units (total numbers), Germany*: 1976–2014 (selected years)

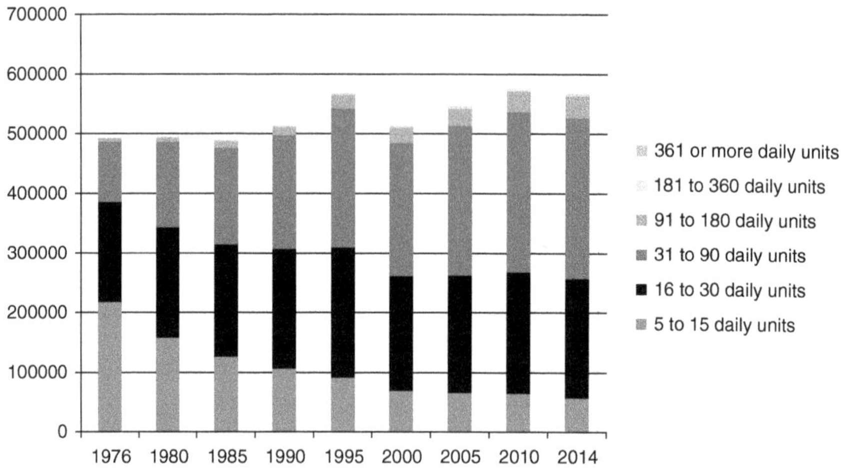

Source: Strafverfolgungsstatistik, Fachserie 10, Reihe 3: 1976–2014.

* Since 1991 including East Germany.

Table 6.3 Fine sentences according to the number of daily units (total numbers), Germany*: 1976–2014 (selected years)

Year	*Total convictions to fines*	*5 to 15 daily units*	*16 to 30 daily units*	*31 to 90 daily units*	*91 to 180 daily units*	*181 to 360 daily units*	*361 or more daily units*
1976	492,561	217,766	167,555	100,866	5,696	608	70
1980	494,114	158,230	185,018	142,347	7,657	748	114
1985	488,414	126,699	188,133	161,193	11,053	1,196	140
1990	512,343	106,280	200,965	189,553	13,984	1,363	198
1995	567,195	91,544	218,578	232,168	22,836	1,806	263
2000	513,336	69,187	192,234	222,416	26,850	2,307	342
2005	545,971	66,289	196,367	250,672	29,671	2,620	352
2010	575,068	65,196	202,618	268,952	34,882	3,063	357
2014	566,635	57,067	199,814	269,439	37,018	3,021	276

Source: Strafverfolgungsstatistik, Fachserie 10, Reihe 3: 1976–2014.

* Since 1991 including East Germany.

Between 1975 and 1980, 98.5 per cent of fines amounted to no more than 90 days (Albrecht 1980: 199ff.; Heinz 1981 and 1982: 641–642; Kürzinger 1984: 1867ff.). The possibility of imposing a day fine of up to 360 days went practically unused as evidenced by the following statistics. In 1976 only 1.3 per cent of all fines imposed in West Germany were between 91 and 360 days. This percentage

Figure 6.4 Fine sentences according to the number of daily units (percentages), Germany*: 1976–2014 (selected years)

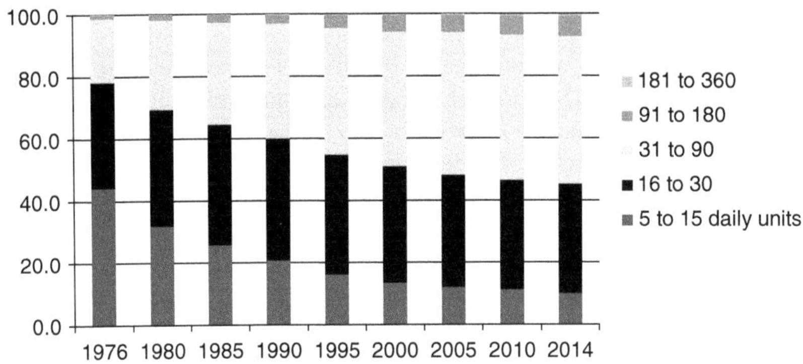

Source: Strafverfolgungsstatistik, Fachserie 10, Reihe 3: 1976–2014.

* Since 1991 including East Germany.

increased slightly to 1.7 in 1980 and more decidedly to 3 per cent in 1990, the year before the reunification (Statistisches Bundesamt 2009: 68–69). It experienced a slow but steady increase in the 2000s: 5.7 per cent in 2000 and 7 per cent in 2014.

Table 6.4 Fine sentences according to the number of daily units (percentages), Germany*: 1976–2014 (selected years)

Year	*5 to 15 daily units*	*16 to 30*	*31 to 90*	*91 to 180*	*181 to 360*	*361 or more*
1976	44.2	34.0	20.5	1.2	0.1	<0.05
1980	32.0	37.4	28.8	1.5	0.2	<0.05
1985	25.9	38.5	33.0	2.3	0.2	<0.05
1990	20.7	39.2	37.0	2.7	0.3	<0.05
1995	16.1	38.5	40.9	4.0	0.3	<0.05
2000	13.5	37.4	43.3	5.2	0.4	0.1
2005	12.1	36.0	45.9	5.4	0.5	0.1
2010	11.3	35.2	46.7	6.0	0.5	0.06
2014	10.0	35.2	47.5	6.5	0.5	<0.05

Source: Strafverfolgungsstatistik, Fachserie 10, Reihe 3: 1976–2014.

* Since 1991 including East Germany.

This means that as an alternative to imprisonment, fines were initially being used only to substitute the shortest sentences, and not prison sentences which were deemed to be in the middle order of severity (Frank 1978: 21–22; Heinz 1982: 667; Van Kalmthout and Tak 1992: 435; Sevdiren 2011: 150–151). The situation has changed in recent years, but the most used range of unit fines is still low, 31 to 90 days in almost half of all cases.

The greatest increase is seen in prison sentences longer than two years, which is mainly the result of a more stringent sanctioning policy primarily directed at drug offences. As Van Kalmthout and Tak (1992: 436) wrote, 'Penalties in this area were tightened up considerably in 1971 and 1981'. The result was an increase in the average duration of custody, which can be partially explained by the strong correlation between the average length of prison sentences and the incarceration rate (Killias 1994: 118–119). There were also other relevant factors, such as the general rise in criminality recorded by the police and brought to courts (the overall number of convicted offenders increased, though not dramatically, from 526,813 in 1968 to 656,895 in 1996), demographic changes, and stiffer penalties for recidivists. The conjunction of all these factors may explain why there was no emptying of prisons.

In contrast, other countries also tried to restrict imprisonment by mainly substituting short-term prison sentences with fines while neither enacting a statutory minimum term of imprisonment nor stating a preference for the fine in the selection of penalties. The Scandinavian countries and Switzerland could be placed in this group of countries. Finland is a good study case, because of its counter-cyclical success in reducing the imprisonment rate, which included a sharp reduction in imprisonment for defaulters.

Finland was the first country in the world to introduce the day-fine system in 1921. By then its imprisonment rate was very high, mainly as a result of the 1918 civil war. The sharp reduction that can be observed in the 1920s was not produced by the day-fine system, but by amnesties (Lappi-Seppälä 2009: 348). An increased crime rate and the deep economic recession of the late 1920s raised the figures back to 250 for every 100,000 by the middle of the 1930s, in part due to a substantial increase in imprisonment for defaulters. A steady increase in crime started in Finland soon after the two wars conducted with Russia between 1939 and 1944. In response to this situation longer sentences of imprisonment were used and the Finnish criminal system toughened up in general (Törnud 1993: 1; Ekunwe and Jones 2012: 174–175). As a result, more offenders were sent to prison for longer periods. At the beginning of the 1950s the imprisonment rate in Finland was much higher than in the other Nordic countries and was among the highest in Western Europe until 1975 (Törnud 1993: 1; Lappi-Seppälä 2004: 140). During the late 1960s a vibrant reform movement called for a reappraisal of the strategies against crime both within and outside the criminal justice system, criticizing the excessive use of custodial sentences. By then it was too late for the rehabilitation ideology to become dominant (Törnudd 1993: 3). The resulting criminal political ideology, known as 'humane neo-classicism' (Lappi-Seppälä 2001: 115; against the use of this term see Lahti 1989: 69), brought profound changes to how the entire problem of crime and punishment was viewed. Neo-classicism emphasized fairness, proportionality, predictability, and equality in the choice of punishment. Systematic sentencing reforms from 1969 onward, which included legislative reforms pertaining to particular offences and the realignment of general sentencing principles, brought the Finnish incarceration rate back to Nordic levels in the 1990s.

The adoption of proportionality-based sentencing principles did not lead to the expected harsher sentences. The Finnish Penal Code included a clear statement against aggravation of punishment for the purpose of general prevention (Lappi-Seppälä 2001: 130ff.). The new chapter added in 1976 stated that 'punishment shall be measured so that it is in just proportion to the damage and danger caused by the offence and to the guilt of the offender manifested in the offence'. But, as Cavadino and Dignan (2006: 162) put it,

> there was an 'asymmetry' to this proportionality principle: the Code allowed courts to impose sentences which were more lenient than proportionality would indicate, but – so as to guarantee citizens against the excessive use of state force – not generally to pass disproportionately harsh penalties.

Regarding other reforms, it must be taken into account that fines have always made up the bulk of the punishments imposed in Finland. One reason is that there is no general administrative sanctioning law in Finland. Almost all offences are classified as crimes and treated under the label of criminal punishments, although for certain petty offences fines can be imposed through simplified summary penal proceedings (penalty orders) by the prosecutor. Another reason is that the Finnish criminal justice system offers few alternatives to imprisonment in comparison with other European countries. The courts usually could sentence the offender only to unconditional imprisonment, conditional imprisonment, or a fine, with community service being added only in the 1990s. Properly speaking, fines are considered a principal punishment, not a mere alternative to imprisonment (Utriainen 2002: 196–197, explaining that in Finland it is impossible to convert a prison sentence into a fine).

By changing the statutes on theft offences and public drunkenness, the two most common crimes ending up in prison sentences, it became possible to increase the use of fines while simultaneously reducing short-term prison sentences. Long prison sentences imposed for traditional property crimes, combined with high minimum penalties and rigid offence definitions for aggravated forms, kept the Finnish prison population at very high levels during the early 1950s (Lappi-Seppälä 2004: 142). In 1972 new definitions and new minimum penalties for theft were introduced (Törnud 1993: 8–9). In 1991 the penalties were reduced again, leading to a considerable decrease in the use of prison sentences. In 1971, 38 per cent of offenders sentenced for theft received an unconditional prison sentence. In 1991, this percentage decreased to 11 per cent. The average length of all prison sentences imposed for theft also decreased. In 1971 it was 7.4 months, but in 1991 only 2.6 months (Lappi-Seppälä 2004: 142). The percentage of fines increased from 37 per cent in 1971 to 82 per cent in 1991 (Törnud 1993: 19). But the increased use of fines for these property offences was reflected in the growing number of fine defaulters who were sent to prison.

In the late 1920s Finland, four out of five admitted prisoners were taken into custody because of unpaid fines (Lappi-Seppälä 2014: 1641). In the 1950s fine defaulters still constituted the vast majority of offenders receiving a short custodial sentence, as well as a substantial percentage of the Finnish prison population, sometimes exceeding 25 per cent (Lappi-Seppälä 2004: 146). This fact explains why, starting in the 1960s, more attention began to be paid to the specific offender group of fine defaulters. Later on in the 1960s, the percentage of default prisoners was reduced due to two reforms: the decriminalization of public drunkenness and the increase in the amount of the day-fine unit (now without an upper limit), combined with the reduction of the maximum duration (from 300 to 120 days). The first reform reduced the number of unpaid fines since public drunkenness often resulted in an unpaid fine (Törnud 1993: 15).[5] The second reform led to shorter prison terms for fine defaulters, while at the same time encouraging courts to use fines in more serious crimes, such as theft[6] and drunken driving.[7] A major component of the reform was the drastic adjustment of the conversion rate. As a result, fine defaulters were practically removed from prisons (Utriainen 2002: 197; Ekunwe and Jones 2012: 177), even though the proportion of sentences that were fines considerably increased. Other factors unrelated to fines also considerably influenced imprisonment rates during this period.

During the 1970s and 1980s, when most European countries experienced rising prison populations, Finland's kept going down, reaching the traditionally low Nordic level by the beginning of the 1990s. Both the number of prison sentences and their average lengths were significantly reduced between 1976 and 1991 (Törnud 1993; Cavadino and Dignam 2006: 165). This development has been correctly defined as a 'criminal policy triumph' (Lappi-Seppälä 2001: 138). But the number of prisoners started to increase again from 2000 onwards, albeit with ups and downs. The explanation of this recent trend seems to be the increasing number of foreign offenders, which in turn increased the use of pretrial detention and the number of fine defaulters (Lappi-Seppälä 2009: 371–372). Between 1999 and 2002, these factors accounted for a little over 50 per cent of the increase (Lappi-Seppälä 2004: 152–153). The global trend towards the international harmonization of criminal justice has also been mentioned in this regard. From 2006 to 2008 acts were passed in order to restrict the use of subsidiary imprisonment: the conversion rate was changed from 2:1 to 3.1, the maximum subsidiary prison sentence was lowered from 90 days to 60 days, and smaller fines (court-ordered fines under 12 days and fines ordered by prosecutors) were excluded from the fine default system.

Today, according to the current Finnish Criminal Code, the number of day fines that may be imposed on an offender is limited to 120 days for one offence and 240 days if the offender is sentenced for more than one offence. The daily amount of the fine should equal one sixtieth of the offender's average monthly salary less taxes and fees and a fixed deduction for basic consumption. This is roughly 50 per cent of the offender's daily net income. The initial deduction for basic needs is 255 euros (Statistics Office Finland 2012). The law does not provide an upper limit for the day-fine amount. As a result, fines for relatively minor offences are occasionally very high. A conversion sentence is passed for a person sentenced to a fine if efforts to collect the fine have been unsuccessful (Penal Code, Chapter 2[a], Section 4). The main rule is that three unpaid day fines are equivalent to one day of imprisonment. When passing a conversion sentence for a penalty payment, imposed as a lump sum, every 30 euros equals one day of imprisonment. A conversion sentence shall be passed for at least 4 days and at most 60 days. Pecuniary penalties given in summary penal proceedings are not converted to imprisonment.

The consequence of these two different national approaches is twofold. First, both countries, Germany and Finland, were able to considerably increase both the number of sentences that are fines and their percentage of total convictions.

Table 6.5 Fine sentences (total numbers and percentage of fines of total convictions), Germany* and Finland: 1950–2010 (in ten-year periods)

Year	*Germany*		*Finland*	
	Fine sentences	*Percentage of fines to total convictions*	*Fine sentences*	*Percentage of fines to total convictions*
1950	172,575	62.7	11,734	61.7
1960	335,978	69.2	11,895	63.8
1970	464,818	83.9	19,890	69.7
1980	494,114	82.4	43,997	74.6
1990	512,343	83.3	51,491	76.0
2000	513,336	80.3	58,609	80.9
2010	575,068	81.6	72,932	83.9

Source: For Germany, Strafverfolgungsstatistik 1950–2011; for Finland, Nordic Criminal Statistics 1950–2012.

* Since 1991 including East Germany.

This development was quite gradual and linear for Finland, but not for Germany.

Figure 6.5 Percentage of fines of total convictions, Germany* and Finland: 1950–2010 (in ten-year periods)

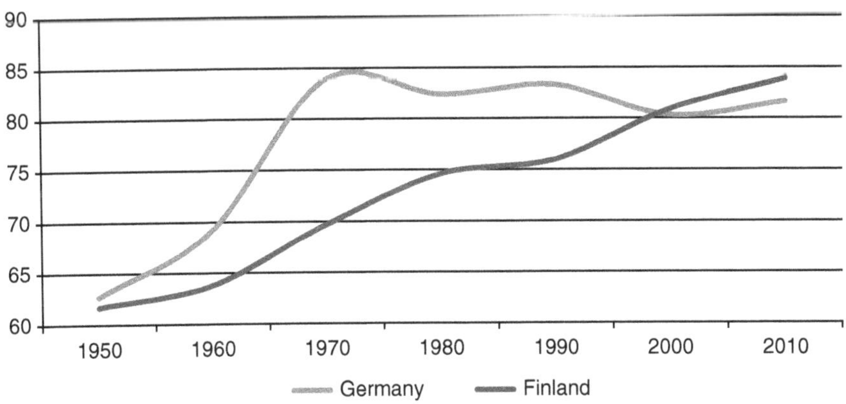

Source: For Germany, Strafverfolungsstatistik 1950–2011; for Finland, Nordic Criminal Statistics 1950–2012.

*Since 1991 including East Germany.

Finland was able to reduce its incarceration rate until the mid-2000s, but Germany's fluctuated.

Table 6.6 Prison population and incarceration rate, including pretrial prisoners, Germany and Finland: 1950–2015 (in five-year periods)

Year	*Germany**		*Finland*	
	Prison population	*Incarceration rate*	*Prison population*	*Incarceration rate*
1950			7,507	187
1955			6,330	149
1960		106	6,818	154
1965	60,878	103	6,665	146
1970	48,288	79	5,140	112
1975	50,164	81	5,242	111
1980	56,705	92	5,088	106
1985	61,705	101	4,411	90
1990	52,003	82	3,441	69
1995	58,909	88	3,243	63
2000	70,252	85	2,855	55
2005	78,992	95	3,888	74
2010	69,385	85	3,291	61
2015	63,628	78	3,106	57

Source: For Germany, Dünkel and Rössner (2001: 291) for the period 1965–1995, World Prison Population List for the period 1996–2015; for Finland, Nordic Criminal Statistics 1950–2010, 68–69, and World Prison Population List for the years 2010–2015.

*Since 1991 including East Germany.

In short, penal reform in Germany contained binding rules regarding the choice of the penalty, with the day fine having priority over any prison sentence of less than six months, unless exceptional circumstances concerning the offender, the offence, or both indicate the need for a different type of punishment. Since courts must justify all sentences of less than six months, they are reluctant to resort to short-term imprisonment. Day fines regularly substitute prison sentences of up to six months, being the typical punishment not only for traffic offences but also for more traditional crimes, such as theft, larceny, burglary, fraud, and assault (Janssen 1994; Albrecht 2001: 310). However, short prison terms are still being used, and one of the main reasons for this is the imprisonment of defaulters (Dünkel and Rössner 2001: 292), which will be shown in the next section. Finland, on the other hand, typically uses the fine for most middle-rank offences, such as theft, minor burglaries, and assaults. The decrease in the Finnish prison population which started during the 1950s is the result of a conscious, long-term, and systematic criminal policy (Lappi-Seppälä 2000: 37–38; Von Hofer 2003: 31). As Albrecht (2013: 219) put it, 'In Finland, it was evidently the desire to fall in line with the rest of the Scandinavian countries that resulted in adopting a decarceration policy that decreased the prison population significantly'. The reform of the day-fine system was only one piece, yet important, in this effort, along with the expanded use of the parole system, the introduction of community service as an alternative to unconditional imprisonment, the increased use of conditional prison sentences, and the decriminalization of certain minor crimes.

In sum, the most interesting conclusion is that adopting the day-fine system does not always reduce the use of prison sentences or the imprisonment rate. Rather this reduction, often used to justify the day-fine system, depends on several factors. The critical fact seems to be the *conditions* under which the day-fine system is delivered, not merely the introduction of statutory restrictions concerning the choice of penalties for less serious crimes. In particular, as will be shown in the next section, the rules governing the conversion of unpaid fines into imprisonment are of utmost importance.

Does the day-fine system reduce imprisonment for defaulters? The contrasting cases of West Germany and Sweden

The large number of people imprisoned for defaulting on fines in a period of serious prison overcrowding was one of the main factors impelling the adoption of the day-fine system in many European countries. The introduction of the day-fine system in West Germany was an important tool to manage the rise in crime rates during the 1960s and the overcrowded prisons it produced. West Germany responded to this rise by decreasing rather than increasing its punitiveness. As we have seen in the previous section, the substantial rise in convictions was treated with sanctions other than imprisonment, so that prison capacity did not substantially increase between 1968 and 1996 (Weigend 2001: 193). However, contrary to expectations (Lang-Hinrichsen 1959: 135), while the adoption of the day-fine system reduced the use of short-term imprisonment, it actually increased the use of imprisonment for defaulters.

In fact, only adopting the day-fine system does not necessarily result in a diminution of unpaid fines. From a purely theoretical viewpoint, a factor that can strongly influence the use of imprisonment for defaulters is an easily understandable conversion rate, since the temporal similarity of the day fine to a prison sentence makes substitution between the two more feasible. It is very important to provide clear and rational conversion rates for the various types of punishments incorporated into the criminal justice system. If conversion is perceived to be rational, it is easier for the courts to substitute unpaid fines with a prison term. Let us now turn to the implementation of day-fine systems in Sweden and Germany and examine some national factors which led to contrasting results.

Prison data dating back to the nineteenth century show very high imprisonment rates in both countries. Since then, prison populations have decreased considerably. Nowadays, in both countries the overwhelming majority of sentences involve fines. An equalization of impact between poor and rich offenders has been secured in Sweden since 1931 and in Germany since 1974 by the day-fine system. However, there are differences between the national legislative frameworks and judicial application. One is the proportion of the offender's disposable income or degree of economic deprivation that a day fine should represent. In Sweden, the degree of economic deprivation imposed is relatively modest. According to the preparatory works of the legislation of 1931, the offender's per diem income should be the starting point for determining the amount of the fine. 'This income ought in the general opinion to be the offender's mean income per day calculated on the basis of his economic circumstances during a not too short time' (Thornstedt 1975: 309). The thousandth part of the income during a year was chosen later as a basis, regarded as the per diem amount which would be left when the offender had spent what was absolutely necessary for him- or herself and his or her family. Nowadays, the practice in Sweden consists of setting each day-fine unit equal to one one-thousandth of the offender's annual income, which is more or less equivalent to one-third of one day's income, with allowances for taxes, the number of dependent family members and financial liabilities and debts (Thornstedt 1975: 309; Hamdorf and Wölber 1999: 931). In Germany the system is harsher for the offender (Hillsman 1990: 79ff.; Hamdorf and Wölber 1999: 932; Henning 1999: 301; Seebode 1999: 521; Warner 2012: 236–237). It comes down to calculating the income the offender stands to lose if he or she is in detention, while taking individual circumstances into account. It is specified that the fraction of the offender's average net daily income to be used for calculating the fine may not equal an amount which would deprive the offender and his or her family of a minimal living standard (Friedman 1983: 288). No provision for reducing the daily fee was established in the event of the offender's economic situation worsening after the sentence was imposed.[8]

In Sweden assessing the means of the offender is based on statements by the offender to the police or to the court, corroborated by unrestricted access to income and tax records (Thornstedt 1974: 608ff.). In theory, the case may be adjourned for further enquiries if it is evident that the offender is untruthful, but this is seldom done. German courts have no access to this kind of information. The West German federal parliament refused to vest courts with the power to compel an offender to disclose his or her income, as previously proposed in the alternative draft, § 49, and the E 1962, § 51(3) (Friedman 1983: 289). Therefore, German courts rely upon information from the police and the public prosecutor supplemented by a brief oral interrogation of the offender. However, Friedman (1983: 290) clearly indicated, 'if the offender does not supply the court with information about his income, and his profession is not one characterized by wage uniformity, it is difficult for a court to set an accurate fine'. The restricted access to data to investigate the offender's income undermines the goal of equalizing the impact of fines and may generally inhibit the court's ability to properly calculate the final amount. In many cases the resulting fine is overly burdensome, so that the offender is unable to pay it. The conversion of a large number of day fines into a similarly large number of days of work for the community causes a low level of motivation among offenders. 'The number of hours to be worked and the length of time it goes on seems too long to many of them' (Van Kalmthout and Tak 1992: 516). The range of day-fine units is also different, wider in Germany (from 5 to 360 days, with the possibility of 720 days in the case of exceptional and serious offences and aggregate offences) than in Sweden (originally 1 to 120, 180 in the case of multiple offences, nowadays 30 to 150, 200 in the case of multiple offences, according to Sections 2 and 6 of Chapter 25 of the Swedish Penal Code). Also the sum to be paid each day is different, with broader margins in Germany than in Sweden, especially if the maximum is considered: currently, in Germany a daily unit cannot be set at less than 1 and not at more than 30,000 euros (§ 40[2] of the German Penal Code), whereas in Sweden the lowest amount for a day fine is 450 Swedish crowns (Section 2 of Chapter 25 of the Swedish Penal Code). These differences are attributed to the fact that day fines in Sweden are intended to be used for less serious offences than is the case in Germany, where more types of offences are covered by the day-fine system (Hillsman 1990: 79ff.). In any case, the maximum is rarely applied in both countries.

In Sweden fines were and still are the most prominent sentence and used very extensively (Arnholm 1997: 7; Von Hofer 2004: 119; Von Hofer et al. 2012: 58–59), though usually not in combination with a prison sentence. They appear to be a viable alternative to incarceration (Thornstedt 1975: 312; Zagaris 1977: 153–155), even for offences that are traditionally regarded as rather serious. And while Sweden reserves the option to imprison fine defaulters, the conditions for its imposition are very restrictive. Imprisonment for default reached significant percentages during the 1930s, when approximately 13,000 fine defaulters were imprisoned on an annual basis (Cornils 1983: 793). The enactment of the 1937 Act on Enforcement of Fines (*Lag om verkställighet av bötesstraff*, no. 119) put an end to this massive imprisonment of fine defaulters by tightening the conditions for converting unpaid fines. This progressive statute required a second examination of the case before commutation and potentially allowed for sentences to be remitted in cases where the offender was unable to pay the fine. Only if the offender failed to pay because of deliberate neglect or stubborn refusal, or if he or she deliberately took steps to evade collection, was a prison sentence for non-payment mandatory (Rusche and Kirchheimer 1939 [2003]: 170). Imprisonment for non-payment could also be considered if the public interest demanded it in particular cases. This clause was intended to cover flagrant cases of repeat offenders or cases in which the offender's inability to pay would practically equate to an 'immunity to sanctioning' (Hamdorf and Wölber 1999: 940–941; Von Hofer 2004: 120). But even then the court may suspend the execution of such sentences. Imprisonment for default ranged from 14 days to three months, with no statutorily fixed conversion rate. The courts ruled according to the offender's special circumstances and took the number and amount of daily units as one of many factors into consideration.

The results were impressive. In 1932 13,358 persons were in prison for non-payment of fines. In 1938, only one year after the introduction of the day-fine

Table 6.7 Unpaid fines converted into prison sentences (percentage of fine convictions), Sweden: 1931 until now

Year	*Unpaid fines converted into prison sentences (percentage of imposed fines)*
1931	11.9
1932	12.5
1933	10.0
1934	7.4
1935	6.4
1936	5.3
1937	3.5
1938	3.3
1939	0.6
1940	0.6
1941	0.4
1942	0.3
1943 until 1982	0.2 or less
1983 until now*	0.0

Source: Ermgassen (1977: 949) for the period 1931–1976, Sveri (1998: 946) for the period 1987–1997, Kristoffersen (2008: 33, 2010: 35, 2013: 24) for the period 2002–2012.

* Since 1983 there are no available statistical data, because the absolute numbers are very small. In 1983 there were 29 cases, of which 2 were converted into prison sentences (Schaeferdiek 1997: 112). In 1989, only in six cases the prosecutor asked the court to have fines changed into imprisonment, but none of them went into prison, 'which must mean that these six fine defaulters did pay "before the prison gates" ', according to Sveri (1998: 946).

Figure 6.6 Unpaid fines converted into prison sentences (percentage of imposed fines), Sweden: 1931 until now

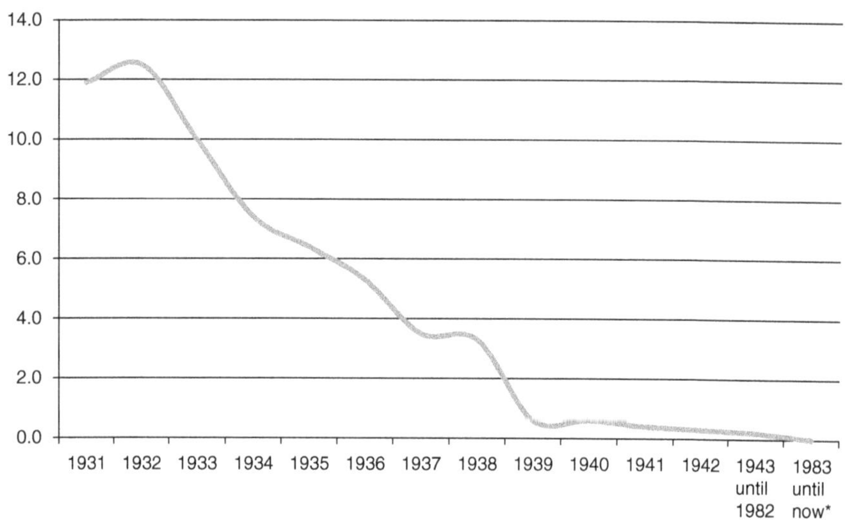

Source: Ermgassen (1977: 949) for the period 1931–1976, Sveri (1998: 946) for the period 1987–1997, Kristoffersen (2008: 33, 2010: 35, 2013: 24) for the period 2002–2012.

system, the number had dropped to 4,728. In 1939, after additional reform, the number dropped to 815. By 1946 only 286 persons were imprisoned yearly for non-payment of fines (Sellin 1947: 14–15). In practice, Sweden has completely ceased to convert fines into imprisonment since 1983 (Sveri 1998: 946; Hamdorf and Wölber 1999: 929 and 940; Lappi-Seppälä 2012: 97), in line with crime policy efforts to restrict the negative effects of prison sentencing.

The legal provision of subsidiary imprisonment was not eliminated for two reasons: first, legislators feared that this would lead to the courts imposing more short-term prison sentences in the belief that the fine would remain unpaid; and second, this vacuum could create groups of the population 'immune to the fine'. The statistics show that a significant percentage of offenders pay the fine just before imprisonment is enforced (6,000 in 1975, according to Hamdorf and Wölber 1999: 937). The demand for more and longer prison sentences from the 1990s onwards did not impact on the (lack of) use of imprisonment for defaulters.

On the contrary, the percentages of subsidiary imprisonment in Germany not only increased but also actually doubled – rising from 5.6 per cent of imposed fines in 1974 to 10.8 per cent in 1997 (Albrecht 1981; Janssen 1994; Hamdorf and Wölber 1999: 935). In 2002, it was 9.3 per cent (Heinz 2010: 71).

Table 6.8 Unpaid fines converted into prison sentences (percentage of imposed fines), Germany*: 1926–2000 (selected years)

Year	*Unpaid fines converted into prison sentences (percentage of imposed fines)*
1926/27	8.8
1928/29	9.0
1930	12.5
1931. . .	15.4
1971**	3.8
1972	4.1
1973	4.5
1974	5.6
1975	5.7
1976	5.6
1980	5.2
1985	6.3
1990	5.8
1995	7.4
2000***	9.0

Source: Adapted from Albrecht (1978: 188), Hamdorf and Wölber (1999: 935), Strafvervolgungsstatistik 1976–2006.

* Since 1991 including East Germany.

** West German statistical data concerning imprisonment for defaulters is available only since 1971 (Heinz 1982: 656).

*** From 2003 onwards there are no statistical data available on imprisonment for defaulters in Germany. The last account, in 2002, showed 9.3 per cent (Heinz 2012: 71).

Figure 6.7 Unpaid fines converted into prison sentences (percentage of imposed fines), Germany*: 1926–2000 (selected years)

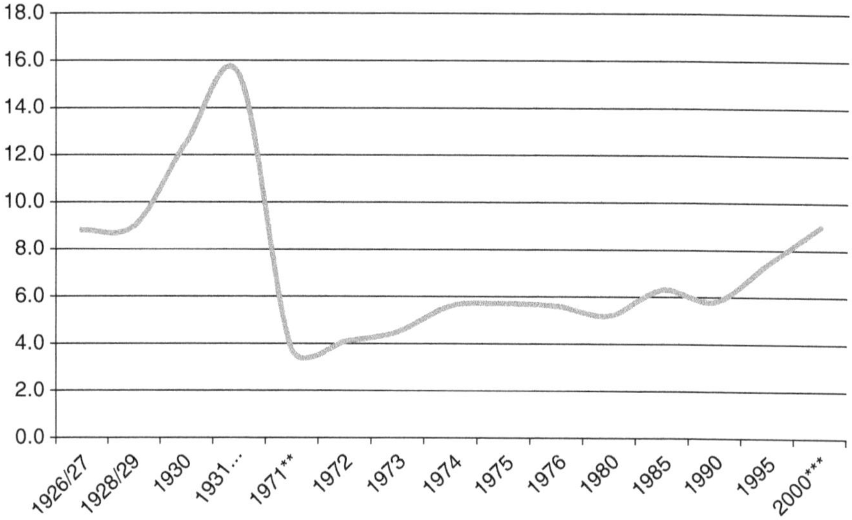

Source: Adapted from Albrecht (1978: 188), Hamdorf and Wölber (1999: 935), Strafvervolgungsstatistik 1976–2006.

*Since 1991 including East Germany.
**West German statistical data concerning imprisonment for defaulters is available only since 1971 (Heinz 1982: 656).
***From 2003 onwards there are no statistical data available on imprisonment for defaulters in Germany. The last account, in 2002, showed 9.3 per cent (Heinz 2012: 71).

According to Heinz (1989: 208), from 1981 to 1986 about 30,000 defaulters were imprisoned every year in West Germany. Starting from 1990 the problem of fine defaulters began to increase considerably, especially in the new federal states of the former German Democratic Republic (Dünkel and Grosser 1999: 28–29; Seebode 1999: 523–525; Dünkel and Rössner 2001: 293; Heinz 2010: 71). Especially astonishing was the 20 per cent increase in the number of imprisoned fine defaulters from 1995 to 1997 (Hamdorf and Wölber 1999: 929). In 1996 about 10 per cent of all adult prisoners (57,299 persons, according to Hennig 1999: 298) served a period of imprisonment in lieu of a fine, with striking differences between states of the former East Germany, 13 per cent, and West Germany, 7 per cent (Dünkel and Grosser 1999: 28–29; Dünkel and Rössner 2001: 293). Default detention imposed for non-payment of fines was one of the main reasons why the desired relief of the prison system failed to materialize after the enactment of the First and Second Criminal Law Reform Acts.

The explanation of the German increase in imprisonment for defaulters was originally sought in the deteriorating economic situation and rising unemployment rate in the early 1970s that peaked in the mid-1980s and rose again immediately after the 1990 German reunification. It meant that more people were unable to pay their fines despite the opportunity to pay in instalments (Gerken and Henningsen 1987: 388; Heinz 1989: 20–21; Van Kalmthout and Tak 1992: 436).

However, the situation did not get better when the economic circumstances did. In reality, the high rate of imprisonment for defaulters is linked to a noticeably larger amount and duration of the fine than in the Swedish example (Hillsman 1990: 81; Warner 2012: 236), but also with much more extensive and rigorous regulation of imprisonment for defaulters, as imprisonment was always applicable in the case of non-payment, even if this was involuntary, without allowing the amount of a fine to be reduced if the offender's financial circumstances worsened after sentencing. Three stipulations must be mentioned here. First, alternatives to imprisonment for defaulters, such as community service, were offered only to convicted offenders who were free to move around the community and have a permanent address. These two criteria proved problematic since many of those fined are either already in custody for another offence, in which case imprisonment for default is simply added to the other prison sentence (Van Kalmthout and Tak 1992: 516), or homeless, thus rendering them unsuitable for alternative penalties (Gerken and Henningsen 1987: 388). Second, the conditional suspension of a fine (*Verwarnung mit Strafvorbehalt*, § 59 of the German Penal Code) was allowed only in exceptional cases. And third, conviction without the imposition of a penalty (*Absehen von Strafe*, § 60) had no practical significance, constituting less than 1 per cent of all sanctions imposed by the courts (Heinz 1982: 639; Janssen 1994: 15; Dünkel and Rössner 2001: 294).

In sum, differences in the levels of imprisonment for defaulters are principally due to differences in what both countries seek to accomplish – with the West German system viewing fines as a replacement for short and medium terms of incarceration, while the Swedish system views them as a milder measure for minor crimes – as well as to differing degrees of information about the offender's financial circumstances and to disparate statutory requirements governing conversion. On the one hand, German courts could not impose a fair fine based on trustworthy data because in over one-half of the cases they had no information concerning income. Swedish courts did not suffer from this dearth of information. On the other hand, in Germany conversion is quasi-automatic whenever attachment efforts fail to yield satisfactory amounts, with German courts still relying heavily on unsuspended short prison sentences for moderately serious and serious crimes, while in Sweden conversion is left to the court's discretion, with Swedish courts convinced that imprisonment is an expensive, ineffective, and detrimental form of punishment, the use of which should be limited to the greatest extent possible. In Germany it is irrelevant if the offender does not pay because he or she either has no means or simply does not want to pay, while in Sweden conversion is possible only if the offender refuses to pay. Last but not least, the conversion rate in Germany is very strict – 1:1 – especially if we consider that the maximum limit of daily units is between 360 and 720 days. This means the maximum limit for the subsidiary penalty ranges from 360 to 720 days. The conversion rate 1:1 has always been extremely controversial in Germany. Objections proceed from the viewpoint that one day's deprivation of liberty represents a greater evil than the loss of one day's income, so that another conversion rate would be justified in the light of the guilt principle (see on this regard Grebing 1978: 149 and 1982: 141; Seebode 1999: 549–550: Schott 2003: 315ff.). Automatism is heavily criticized too (Tröndle 1972: 461ff., 466, and 1974: 567–568 and 588; Seebode 1999: 550). Conversely, duration is left to the court's discretion in Sweden, within much more reduced limits: 14 days to three months. Despite the different levels of imprisonment for defaulters, the rate of unpaid fines is much higher in Germany than in Sweden: between 10 and 30 per cent for Germany, 10 per cent or less for Sweden (Hennig 1990: 99 and 103; Bublies 1992: 178 and 184; Hamdorf and Wölber 1999: 948; Sveri 2005: 376).

The rate of unpaid fines seriously undermined enthusiasm for the day-fine system in Germany as it dashed hopes for the reduced use of subsidiary imprisonment (Von Hippel 1925: 554; Lang-Hinrichsen 1959: 53ff., 135; Heinz 1982: 667). Clearly, although there were both a politically acceptable justificatory system and a narrative that endorsed decarceration policies based on the use of fines as an alternative to imprisonment (Albrecht and Johnson 1980: 13), the normative framework was too harsh and unduly restricted judicial discretion. This problem can, nevertheless, be remedied by legislative reforms and is not a principled objection.

There is, however, another aspect that can further compromise the fairness of the day-fine system. Obviously, it is usually the poorest offenders who are unable to pay their fines and consequently are imprisoned for fine default (Grünhut 1948: 6; Schmidt 1967: 1938; Gerken and Henningsen 1987: 388; Seebode 1999: 525–526). As Janssen (1994: 167) denounced, by the time of his writing fines with daily amounts between 10 and 20 DM were converted in 39.1 per cent of the cases, while there was no conversion *at all* with daily amounts of more than 100 DM: 'This completely contradicts the political-criminal aim of introducing the [system of the day] fine, which was intended to prevent favouring the position of offenders with higher levels of income by calculating their income'. Essentially, the equality principle had been compromised (Albrecht 1981: 265–266; Gerken and Henningsen 1987: 388–390; Van Kalmthout and Tak 1992: 504; Hamdorf and Wölber 1999: 934; Seebode 1999: 519ff., 526–527). We have already seen that the notion that short-term imprisonment for fine defaulters should be restricted or even abolished has a long tradition in German-speaking literature. In fact, '[t]he reform movement of the 1960s was built on this nineteenth century ideological foundation and when the legislation was introduced, it met little opposition' (Weigend 2001: 193). This tradition was revitalized once the aforementioned limitations of the day-fine system were made evident (Wagner 1984: 3; Schädler 1985: 186; Gerken and Henningsen 1987: 389–390). This support had and has a lot to do with the basic injustice of converting an unpaid fine into a prison sentence. It is necessary to take the principle of equality of impact more seriously. Abolishment of subsidiary imprisonment in practice without undermining the use of fines is possible, as the Swedish experience shows. If this possibility is rejected, as it was in Germany, restrictions in the use of imprisonment for poor defaulters constitute a very important factor in implementing a fairer fine system. And the same can be said about other sorts of measures which Sweden adopted to avoid non-payment and Germany did not, such as allowing the amount of a fine to be reduced if the offender's economic circumstances deteriorate after sentencing.

In the end, equalizing the impact of fines requires us not only to examine poor offenders but also to look at the other end of the spectrum, the rich.

Does the day-fine system increase the fine amount for rich offenders? Comparing the German approach to day fines with the English (bad) experience of unit fines

One of the consequences of adjusting fines to the economic and personal circumstances of the offender should be an increased fine to be paid by rich offenders (Hudson 2000: 205). It is an important factor to achieve equalization of impact. As Warner (2012: 230) explained,

> allowing the amount of a fine to be increased as well as reduced helps to ensure that the imposition of a fine on an affluent offender achieves the principle of equal impact. It helps to ensure that the 'penal bite' of the fine is the same for all offences to which the system applies. Arguably also, setting fairer fining levels has other advantages, such as encouraging the use of fines, particularly in higher courts where fining levels are low, raising revenue, and facilitating enforcement because fines are better calibrated to the offender's means.

Figure 6.8 Distribution of fines according to their amount, West Germany: 1972–1975

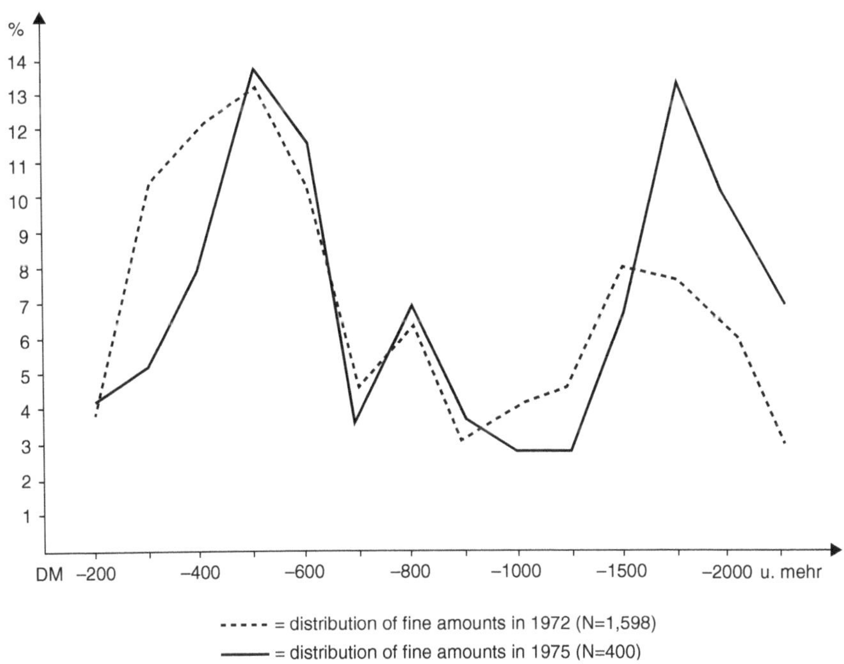

Source: Albrecht (1980: 202).

The day-fine system should have the effect of burdening more affluent offenders with progressively higher fines, precisely adjusted to the offender's circumstances. The comparison between the West German level of fines before and after the Second Criminal Law Reform Act is quite telling. The Reform Act instituted a formalized method of adjusting fines to the offender's financial and personal circumstances. In fact, it introduced remarkable changes in the distribution of fine amounts. As Albrecht (1980: 202), Albrecht and Johnson (1980: 7ff.), and Friedman (1983: 294) note, Figure 6.8 suggests that the reform had little effect on the distribution of fines below 1,500 DM, which remained relatively low, but noticeably increased fines above 1,500 DM.

One could presume that German courts may simply have begun to punish particular crimes more harshly, rather than punish offenders according to their financial circumstances. This explanation is contradicted by data showing that the part of the fine related to the offender's circumstances was the element that changed, not the part related to the seriousness of the crime (Albrecht 1980: 203). This means that the Second Criminal Law Reform Act had the desired effect of burdening affluent offenders with higher fines (Friedman 1983: 294). Nevertheless, it bears mentioning that in over 54 per cent of the cases in which German courts imposed a day fine they had no information at all about the offender's income, and in over 75 per cent of cases about the offender's wealth (Albrecht 1980: 204–205). From other research carried out in Baden-Württemberg it appeared that in a third of the cases the courts did not have any information and therefore estimated the fine based on the offender's type of work (Albrecht 1982). Since the implementation of the day-fine system it has been confirmed that courts do not make use of the entire range of daily unit rates, and that less than 2 per cent of offenders sentenced to fines actually pay more than 50 euros per day.

Table 6.9 Fine sentences according to the amount of the daily unit (total numbers), Germany*: 1976–2014 (selected years)

Year	*Total convictions to fines*	*Until €5*	*More than €5 until €10*	*More than €10 until €25*	*More than €25 until €50*	*More than €50*
1976	492,491	39,177	106,934	322,159	22,487	1,734
1980	494,000	33,667	93,463	331,393	33,398	2,079
1985	488,274	53,661	115,731	272,655	43,466	2,761
1990	512,145	61,039	105,928	265,221	76,222	3,735
1995	566,932	61,888	128,053	259,268	111,931	5,792
2000	512,994	41,598	116,142	242,743	106,223	6,288
2005	545,619	30,196	154,366	221,380	205,494	10,477
2010	575,068	17,852	185,703	222,580	135,966	12,610
2014	566,635	13,603	174,767	210,964	152,295	14,730

Source: Strafverfolgungsstatistik 1976–2014.

* Since 1991 including East Germany.

Figure 6.9 Fine sentences according to the amount of the daily unit (total numbers), Germany*: 1976–2014 (selected years)

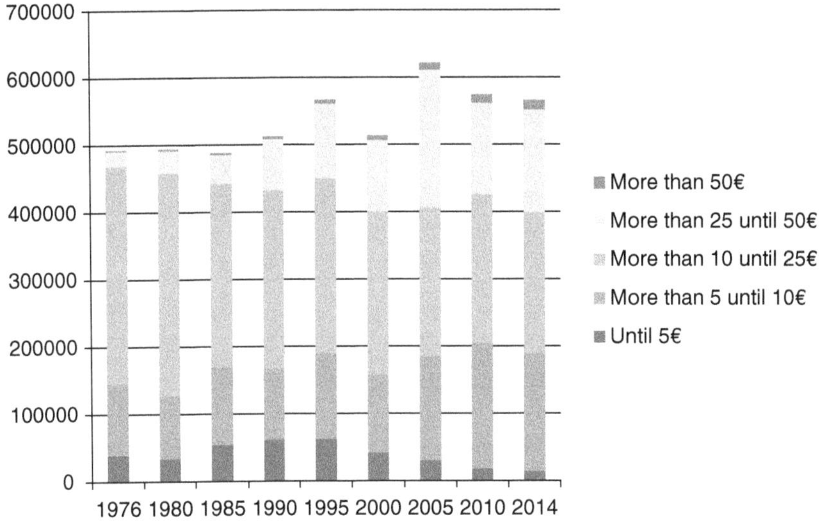

Source: Strafverfolgungsstatistik 1976–2014.

* Since 1991 including East Germany.

In 2014, 37.2 per cent of the fines imposed were made up of a daily unit of 10 to 25 euros. Less than 3 per cent of fines were at a rate of under 5 euros, a third between 5 and 10, and a bit more than a quarter between 25 and 50 euros. Two and a half per cent of those sentenced to a fine are requested to pay a daily unit of more than 50 euros. This situation is considerably different from the one in 1976, when the vast majority of fines were made up of a daily unit ranging between 10 and 25 euros (65.4 per cent), only a fifth between 5 and 10 euros (21.7 per cent), and less than 10 per cent under 5 euros.

More offenders receive the highest amount, but fewer offenders receive the lowest, while the percentage receiving between 25 and 50 euros quintupled.

Although this result can be considered appropriate in theory, the truth is that it has not always been accepted in practice. In fact, the perceived lack of proportionality of very high fines imposed on affluent offenders for petty offences was the main reason for the abandonment of the unit system in England and Wales in the 1990s.[9]

The approach of English sentencing law and practice until 1991 was to use a fixed fine which could be reduced by the court if the offender was unable to pay. The Home Office proposed a day-fine system for England and Wales in its 1990 White Paper titled *Crime, Justice and Protecting the Public* (Cm. 965, 1990). The government claimed,

Figure 6.10 Fine sentences distribution according to the amount of the daily unit (percentages), Germany: comparison 1976 and 2014

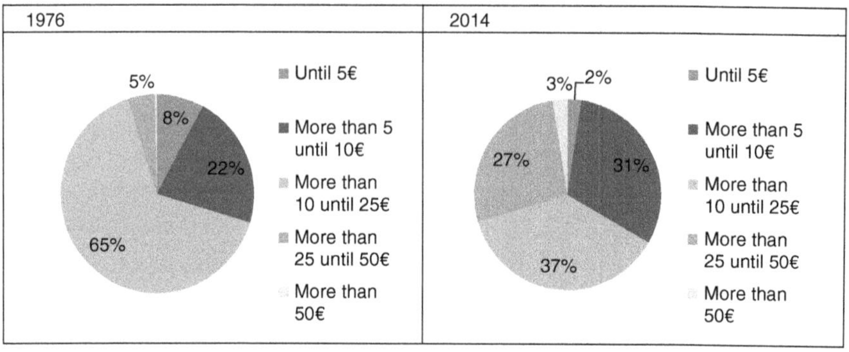

Source: Strafverfolgungsstatistik 1977 and 2015.

> If magistrates impose a fine which is ill-matched to an offender's means then the likelihood of default and the subsequent need for enforcement measures will be that much greater than if the financial penalty succeeds in combining affordability with a punitive element.
>
> (1990: 7–8)

Table 6.10 Fine sentences according to the amount of the daily unit (percentages), Germany*: 1976–2014 (selected years)

Year	*Total convictions to fines*	*Until €5*	*More than €5 until €10*	*More than €10 until €25*	*More than €25 until €50*	*More than €50*
1976	492,491	8.0	21.7	65.4	4.6	0.4
1980	494,000	6.8	18.9	67.1	6.8	0.4
1985	488,274	11.0	23.7	55.8	8.9	0.6
1990	512,145	11.9	20.7	51.8	14.9	0.7
1995	566,932	10.9	22.6	45.7	19.7	1.0
2000	512,994	8.1	22.6	47.3	20.7	1.2
2005	545,619	5.5	28.3	40.6	23.7	1.9
2010	575,068	3.1	32.2	38,7	23.6	2.1
2014	566,635	2.4	30.8	37.2	26.8	2.5

Source: Strafverfolgungsstatistik 1976–2014.

* Since 1991 including East Germany.

Therefore, 'it is in the interests of justice that offenders should be fined according to their means, otherwise fines have a different impact on offenders, according to their means and not the seriousness of their offences' (1990: 26). The issue was discussed for the first time in 1970 in the report of the Advisory Council on the Penal System about non-custodial and semi-custodial penalties, in which a means-related fine system, which would equalize the impact on offenders, was proposed and rejected, on

Figure 6.11 Fine sentences according to the amount of the daily unit (percentages), Germany*: 1976–2014 (selected years)

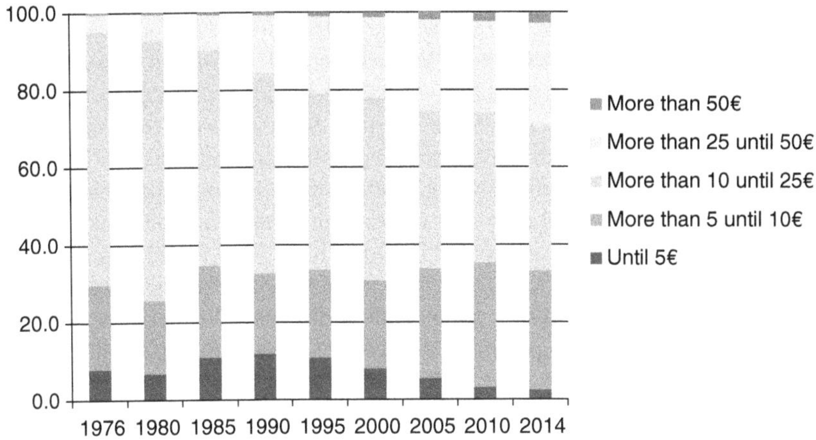

Source: Strafverfolgungsstatistik 1976–2014

*Since 1991 including East Germany

the grounds of 'practical difficulties'. As day fines spread in Europe, the debate about them resurfaced. There were some proposals by the National Association for the Care and Resettlement of Offenders (NACRO; 1981), Justice (1989), the Penal Affairs Consortium (1990), and the Prison Reform Trust (1990). In the years preceding the 1991 reform there was a growing recognition of the need to pay further attention to equalization of impact. It was found that, in setting fine amounts, English courts emphasized the seriousness of the offence and did not normally thoroughly review the information available to them on offenders' means. Thus, the total fine amount set was often too high and inconsistent with the offender's economic circumstances, producing an increase in imprisonment for fine default, which in turn accounted for a significant proportion of all prison receptions. In fact, as elsewhere, the primary motivation for the 1991 reform was to achieve equality of penal impact (Hudson 1999: 588; Grover 2008: 185), which would also mean higher fines for the wealthy. It was also thought desirable to induce a return to the high level of recourse to fines by courts of the 1970s,[10] because since then the use of fines had decreased from 50 per cent of indictable offences receiving fines in 1979 to 39 per cent by 1989 (Moxon, Sutton and Hedderman 1990: 1). The most likely reason for this fall was the rise in fine defaults caused by an increase in unemployment and the general worsening of economic conditions. As Moxon (1995a: 31) put it, 'Although the proportion imprisoned for default has never exceeded 1.6 percent of those fined, the number doubled in a decade, reaching a peak of around 26,000 in 1982, when fine defaulters represented about a quarter of all prison receptions'. This led to courts imposing fewer fines. There was an offsetting increase in the use of probation and community service. But by the 1990s disillusion regarding these kinds of alternatives to custody were widespread. Money efficiency and preventive effects were two of the reasons given: 'These sanctions are, for the most part, much more costly and no more effective at deterring people from further offending' (Moxon 1995a: 31). Experiments were conducted in four magistrates' courts, the details of which have since been published (Gibson 1990; Moxon et al. 1990; Bazell and Lomax 1992). The four districts were Bradford, Basingstoke, Teesside, and Swansea. It is noted in the White Paper that magistrates who were sceptical at the start came to take a positive view. Evaluation was confined to 17 offence categories. Almost 7,000 cases in which unit fines were imposed were compared to more than 6,000 in which fines were imposed under the traditional system. The experiments were, however, constrained by doubts about imposing larger fines on the better off. Courts therefore set local norms for the average weekly disposable income they thought an employed person in their district would have. They would then reduce the fine for anyone they assessed to have less than this norm. Nonetheless, in Basingstoke, where the norm was higher than in the other three districts (20 rather than 10 pounds per week), the better off did pay more than before. In each trial, the minimum unit value was 3 pounds. The unit used for assessment was a week's disposable income, after deducting tax and necessary living expenses. Courts were accustomed to assessing weekly income in determining payments, so this approach worked better with existing practice. It was also felt that few people think in terms of daily income and expenditure, and those fined would more readily understand a system similar to how they planned their finances. Disposable income was calculated by subtracting a certain allowance for each person dependent on that income from the net income – for example, 50 pounds for a spouse and 25 pounds for a child (Gibson 1990). All the courts began with the same form, which solicited basic information on income and family commitments, with provision for the defendant to submit any special circumstances. In its simplicity, this form was closer to that used to determine eligibility for legal aid than to a detailed means inquiry. One court (Swansea) also sought information on savings and occupation. It was found that information was made available without compulsion in most cases, that the simple means forms employed did not greatly affect court workloads, and that the actual arithmetic of calculating times was quite straight forward. Other findings showed that the use of fines did not increase, though fine revenues did in Basingstoke, because of the more realistic ceiling. Disparities between courts in fines imposed on poorer offenders were significantly reduced. There was a drop of about one-quarter in default imprisonment, and fines were paid in full more quickly (Moxon et al. 1990; Moxon 1995a: 33–34).

With the background of these encouraging first results, England and Wales experimented with the unit-fine system between 1991 and 1993. The unit-fine scheme was introduced by the 1991 Criminal Justice Act. Under the Act's first step, the courts were to assess the seriousness of the offence, or the combination of the offence and other offences associated with it, by also taking into consideration any aggravating and mitigating circumstances (Section 18[2][a]). The seriousness of the offence was then reflected by the number of units, which could range from 2 to 50 (Section 18[4]). In the second step, the value of each unit was determined according to 'the offender's weekly disposable income' – that is, the weekly income after basic expenditures had been deducted (Moxon et al. 1990: 36) – within a minimum of 4 pounds to avoid criticisms that some fines could be so small as to appear insignificant and a maximum of 100 to avoid very large fines being imposed for minor offences (Section 18[2][b]). Allowances were fixed according to the number of adults and children in the family supported from that income. Any expenditure out of the ordinary was taken into account.

Although the unit-fine system achieved certain desired goals – the use of fines increased compared to other punishments, and the amount of the average fine for unemployed people fell while it increased for employed people (Grover 2008: 202, citing Cavadino and Dignan 2002) – it ultimately failed. Six months after the system went into effect, the Home Office announced a preliminary suspension. Despite combining 'simplicity', 'fairness', 'clarity', 'greater precision', 'effectiveness', and 'consistency' (Gibson 1990: 11), the system was repealed in May 1993, in what has been described as 'perhaps the most astonishing *volte face* in the history of the English justice system' (Cavadino and Dignan 1997: 211, italics in the original). The most salient reasons for the demise of the system seem to be following (Bazell and Lomax 1992: 46–47; Lacey 1994: 548; Moxon 1995b; Tonry 1996: 127; Greene 1998: 268–270; Cavadino and Dignan 2002: 128–129; Grover 2008: 188–190; Warner 2012: 233ff; Ashworth 2015: 348–350):

- First, the exaggerated emphasis on the weekly disposable income when assessing the offender's means, with exclusion of other indicators of wealth, and the complexity of calculation. The scheme rolled out was clearly more draconian than the scheme piloted (Easton and Piper 2005: 224).
- Second, the strong opposition of what has been described as 'a vociferous minority of magistrates' (Cavadino and Dignan 2002: 128), who complained that unit fines unduly constrained judicial discretion (Lacey 1994: 546–548).
- Third, a media campaign which highlighted high fines for middle-class motoring offenders and small fines for similar offences committed by poor people, without explaining that differences were due to different incomes, as a way of avoiding other disparities. As Warner (2012: 231) put it, '[the scheme] was not well explained to the public and the press were able to ridicule it'. In fact, the media, ignoring the differences in income of the people involved, 'objected to the fact that relatively well-paid, middle-class motoring offenders were being fined substantial sums while the unemployed and low-paid were in their view "let off" with derisory fines for offences which they considered to be much more serious' (Cavadino and Dignan 2002: 128–129). Statements both in the media and among magistrates repeatedly ignored the elementary justice of the principle of equal impact. In this way,

  > [t]he demise of the unit fine system, introduced in order to ensure equality of treatment for offenders with different financial resources, provides an object lesson in how a sound principle can be undermined by reporting which fails to explain the reasons behind the sentences imposed.
  >
  > (Ashworth and Player 1998: 272)

- And fourth, the unit fine used in the 1991 Criminal Justice Act was thought to be unfair *for the better off*. Large fines for very minor offences were the

> result of raising the maximum unit value to 100 pounds, of adopting the maximum in the absence of means information, and of applying the unit fine to every kind of offence in magistrates' courts but not in the higher Crown Court (Moxon 1995b: 40). Middle-class people were seen as being the victims of an unfair system of punishment (Lacey 1994; Easton and Piper 2005: 224). This can be understood only as 'a retrieval of the brutal inegalitarian Tory philosophy which [. . .] characterised the Thatcher years', as indicated by Sanders (1998: 537), 'a short-term triumph of political expediency over principle', as highlighted by Cavadino and Dignan (1997: 213), and an 'eloquent testimony to the power of short-term political gain over sound penal policy', as noted by Ashworth and Gibson (1994: 101ff.).

In the 1993 Criminal Justice Act the consideration of the financial circumstances of the offender once again became a subsidiary requirement. How this was to be done was left to the court's discretion, with courts now able to increase fines for the wealthy and to reduce them for the poor. The immediate consequence was that in 1993 the level of fining declined. Statistical data indicate that the use of fines for indictable offences declined from 63.2 per cent in 1975 to 51 per cent in 1989 to 31 per cent in 2000, although three-quarters of all cases sentenced by the magistrates' courts resulted in a fine being imposed, a number that increased to 89 per cent of all summary motoring offences (Mackie et al. 2003: 24–25; Moore 2003: 13; Easton and Piper 2005: 220–221). Most importantly for the argument pursued here, the average fine rose for the unemployed and decreased for the employed (Warner 2012: 239; Ashworth 2015: 350). In essence, rejection of the unit-fine system produced less fairness, fewer fines, and greater difficulty in enforcing them. The framework created by the 1993 Act is still in place and its respective provisions (Section 164) were re-enacted via the 2003 Criminal Justice Act.

After receiving some academic support (Ashworth 1997: 1122, Moore 2003), the unit-fine system reappeared in the legislative discussions in 2004, when the Carter Report recommended that fines be linked to income for certain offences and that fixed penalties and low-level fines be excluded, with the English experience of unit fines in mind, to 'avoid excessive fines for very low-level crimes' (about the genesis and contents of the Carter Report, see Dobson 2004: 145; Grover 2008: 191–192). However, the bill to amend the 2003 Criminal Justice Act and set fines in accordance with daily disposable income, introduced in 2005, was not approved because of prorogation of Parliament. In 2006 a new Home Office report (*A Five-Year Strategy for Protecting the Public and Reducing Reoffending*, Cm. 6717, 2006) reaffirmed the government's intention to introduce day fines, to no avail. Since 2008 the Magistrates' Court Sentencing Guidelines only require fines to be first calculated as a percentage of weekly income before considering the offender's financial circumstances in determining the amount of the fine (Ashworth 2015: 351–352). Before these new sentencing guidelines in 2008, the problem of default had already been successfully tackled by diverting defaulters from imprisonment to non-custodial measures, such as community service orders, electronic monitoring, and deprivation of rights.[11] These improvements led to the number of receptions into custody for fine default falling sharply from 22,723 in 1995 to 2,040 in 2005 – a 90 per cent reduction (Home Office 2006: para. 7.6). Thereafter it remained at very low levels, even if the full payment rate for fines declined. It was 62 per cent in 1999–2000 and dropped to 55 per cent in 2002–2003 (Easton and Piper 2005: 226). The use of fines for indictable offences declined to 16 per cent. At magistrates' courts fines fell to the third most common disposal, accounting for only 21 per cent of all sentences in 2008, after having been the most common disposal in 1998, when they accounted for 35 per cent of sentences given for indictable offences. It is quite evident that since the late 1970s there has been a strong decline both in the use of fines and in their payment rate.

The English experiment with unit fines shows that it is very important to sufficiently explain the functioning of the day-fine system, bearing in mind that acceptance by both the public and the courts is crucial to success. A very high fine for a petty offence can be viewed as outrageous if the reasoning is not effectively communicated to the public, while those operating the system should also understand and accept both its principles and its practical implications. At the same time, the English experience has also confirmed that it is perfectly possible to reduce the level of imprisonment for default without a day-fine system.

Does imprisonment for insolvent defaulters violate constitutional principles? The apparently contradictory answers given by the Italian and Spanish constitutional courts

The conversion of a fine into a custodial sentence has always been subject to controversy. As already shown in Chapter 2, the threat of imprisonment is generally used to compel offenders to pay their fines, although this measure poses problems of fairness and equity, particularly if the fine system does not take into account the financial circumstances of the offender and winds up placing those who cannot afford to pay the fine in prison. In the 1970s and 1980s, two European constitutional courts provided diverging answers to the question asked in the title of this section. However, in the end, both coincided in the essence of their reasoning. Let us see how they justified their positions.

After other unsuccessful attempts,[12] the unconstitutionality of imprisonment for defaulters was declared in Italy via Judgement no. 131 of November 21, 1979. The Italian Constitutional Court categorically stated that the automatic conversion of fines into imprisonment in cases where the offender was insolvent contravened Article 3 of the 1947 Italian Constitution.[13] In the court's opinion, the increased severity of the punishment brought by the conversion altered 'the ratio of proportionality between the seriousness of the offence and the offender's capacity to offend, for one thing, and the nature and amount of the imposed punishment, for another'. This alteration, which implies an 'unequal sanctioning consequence for cases of similar intensity breaching the same incriminatory rule', would be directly caused by the offender's economic conditions (his inability to pay even if he wanted) and amounts to inadmissible discrimination clearly contravening the provisions of Article 3 of the Italian Constitution (Caraccioli 1979: 1210–1211). The court, echoing the critics (e.g., Bricola 1961: 1079), placed particular emphasis on the fact that equating freedom to property contradicted constitutional values, since converting the fine into a prison sentence would be based on an alleged fungibility or convertibility between freedom and wealth that would be inadmissible.

Concerning the non-derogability (*inderogabilità*) of the punishment – that is, adhering to the constitutional requirement that an imposed sanction must be enforced – the court clarified that cases of insolvency must not be confused with those of 'material enforceability' or 'deferability based on situations that were deemed worthy of consideration'. From the confusion between non-derogability and the possibility of deferral it was concluded, erroneously in the court's view, that the offender's inability to pay a fine in full provided valid grounds for the punishment to be annulled, instead of considering this to be a situation that temporarily stopped the punishment from being enforced.

This ruling led to the abolition of default imprisonment and default detention. The message to the legislator was clear, according to De Maglie (1988: 648–649): not all forms of conversion are unlawful – only those that are automatic and objective; subsidiary sanction, in the case of conversion, should not be swapped for custodial sentences; and it is appropriate to adopt mechanisms that allow the fine to be adapted in line with the offender's economic circumstances. The legislature incorporated some of the guidelines of the court in Law no. 689 of November 24, 1981, on modifications to the penal system (*di modifiche al sistema penale*).

On the contrary, the Spanish Constitutional Court upheld the constitutionality of imprisonment for defaulters with ruling no. 19 of February 16, 1988.

The Writ of the Magistrates' Court no. 9 of Madrid, which raised the question of unconstitutionality of Article 91 of the 1944 Penal Code in view of the possible contradiction of Articles 1.1, 9.2, 14, 17, and 25.2 of the Spanish Constitution,[14] stated,

> In short, the constitutionality of Article 91 of the Penal Code is questioned for the following reasons: 1) because it seems to contradict, given the generality of its wording, the equality principle embodied in Article 14 of the Constitution, since the subsidiary deprivation of liberty for non-payment of the fine takes place even if the insolvency is caused by aspects that are not attributable to the offender, therefore custody is an immediate consequence of the offender's economic situation; 2) because it could contravene, for the same reasons, the principles of culpability and proportionality of the punishment implicit as a fundamental value in the requirements of justice (Article 1.1 of the Constitution); 3) because as it considers freedom and wealth to be equally fungible, it appears to subvert the scale of values established in Articles 17 and 33 of the Constitution; and 4) because, as it brought about the desocialising effects of imprisonment inflicted on the most underprivileged levels of society, it could contravene the principles of social organisation contained in Article 9.2 of the Constitution.
>
> (precedent of fact 2 e) of the Writ of April 22, 1987)

The question of unconstitutionality was considered as 'truly exemplary in view of its careful argumentative grounds' (Rodríguez Ramos 1988: 918). However, the Constitutional Court dismissed the alleged arguments one by one.

First, the court addressed the question concerning the legal nature of subsidiary imprisonment. It concluded that subsidiary imprisonment is not a custodial sentence but rather the method chosen by law for fines to be paid in cases of insolvency.[15] Furthermore, it considered the uncertainty of Article 91 on the contents of subsidiary personal liability to be a positive point, as this made it possible to state that it did not necessarily lead to a custodial sentence. It stated that it was possible 'to choose ways of restricting freedom, that sit better with the general sense of the precept and with an interpretation of it that favours lower levels of individual restriction, which occurs, very specifically, in the case of house arrest.' It was a purely formal observation, because at that time the judicial practice showed that there was no alternative to deprivation of liberty (Quintero Olivares 1977: 127–128; Rodríguez Ramos 1988: 920).

The Spanish Constitutional Court drew attention to the extensive number of 'palliative aspects and softeners which appear to surround' subsidiary liability, and in particular to the fact that a maximum term was set for subsidiary imprisonment – six months for a crime and 15 days for a misdemeanour (Article 91) – a conditionally suspended sentence was permitted (Article 93), and payment by instalments was permissible (Article 90.2). The court also acknowledged that

> [i]t is true that all these palliative or softening aspects [. . .] are left to the careful arbitration of the Court, but it is also true [. . .] that there is nothing to say that this authority is entirely discretional. On the contrary, the court's decision must be adopted in line with the interpretation of the global sense of the legal ruling and in accordance with an admissible interpretation of the Constitution, within which [. . .] a principle reigns in favour of individual freedom and lower levels of restricting it.
>
> (Ruling no. 19 of February 16, 1988, of the Spanish Constitutional Court)

The court examined the possible contradiction of subsidiary imprisonment with Article 17 of the Constitution, which declares the right of all to freedom, in purely formal terms:

> the Constitution has specified such a guarantee, in terms of what matters now, ordering that a deprivation or restriction of liberty should not be imposed unless 'in the circumstances and manner established by law'; and among the hypotheses that constitutionally justify the deprivation or restriction pro tempore of liberty there is the one stating that the individual be 'lawfully punished under the terms of a Judgement passed by a competent Court' (section 1.a of Article 5 of the Convention for the Protection of Human Rights and Fundamental Freedoms of November 4, 1950).
>
> (Ruling no. 19 of February 16, 1988, of the Spanish Constitutional Court)

Pertaining to the alleged equating of the values of freedom and property, the court believed that this equation did not apply, for three reasons. First, the existence of alternative punishments to imprisonment or a fine for the same offence showed that the rule did not intend to establish abstract equivalents.

> [B]ut rather to address the demands of criminal policy, unobjectionable in themselves, consisting of the most appropriate legal individualisation of the punishment, since, as in the previous case, the predisposition of a substitute sanction which, were it to be imposed principally, would be impossible to enforce.
>
> (Ruling no. 19 of February 16, 1988, of the Spanish Constitutional Court)

Second, Article 25.3 of the Spanish Constitution did not exclude the conversion of the fine into imprisonment. And third, the content of subsidiary personal liability should not necessarily be considered as a custodial sentence. The court did not believe that when equating the values of freedom and wealth, the conversion mechanism made them fungible, even though Judgement no. 131 of November 21, 1979, of the Italian Constitutional Court was passed on these grounds. The fundamental problem was that the Spanish court completely relied on the assertion that in case of default there were other possibilities than imprisonment. This argument, although not wrong in theory, had no translation into practice, because the courts systematically opted for the imposition of a subsidiary custodial penalty. In fact, the suspected equivalence between two constitutional rights of diverse range, freedom and property, had indeed taken place (Rodríguez Ramos 1988: 922).

Concerning the contradiction with the equality principle, enshrined in Article 14 of the Spanish Constitution, the Constitutional Court understood that the legislature ordered 'a specific provision – non-"differentiating" – for the hypothesis in which the general rule (imposing the fine) suffers from an inevitably diverse application as the abstract mandate establishes the sanctioning rules for different factual realities', so that 'no differentiation is, therefore, attributable to the action of the legislature'. Consequently, as this was not a differentiating rule but rather a specific rule, it was not appropriate to raise the question of equality, given that there was no preceding inequality. This idea was almost literally identical to the one defended by the Italian Constitutional Court in its Judgement no. 29 of March 27, 1962. However, the Italian court did then deliberate the question of equality and concluded that it was constitutionally admissible, a conclusion that was overturned a mere 17 years later. And, in effect, the truth is that a rule that specifies is also a rule that differentiates, and therefore it would need to have been subjected to the consideration of equality (Jareño Leal 1994: 137).

The exclusion of a possible breach of the principle of culpability also responded to purely formal considerations:

> insofar as when the fine is imposed as a consequence of a process, in which the possible culpability of the individual was analysed, it is not necessary to question the legitimacy of the ruling in the event of subsidiary liability, it is sufficient

> to prove the individual's culpability and liability for a fine, so that, by association, he is also liable for the punishment that may be used to substitute the fine.
>
> (Ruling no. 19 of February 16, 1988, of the Spanish Constitutional Court)

The Spanish Constitutional Court added, in a reference to the non-derogability of punishments, 'The aim of the substitution is to ensure that the offender does not go unpunished, in this hypothesis'. It was not taken into account that this meant that the fine, if not paid, could lead to subsidiary punishments, whereas with other penalties it is not possible to resort to other subsidiary measures should the original penalty be unenforceable (Quintero Olivares 1977: 124). The distinction introduced was discriminatory insofar as it was disproportionate to achieve the aim of punishments being enforced.

Consequently, the Spanish Constitutional Court upheld the constitutionality of the mechanism to convert the fine into imprisonment in the case of non-payment. The discrepancy with the Italian court was justified essentially on the grounds of the different conversion regulations in the two countries: automatic conversion into imprisonment in the Italian case, and the purely theoretical possibility of conversion into measures not involving a deprivation of freedom, without automatic steps, in the Spanish case. The real practice of conversion interested no one.

Can a fine system without an effective collection procedure and strong default penalties survive? The Italian case

The idea that without subsidiary imprisonment the fine would be 'like a knife without a blade' – *ein Messer ohne Klinge*, in the words of Seebode (1999: 531, citing Schäger) – is quite widespread in literature and is used to justify maintaining custodial sentences in case of default. What would happen if imprisonment for defaulters were to be banished without being substituted by an appropriate subsidiary penalty? Furthermore, what would happen if the payment rate of fines is so low that it undermines the credibility of the whole system? Italy offers a good example of the failure of a fine system that collapsed because of the lack of both a strong backup sanction in case of default and effective enforcement.

From the beginning of codification, Italy had a fixed-fine system with separate minimum and maximum limits for the three categories of fines, *multa*, *ammenda*, and administrative fine. The fine was not adapted to the offender's *bad* financial circumstances (Bricola 1961: 1077), but to the good ones. The 1889 Zanardelli Penal Code permitted the trebling of the fine for cases in which the offender's economic situation warranted such, as did the 1930 Rocco Penal Code.

Proposals aimed at substituting the tariff system with a system that considered 'the rate between the offender's economic situation and the pecuniary punishment' (de Marsico 1925: 281), and even led to reform projects of the Penal Code, fell on deaf ears. The result was that the percentage of the fine out of all the punishments did not increase much. It stood at 13.51 per cent in the 1891–1895 period (Direzione Generale della Statistica 1899: xxii–xxiv, which explained that this was the specific percentage of simple fines imposed, since the percentage of fines imposed accompanied by imprisonment was unknown), during which confinement of less than one month amounted to 45.07 per cent of the total, and terms of one to six months amounted to 19.49 per cent. The percentage of imposed fines rose slightly from 18.87 per cent to 20.27 per cent between 1900 and 1933 (Rusche and Kirchheimer 1939 [2003]: 249; Padovani 1981: 195). In the same period, other countries experienced more intense increases. Resorting to other alternative measures did not increase either. In fact, the use of a conditional suspended sentence decreased by more than half, sliding from 22 per cent of all convictions in the 1905–1907 period to 9 per cent in 1927, with a sharp subsequent drop that coincided with the onset of the fascist period (Bellini 1930: 265–267, 274; de Castro 1934: 321–322).

Rusche and Kirchheimer (1939 [2003]: 173), when explaining the scarce use of the fine in Italy in the first quarter of the twentieth century, stated, 'the frequency of fines is not primarily the result of legislative or judicial measures or theories, but is rather an accurate reflection of the prevailing social and economic conditions'. They did not consider that in Italy, unlike other countries, there were no statutory instruments enabling the expansion of the fine. Naturally, the fact that these instruments had not been established could be consequently seen as an effect of the inadequate socio-economic conditions of the country. In reality, this explanation, as well as being tautological, did not fully explain the phenomenon (Padovani 1981: 142–143). The first Italian Penal Code, the 1889 Zanardelli Code, was internationally praised for the special attention given to reducing the use of short-term prison sentences. But the 1930 Rocco Code abolished all the alternatives to imprisonment in the Zanardelli Code apart from the fine and the suspended sentence. It severely restricted the scope for imposing the fine, which was largely used more as an accessory penalty than as a principal penalty in spite of being regulated as such together with imprisonment and life imprisonment. In many cases the court was obliged to impose a fine as well as a prison sentence. Very few crimes had an alternative sentence provision in which the court could choose to impose either a prison sentence *or* a fine.[16] The fine was seldom imposed as the sole penalty for a crime. In addition to this compulsory cumulative fine, there was also an optional variant. For crimes motivated by greed, even though the law prescribed only imprisonment as a punishment, the court could in addition impose a fine (Article 24.2 of the Rocco Code). This regulation was based on the premise that 'it is justified due to the demand to make the punishment stricter in terms of fulfilling its intended purpose, in cases in which the reason for the offence stemmed from greed' (according to the governmental report on the penal code draft, *Relazione ministeriale sul progetto del codice penale*: 1, 72). This is a rationale reminiscent of the eighteenth century which was fully incorporated into the Italian doctrine of the nineteenth (Rossi 1853) and early twentieth centuries (de Marsico 1925: 281). The fact that Italian judges rarely imposed fines meant that this enshrined rationale gradually fell into oblivion (Molinari 1978: 503).

As a result of this regulation, after World War II the fine continued to be used on a limited basis, despite an increase in popularity thanks to the intensifying of the debate on alternatives to imprisonment (Molinari 1978: 507; Goisis 2012: 3).

Table 6.11 Total convictions, prison sentences (including prison sentences combined with fines), and fines (total numbers and percentages), Italy: 1946–1972 (selected years)

Year	*Total convictions*	*Prison sentences*	*Percentage of prison sentences of total convictions*	*Fines*	*Percentage of fines of total convictions*
1946	175,451	114,541	65.28	60,910	34.72
1950	213,156	170,494	79.99	42,662	20.01
1955	141,964	95,208	67.07	46,756	32.93
1960	130,928	95,326	72.81	35,602	27.19
1965	102,196	71,487	69.95	30,709	30.05
1970	65,264	39,038	59.82	26,226	40.18
1972	88,804	47,216	53.17	41,558	46.83

Source: Adapted from Molinari (1978: 513).

Figure 6.12 Total convictions, prison sentences (including prison sentences combined with fines), and fines (total numbers), Italy: 1946–1972 (selected years)

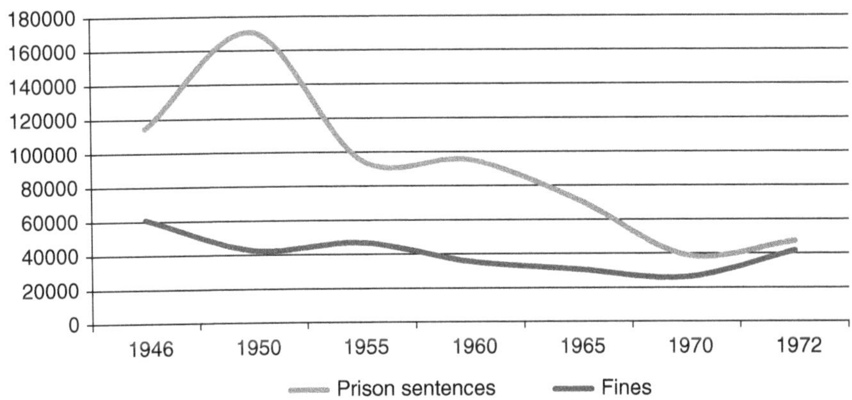

Source: Adapted from Molinari (1978: 513).

Figure 6.13 Total convictions, prison sentences, and fines (percentages), Italy: 1946–1972 (selected years)

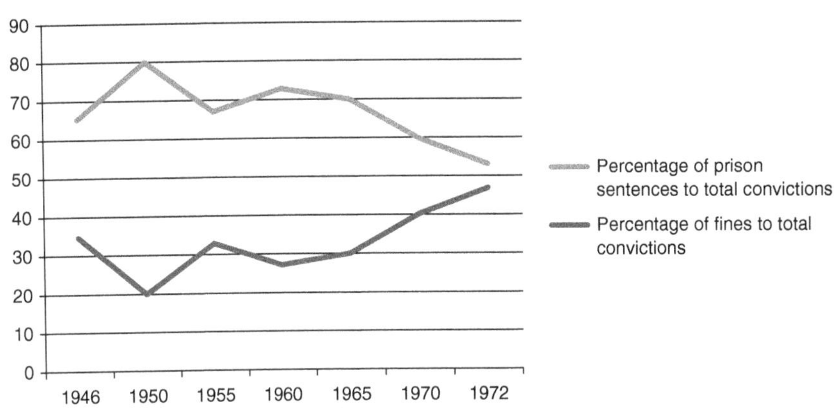

Source: Adapted from Molinari (1978: 513).

Table 6.12 Total convictions, prison sentences, prison sentences combined with fines, and fines (total numbers and percentages), Italy: 1968–1972

Year	*Total convictions*	*Prison sentences (total numbers)*	*Percentage of prison sentences to total convictions*	*Prison sentences combines with fines*	*Percentage of prison sentences combined with fines to total convictions*	*Fines imposed as a sole penalty*	*Percentage of fines imposed as a sole penalty to total conviction*
1968	94,806	20,833	21.97	27,355	28.86	46,618	49.17
1969	87,331	18,420	21.09	25,143	28.79	43,768	50.12
1970	65,264	17,957	27.52	21,081	32.30	26,226	40.18
1971	82,209	22,852	27.80	23,294	28.33	36,063	43.87
1972	88,804	23,873	26.88	23,343	26.29	41,558	46.83

Source: Adapted from Molinari (1978: 513).

Statistical data showed the prevalence of custodial sentences. They did start to recede, but not without some fluctuations (Molinari 1978: 501). When separating the fines combined with prison sentences from those fines that were imposed as the sole punishment, we can see that the percentage of sole penalty fines varied between 50.12 per cent in 1969 and 46.83 per cent in 1972. In fact, it outnumbered by far the percentages of imprisonment imposed as the sole penalty, which amounted to just 21.09 per cent in 1969 and 26.88 in 1972.

Up to November 21, 1979, an unpaid *multa* or *ammenda* could be converted into a subsidiary prison sentence of up to three years or a subsidiary detention of up to two years (Articles 136 of the Penal Code and 586 of the Code of Criminal Procedure). In the case of multiple offences, the maximum sentence could be increased to four and three years respectively (Article 78 of the Penal Code). The minimum terms of imprisonment did not apply to imprisonment for fine defaulters, whose length was determined by the criterion that one day of imprisonment should be served for each unpaid stipend of 5,000 lire. During the 1970s only a small percentage of fines were converted for defaulters. Molinari (1978: 510–511) gives a percentage varying between 0.84 and 1.96 per cent of all imposed fines in the period 1970–1973, with subsidiary imprisonment not longer than 15 days in over 50 per cent of cases.

The infrequent use of imprisonment for defaulters only strengthened the serious doubts expressed in literature about its constitutionality. On November 21, 1979, the Italian Constitutional Court declared in Judgement no. 131 that the imprisonment of defaulters was unconstitutional. This judgement compelled the Italian legislator to look for a new model of conversion. The Constitutional Court itself suggested 'other measures which do not affect personal liberty of the offender but aim at creating, respectively increasing, his solvency by enabling him to work for public institutions during one or more working days or public holidays'. Law no. 689 of November 24, 1981, on modifications to the penal system adopted this suggestion by providing a regulation both of community service (called *lavoro sostitutivo*), restricted to replace only uncollectable fines (Paliero 1986: 156), and of monitored liberty (*libertà controllata*).[17] Community service, which was an option only when requested by the offender in lieu of paying fines of less than 1,000,000 lire – 3,000,000 lire in case of more than one offence – has been barely applied in practice. Monitored liberty is applied in 99 per cent of cases of conversion of unpaid fines.

This does not mean that fines are being paid. In Italy, less than 5 per cent of imposed fines are paid in full. To know why, it can be illustrative to first give some data. In 1999, 166,098 fines – including both *multe* and *ammende* – were imposed as the sole sentence, of which 108,520 were suspended and 23,732 were converted into either monitored liberty – 23,700 – or community service – 32 – because of the offender's insolvency. There are no data on fines paid in full. In 2000, 200,443 fines were imposed as the sole sentence, of which 146,805 were suspended (73.2 per cent), 16,386 were converted (8.17 per cent), and 6,723 paid in full (3.35 per cent). Thus, the remaining 15.2 per cent of imposed fines were unsuspended, unpaid, *and* unconverted. The numbers got even worse in 2004, when of 155,299 fine sentences, 92,339 were suspended (59.45 per cent) and 1,539 were paid in full (0.99 per cent). Interestingly, of the remaining 61,421 unsuspended and unpaid fines (39.56 per cent), only 3,709 (2.38 per cent) were converted (Statistica Giudiziaria Penale 1999 and 2004; Goisis 2012: 4–5). It is evident that suspension and non-enforcement of fines are the two reasons that explain the high levels of uncollected fines in Italy (Dolcini 2006: 1099; Goisis 2008: 411–412 and 2012: 5–6).

Conditional suspension of fine sentences is not undisputed. After being strongly advocated by the Positivist School and introduced in 1904 into the Zanardelli Code, the so-called *sospensione condizionale della pena* was later taken up by the Rocco Code. Article 163 empowered the judge to suspend the sentence for a certain period of time provided that circumstances allowed this and that certain conditions were fulfilled. A suspended sentence in Italy is not accompanied by the imposition of obligations other than refraining from committing another crime. It was quite clear that only custodial sentences were to be suspended, including in this concept the subsidiary penalty of imprisonment for defaulters. Nevertheless, arguing that it was unfair to suspend relatively long custody sentences but not fine sentences imposed for minor crimes, the idea to also suspend fine sentences quickly found support. The historical reasons that led to the establishment of custodial sentences being conditionally suspended, based on the need to avoid the desocialization that imprisonment meant for a first-time offender of a fairly negligible offence, were not considered, as correctly pointed out by Fornasari (2003: 569–579). The possibility of suspended fine sentences created a vacuum that further compromised the functioning of the fine system (Fiorentin 2004: 892; Miedico 2008: 69).

The debate reopened after the Judgement of the Constitutional Court in 1979. The Joined Chambers of the Court of Cassation decided in favour of the possibility of suspension of fine sentences (April 12, 1980, commented by Vergine 1981). In 2000, legislative decree no. 274 prohibited the suspension of fines and other penalties imposed by the justice of the peace (*giudice di pace*). It is still possible to suspend fines imposed by higher courts, although the main opinion in penal literature is contrary to this (Miedico 2008: 176).

Moreover, the procedure applied to enforce the fine was completely unsatisfactory. Between 1981, the date when reforms resulting from the declaration of the unconstitutionality of imprisonment for insolvent offenders came into effect, and 2002, the enforcement procedure was characterized by extraordinary complexity.[18] As a result, the proportion of fines (*multe*) to total convictions sharply declined: it was 52.47 per cent in 1981, but only 31.66 per cent in 2002 (ISTAT 2012: 331).

The Italian government tried to simplify the enforcement procedure for fines via the Sole Text of legislative rulings and regulations concerning judicial costs (*Testo Unico delle disposizioni legislative e regolamentari in materia di spese di giustizia*), which was enacted by Decree no. 115 of May 30, 2002. The Sole Text authorized the enforcement judge to decide on the issue of conversion (Article 237). If the enforcement judge deemed that the offender was solvent, the concession holder proceeded to enforce payment (Article 224).[19] If the enforcement judge found that the offender was insolvent, he or she could grant payment by instalments or defer the conversion for a period of no longer than six months, which would be renewable just once. At the end of this period, he or she would have to order conversion in line with the outstanding amount.

The Italian Constitutional Court, in its Judgement no. 212 of June 18, 2003, declared the unconstitutionality of these changes, based on the premise that the appointed legislator was not authorized to alter the jurisdiction rules. This led to a situation of significant confusion, as some understood that the judgement was applicable only to the question of jurisdiction, upholding the validity of the other

Table 6.13 Offenders sentenced to fines, payment by instalments granted, delays, and conversions, Italy: 1999–2004

Year	*Offenders sentenced solely to fines*	*Instalment periods granted A*	*Delays B*	*Conversions C*	*Sum of A+B+C*	*Percentage of the total number of offenders sentenced to fines A+B+C*	*Fines paid*	*Percentage of fines paid to the total number of fines imposed*
1999	166,098	2,594	2,325	23,732	28,651	17.24	–	–
2000	200,443	1,890	1,857	16,386	20,133	10.04	6,723	3.35
2001	143,050	1,256	1,213	12,691	15,163	10.59	2,578	1.80
2002	132,429	676	608	6,845	8,129	6.13	2,395	1.80
2003	140,915	249	153	3,058	3,460	2.45	1,628	1.15
2004	155,299	635	388	3,709	4,732	3.04	1,539	0.99

Source: Statistiche Giudiziarie Penali 1999–2004.

rules not related to this issue, while others stated that the regulations prior to 2002 had regained validity (see the terms of this debate in Miedico 2008: 93–95). The result was the gradual paralysation of the fine enforcement mechanisms, as shown in the statistics (Goisis 2008: 133 and 2012: 7). Consequently, the percentage of fines that were effectively paid also dropped to negligible levels.

A sharp decrease in the total number and percentage of fine sentences imposed for crimes can be observed in the 2000s, with scholars lamenting the complete inefficacy of the Italian fine system (Dolcini 2006: 1098–1099; Goisis 2012).

Table 6.14 Prison (*ergastolo* and *reclusione*) and fine (*multa*) sentences for crimes only (total numbers and percentages), Italy: 2000–2009

Year	*Total*	*Prison sentences*	*Fine sentences*	*Percentage of prison sentences to total convictions*	*Percentage of fine sentences to total convictions*
2000	308,300	187,515	120,785	60.82	39.17
2001	239,174	162,615	76,559	67.99	32.00
2002	221,190	151,158	70,032	68.33	31.66
2003	219,679	144,665	75,014	65.85	34.14
2004	239,391	156,718	82,673	65.46	34.53
2005	221,381	143,658	77,723	64.89	35.10
2006	198,263	132,829	65,434	66.99	33.00
2007	234,730	193,938	40,792	82.62	17.37
2008	252,725	202,433	50,292	80.10	19.89
2009	249,154	205,710	43,444	82.56	17.43

Source: Italian National Institute of Statistics, ISTAT (2012: 331).

We can safely conclude that the fines imposed by the courts are taken seriously if they are effectively enforced (Walker and Padfield 1996). As Hillsman and Mahoney (1988: 18) explained, 'The efficacy of fines as criminal penalties rests on the ability of courts to collect them, to do so expeditiously, and to compel payment if the offender fails to meet his or her obligation to the court'. If courts cannot assume the fines will be collected, and if offenders assume they need not pay them, the potential of fines to punish and deter is seriously eroded (Hillsman 1990: 66). 'Low payment rate undermines the credibility of the whole system' (Lappi-Seppälä 2014: 1641). A strong backup penalty is an important factor. Many fine defaulters pay their fines if they perceive the threat of immediate incarceration, which is more efficient than milder admonitions (Weisburd, Einat and Kowalski 2008). Not prison as such but the threat of imprisonment for defaulters is a powerful means to reduce defaulting. In Italy, the wide use of suspended sentences weakened the deterrent effect of the threat of incarceration (Dolcini 2001: 828; Goisis 2012: 21). The disappearance of imprisonment for defaulters, ineffectively substituted by monitored liberty and community service, combined with a much discussed enforcement procedure, resulted in a total failure of the fine system. Success depends on the capability of enforcement. If the enforcement of fines is weak and patchy, or completely ineffective, offenders are able to escape unpunished and the criminal justice system is brought into disrepute, as the Italian experience has demonstrated.

Notes

1 The fixation on the German experience needs an explanation. The West German adoption of the day-fine system is a very interesting case study for three reasons. First, it was preceded by a protracted and well-documented academic discussion detailing the advantages of the day fine over incarceration. Second, there are good statistical data that allow an evaluation of the results. And third, it was the starting point of a wave of legislative changes with the same orientation in Western Europe. This is why different aspects of the German day-fine system will be compared with contrasting developments in Finland, Sweden, and England and Wales.

2 In the 1960s already the majority of sentenced offenders were fined. In 1968 63 per cent of sentences were fines. This percentage would increase to more than 80 per cent only two years later (84 per cent in 1970), once the First Criminal Law Reform Act was implemented.

3 This sort of regulation was copied by many countries. For example, Austria adopted the day-fine simultaneously with West Germany in 1975. Austria's adoption was profoundly influenced by the West German proposal and the arguments of its proponents (Nowakowski 1972: 198–199; Dearing 1983: 615). Paragraph 37 of the Austrian Penal Code enacted the rule that the fine must take precedence over a short prison term. If short imprisonment is imposed, execution of sentence must be preceded by suspension on probation. Also Article 43 of the 1982 Portuguese Penal Code stated the principle that imprisonment of less than six months should be substituted by a corresponding number of days of a fine, unless the prison sentence is considered necessary in order to prevent further crimes of the same nature, with community service as an alternative to fines (Figueiredo Dias 1989: 291–292). Article 70 stated that it was the duty of the court to give priority to non-custodial forms of punishment when they were shown to be sufficient to achieve punishment scope, mainly the resocialization of the offender and the confidence of the community in the validity of the law (special and general prevention). In Spain, Article 71.2 of the 1995 Penal Code established that a sentence of imprisonment under six months (nowadays three months) 'shall be substituted in all cases [. . .], without prejudice to suspension of execution of the punishment in the appropriate cases', with a fine or community service (Article 88).

4 In 1970 there were 46,521 prisoners (stock statistics) in West Germany. They were 43,040 in 1971, but 46,606 in 1972, 49,925 in 1973, 50,519 in 1974, 50,140 in 1975, 49,677 in 1976, 49,772 in 1977, 50,929 in 1978, 50,395 in 1979, and 51,051 in 1980 (Council of Europe 1987: 25).

5 In spite of a low rate of consumption of alcohol – smaller than in most European countries, including her Nordic neighbours – drunkenness was a comparatively common phenomenon in Finland. In 1950 the rate of arrest for public drunkenness was about ten times higher in Finland than in Sweden and three times higher than in Norway. Per capita arrests for drunkenness fell at a fairly constant rate from 1950 to 1958 and experienced a slight increase between 1958 and 1967. The arrest rate for 1975 was approximately half that of 1950 (Beauchamp 1981: 237), a decrease caused by shifting priorities of the police, not by a reduction in alcohol consumption.

6 From the 1950s onwards there was a considerable increase in the rate of theft offences. It grew up from 507 reported offences every 100,000 population in 1950 to 700 in

1960, 1,345 in 1970, and 2,280 in 1980 (Von Hofer et al. 2012). Instead of responding to this increase with increased penalties, the reform enacted in 1972 gave the courts more discretion in applying the different categories of theft and also introduced lesser penalties (Törnud 1993: 8, 19).

7 A substantial part of the Finnish prison problem during the period we are analysing here resulted from fairly long unconditional prison sentences imposed for drunken driving, combined with a considerable growth in the number of convictions for this offence from the 1950s onwards. The Finnish criminal justice system responded to this challenge by drastically increasing the use of fines and conditional imprisonment – typically in combination with fines (Lappi-Seppäla 2004: 143–144). Fines made up 6 per cent of all convictions for drunken driving in 1971, but only ten years later the percentage was already 49 per cent. In 1991 there was a slight decrease: 44 per cent (Törnud 1993: 20).

8 A proposal was made pertaining to this point. In 1996, the Social Democratic Party of Germany (*Sozialdemokratische Partei Deutschlands*, SPD) submitted a draft bill in the 59th German Jurists' Conference (*Deutscher Juristentag*) that allowed the possibility of either converting the fine into a suspended sentence or reducing the amount of the day fine, if the offender's economic situation had become worse. The processing of this proposal ended after it was sent to the commission (Hamdorf and Wölber 1999: 929). It was equally unsuccessful as the proposal of changing the conversion rate between day fines and default imprisonment, statutorily fixed at 1:1 (one daily unit corresponds to one day of imprisonment, according to Paragraph 43 of the German Penal Code), to 2:1 (Hamdorf and Wölber 1999: 930).

9 It is worth mentioning here that other countries, such as Sweden, included a clause in the law that allowed the amount of the day fine to be abated if the offence is petty and if the offender is a wealthy person for which the amount to be paid might seem to be too great in relation to the seriousness of the offence. This is an exception to the principle that the seriousness of the offence should influence the number of days, and not the amount to be paid for each of them, as Thornstedt (1975: 311) pointed out regarding the Swedish system.

10 Induced by the 1967 Criminal Justice Act, which encouraged the use of fines by increasing the maximum that could be imposed in the magistrates' courts from 100 to 400 pounds, while at the same time placing restrictions on magistrates' power to imprison defaulters.

11 In 1995 a Queen's Bench Judgement in Cawley and Others determined that imprisonment could be imposed on fine defaulters only following an active consideration of all fine enforcement measures by the courts. According to a Report of the Ministry of Justice (2013: 18), this led to the release of a number of fine defaulters who had been 'unlawfully' imprisoned and a rapid decrease in numbers of fine defaulters for whom imprisonment was imposed. A number of initiatives under the Government's Working Group on the Enforcement of Financial Penalties were taken forward in 1996. As a result, the volumes of offenders imprisoned for defaulting on fines declined 70 per cent from 1995 to 1997.

12 Constitutionality of the conversion of unpaid fines into imprisonment was questioned before the Italian Constitutional Court twice during the 1960s. Judgement no. 29 of March 27, 1962 (commented by Pisani 1962, Annunziata 1964, and Ranieri 1966), denied at that moment that the imposition of imprisonment as a substitute penalty for unpaid fines imposed upon insolvent offenders should be deemed to contravene the equality principle found in Article 3 of the Italian Constitution. Judgement no. 12 of February 12, 1966 (commented by Sigismondi 1966), declared that the fine, far from fulfilling a merely retributive function, also served a re-educational function. Consequently, it denied that the imposition of default detention upon insolvent offenders should be deemed to contravene the rehabilitation principle found in Article 27 of the Italian Constitution.

13 According to Article 3 of the 1947 Italian Constitution,

> All citizens have equal social dignity and are equal before the law, without distinction of sex, race, language, religion, political opinion, personal and social conditions.
>
> It is the duty of the Republic to remove the economic and social obstacles which by limiting the freedom and equality of citizens prevent the full development of the human person and the effective participation of all workers in the political, economic and social organisation of the country.

14 According to Article 1.1, 'Spain is hereby established as a social and democratic State, subject to the rule of law, which advocates freedom, justice, equality and political pluralism as highest values of its legal system'. Article 9.2 states,

> It is the responsibility of the public authorities to promote conditions ensuring that freedom and equality of individuals and of the groups to which they belong are real and effective, to remove the obstacles preventing or hindering their full enjoyment, and to facilitate the participation of all citizens in political, economic, cultural and social life.

Article 14 promotes the equality principle in following terms: 'Spaniards are equal before the law and may not in any way be discriminated against on account of birth, race, sex, religion, opinion or any other personal or social condition or circumstance'. Article 17 provides the following:

1 Every person has the right to freedom and security. No one may be deprived of his or her freedom except in accordance with the provisions of this section and in the cases and in the manner provided for by the law.
2 Preventive arrest may last no longer than the time strictly necessary in order to carry out the investigations aimed at establishing the events; in any case the person arrested must be set free or handed over to the judicial authorities within a maximum period of 72 hours.
3 Every person arrested must be informed immediately, and in a way understandable to him or her, of his or her rights and of the grounds for his or her arrest, and may not be compelled to make a statement. The arrested person shall be guaranteed the assistance of a lawyer during police and judicial proceedings, under the terms to be laid down by the law.
4 A habeas corpus procedure shall be provided for by law in order to ensure the immediate handing over to the judicial authorities of any person illegally arrested. Likewise, the maximum period of provisional imprisonment shall be determined by law.

Article 25.2 states,

> Punishments entailing imprisonment and security measures shall be aimed at re-education and social rehabilitation and may not involve forced labour. The person sentenced to prison shall enjoy, during the imprisonment, the fundamental rights contained in this Chapter except those expressly restricted by the content of the sentence, the purpose of the punishment and the penitentiary law. In any case, he or she shall be entitled to paid work and to the appropriate Social Security benefits, as well as to access to cultural opportunities and the overall development of his or her personality.

15 The court's approach was contrary to the majority in the literature (Beristain Ipiña 1976: 350ff.; Boix Reig 1977: 31ff.; Alonso Escamilla 1988: 1870–1871; Jareño Leal 1994: 36–49). It followed a previous line of case law of the Supreme Court. See the Supreme Court Judgements of January 16, 1954, according to which 'this subsidiary liability cannot be classed as a deprivation of liberty, nor even a punishment'; of May 9, 1977, for whom 'it is not truly a punishment as it is not included in the general scale of Article 27, nor is it listed in any of the offences or misdemeanours classified

in' the Penal Code; and of May 25, 1985, according to which 'it is not a punishment strictly speaking, therefore it is not mentioned in the general scale of punishments'.

16 Molinari (1978: 504) indicates for 1972 that the Italian Penal Code had 365 crimes, of which 201 were punished only by a prison sentence, 80 by a prison sentence combined with a fine, 55 by a prison sentence or a fine, and 29 solely by a fine. Crimes punished only by a fine are much more frequently committed.

17 This successfully addressed a new constitutional challenge in 1987, when, playing off the new regulation in Article 3 of the Italian Constitution, the Constitutional Court affirmed that 'the provision of replacement measures for pecuniary penalties that remain unpaid due to economic inability is not specifically avoidable, nor is the fact that these can involve a margin of greater severity' (Corte Cost., ruling no. 108 of April 7, 1987, commented by De Maglie 1988).

18 It consisted of the following phases:

1. Within 30 days following the final judgement, the clerk of the enforcement court issued the debtor with the notice to pay, with a time limit of ten days (Article 181 of the Code of Penal Procedure, CPP);
2. In the event of non-payment, the clerk of the enforcement court referred the matter to the public prosecution service (Article 182 CPP);
3. The public prosecution service sent it to the supervising magistrate (*magistrato di sorveglianza*, Article 660 CPP) for the offender's solvency to be assessed;
4. After assessing the prospects of immediate payment, three options were offered:
   a. If the offender was solvent, the supervising magistrate sent the matter back to the public prosecution service, which, in turn, sent it back to the clerk of the enforcement court (Article 30 CPP).
   b. In cases of temporary insolvency, the supervising magistrate could order the offender to pay by instalments (Article 133ter of the Penal Code), or issue an extension of time before conversion lasting not more than six months. If, after this period had elapsed, the offender's insolvency persisted, either a new deferral could be issued or conversion could be ordered (Article 660 CPP).
   c. In contrast, if the offender was found insolvent the fine was converted into monitored liberty or community service (Presutti 1991: 424; Nannucci 1998: 2240; Miedico 2008: 87).

The enforcement of fines imposed by the justice of the peace followed a different discipline, as this allowed for assessment of the offender's solvency, as well as the possibility of granting payment by instalments and agreeing on the conversion (Gallucci 2001).

19 By means of the legislative decree no. 237 of July 9, 1997, on the amendment of the regulation of independent cash services of financial offices (*modifica della disciplina nei servizi autonomi di cassa degli uffici finanziari*) the cash service of registration offices for collecting fines and legal costs was abolished, and this function was transferred to a private concession holder of the department of tax collection (Bernardi 1999).

References

Advisory Council on the Penal System (1970) *Non-Custodial and Semi-Custodial Penalties*. London: HMSO.

Albrecht, H.-J. (1978) 'Statistische Angaben über die Geldstrafe in der Bundesrepublik Deutschland'. In Jescheck, H.-H. and G. Grebing (eds.) *Die Geldstrafe im deutschen und ausländischen Recht*. Baden-Baden: Nomos, 165–191.

Albrecht, H.-J. (1980) *Strafzumessung und Vollstreckung bei Geldstrafen*. Berlin: Duncker & Humblot.

Albrecht, H.-J. (1981) 'Alternativen zur Freiheitsstrafe: Das Beispiel der Geldstrafe'. *Monatsschrift für Kriminologie und Strafrechtsreform* 64: 265–278.

Albrecht, H.-J. (1982) 'The Fine in the German Penal Sanctioning System'. In Criminological Research Unit (ed.) *Research in Criminal Justice*. Freiburg i. Br.: iuscrim, 225–245.

Albrecht, H.-J. (2001) 'Post-Adjudication Dispositions in Comparative Perspective'. In Tonry, M. and R. S. Frase (eds.) *Sentencing and Sanctions in Western Countries*. New York: Oxford University Press, 293–330.

Albrecht, H.-J. (2013) 'Sentencing in Germany: Explaining Long-Term Stability in the Structure of Criminal Sanctions and Sentencing'. *Law and Contemporary Problems* 76: 211–236.

Albrecht, H.-J. and E. H. Johnson (1980) 'Fines and Justice Administration: The Experience of the Federal Republic of Germany'. *International Journal of Comparative and Applied Criminal Justice* 4: 3–14.

Alonso Escamilla, A. (1988) 'Tratamiento penitenciario del llamado arresto sustitutorio'. *Actualidad Penal* 36: 1869–1877.

Annunziata, G. (1964) 'Considerazioni sulla illegitimità costituzionale della conversione delle pene pecuniarie in pene detentive'. *Il Foro Penale* 19: 38–63.

Arnholm, M. (ed.) (1997) *The System of Administrative and Penal Sanctions in Sweden*. Uppsala: Swedish Society for European Criminal Law.

Ashworth, A. (1997) 'Sentencing'. In Maguire, M., Morgan, R. and R. Reiner (eds.) *The Oxford Handbook of Criminology*. 2nd ed. Oxford: Clarendon Press, 1095–1135.

Ashworth, A. (2015) *Sentencing and Criminal Justice*. 6th ed. Cambridge: Cambridge University Press.

Ashworth, A. and B. Gibson (1994) 'The Criminal Justice Act 1993: Altering the Sentencing Framework'. *The Criminal Law Review*, February: 101–109.

Ashworth, A. and E. Player (1998) 'Sentencing, Equal Treatment and the Impact of Sanctions'. In Ashworth, A. and M. Wasik (eds.) *Fundamentals of Sentencing Theory*. Oxford: Clarendon Press, 252–272.

Baumann, J. (1969) 'Was erwarten wir von der Strafrechtsreform'. In Baumann, J. (ed.) *Weitere Streitschriften zur Strafrechtsreform*. Bielefeld: Gieseking, 9–39.

Bazell, C. and I. Lomax (1992) *Unit Fines*. London: Fourmat.

Beauchamp, D. E. (1981) 'The Paradox of Alcohol Policy: The Case of the 1969 Alcohol Act in Finland'. In Moore, M. H. and D. R. Gerstein (eds.) *Alcohol and Public Policy: Beyond the Shadow of Prohibition: Panel on Alternative Policies Affecting the Prevention of Alcohol Abuse and Alcoholism*. Washington, DC: National Academy Press, 225–254.

Bellini, U. (1930) 'Condanna e liberazione condizionale'. *Rivista di diritto penitenziario* 1: 265–277.

Beristain Ipiña, A. (1976) 'La multa penal y la administrativa en relación con las sanciones privativas de libertad'. In AA.VV (ed.) *III Jornadas de Profesores de Derecho Penal*. Madrid: Universidad de Santiago de Compostela, 11–56.

Bernardi, A. (1999) 'Riscossione delle sanzioni penali pecuniarie: incostituzionalità del nuovo regime 'privatistico'?' *Rivista Trimestrale di Diritto Penale dell'Economia* 12: 1017–1028.

Boix Reig, J. (1977) 'Algunos aspectos de la responsabilidad personal subsidiaria'. *Cuadernos de Política Criminal* 3: 29–52.

Bricola, F. (1961) 'L'istituto della conversione della pena pecuniaria in pena detentiva alla luce dei principi costituzionali'. *Rivista Italiana di Diritto e Procedura Penale* 4: 1073–1084.

Bublies, W. (1992) 'Das Gefängnis darf kein Schuldturm sein – Strategien zur Vermeidung der Ersatzfreiheitsstrafe'. *Bewährungshilfe* 39: 178–194.

Bundeskriminalamt (1997) *Polizeiliche Kriminalstatistik 1996*. Wiesbaden: Bundeskriminalamt.

Caraccioli, I. (1979) 'Conversione della pena pecuniaria e principio di uguaglianza'. *Giurisprudenza Costituzionale* 1: 1205–1216.

Castro, D. de (1934) 'La decrescente applicazione della condanna condizionale'. *La Scuola positiva* 14: 7ff.

Cavadino, M. and J. Dignan (1997) *The Penal System: An Introduction*. 2nd ed. London: SAGE.

Cavadino, M. and J. Dignan (2002) *The Penal System: An Introduction*. 3rd ed. London: SAGE.

Cavadino, M. and J. Dignan (2006) *Penal Systems: A Comparative Approach*. London: SAGE.

Cornils, K. (1983) 'Die Freiheitsstrafe und ihre Surrogate in Schweden'. In Jescheck, H.-H. (ed.) *Die Freiheitsstrafe und ihre Surrogate im deutschen und ausländischen Recht*. Baden-Baden: Nomos, 781–860.

Council of Europe (1987) 'Statistics on Prison Populations in the Member States of the Council of Europe'. *Prison Information Bulletin* 9: 16–26.

Dearing, A. (1983) 'Die Freiheitsstrafe und ihre Surrogate in Österreich'. In Jescheck, H.-H. and G. Grebing (eds.) *Die Freiheitsstrafe und ihre Surrogate im deutschen und ausländischen Recht. Band 1*. Baden-Baden: Nomos, 599–720.

Direzione Generale della Statistica (1899) *Notizie complementari alle Statistiche Giudiziarie Penali degli anni 1890–1895*. Rome: Tipografia Nazionale di G. Bertero.

Dobson, G. (2004) 'Get Carter'. *Probation Journal* 51(2): 144–154.

Dolcini, E. (2001) 'Riforma della parte generale del codice e rifondazione del sistema sanzionatorio penale'. *Rivista italiana di diritto e procedura penale* 44(2): 823–849.

Dolcini, E. (2006) 'La pena in Italia, oggi, tra diritto scritto e prassi applicativa'. In Dolcini, E. and C. E. Paliero (eds.) *Studi in onore di Giorgio Marinucci. Volume II*. Milan: Giuffrè, 1073–1107.

Dünkel, F. and R. Grosser (1999) 'Vermeidung von Ersatzfreiheitsstrafen durch gemeinnützige Arbeit'. *Neue Kriminalpolitik* 11(1): 28–33.

Dünkel, F. and D. Rössner (2001) 'Germany'. In Van Zyl Smit, D. and F. Dünkel (eds.) *Imprisonment Today and Tomorrow: International Perspectives on Prisoners' Rights and Prison Conditions*. 2nd ed. The Hague: Kluwer Law International, 288–350.

Easton, S. and C. Piper (2005) *Sentencing and Punishment: The Quest for Justice*. Oxford: Oxford University Press.

Ekunwe, I. O. and R. S. Jones (2012) 'Finnish Criminal Policy: From Hard Time to Gentle Justice'. *The Journal of Prisoners on Prisons* 21(1&2): 173–189.

Ermgassen, O. (1977) *Die Geldstrafe in den nordischen Ländern (Dänemark, Norwegen, Schweden, Finnland)*. Freiburg im Br.: Univ. Diss.

Figueiredo Dias, J. de (1989) 'Problemas de igualdade na estruturaçâo e aplicaçâo da pena de multa'. In AA.VV (ed.). *Estudios Penales en Memoria del Profesor Agustín Fernández-Albor*. Santiago de Compostela: Servicio de Publicaciones de la Universidad de Santiago de Compostela, 289–305.

Fiorentin, F. (2004) 'Appunti in tema di esecuzione delle pene pecuniarie'. *Diritto penale e processo* 10: 892–899.

Fornasari, G. (2003) 'Riflessioni sulla disciplina della sospensione condizionale della pena nel "Progetto Grosso" con particolare riferimento ai rapporti con la pena pecuniaria'.

In Stile, A. (ed.) *La riforma della parte generale del codice penale: La posizione della dottrina sul Progetto Grosso*. Napoli: Jovene, 561–576.

Frank, U. (1978) *Die Höhe des Tagessatzes im neuen Geldstrafensystem*. Tübingen: Univ. Diss.

Friedman, G. M. (1983) 'The West German Day-Fine System: A Possibility for the United States?' *The University of Chicago Law Review* 50(1): 281–304.

Gallucci, E. (2001) 'Il procedimento di conversione e rateizzazione delle pene pecuniarie: disciplina ordinaria e prospettive innovative nella giurisdizione penale di pace'. *Cassazione penale* 41: 3428–3433.

Gerken, U. and J. Henningsen (1987) 'Ersetzung der Ersatzfreiheitsstrafe durch freie Arbeit'. *Zeitschrift für Rechtspolitik* 20(11): 386–390.

Gibson, B. (1990) *Unit Fines*. Waterside Press: Winchester.

Gillespie, R. W. (1980) 'Fines as an Alternative to Incarceration: The German Experience'. *Federal Probation* 44(4): 20–25.

Goisis, L. (2008) *La pena pecuniaria. Un'indagine storica e comparata. Profili di effettività della sanzione*. Milan: Giuffrè.

Goisis, L. (2012) 'L'effettività (rectius ineffettività) della pena pecuniaria in Italia, oggi'. *Diritto Penale Contemporaneo*: 1–25, available at www.penalecontemporaneo.it/d/1835-l-effettivita-rectius-ineffettivita-della-pena-pecuniaria-in-italia-oggi

Grebing, G. (1978) 'Die Geldstrafe im deutschen Recht nach Einführung des Tagessatzsystems'. In Jescheck, H.-H. and G. Grebing (eds.) *Die Geldstrafe im deutschen und ausländischen Recht*. Baden-Baden: Nomos, 1–184.

Grebing, G. (1982) *The Fine in Comparative Law: A Survey of 21 Countries*. Cambridge: Institute of Criminology Occasional Papers n° 9.

Greene, J. (1998) 'The Unit Fine: Monetary Sanctions Apportioned to Income'. In von Hirsch, A. and A. Ashworth (eds.) *Principled Sentencing: Readings on Theory and Policy*. 2nd ed. Oxford: Hart, 268–272.

Grover, C. (2008) *Crime and Inequality*. Cullompton: Willan.

Grünhut, M. (1948) *Penal Reform: A Comparative Study*. Oxford: Clarendon Press.

Hall, K. A. (1954) 'Die Freiheitsstrafe als kriminalpolitisches Problem'. *Zeitschrift für die gesamte Strafrechtswissenschaft* 66: 77–110.

Hamdorf, K. and O. Wölber (1999) 'Die Ersatzfreiheitsstrafe in Schweden und Deutschland'. *Zeitschrift für die gesamte Strafrechtswissenschaft* 111: 181–200.

Heinz, W. (1981) 'Entwicklung, Stand und Struktur der Strafzumessungspraxis: Eine Übersicht über die nach allgemeinem Strafrecht verhängten Hauptstrafen von 1882–1979'. *Monatsschrift für Kriminologie und Strafrechtsreform* 64: 148–173.

Heinz, W. (1982) 'Strafrechtsreform und Sanktionsentwicklung: Auswirkungen der sanktionenrechtlichen Regelungen des 1. und 2. StrRG 1969 sowie des EGStGB 1974 auf die Sanktionspraxis'. *Zeitschrift für die gesamte Strafrechtswissenschaft* 94: 632–668.

Heinz, W. (1989) 'The Problems of Imprisonment Including Strategies That Might Be Employed to Minimise the Use of Custody'. In Hood, R. (ed.) *Crime and Criminal Policy in Europe: Proceedings of a European Colloquium*. Oxford: University of Oxford, 186–219.

Heinz, W. (2010) *Das strafrechtliche Sanktionensystem und die Sanktionierungspraxis in Deutschland 1882–2008*. Stand: Berichtsjahr. Available at www.ki.uni-konstanz.de/kis

Heinz, W. (2012) 'Das strafrechtliche Sanktionensystem und die Sanktionierungspraxis in Deutschland 1882–2012'. Online available at www.ki.uni-konstanz.de/kis/

Hennig, D. (1990) 'Vollstrecker ohne Macht'. *Zeitschrift für Rechtspolitik* 23(3): 99–103.

Hennig, D. (1999) 'Rettet die Geldstrafe – und macht sie einbringlich'. *Bewährungshilfe* 46: 298–305.

Hillsman, S. T. (1990) 'Fines and Day Fines'. In Tonry, M. (ed.) *Crime and Justice: A Review of Research. Volume 12.* Chicago: University of Chicago Press, 50–98.

Hillsman, S. T. and B. Mahoney (1988) 'Collecting and Enforcing Criminal Fines: A Review of Court Processes, Practices and Problems'. *Justice System Journal* 13(1): 17–36.

Home Office (2006) 'Offender Management Caseload Statistics 2005'. Home Office Statistical Bulletin 18. London: Home Office.

Hudson, B. (1999) 'Punishment, Poverty and Responsibility: The Case for a Hardship Defence'. *Social and Legal Studies* 8(4): 583–591.

Hudson, B. (2000) 'Punishing the Poor: Dilemmas of Justice and Difference'. In Heffernan, W. C. and J. Kleinig (eds.) *From Social Justice to Criminal Justice: Poverty and the Administration of Criminal Law.* New York: Oxford University Press, 189–216.

ISTAT (2012) *L'Italia in 150 anni: Sommario di statistiche storiche 1861–2010.* Rome: Istituto nazionale di statistica.

Janssen, H. (1994) *Die Praxis der Geldstrafenvollstreckung.* Frankfurt: Peter Lang.

Jareño Leal, A. (1994) *La pena privativa de libertad por impago de multa.* Madrid: Civitas.

Jescheck, H.-H. (1977) 'Die Geldstrafe als Mittel moderner Kriminalpolitik in rechtsvergleichender Sicht'. In Herren, R., Kienapfel, D. and H. Müller-Dietz (eds.) *Kultur-Kriminalität-Strafrecht: Festschrift für Thomas Würtenberger zum 70. Geburtstag.* Berlin: Duncker & Humblot, 257–276.

Justice (1989) *Sentencing: A Way Ahead.* London: Justice.

Kaiser, G. (1973) 'Tendenzen in der Entwicklung des heutigen Strafrechts aus der Sicht der Strafrechtswissenschaft und Kriminologie'. In Horstkotte, H., Kaiser, G. and W. Sarstedt (eds.) *Tendenzen in der Entwicklung des heutigen Strafrechts.* Frankfurt: Verlag der Evangelischen Akademie in Hessen und Nassau, 29–50.

Kalmthout, A. M. van and P.J.P. Tak (1992) *Sanctions-Systems in the Member States of the Council of Europe: Part II. Deprivation of Liberty, Community Service and Other Substitutes.* Deventer: Kluwer.

Killias, M. (1994) 'Der Kreuzzug gegen kurze Freiheitsstrafen: Historische Hintergründe, neue Erwartungen – und die verdrängten Folgen'. In Groupe Suisse de Travail de Criminologie (ed.) *Réforme des sanctions pénales.* Zürich: Rüegger, 111–131.

Kristoffersen, R. (2008) *Correctional Statistics of Denmark, Finland, Iceland, Norway and Sweden 2002–2006.* Oslo: Correctional Service of Norway Staff Academy.

Kristoffersen, R. (2010) *Correctional Statistics of Denmark, Finland, Iceland, Norway and Sweden 2004–2008.* Oslo: Correctional Service of Norway Staff Academy.

Kristoffersen, R. (2013) *Correctional Statistics of Denmark, Finland, Iceland, Norway and Sweden 2008–2012.* Oslo: Correctional Service of Norway Staff Academy.

Kürzinger, J. (1984) 'Die Freiheitsstrafe und ihre Surrogate in der Bundesrepublik Deutschland'. In Jescheck, H.-H. (ed.) *Die Freiheitsstrafe und ihre Surrogate im deutschen und ausländischen Recht.* Baden-Baden: Nomos, 1737–1939.

Lacey, N. (1994) 'Government as Manager, Citizen as Consumer: The Case of the Criminal Justice Act 1991'. *The Modern Law Review* 57(4): 534–554.

Lahti, R. (1989) 'On Finnish and Scandinavian Criminal Policy'. *Cahiers de Défense Sociale* 1989: 64–73.

Lang-Hinrichsen, D. (1959) 'Betrachtungen zur Strafrechtsreform'. In Peters, K. and D. Lang-Hinrichsen (eds.) *Grundfragen der Strafrechtsreform.* Padeborn: Bonifacius.

Lappi-Seppälä, T. (2000) 'The Fall of the Finnish Prison Population'. *Journal of Scandinavian Studies in Criminology and Crime Prevention* 1: 27–40.

Lappi-Seppälä, T. (2001) 'Sentencing and Punishment in Finland: The Decline of the Repressive Ideal'. In Tonry, M. and R. S. Frase (eds.) *Sentencing and Sanctions in Western Countries*. Oxford: Oxford University Press, 92–150.

Lappi-Seppälä, T. (2004) 'Reducing the Prison Population: Long-Term Experiences from Finland'. In AA.VV (ed.) *Crime Policy in Europe: Good Practices and Promising Examples*. Strasbourg: Council of Europe, 139–156.

Lappi-Seppälä, T. (2009) 'Imprisonment and Penal Policy in Finland'. *Scandinavian Studies in Law* 54: 336–379.

Lappi-Seppälä, T. (2012) 'Penal Policies in the Nordic Countries 1960–2010'. *Journal of Scandinavian Studies in Criminology and Crime Prevention* 13(1): 85–111.

Lappi-Seppälä, T. (2014) 'Fines in Europe'. In Bruinsma, G. and D. Weisburd (eds.) *Encyclopedia of Criminology and Criminal Justice*. Heidelberg: Springer, 1637–1648.

Mackie, A., Raine, J., Burrows, J., Hopkins, M. and E. Dunstan (2003) 'Clearing the Debts: The Enforcement of Financial Penalties in Magistrates' Courts'. Home Office Online Report 09/03. London: Home Office.

Maglie, C. de (1988) 'Ha un futuro l'attuale modello di pena pecuniaria?' *Rivista Italiana di Diritto e Procedura Penale* 31: 648–685.

Marsico, A. de (1925) 'Relazione della Commissione della Camera dei deputati per la riforma del cod. pen'. *La Scuola Positiva* 5: 277–305.

Miedico, M. (2008) *La pena pecuniaria: Disciplina, prassi e prospettive di riforma*. Milan: Egea.

Ministry of Justice (2013) *Story of the Prison Population: 1993–2012. England and Wales*. London: Ministry of Justice.

Molinari, F. (1978) 'Statistische Angaben über die Geldstrafe in Italien'. In Jescheck, H.-H. and G. Grebing (eds.) *Die Geldstrafe im deutschen und ausländischen Recht*. Baden-Baden: Nomos, 479–516.

Moore, R. (2003) 'The Use of Financial Penalties and the Amounts Imposed: The Need for a New Approach'. *The Criminal Law Review*, January: 13–27.

Morgenstern, C. (2016) 'Der Resozialisierungsgrundsatz: Social Reintegration as the Dominant Narrative for Community Punishment in Germany?' In Robinson, G. and F. McNeill (eds.) *Community Punishment: European Perspectives*. London: Routledge, 72–94.

Moxon, D. (1995a) 'England Adopts Day Fines'. In Tonry, M. and K. Hamilton (eds.) *Intermediate Sanctions in Overcrowded Times*. Boston: Northeastern University Press, 31–35.

Moxon, D. (1995b) 'England Abandons Day Fines'. In Tonry, M. and K. Hamilton (eds.) *Intermediate Sanctions in Overcrowded Times*. Boston: Northeastern University Press, 36–42.

Moxon, D., Sutton, M. and C. Hedderman (1990) 'Unit Fines: Experiments in Four Courts'. Home Office Research and Planning Unit Paper no. 59. Home Office: London.

NACRO (1981) *Fine Default*. London: NACRO.

Nannucci, U. (1998) 'L'esecuzione della pena pecuniaria ovverosia con quale impegno lo Stato punisce se stesso'. *Cassazione penale* 38: 2238–2247.

Nowakowski, F. (1972) 'Das Tagesbußensystem nach § 19 der Regierungsvorlage (1971) eines Strafgesetzbuches'. *Österreichische Juristen-Zeitung* 27: 197–204.

Nüßlein, A. (1969) *Freiheitsstrafen in Hessen 1969*. Hamburg: Kriminalistik.

Padovani, T. (1981) *L'utopia punitiva*. Milan: Giuffrè

Paliero, C. E. (1986) 'Community Service in Italy – Legislation and Practice'. In Albrecht, H. J. and W. Schädler (eds.) *Community Service: A New Option in Punishing Offenders in Europe*. Freiburg: Max Planck Institute for Foreign and International Penal Law, 151–172.

Penal Affairs Consortium (1990) *Means-Related Fines*. London: Penal Affairs Consortium.

Pisani, M. (1962) 'Ricchi e poveri di fronte al processo e di fronte alla pena (appunti in margine ad una sentenza della Corte Costituzionale)'. *Rivista Italiana di Diritto e Procedura Penale* 5: 569–578.

Presutti, A. (1991) 'La nuova disciplina della conversione della pena pecuniaria'. In AA.VV (ed.) *Studi in memoria di Pietro Nuvolone. Volume Terzo. Il nuovo processo penale: Studi di diritto straniero e comparato*. Milan: Giuffrè, 419–437.

Prison Reform Trust (1990) *Tackling Fine Default*. London: Prison Reform Trust.

Quintero Olivares, G. (1977) 'El arresto sustitutorio'. *Cuadernos de Política Criminal* 2: 111–141.

Ranieri, S. (1966) 'Pene pecuniarie e rieducazione del condannato'. *La Scuola Positiva* 70: 265–268.

Rodríguez Ramos, L. (1988) '¿Prisión por "penosas deudas" al Estado?' *La Ley* 3: 917–924.

Rossi, P.L.O. (1853) *Trattato di diritto penale*. Turin: Società Editrice.

Roxin, C. (1969) 'Franz von Liszt und die kriminalpolitische Konzeption des Alternativentwurfs'. *Zeitschrift für die gesamte Strafrechtswissenschaft* 81: 613–649.

Rusche, G. and O. Kirchheimer (1939 [2003]) *Punishment and Social Structure*. New Brunswick: Transaction.

Sanders, A. (1998) 'What Principles Underlie Criminal Justice Policy in the 1990s? *Oxford Journal of Legal Studies* 18(3): 533–542.

Schädler, W. (1985) 'Der 'weiße Fleck' im Sanktionensystem: Ein Beitrag zur Diskussion um Geldstrafe, freie Arbeit und Ersatzfreiheitsstrafe'. *Zeitschrift für Rechtspolitik* 18: 186–192.

Schaeferdieck, S. (1997) *Die kurze Freiheitsstrafe im schwedischen und deutschen Strafrecht*. Berlin: Duncker & Humblot.

Schmidt, E. (1952) 'Eröffnungsansprache auf der Tagung der Arbeitsgemeinschaft zur Reform des Strafvollzuges'. *Zeitschrift für die gesamte Strafrechtswissenschaft* 64: 1–16.

Schmidt, E. (1967) 'Freiheitsstrafe, Ersatzfreiheitsstrafe und Strafzumessung im Alternativ-Entwurf eines Strafgesetzbuchs'. *Neue Juristische Wochenschrift* 20: 1929–1940.

Schott, T. (2003) 'Abkehr von der 1:1 Umrechnung von Geld und Freiheitsstrafe?' *Juristische Rundschau* 57: 315–320.

Seebode, M. (1999) 'Problematische Ersatzfreiheitsstrafe'. In Feuerhelm, W., Schwind, H.-D. and M. Bock (eds.) *Festschrift für Alexander Böhm zum 70: Geburtstag am 14. Juni 1999*. Berlin: Walter de Gruyter, 519–552.

Sellin, J. T. (1947) *Recent Penal Legislation in Sweden*. Stockholm: Norstedts.

Sevdiren, O. (2011) *Alternatives to Imprisonment in England and Wales, Germany and Turkey*. Berlin: Springer.

Sigismondi, A. (1966) 'Pene pecuniarie e funzione rieducativa'. *Giurisprudenza Costituzionale* 11: 146–155.

Stammberger, W. (1963) 'Die Geschichte der Strafrechtsreform bis zum Strafgesetzbuchentwurf 1962'. In Friedrich-Naumann-Stiftung (ed.) *Probleme der Strafrechtsreform*. Stuttgart: Deutsche Verl.-Anst, 11–29.

Statistisches Bundesamt (1970) *Statistisches Jahrbuch für die Bundesrepublik Deutschland 1970*. Stuttgart: Statistisches Bundesamt.

Statistisches Bundesamt (1988) *Staatsanwaltschaften: Arbeitsunterlagen*. Wiesbaden: Bundesamt.

Statistisches Bundesamt (1996) *Statistisches Jahrbuch für die Bundesrepublik Deutschland 1996*. Wiesbaden: Statistisches Bundesamt.

Statistisches Bundesamt (1997) *Statistisches Jahrbuch für die Bundesrepublik Deutschland 1997*. Wiesbaden: Statistisches Bundesamt.

Statistisches Bundesamt (2009) *Statistisches Jahrbuch für die Bundesrepublik Deutschland 2009*. Wiesbaden: Statistisches Bundesamt.

Stenner, D. (1970) *Die kurzfristige Freiheitsstrafe und die Möglichkeiten zu ihrem Ersatz durch andere Sanktionen*. Hamburg: Kriminalistik-Verlag.

Sveri, K. (1998) 'Incarceration for Non-Payment of a Fine'. In Schwind, H.-D., Kube, E. and H.-H. Kühne (eds.) *Festschrift für Hans Joachim Schneider zum 70: Geburtstag am 14. November 1998. Kriminologie an der Schwelle zum 21. Jahrhundert*. Berlin: Walter de Gruyter, 943–951.

Sveri, K. (2005) 'Criminal Law and Penal Sanctions'. In Bondeson, U. V. (ed.) *Crime and Justice in Scandinavia*. Copenhagen: Thomas GadJura, 15–30.

Thornstedt, H. (1974) 'Skandinavische Erfahrungen mit dem Tagesbuβensystem'. *Zeitschrift für die gesamte Strafrechtswissenschaft* 86: 595–613.

Thornstedt, H. (1975) 'The Day-Fine System in Sweden'. *The Criminal Law Review*, June: 307–312.

Tonry, M. (1996) *Sentencing Matters*. New York: Oxford University Press.

Törnud, P. (1993) *Fifteen Years of Decreasing Prisoner Rates in Finland*. Research Communication 8. Helsinki: National Research Institute of Legal Policy.

Tröndle, H. (1972) 'Die Geldstrafe im neuen Strafensystem'. *Monatsschrift für Deutsches Recht* 6: 461–468.

Tröndle, H. (1974) 'Die Geldstrafe in der Praxis und Probleme ihrer Durchsetzung unter besonderer Berücksichtigung des Tagessatzsystems'. *Zeitschrift für die gesamte Strafrechtswissenschaft* 86: 545–594.

Utriainen, T. (2002) 'Community Sanctions in Finland'. In Albrecht, H.-J. and A. van Kalmthout (eds.) *Community Sanctions and Measures in Europe and North America*. Freiburg: iuscrim, 193–207.

Vergine, A. L. (1981) 'La sospensione condizionale delle pene pecuniarie: contrasti giurisprudenziali e proposte di riforma'. *Rivista Italiana di Diritto e Procedura Penale* 24: 1167–1202.

Von Hippel, R. (1925) *Deutsches Strafrecht. Band 1: Allgemeiner Grundlagen*. Berlin: Springer.

Von Hofer, H. (2003) 'Prison Populations as Political Constructs: The Case of Finland, Holland and Sweden'. *Journal of Scandinavian Studies in Criminology and Crime Prevention* 4(1): 21–38.

Von Hofer, H. (2004) 'Imprisonment for Non-Payment of Fines in Sweden'. In AA.VV (ed.) *Crime Policy in Europe: Good Practices and Promising Examples*. Strasbourg: Council of Europe, 119–125.

Von Hofer, H., Lappi-Seppälä, T. and L. Westfelt (2012) *Nordic Criminal Statistics 1950–2010*. Stockholm: Kriminologiska institutionen.

Wagner, G. (1984) *Das absurde System: Strafurteil und Strafvollzug in unserer Gesellschaft*. Heidelberg: C. F. Müller.

Walker, N. and N. Padfield (1996) *Sentencing: Theory, Law and Practice*. London: Butterworths.

Warner, K. (2012) 'Equality before the Law and Equal Impact of Sanctions: Doing Justice to Differences in Wealth and Employment Status'. In Zedner, L. (ed.) *Principles and Values in Criminal Law and Criminal Justice: Essays in Honour of Andrew Ashworth*. Oxford: Oxford University Press, 225–244

Weigend, T. (1995a) 'Fines Reduce Use of Prison Sentences in Germany'. In Tonry, M. and K. Hamilton (eds.) *Intermediate Sanctions in Overcrowded Times*. Boston: Northeastern University Press, 43–49.

Weigend, T. (1995b) 'In Germany, Fines Often Imposed in Lieu of Prosecution'. In Tonry, M. and K. Hamilton (eds.) *Intermediate Sanctions in Overcrowded Times*. Boston: Northeastern University Press, 50–55.

Weigend, T. (2001) 'Sentencing and Punishment in Germany'. In Tonry, M. and R. S. Frase (eds.) *Sentencing and Sanctions in Western Countries*. New York: Oxford University Press, 188–221.

Weisburd, D., Einat, T. and M. Kowalski (2008) 'The Miracle of the Cells: An Experimental Study of Interventions to Increase Payment of Court-Ordered Financial Obligations'. *Criminology and Public Policy* 7(1): 9–36.

Zagaris, B. (1977) 'Penal Reform in Sweden'. *Southern University Law Review* 9: 111–156.

7 What next?

Achieving equalization of impact: a fair fine is possible

For a sentence to be fair, just, and proportionate, it needs to be tailored not only to the offence but also to the individual offender. In this regard, the day-fine system has many advantages compared to other types of fines. It expressly requires a consideration of the offender's financial circumstances, which in turn enhances fairness. It provides a transparent explanation of the court's decision-making process, which ensures a better understanding of the sentencing process and builds trust in the criminal justice system. It makes fines available as a sentencing option for more serious offences, which consequently improves their suitability as an alternative sentencing option to imprisonment. It applies a clear and fair method of converting an unpaid fine into a subsidiary custodial or non-custodial sentence. In other words, the seriousness of the offence – not the offender's financial circumstances – determines the number of days the offender must spend in prison or do community service, which ensures equality.

Day fines are the most efficient tool to achieve all these advantages in addition to the benefits traditionally attributed to fines. Nevertheless, some conditions should be met, as the national experiences and comparative approaches presented in the last chapter clearly show. The first essential provision for an efficient application of day fines should include sufficiently detailed guidelines for calculating the fine. In order to prevent the undesirable situation of non-uniform fines across different courts, the law ought to provide precise instructions of what should be taken into account in calculating the day fine (Kantorowicz-Reznichenko 2015: 493).

Developing an accurate picture of the offender's financial circumstances is crucial to achieve equalization of impact of the fine. Actually, determining the offenders' ability to pay has often been considered in itself a major obstacle to the implementation of the day-fine system, a fact that has undercut the theoretical benefits of this form of punishment (Levitt 1997: 181; Pritikin 2010: 357). It is necessary to achieve an efficient use of financial information regarding the offender. The legal system should allow judicial access to this information. Without such accessibility, the day-fine system will remain impaired.

The unit of the fine should encompass the entire wealth of the offender and not only his or her personal income (Grebing 1978: 45; Molinari 1983: 28–29 and 81ff.). 'If only the income is included, persons with profits from other assets would be under-deterred since the daily unit would underestimate their wealth' (Kantorowicz-Reznichenko 2015: 494). But not only is this important. As Hillsman and Greene (1992: 139) put it,

> For the very wealthy, inequities may also remain with a means-based system, although they will be significantly smaller than under a fixed-fine system [. . .] For more specialized and less frequent cases, however, further consideration of ways to take account of very high incomes and capital assets would be useful.

A crucial element to adequately tackle the problem of very rich offenders is the lack of an upper limit on the daily unit (Baumann 1968: 29–30; Molinari 1983: 65ff.). Whenever the law sets a limit on the daily unit that may be imposed on the offender, it allows for under-deterrence of high-income offenders. One of the reasons for establishing an upper limit has usually been the considerable concern about imposing sanctions that seem too high on rich people who commit petty crimes and misdemeanours. Another one is that once an offender's fine is fixed above a certain amount, he or she will simply prefer to go to prison for non-payment rather than pay the fine, so the fine should be set low enough that an offender is willing to pay it rather than go to prison (Levitt 1997: 181; Pritikin 2010: 357). The result is that fines are fixed too low for the richest offenders, undermining the efforts to achieve equal impact. The upper limit must be eliminated, and the offender should not be given the possibility of choosing between payment and prison: payment should be coerced if he or she has the means to satisfy the fine. The fine is the primary sanction, and the enforcement agency should be authorized to garnish wages and seize property in order to collect the fine. The enforcement agency must use the most expedient method of execution to collect the fine while also considering the personal circumstances of the offender and his or her dependents.

In serious cases, the impact must be clearly felt, perhaps demanding some modification of spending habits. The fine has to have a 'bite' but should not cause financial hardship. Whenever an offender is unable to pay immediately without suffering such hardship, payment of the fine by instalments should be allowed. If the total amount of the fine must be paid at once, the day fine would lose the advantage of potentially increasing the payment rate since low-income offenders might not have the full amount. Indeed, many of the countries that adopted the day fine permit payment in instalments. There are even proposals to make payment by instalments the normal form of payment, as we will see in the next section.[1]

If the offender's circumstances change after receiving the sentence, the fine amount needs to be altered accordingly. An alternative punishment should be employed whenever an offender is unable to pay, even if payment is set at a minimum rate. The full range of intermediate punishments should be available as options for offenders who do default. Indigent offenders should not be punished with imprisonment, but be given the possibility to work off their fines (Pritikin

2010: 348). Today, since we have the means and knowledge to achieve reform, imprisonment of the poor for non-payment of fines should be completely eliminated. If subsidiary imprisonment is to be retained, it should be restricted to those offenders who have the means to pay but decide not to do so.

And lastly, whether fines can reduce imprisonment levels in a cost-effective manner may depend not only on whether a system is designed to balance the competing concerns mentioned earlier, but also on proper implementation.

Towards a more personal penalty: fines and the freedom of consumption

Despite all the advantages of fines and the widespread recognition of the shortcomings and drawbacks of prison sentences, imprisonment has experienced a revival since the 1990s. It persists as the dominant punishment in many countries. The assertion 'prison works' (used by Home Secretary Michael Howard in his speech to the Tory Party Conference in 1993) had very clear implications for fines and other intermediate punishments. 'Prison works' symbolized a new turn towards a more punitive penal climate in which Europe has been living ever since. Imprisonment rates reached new highs until the Great Recession of 2008.

The persistence of an institution such as the prison system is the subject of much academic scrutiny. In my opinion, it can be attributed to the fact that imprisonment performs the same functions as it did in the nineteenth century. Just as then, liberty is still considered a universally and intensely valued resource of which all offenders, rich and poor, can be deprived (see, e.g., Young 1989: 63; Kahan 1996: 621, citing Cooter 1984; Pritikin 2010: 357). But while the very essence of freedom and liberty has barely changed, the meaning of money has dramatically shifted. It has become generalized, but is still unequally distributed. The unequal distribution of money makes it even more important to achieve a certain sense of fairness in the way fines are conceived and applied.

The social message projected by different forms of punishment is as important as their successful technical implementation. As we have seen, the universal use of money deprived it of its sacral, moral meaning, without giving it a new, powerful significance that could compete with the one of freedom. In this sense, an important obstacle to using fines as a punishment for non-trivial offences is that sentencing judges and courts, and the community itself, do not accept them as punishment enough for certain offences. As Young correctly highlighted, a 'cultural separation' exists between money and punishment, meaning that 'an ambivalent, even contradictory, set of cultural values form the context in which money is used as a judicial punishment' (Young 1994: 187).

But giving fines a new and more significant meaning is not an impossible task. It has been said that 'maybe money is a medium through which new forms of liberalism, new forms of freedom, simultaneously constitute meaning and are constituted by it' (O'Malley 2009: 15). In fact, money can obviously buy not only commodities but also independence from the will of others. This is something we can regard as liberty, as Simmel (1907 [1990]: 300–301) does (Poggi 1993: 144ff.). Thus, money can be understood as a sort of objectivized freedom (Dürig 1958: 31, 47), because the freedom enjoyed by all in liberal societies can be fully exercised only if the individual has the means, and therefore the ability to do it. The poor are formally free to pursue numerous interests, but they are not really free to achieve many of them because they cannot afford to. Freedom is compromised not only by interferences from other people but also by lack of means (Reddy 1987: 113). Thus, we could say that money contributes to constructing freedom.

Following this argument the fine can be considered as a freedom-restricting penalty, as it involves the 'loss of financial opportunities' (Nowakowski 1972: 200), or in terms of restricting the freedom of the market since it impacts consumption (Baumann 1963, 1968). It could be argued that although different sorts of punishments curtail liberty in different ways, all punishment is coercive and deprives the offender of liberty in some way, the fine depriving the offender of a substantial part of his or her freedom of consumption. In a society in which individuals discover themselves and realize themselves in the lines of expenditure – that is, in the ways they spend their money – the personal autonomy and daily choice unique to consumers are restricted through deprivation of money in the form of a fine, which reduces the freedom of choice.[2] The fine will decrease their command over money, the one and only means of self-expression and enjoyment.

While one argument highlights the decay of impact of fines after imposition, particularly if the quantity is to be settled over a period of weeks or months, it can be counter-argued that instalment payments may potentially be viewed as part of the punishment, because they provide weekly or monthly reminders of the consequence of offending for the duration of the penalty, demanding some modification of spending habits. Therefore, payment by instalments is beneficial not only because it contributes to reducing default but also because 'it serves as a constant reminder that society will not condone the criminal act' (Ryan 1983: 1300). As Bathurst (1996: 2) stated,

> it could be said, with some justification, that only by having to dip into his pocket each week or each fortnight over a protracted period of time can a defendant really be made to feel the pain and inconvenience that a court punishment sets out to inflict.

A fine calculated accurately according to the offender's wealth and wages and paid in instalments can be conceptualized as a 'mechanics of training' upon the bodies and souls of individuals, in the manner suggested by Foucault. It disciplines the individual by reducing his or her capacity of consumption – that is to say, his or her freedom of choice – but not his or her ability to work for a relatively long period of time. Consumerism expresses a personal liberty in consumer societies that both reacts to and reflects changing work and leisure patterns. By limiting the exercise of this liberty, the penal fine constitutes itself as the perfect disciplinarian mechanism of our time. Money becomes then the two-sided symbol of discipline and freedom.

If it is possible to build such a nexus between money and freedom, it may be also possible to make money sanctions for serious offences more palatable, thus contributing to further reducing the use of imprisonment. One possible path to this objective is a revised take on the meaning of money in criminal law. Such a revision would force us to rethink the nature of the relationship between fines and other sanctions, particularly imprisonment. As a result, new questions may emerge, which need to be debated and answered. This book has been written in the hope of stimulating such questions and debate.

We have seen how the evolving notion of money provides interesting clues to understanding the development of both monetary and custodial penalties. For better or worse, the changing meanings of money and fines have influenced the development of the criminal justice system. To understand them provides actors with a valuable set of analytical tools to reform or reorganize existing arrangements. Let us use them.

Notes

1 A similar proposal found strong opposition in Germany (Lackner 1963: 620, 1967: 518; Schmidt 1963: 630) and was never implemented in legislation.

2 Indeed, freedom of choice is reduced, but not completely eliminated. The way in which a fine system is generally organized creates a space where it is possible for offenders to control the enforcement process – that is, to administer themselves their own punishments, at least to a certain point. How? Mainly by deciding if they pay or not, and in case they decide to pay, by negotiating the amount and quantity of instalments to be paid, since almost all fine systems allow payment in instalments, or the sorts of goods and services he will do without to pay the fine. In this way, the punishment effect of the money sanction greatly depends on choices the offender makes. He can choose not to cooperate. He can also choose to cooperate until a certain point where he can trade money for an acceptable term of imprisonment or another penalty. He can choose to cooperate by conforming, obeying, and paying the instalments.

As Simmel argues, the controlling aspect of money is that it requires us to enter into exchange relationships in which we are faced with choice. Following this idea, Young (1999: 195–196) explained:

> money forces us continually to evaluate what we do against market mechanisms and against different opportunity costs. It requires us continually to evaluate those other commodities and relationships with which it is proposed at this or that point to strike an equivalence. If we decide one way, we pay our money and we have to accept the loss of opportunity – but there is always the possibility of difference, of different outcomes.

The fine is the best example of a punishment in which the person punished co-operates in the administration of punishment, but it is not the only one. As Young (1999: 186) correctly highlights, many of the intermediate, non-custodial punishments 'also hand over the administration of the punishment to the offender or centrally presuppose his/her co-operation'.

References

Bathurst, D. (1996) *Financial Penalties: Collection and Enforcement in Magistrates' Courts*. Chichester: Barry Rose Law.

Baumann, J. (1963) 'Von den Möglichkeiten einer Laufzeitgeldstrafe'. *Juristenzeitung* 18: 733–739.

Baumann, J. (1968) *Beschränkung des Lebensstandards anstatt kurzfristiger Freiheitsstrafe*. Neuwied: Luchterhand.

Cooter, R. (1984) 'Prices and Sanctions'. *Columbia Law Review* 84(6): 1523–1560.

Dürig, G. (1958) 'Der Staat und die Vermögenswerten öffentlich-rechtlichen Berechtigungen seiner Bürger'. In Maunz, T., Nawiasky, H. and J. Heckel (eds.) *Staat und Bürger: Festschrift für Willibalt Apelt zum 80. Geburtstag*. Munich: Beck, 13–56.

Grebing, G. (1978) 'Die Geldstrafe im deutschen Recht nach Einführung des Tagessatzsystems'. In Jescheck, H.-H. and G. Grebing (eds.) *Die Geldstrafe im deutschen und ausländischen Recht*. Baden-Baden: Nomos, 1–184.

Hillsman, S. T. and J. A. Greene (1992) 'The Use of Fines as an Intermediate Sanction'. In Byrne, J. M., Lurigio, A. J. and J. Petersilia (eds.) *Smart Sentencing: The Emergence of Intermediate Sanctions*. London: SAGE, 123–141.

Kahan, D. M. (1996) 'What Do Alternative Sanctions Mean?' *University of Chicago Law Review* 63: 591–653.

Kantorowicz-Reznichenko, E. (2015) 'Day Fines: Should the Rich Pay More?' *Review of Law and Economics* 11(3): 481–501.

Lackner, K. (1963) 'Der Allgemeine Teil des künftigen Strafgesetzbuches in der Auseinandersetzung: Ein kritischer Beitrag zum Gegenentwurf Baumann'. *Juristenzeitung* 18: 617–624.

Lackner, K. (1967) Der Alternativ-Entwurf und die praktische Strafrechtspflege. *Juristenzeitung* 22: 513–522.

Levitt, S. (1997) 'Incentive Compatibility Constraints as an Explanation for the Use of Prison Sentences Instead of Fines'. *International Review of Law and Economics* 17(2): 179–192.

Molinari, F. (1983) *La pena pecuniaria*. Verona: Team.

Nowakowski, F. (1972) 'Das Tagesbußensystem nach § 19 der Regierungsvorlage (1971) eines Strafgesetzbuches'. *Österreichische Juristen-Zeitung* 27: 197–204.

O'Malley, P. (2009) *The Currency of Justice: Fines and Damages in Consumer Societies*. New York: Routledge-Cavendish.

Poggi, G. (1993) *Money and the Modern Mind: Georg Simmel's Philosophy of Money*. Berkeley: University of California Press.

Pritikin, M. H. (2010) 'Fine-Labor: The Symbiosis between Monetary and Work Sanctions'. *University of Colorado Law Review* 81: 343–424.

Reddy, W. M. (1987) *Money and Liberty in Modern Europe*. New York: Cambridge University Press.

Ryan, D. M. (1983) 'Criminal Fines: A Sentencing Alternative to Short-Term Incarceration'. *Iowa Law Review* 68: 1285–1313.

Schmidt, E. (1963) 'Ein Gegenentwurf zum Entwurf eines StGB 1962 – Kritische Erörterung'. *Monatsschrift für Deutsches Recht* 17: 629–632.

Simmel, G. (1907 [1990]) *The Philosophy of Money*. New York: Routledge.

Young, P. (1989) 'Punishment, Money and a Sense of Justice'. In Carlen, P. and D. Cook (eds.) *Paying for Crime*. Milton Keynes: Open University Press, 46–65.

Young, P. (1994) 'Putting a Price on Harm: The Fine as a Punishment'. In Duff, A., Marshall, S., Emerson Dobash, R. and R. P. Dobash (eds.) *Penal Theory and Practice: Tradition and Innovation in Criminal Justice*. Manchester: Manchester University Press, 185–198.

Young, P. (1999) 'The Fine as an Auto-Punishment: Power, Money and Discipline'. In Duff, P. and N. Hutton (ed.) *Criminal Justice in Scotland*. Aldershot: Darmouth, 182–197.

Index

For Product Safety Concerns and Information please contact our EU representative GPSR@taylorandfrancis.com
Taylor & Francis Verlag GmbH, Kaufingerstraße 24, 80331 München, Germany

www.ingramcontent.com/pod-product-compliance
Ingram Content Group UK Ltd.
Pitfield, Milton Keynes, MK11 3LW, UK
UKHW011004180926
475701UK00004B/547
* 9 7 8 0 3 6 7 2 2 7 0 8 1 *